Shojo Beat

Story & Art by
MITSUBA TAKANASHI

CONTENTS

STORY THUS FAR

Nobara Sumiyoshi is a first-year high school student who lives for her one passion, volleyball. She's the successor to Seiryu, the high-class ryotei restaurant that her family runs, but she enrolled in Crimson Field High School expressly to play volleyball. Her mother pulled strings and eliminated the girls' volleyball club before Nobara started her first day of school there. Furious, Nobara ran away from home. While living and working in the Crimson Dorm, a dorm for boys' volleyball scholarship students, she began assembling a girls' volleyball club. Enduring harassment from members of the boys' club, she worked hard until she was only one member short of a full team.

That's when she met Tomoyo Osaka, a former member of the Japan Junior Youth team. Nobara wanted her to join, but Tomoyo refused. Unable to overcome a setback after being injured, Tomoyo had already given up on volleyball. Finally, Nobara told her bluntly, "You've got to decide for yourself what you're worth!"

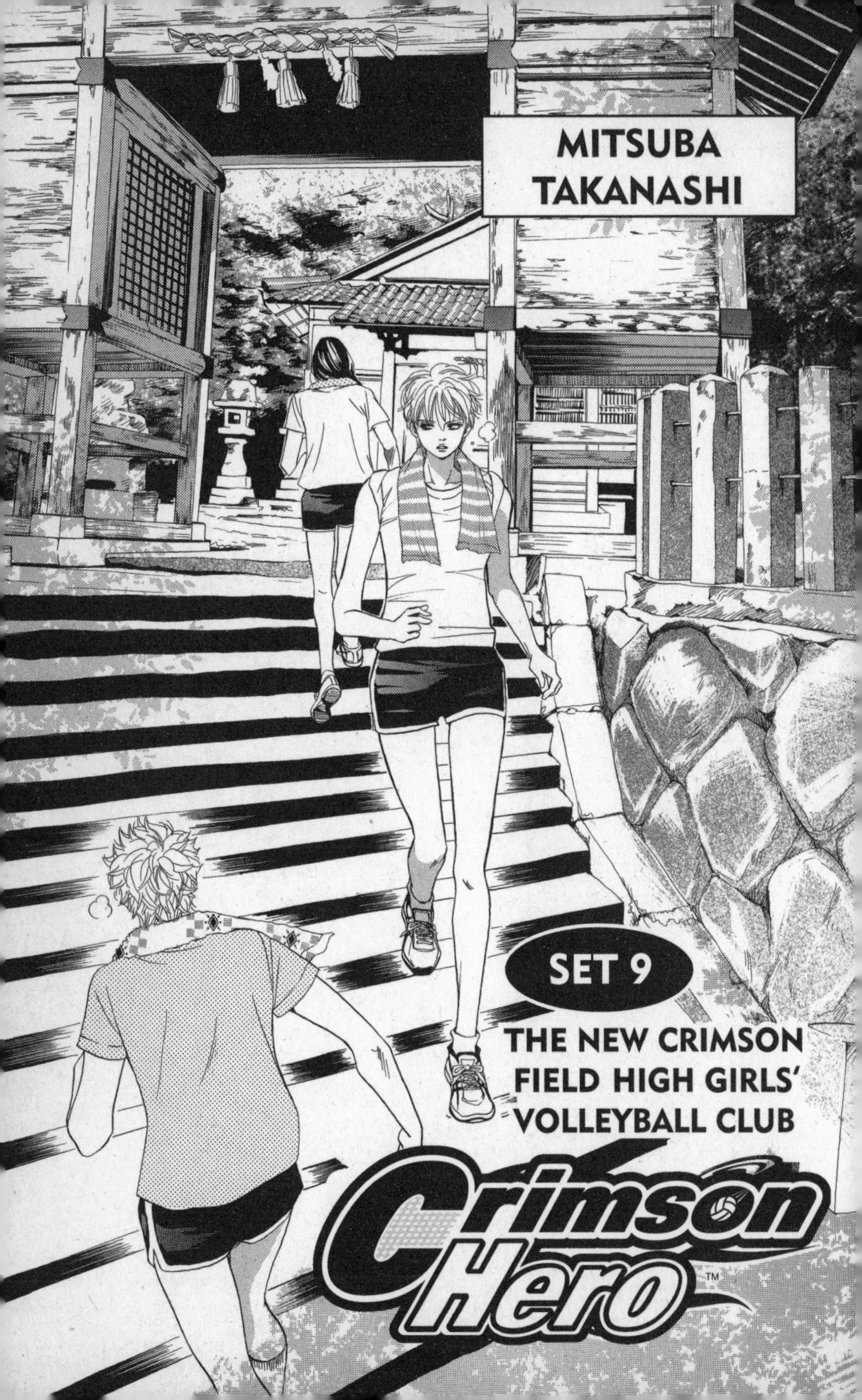
MITSUBA TAKANASHI
SET 9
THE NEW CRIMSON FIELD HIGH GIRLS' VOLLEYBALL CLUB
Crimson Hero™

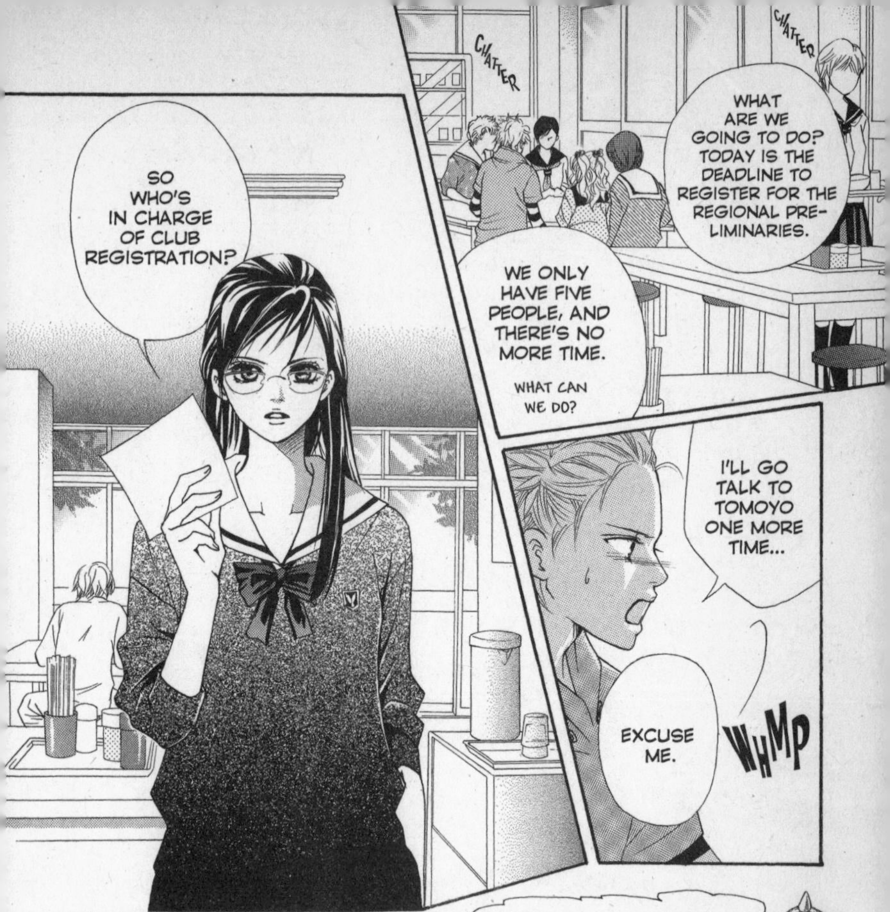
CHATTER
CHATTER
WHAT ARE WE GOING TO DO? TODAY IS THE DEADLINE TO REGISTER FOR THE REGIONAL PRE-LIMINARIES.
WE ONLY HAVE FIVE PEOPLE, AND THERE'S NO MORE TIME.
WHAT CAN WE DO?
I'LL GO TALK TO TOMOYO ONE MORE TIME...
EXCUSE ME.
WHMP
SO WHO'S IN CHARGE OF CLUB REGISTRATION?

THE MAKING OF CRIMSON HERO

HI EVERYONE! HERE'S VOLUME 3. HOW HAVE YOU ALL BEEN?

AS USUAL I'VE BEEN BUSY ALL THE TIME, BUT THE OTHER DAY I GOT TO GO SEE THE TOKYO PRELIMINARIES FOR THE SPRING HIGH SCHOOL VOLLEYBALL TOURNAMENT. (I WENT A YEAR AGO...HOW QUICKLY A YEAR PASSES!) ANYWAY, ONCE AGAIN IT REALLY MOVED ME. YOU KNOW WHY? BEFORE THE PLAYERS ENTERED THE COURT, THEY WERE STANDING IN A ROW HOLDING HANDS!!! OH THOSE HIGH SCHOOL GIRLS, JUST BEFORE THE GAME!!!!

AND IT JUST SO HAPPENED THAT THIS TEAM WAS FROM A VOLLEYBALL CLUB WITH ONLY SIX MEMBERS!

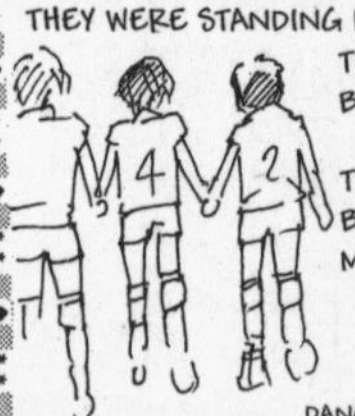

THESE COMIC PAGES WILL COME OUT IN MARCH, AND THAT'S RIGHT SMACK DURING THE SPRING TOURNAMENT. I WANT TO GO EVERY DAY, SO I'VE ALREADY STARTED CRAMMING ON MY WORK. I'M GOING TO GO NO MATTER WHAT! (I'M WAY BEHIND.)

THIS YEAR FOR SURE!! THIS YEAR FOR SURE I'LL HAVE A CAMERA THAT'S NOT BROKEN!!!!

IF YOU SEE A STRANGE WOMAN CRYING HER EYES OUT AT YOYOGI, PLEASE LOOK UPON HER KINDLY.

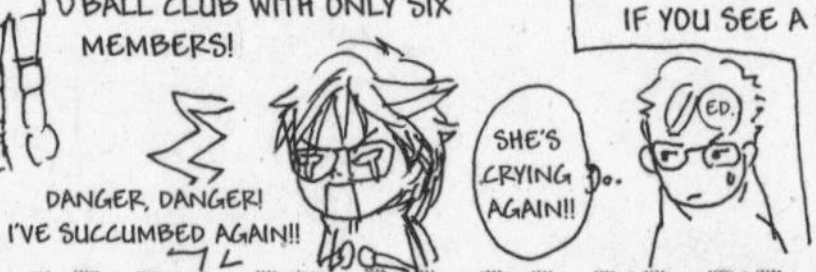
DANGER, DANGER!
I'VE SUCCUMBED AGAIN!!
SHE'S CRYING AGAIN!!
ED.

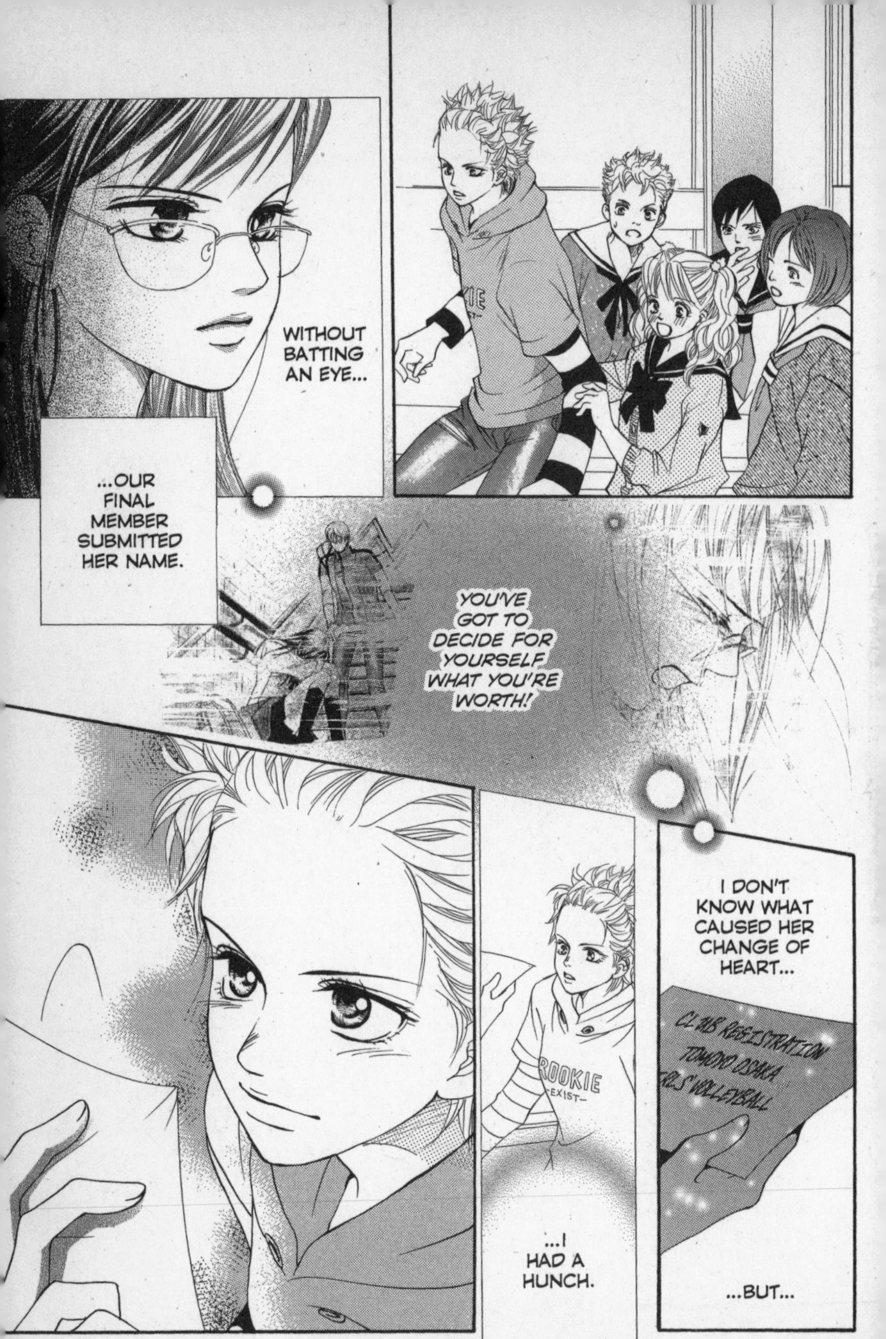
WITHOUT BATTING AN EYE...
...OUR FINAL MEMBER SUBMITTED HER NAME.
YOU'VE GOT TO DECIDE FOR YOURSELF WHAT YOU'RE WORTH!
I DON'T KNOW WHAT CAUSED HER CHANGE OF HEART...
CLUB REGISTRATION
TOMOYO OSAKA
GIRLS' VOLLEYBALL
...BUT...
ROOKIE
-EXIST-
...I HAD A HUNCH.

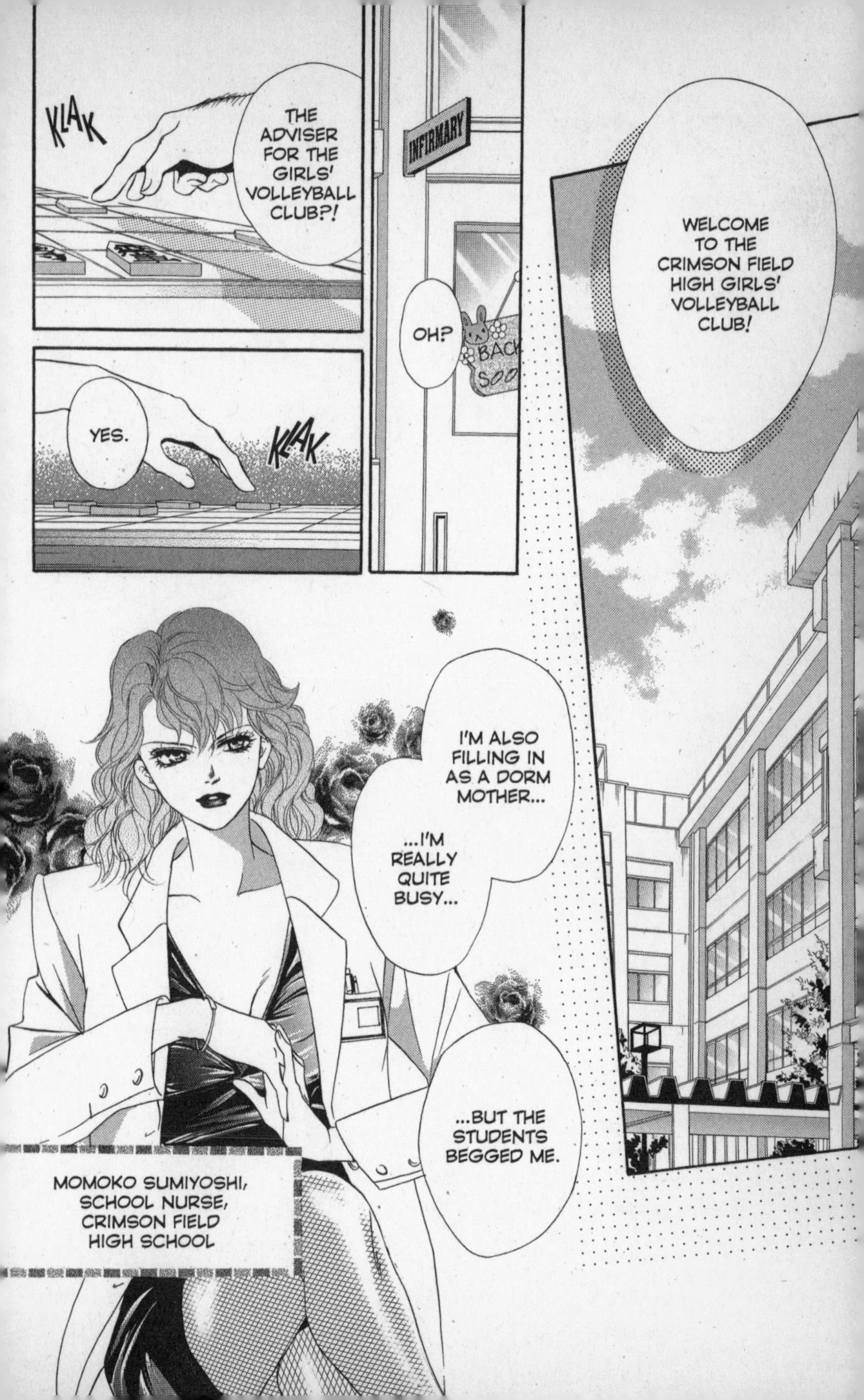
WELCOME TO THE CRIMSON FIELD HIGH GIRLS' VOLLEYBALL CLUB!
INFIRMARY
BACK SOO
OH?
KLAK
THE ADVISER FOR THE GIRLS' VOLLEYBALL CLUB?!
YES.
KLAK
I'M ALSO FILLING IN AS A DORM MOTHER...
...I'M REALLY QUITE BUSY...
...BUT THE STUDENTS BEGGED ME.
MOMOKO SUMIYOSHI, SCHOOL NURSE, CRIMSON FIELD HIGH SCHOOL

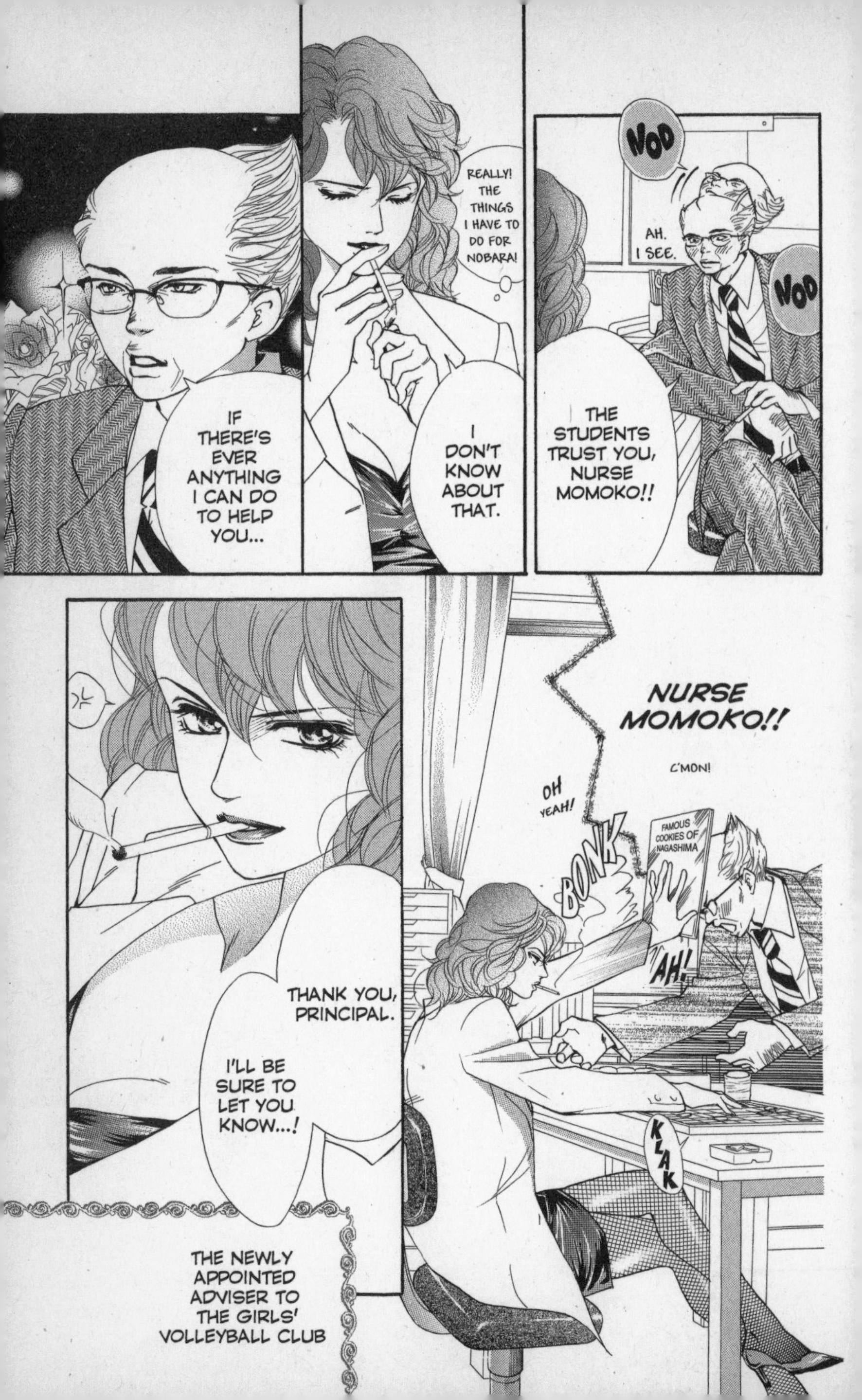
NOD
AH. I SEE.
NOD
THE STUDENTS TRUST YOU, NURSE MOMOKO!!
REALLY! THE THINGS I HAVE TO DO FOR NOBARA!
I DON'T KNOW ABOUT THAT.
IF THERE'S EVER ANYTHING I CAN DO TO HELP YOU...
NURSE MOMOKO!!
C'MON!
OH YEAH!
FAMOUS COOKIES OF NAGASHIMA
BONK
AH!
KLAK
THANK YOU, PRINCIPAL.
I'LL BE SURE TO LET YOU KNOW...!
THE NEWLY APPOINTED ADVISER TO THE GIRLS' VOLLEYBALL CLUB

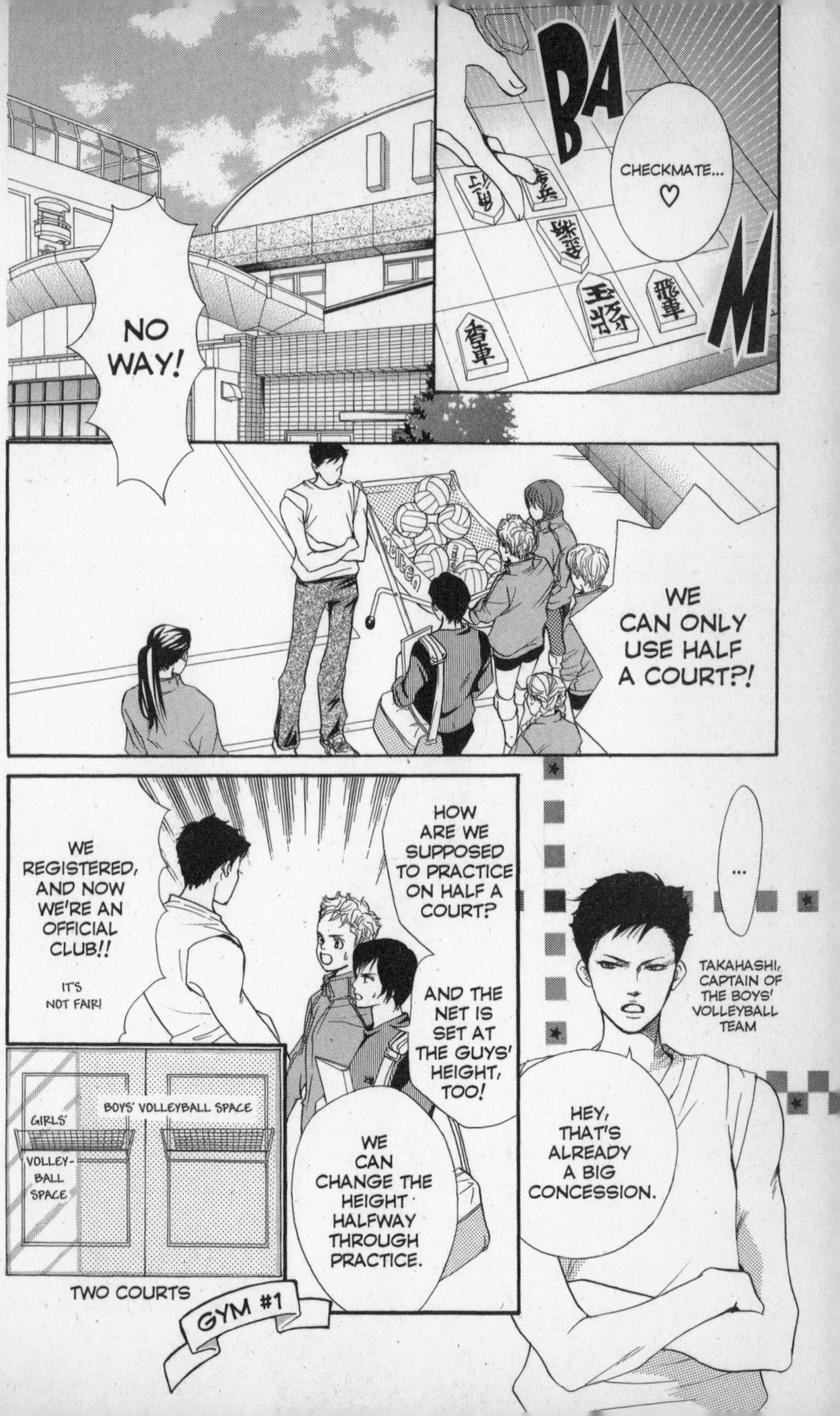
BAM
CHECKMATE... ♡
NO WAY!
WE CAN ONLY USE HALF A COURT?!
...
TAKAHASHI, CAPTAIN OF THE BOYS' VOLLEYBALL TEAM
HEY, THAT'S ALREADY A BIG CONCESSION.
HOW ARE WE SUPPOSED TO PRACTICE ON HALF A COURT?
WE REGISTERED, AND NOW WE'RE AN OFFICIAL CLUB!!
IT'S NOT FAIR!
AND THE NET IS SET AT THE GUYS' HEIGHT, TOO!
WE CAN CHANGE THE HEIGHT HALFWAY THROUGH PRACTICE.
BOYS' VOLLEYBALL SPACE
GIRLS' VOLLEY-BALL SPACE
TWO COURTS
GYM #1

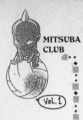

MITSUBA CLUB

Vol. 1

OUR CHIEF ASSISTANT MAKES OUR LUNCHES AT WORK AND LET ME TELL YOU—THEY ARE GOOD.

WE HAVE A SCHEDULE FOR EACH MONTH THAT'S CRAMMED WITH DETAILS ABOUT HOW MY WORK SHOULD BE PROGRESSING AND WHAT THE ASSISTANTS' SCHEDULES ARE. AT THE BOTTOM IT ALSO SHOWS WHAT EACH DAY'S MENU WILL BE. IT ACTUALLY TAKES ABOUT TEN DAYS TO GET THE PAGES DONE, BUT IT'S A HUGE UNDERTAKING TO GO GROCERY SHOPPING FOR TEN DAYS' WORTH OF FOOD. AT FIRST I WENT ALONG TOO, BUT THESE DAYS I JUST LEAVE IT TO HER. SHE HAULS BACK ABOUT TWO CARDBOARD BOXES WORTH OF FOOD IN A CART.

IT'S SO MUCH FOOD THAT EVEN THE SUPERMARKET CLERKS GET SURPRISED EVERY TIME.

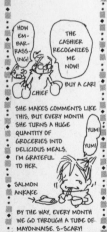

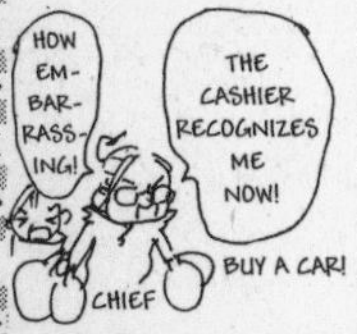
THE CASHIER RECOGNIZES ME NOW!
HOW EM-BAR-RASS-ING!
BUY A CAR!
CHIEF

SHE MAKES COMMENTS LIKE THIS, BUT EVERY MONTH SHE TURNS A HUGE QUANTITY OF GROCERIES INTO DELICIOUS MEALS. I'M GRATEFUL TO HER.

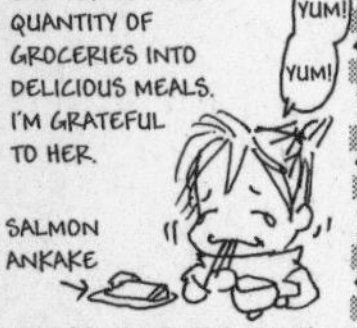
YUM!
YUM!
SALMON ANKAKE

BY THE WAY, EVERY MONTH WE GO THROUGH A TUBE OF MAYONNAISE. S-SCARY!

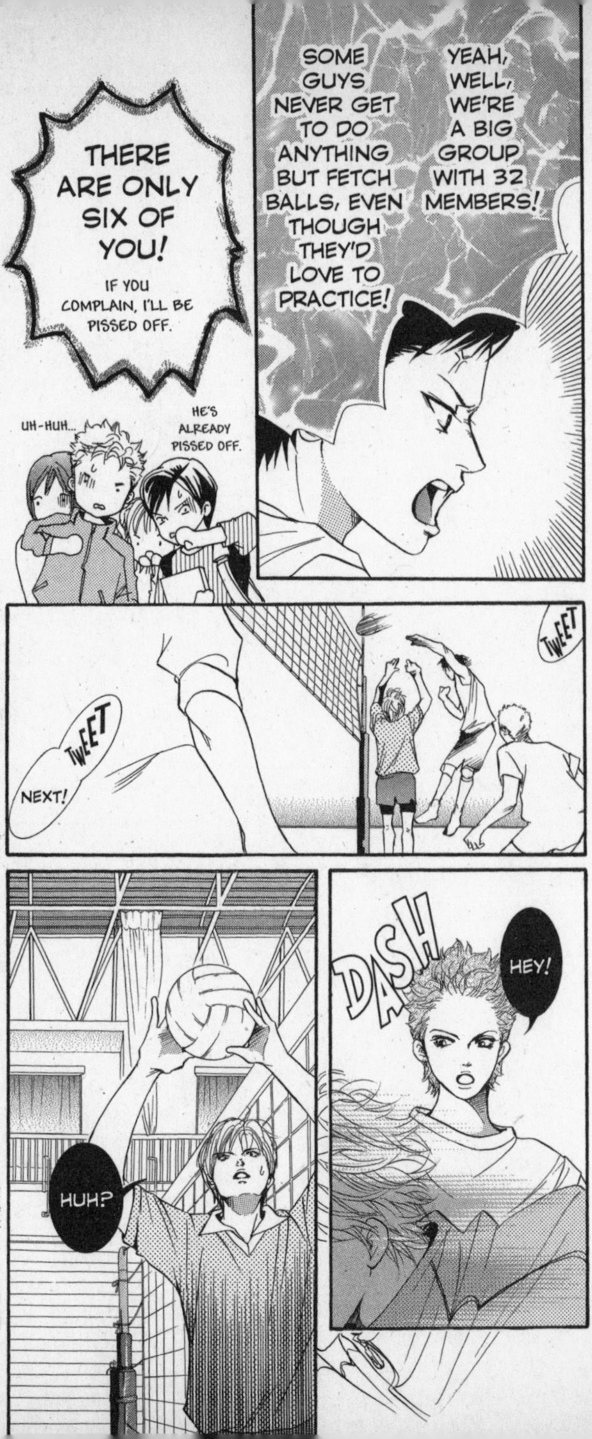
YEAH, WELL, WE'RE A BIG GROUP WITH 32 MEMBERS!
SOME GUYS NEVER GET TO DO ANYTHING BUT FETCH BALLS, EVEN THOUGH THEY'D LOVE TO PRACTICE!
THERE ARE ONLY SIX OF YOU!
IF YOU COMPLAIN, I'LL BE PISSED OFF.
HE'S ALREADY PISSED OFF.
UH-HUH...
TWEET
TWEET
NEXT!
DASH
HEY!
HUH?

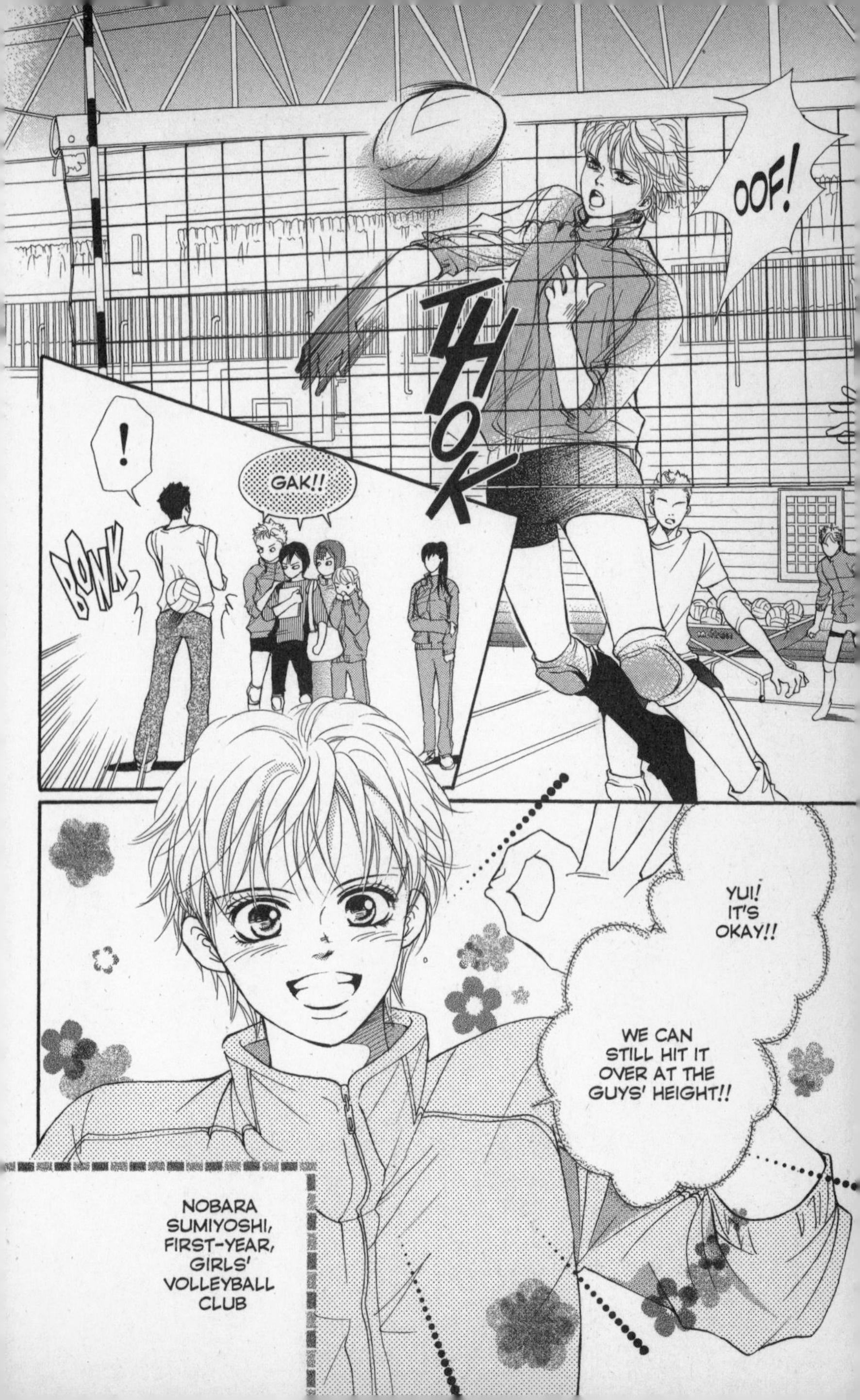
OOF!
THOK
!
GAK!!
BONK
YUI! IT'S OKAY!!
WE CAN STILL HIT IT OVER AT THE GUYS' HEIGHT!!
NOBARA SUMIYOSHI, FIRST-YEAR, GIRLS' VOLLEYBALL CLUB

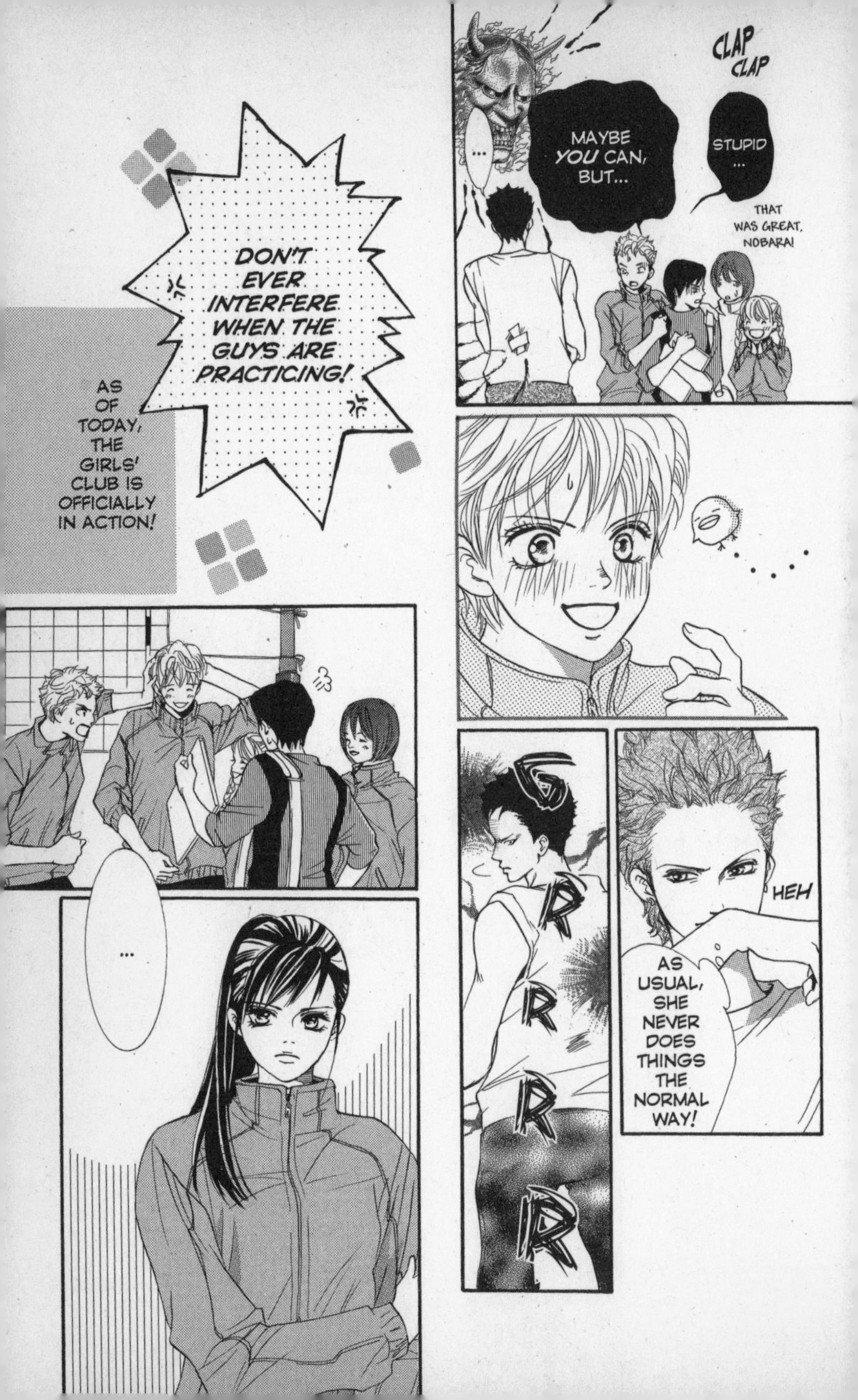
CLAP CLAP
STUPID ...
MAYBE YOU CAN, BUT...
...
THAT WAS GREAT, NOBARA!
HEH
AS USUAL, SHE NEVER DOES THINGS THE NORMAL WAY!
SRRRR
DON'T EVER INTERFERE WHEN THE GUYS ARE PRACTICING!
AS OF TODAY, THE GIRLS' CLUB IS OFFICIALLY IN ACTION!
...

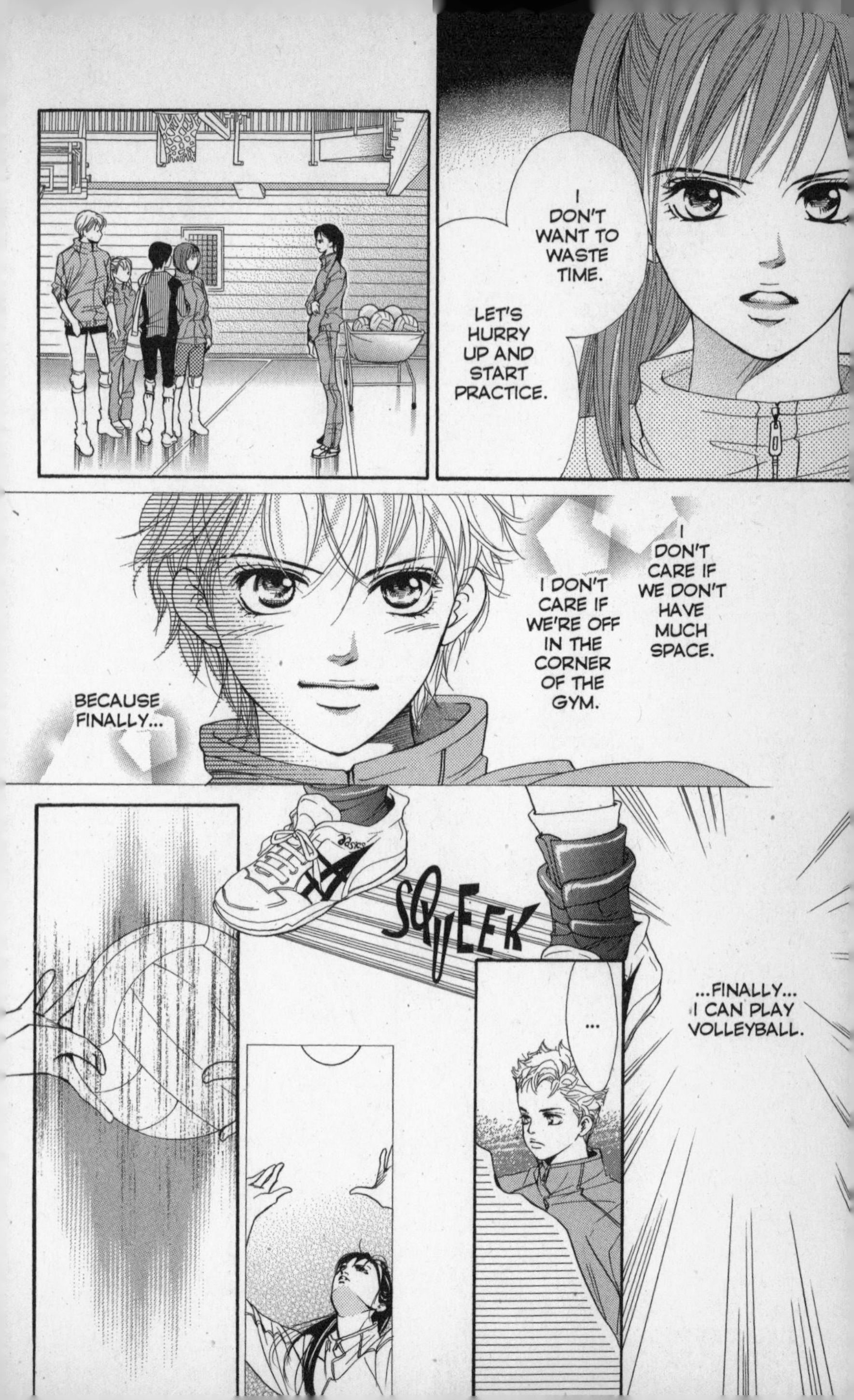
I DON'T WANT TO WASTE TIME.
LET'S HURRY UP AND START PRACTICE.
I DON'T CARE IF WE DON'T HAVE MUCH SPACE.
I DON'T CARE IF WE'RE OFF IN THE CORNER OF THE GYM.
BECAUSE FINALLY...
SQUEEK
...FINALLY... I CAN PLAY VOLLEYBALL.
...

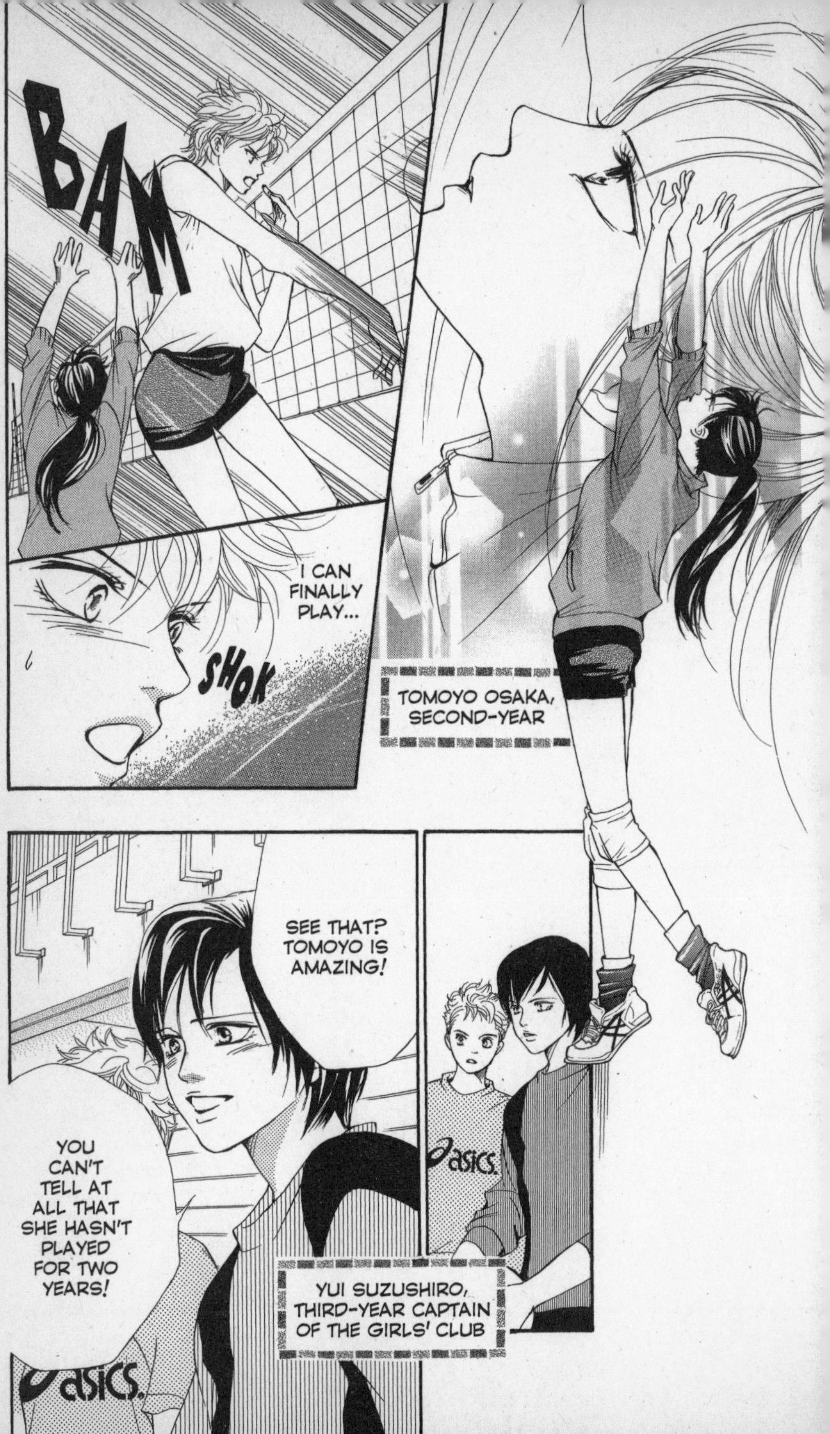
TOMOYO OSAKA, SECOND-YEAR
BAM
I CAN FINALLY PLAY...
SHOK
SEE THAT? TOMOYO IS AMAZING!
YOU CAN'T TELL AT ALL THAT SHE HASN'T PLAYED FOR TWO YEARS!
YUI SUZUSHIRO, THIRD-YEAR CAPTAIN OF THE GIRLS' CLUB
asics
asics

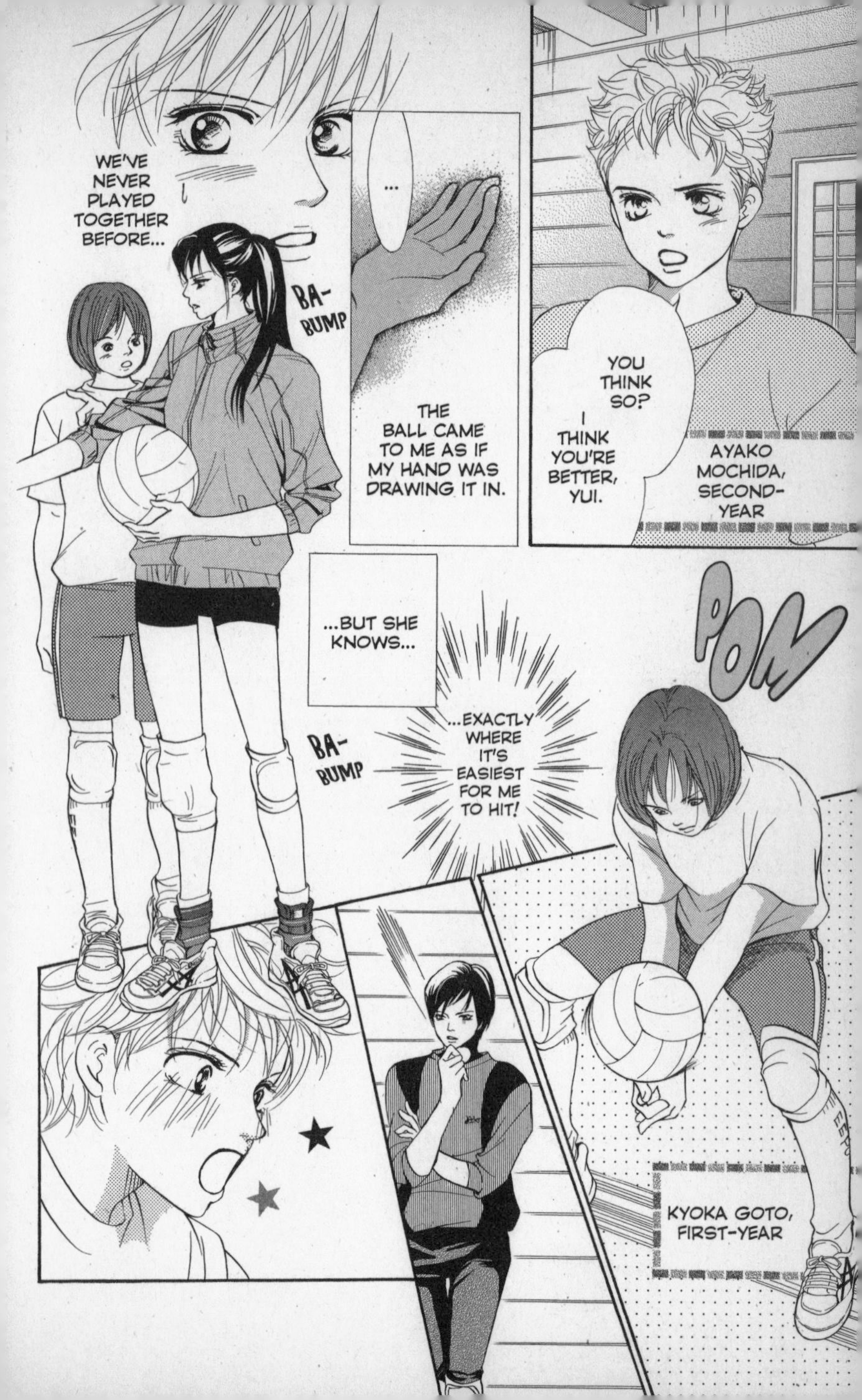
YOU THINK SO?
I THINK YOU'RE BETTER, YUI.
AYAKO MOCHIDA, SECOND-YEAR
...
THE BALL CAME TO ME AS IF MY HAND WAS DRAWING IT IN.
WE'VE NEVER PLAYED TOGETHER BEFORE...
BA-BUMP
POM
KYOKA GOTO, FIRST-YEAR
...BUT SHE KNOWS...
...EXACTLY WHERE IT'S EASIEST FOR ME TO HIT!
BA-BUMP

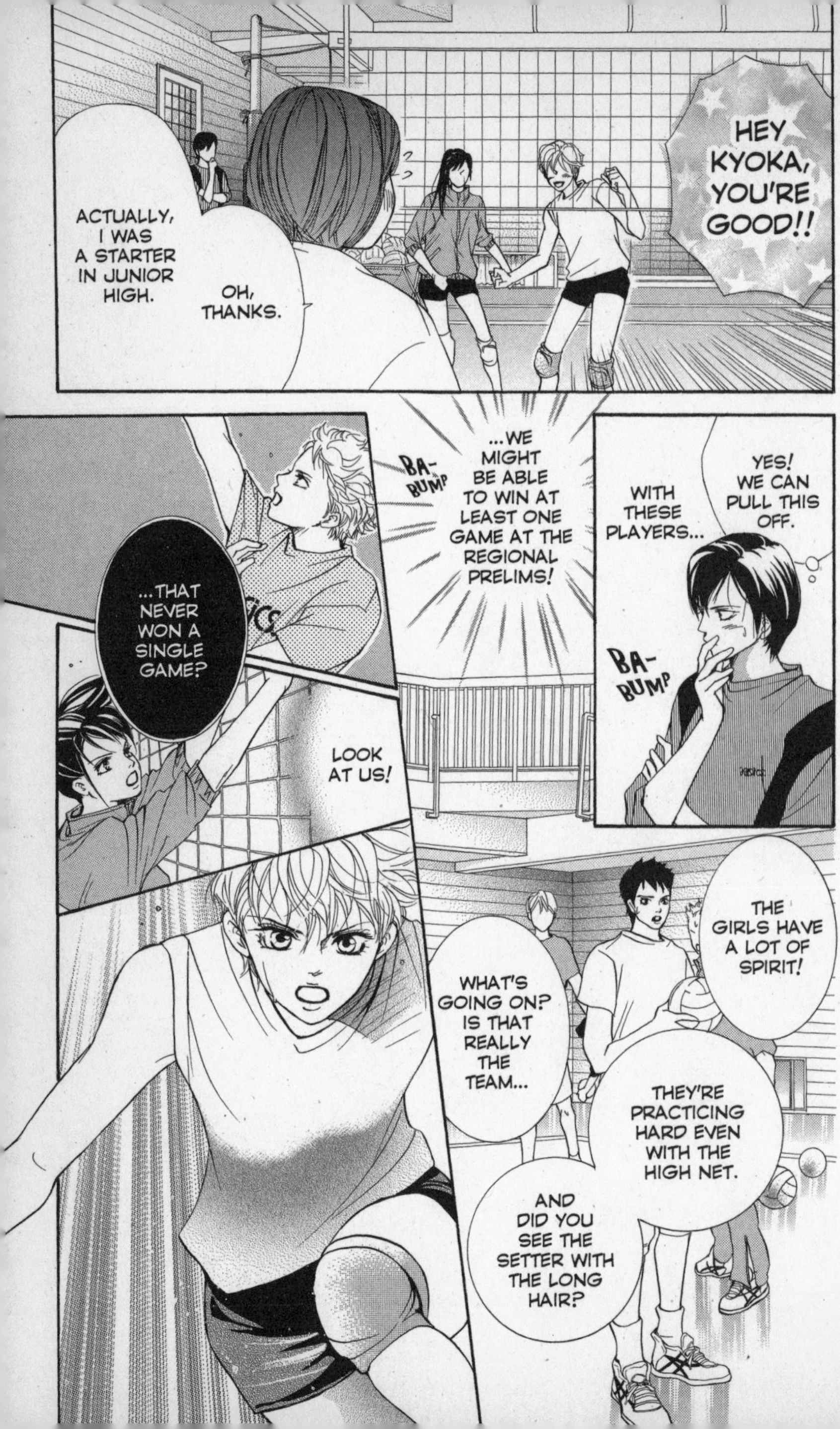
HEY KYOKA, YOU'RE GOOD!!
OH, THANKS.
ACTUALLY, I WAS A STARTER IN JUNIOR HIGH.
YES! WE CAN PULL THIS OFF.
WITH THESE PLAYERS...
BA-BUMP
...WE MIGHT BE ABLE TO WIN AT LEAST ONE GAME AT THE REGIONAL PRELIMS!
BA-BUMP
THE GIRLS HAVE A LOT OF SPIRIT!
WHAT'S GOING ON? IS THAT REALLY THE TEAM...
THEY'RE PRACTICING HARD EVEN WITH THE HIGH NET.
AND DID YOU SEE THE SETTER WITH THE LONG HAIR?
...THAT NEVER WON A SINGLE GAME?
LOOK AT US!

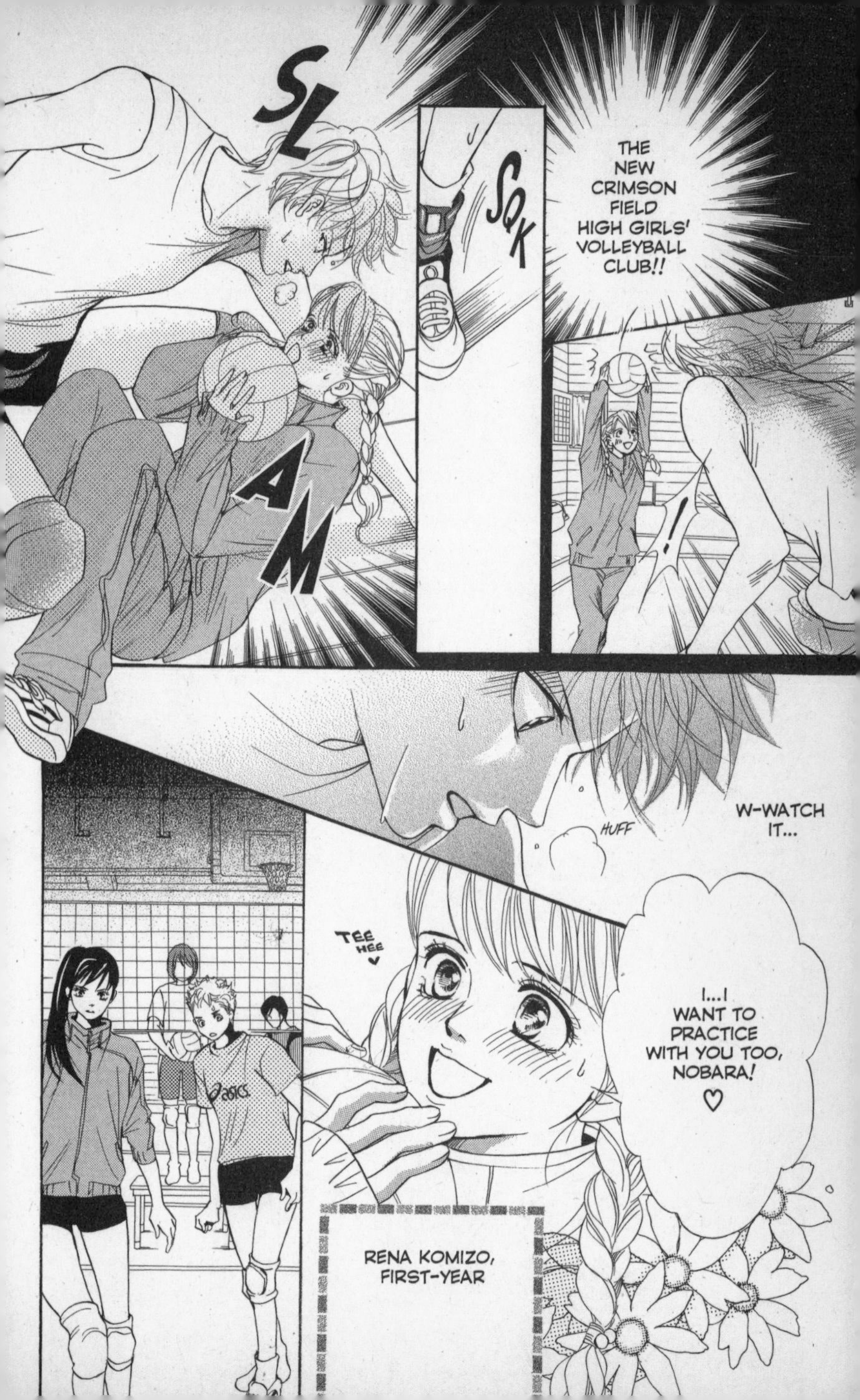
THE NEW CRIMSON FIELD HIGH GIRLS' VOLLEYBALL CLUB!!
!
SQK
SLAM
W-WATCH IT...
HUFF
TEE HEE ♥
I...I WANT TO PRACTICE WITH YOU TOO, NOBARA! ♡
RENA KOMIZO, FIRST-YEAR

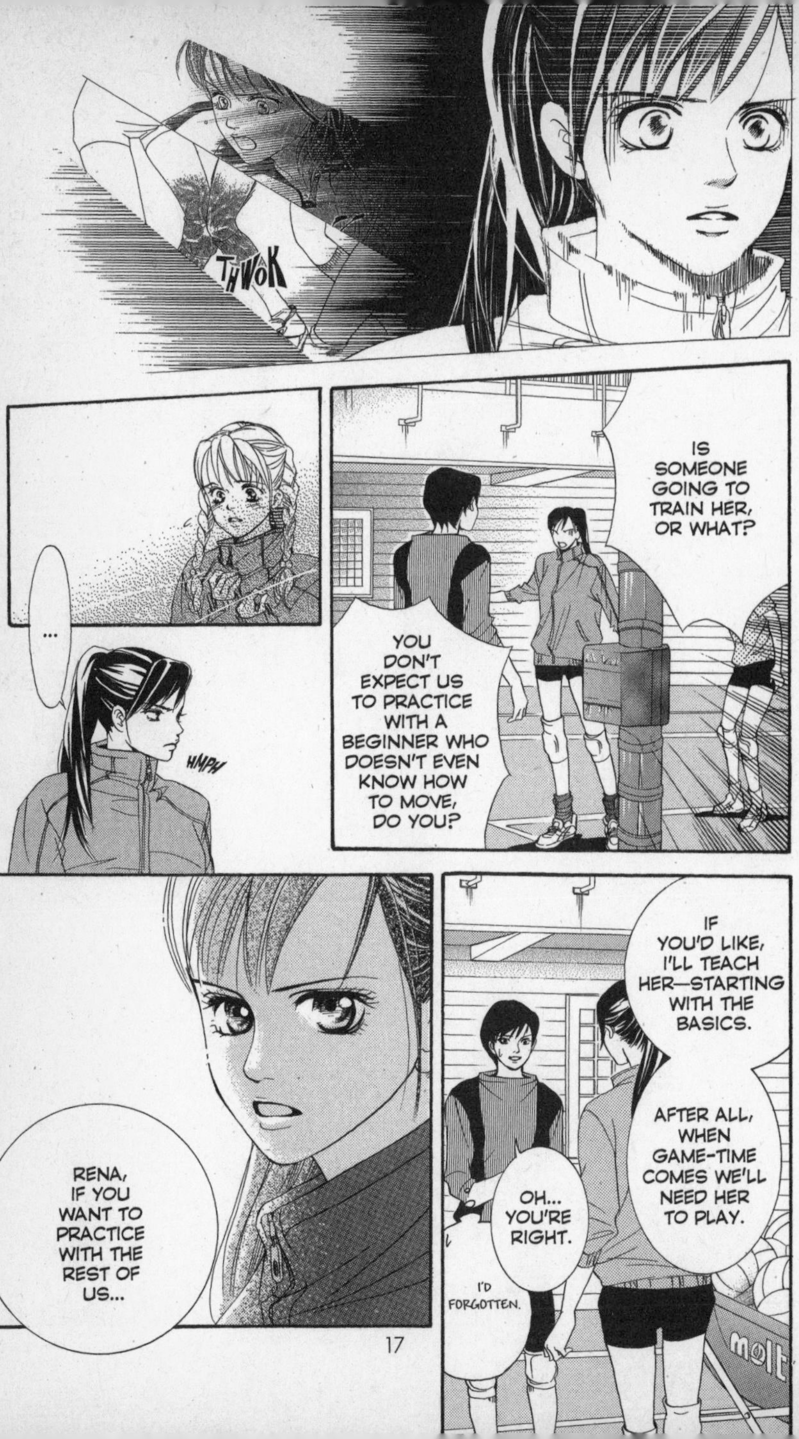
THWOK
IS SOMEONE GOING TO TRAIN HER, OR WHAT?
YOU DON'T EXPECT US TO PRACTICE WITH A BEGINNER WHO DOESN'T EVEN KNOW HOW TO MOVE, DO YOU?
...
HMPH
IF YOU'D LIKE, I'LL TEACH HER—STARTING WITH THE BASICS.
AFTER ALL, WHEN GAME-TIME COMES WE'LL NEED HER TO PLAY.
OH... YOU'RE RIGHT.
I'D FORGOTTEN.
RENA, IF YOU WANT TO PRACTICE WITH THE REST OF US...

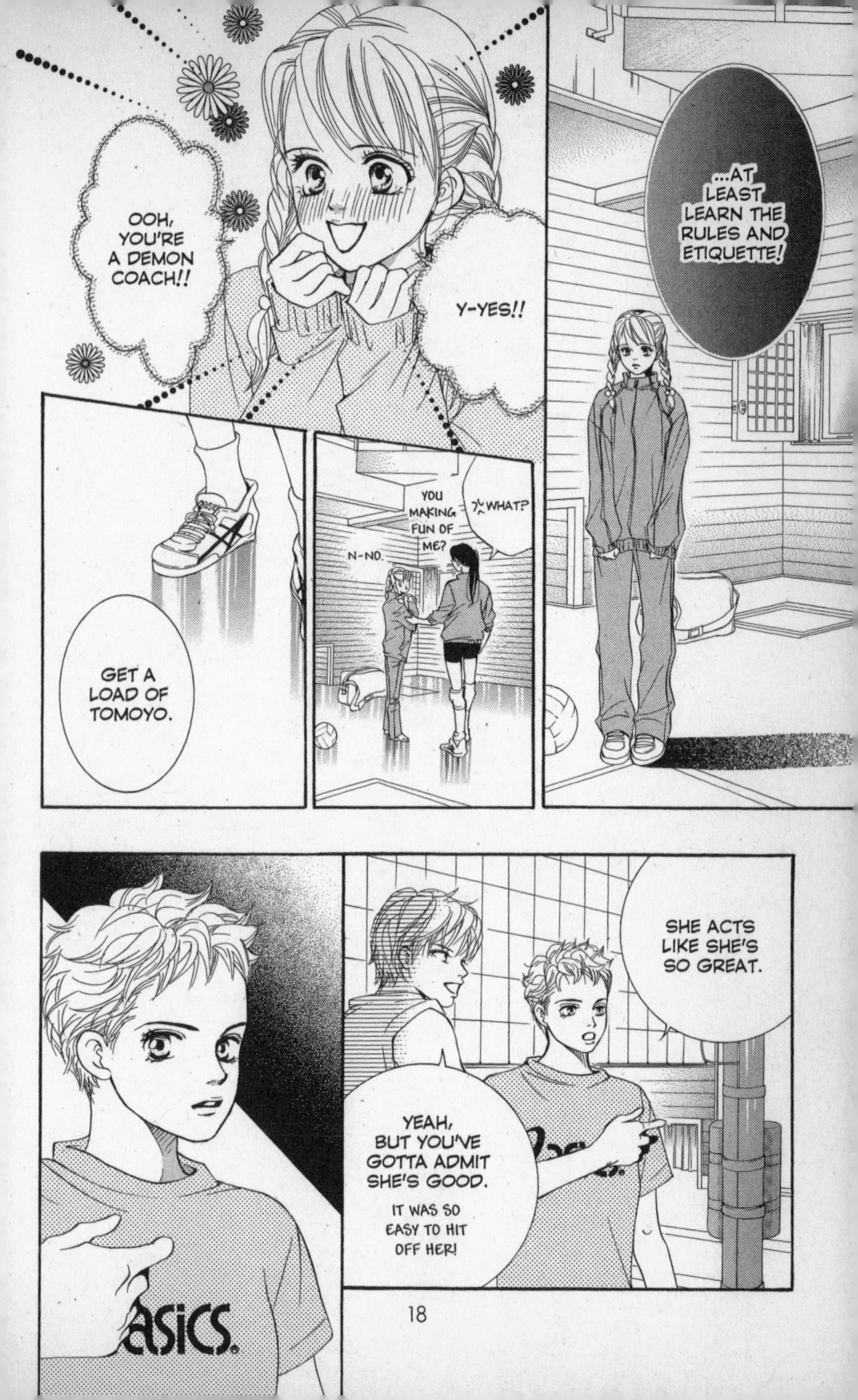
...AT LEAST LEARN THE RULES AND ETIQUETTE!
Y-YES!!
OOH, YOU'RE A DEMON COACH!!
WHAT?
YOU MAKING FUN OF ME?
N-NO.
GET A LOAD OF TOMOYO.
SHE ACTS LIKE SHE'S SO GREAT.
YEAH, BUT YOU'VE GOTTA ADMIT SHE'S GOOD.
IT WAS SO EASY TO HIT OFF HER!

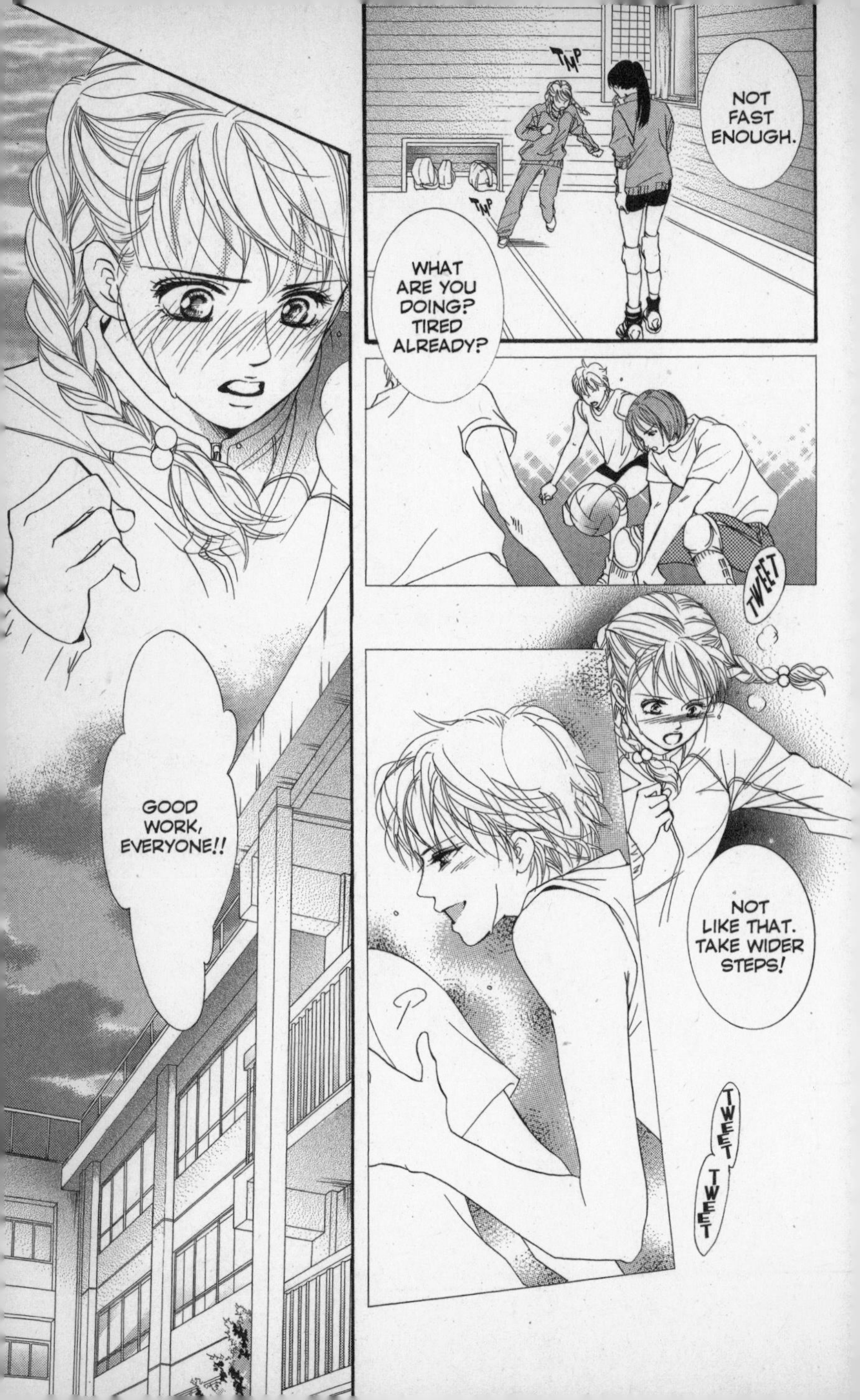
NOT FAST ENOUGH.
TMP
TMP
WHAT ARE YOU DOING? TIRED ALREADY?
TWEET
NOT LIKE THAT. TAKE WIDER STEPS!
TWEET
TWEET
GOOD WORK, EVERYONE!!

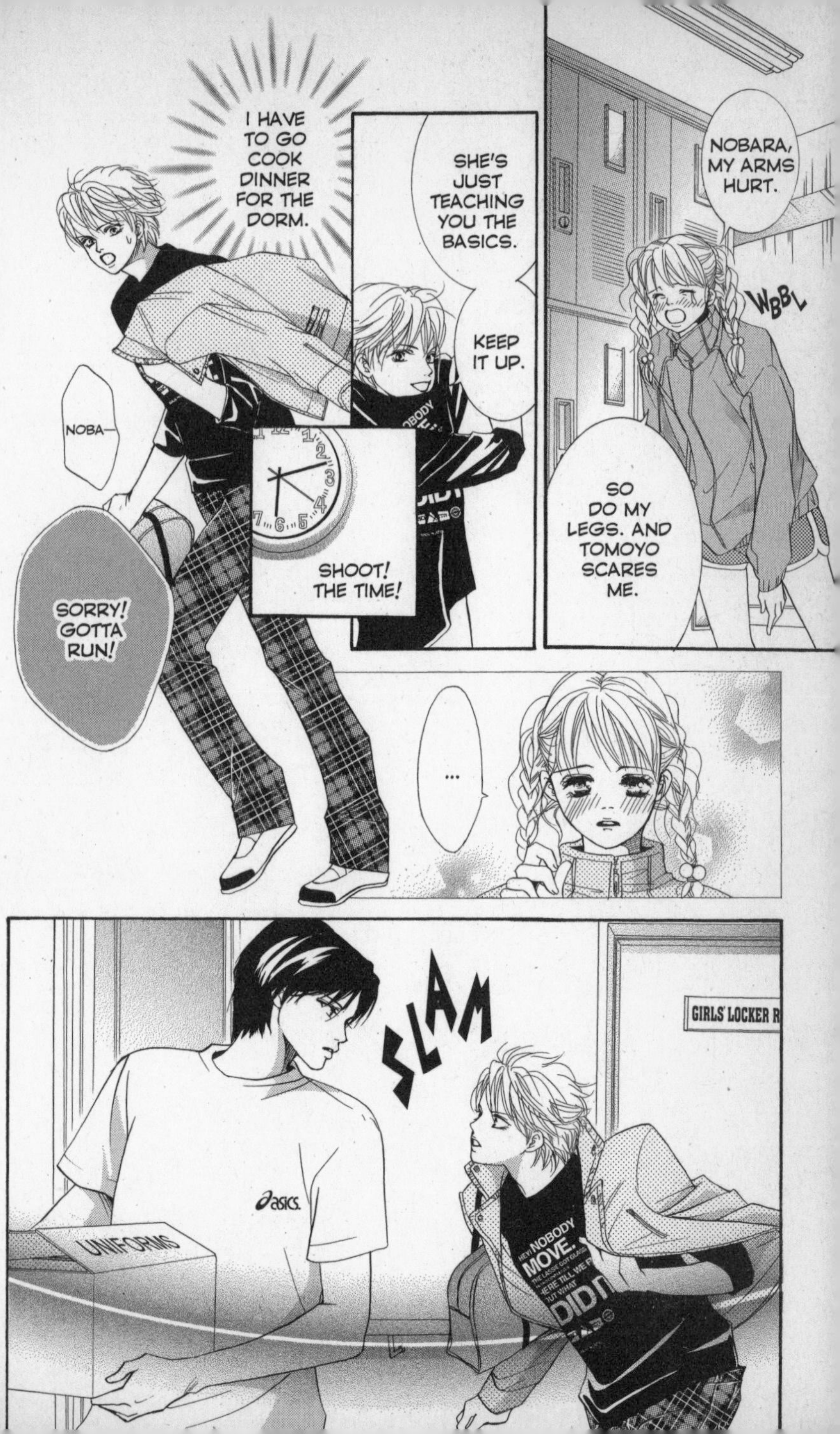
NOBARA, MY ARMS HURT.
WBBL
SO DO MY LEGS. AND TOMOYO SCARES ME.
SHE'S JUST TEACHING YOU THE BASICS.
KEEP IT UP.
SHOOT! THE TIME!
...
I HAVE TO GO COOK DINNER FOR THE DORM.
NOBA—
SORRY! GOTTA RUN!
GIRLS' LOCKER R
SLAM
UNIFORMS

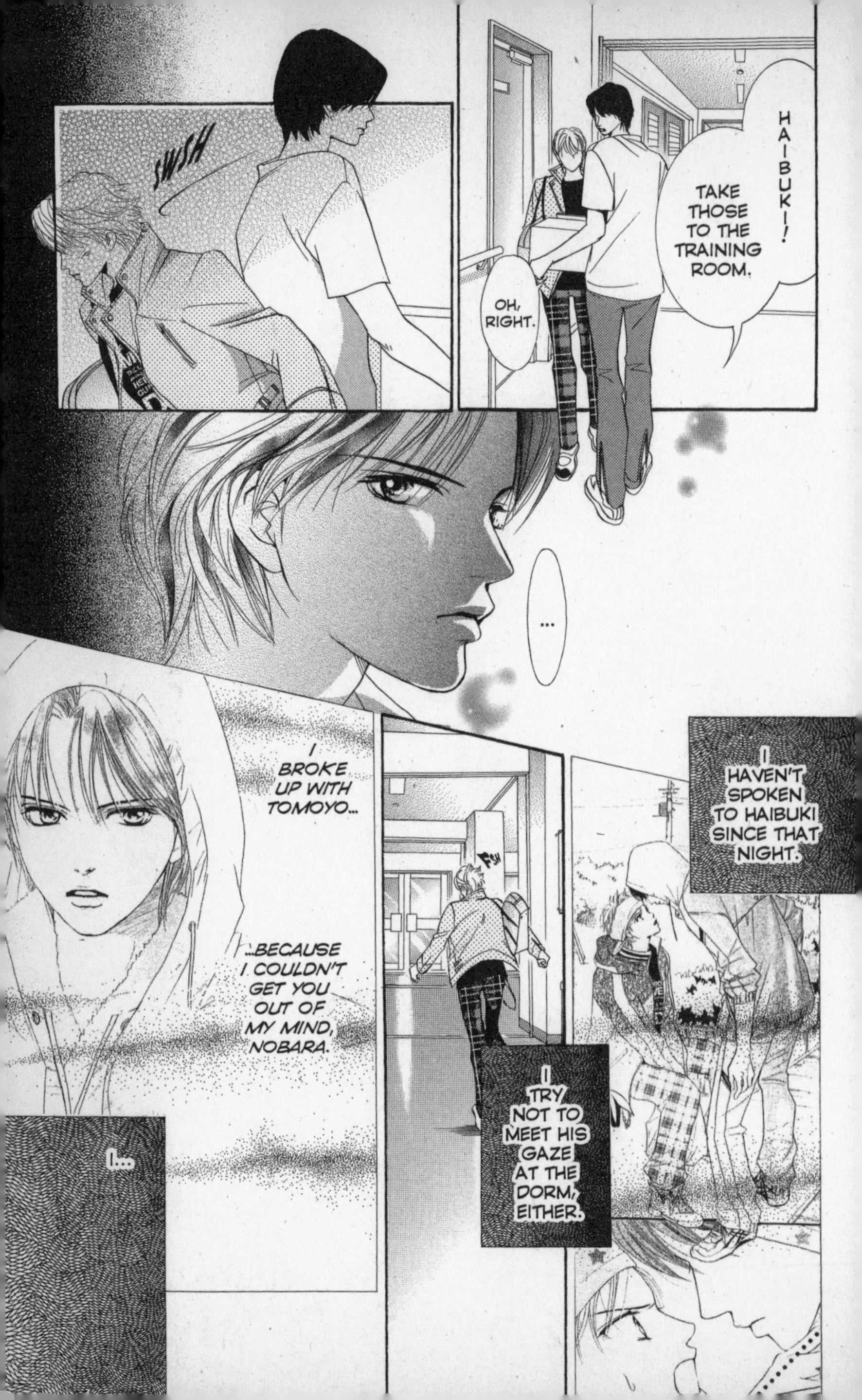
HAIBUKI!
TAKE THOSE TO THE TRAINING ROOM.
OH, RIGHT.
SWSH
...
I HAVEN'T SPOKEN TO HAIBUKI SINCE THAT NIGHT.
FSH
I TRY NOT TO MEET HIS GAZE AT THE DORM, EITHER.
I BROKE UP WITH TOMOYO...
...BECAUSE I COULDN'T GET YOU OUT OF MY MIND, NOBARA.
I...

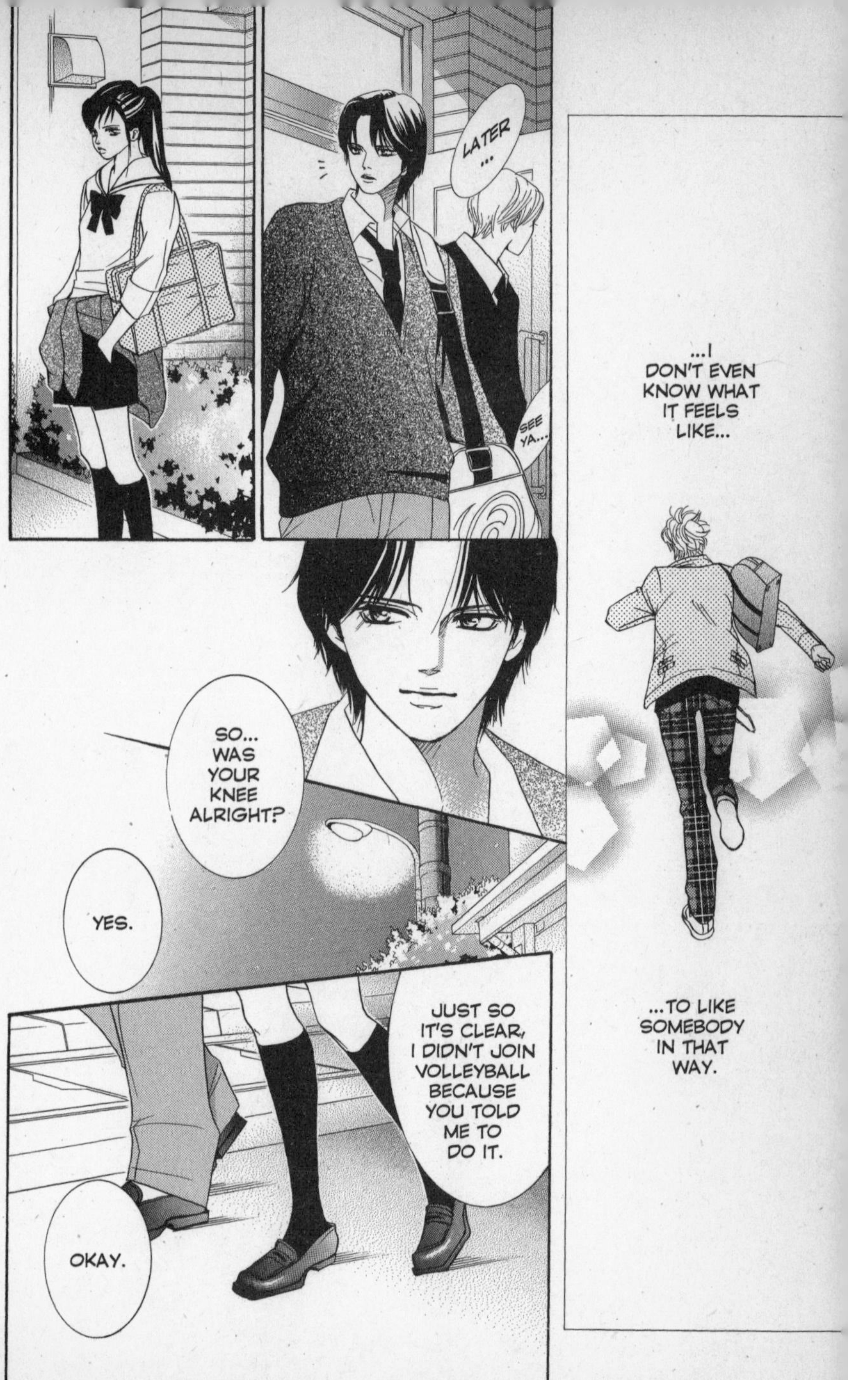
...I DON'T EVEN KNOW WHAT IT FEELS LIKE...
...TO LIKE SOMEBODY IN THAT WAY.
LATER ...
SEE YA...
SO... WAS YOUR KNEE ALRIGHT?
YES.
JUST SO IT'S CLEAR, I DIDN'T JOIN VOLLEYBALL BECAUSE YOU TOLD ME TO DO IT.
OKAY.

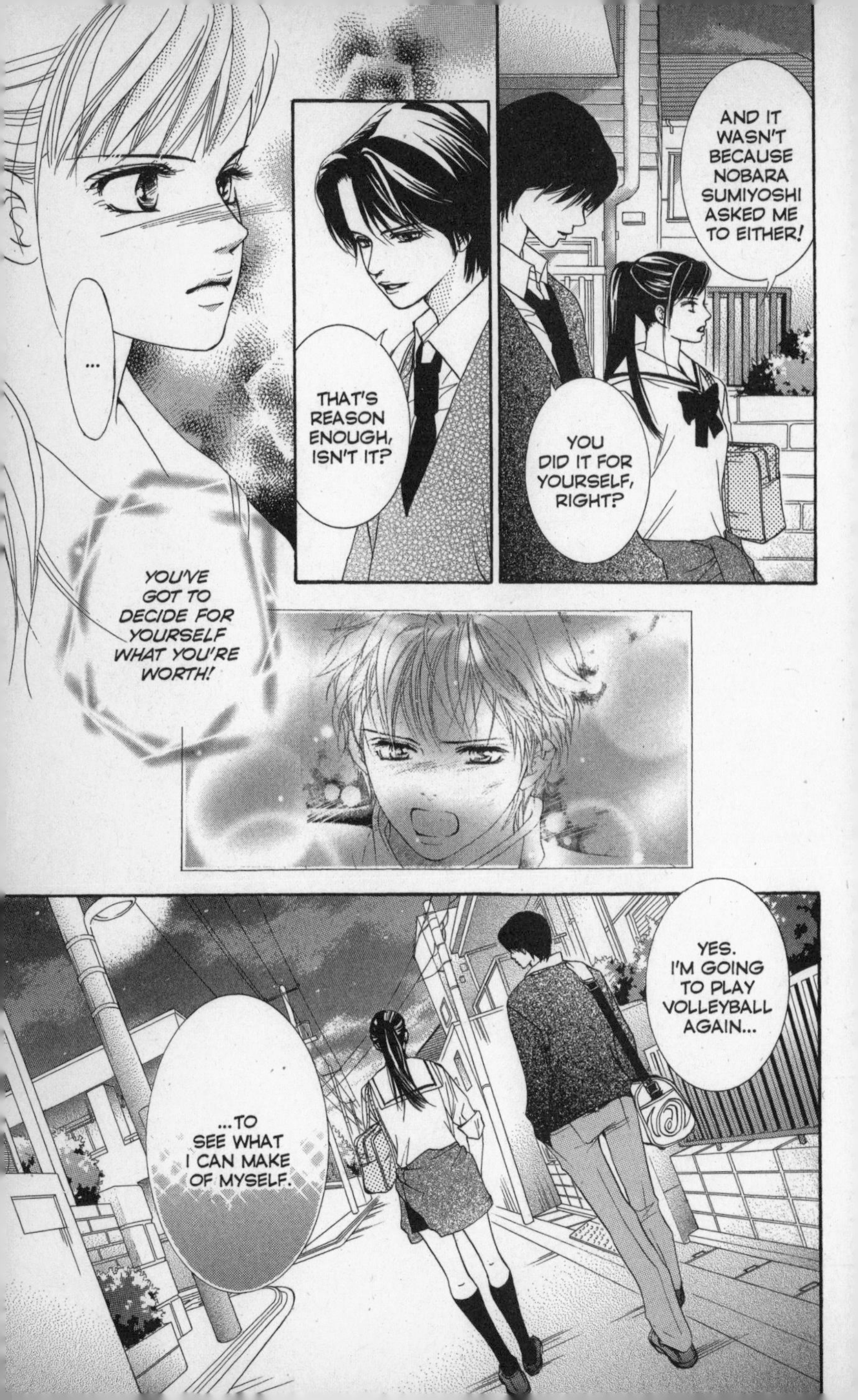
AND IT WASN'T BECAUSE NOBARA SUMIYOSHI ASKED ME TO EITHER!
YOU DID IT FOR YOURSELF, RIGHT?
THAT'S REASON ENOUGH, ISN'T IT?
...
YOU'VE GOT TO DECIDE FOR YOURSELF WHAT YOU'RE WORTH!
YES. I'M GOING TO PLAY VOLLEYBALL AGAIN...
...TO SEE WHAT I CAN MAKE OF MYSELF.

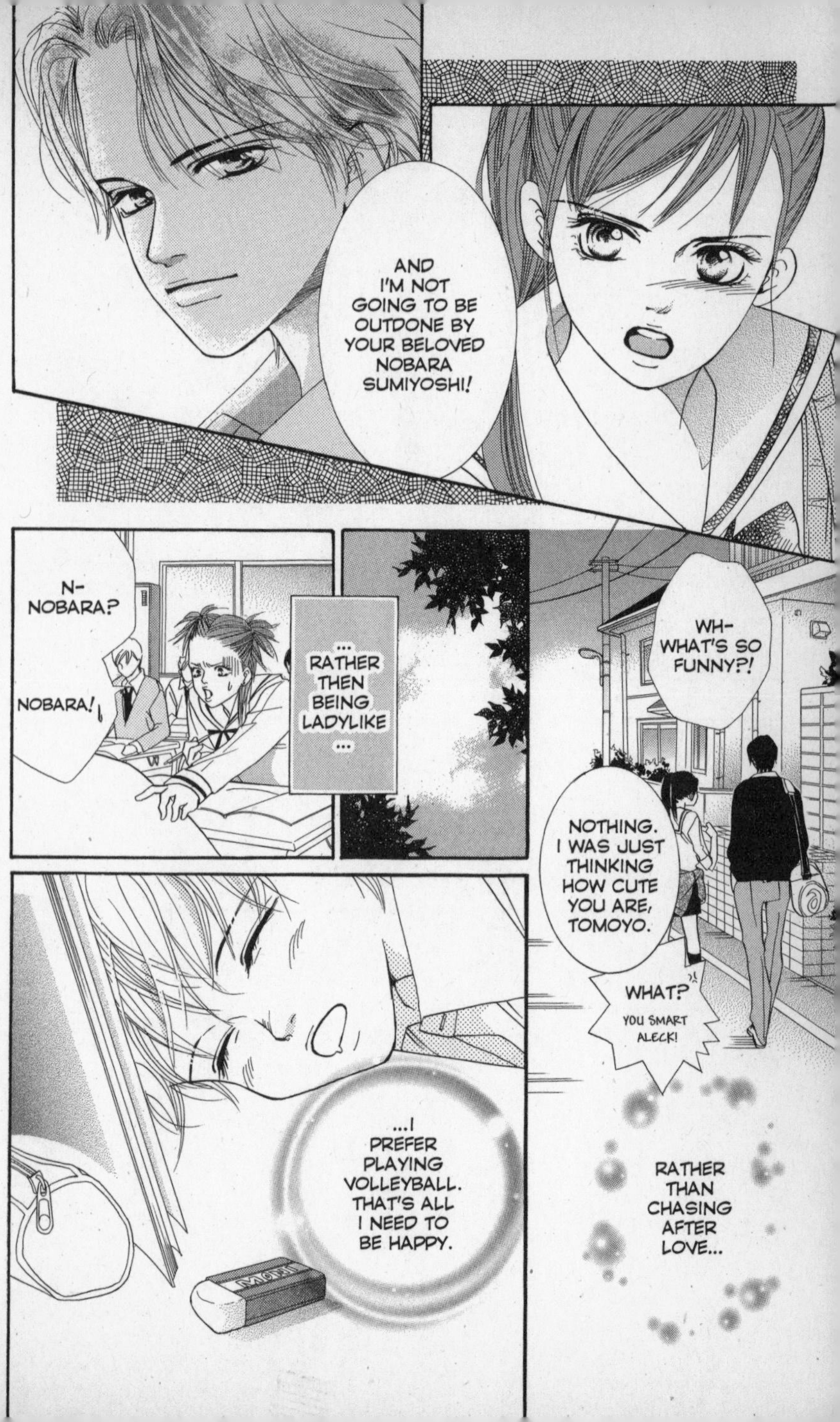
AND I'M NOT GOING TO BE OUTDONE BY YOUR BELOVED NOBARA SUMIYOSHI!
WH- WHAT'S SO FUNNY?!
NOTHING. I WAS JUST THINKING HOW CUTE YOU ARE, TOMOYO.
WHAT?
YOU SMART ALECK!
RATHER THAN CHASING AFTER LOVE...
... RATHER THEN BEING LADYLIKE ...
N- NOBARA?
NOBARA!
...I PREFER PLAYING VOLLEYBALL. THAT'S ALL I NEED TO BE HAPPY.

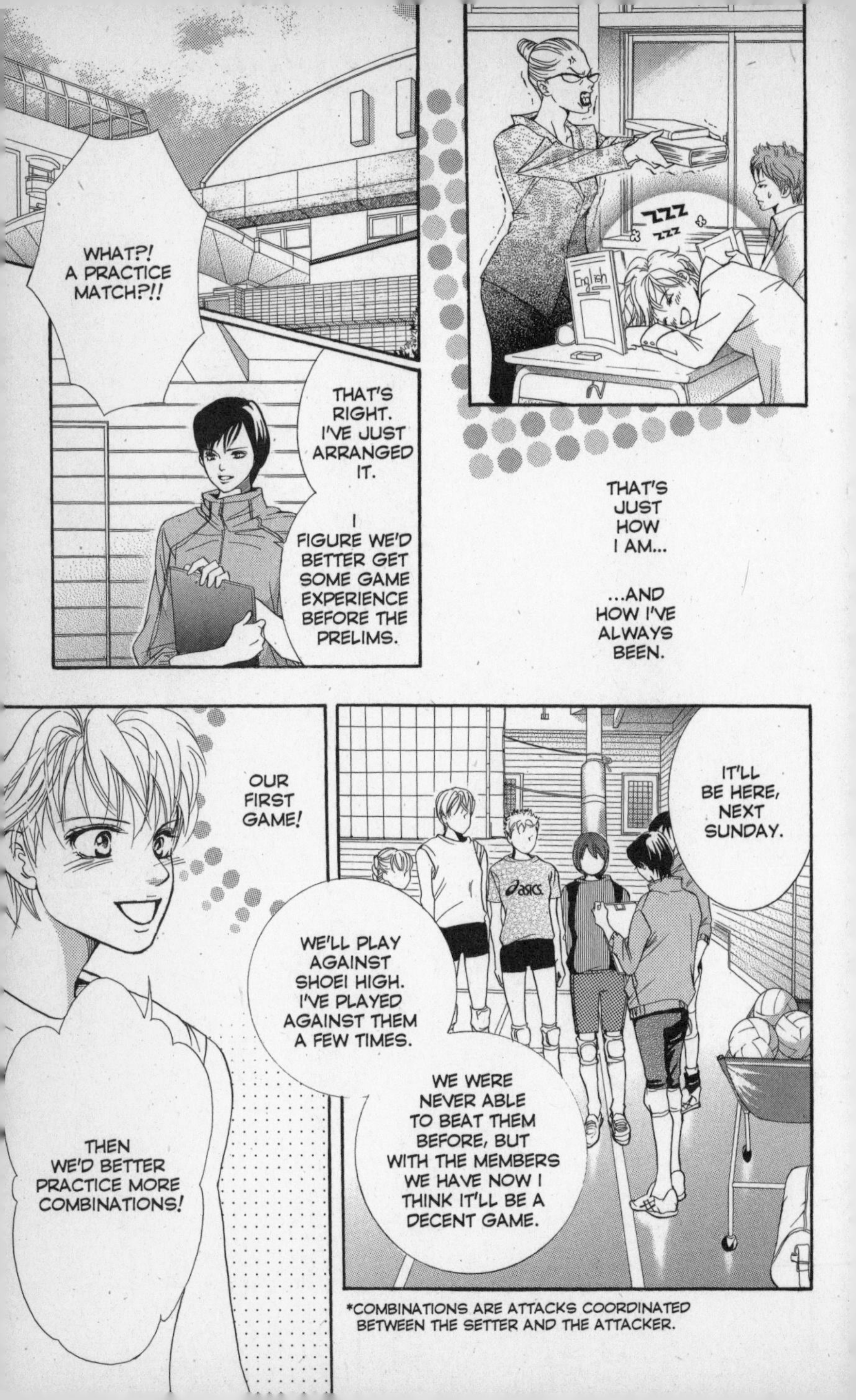
ZZZ
ZZZ
English
THAT'S JUST HOW I AM...
...AND HOW I'VE ALWAYS BEEN.
WHAT?! A PRACTICE MATCH?!!
THAT'S RIGHT. I'VE JUST ARRANGED IT.
I FIGURE WE'D BETTER GET SOME GAME EXPERIENCE BEFORE THE PRELIMS.
IT'LL BE HERE, NEXT SUNDAY.
WE'LL PLAY AGAINST SHOEI HIGH. I'VE PLAYED AGAINST THEM A FEW TIMES.
WE WERE NEVER ABLE TO BEAT THEM BEFORE, BUT WITH THE MEMBERS WE HAVE NOW I THINK IT'LL BE A DECENT GAME.
asics
OUR FIRST GAME!
THEN WE'D BETTER PRACTICE MORE COMBINATIONS!
*COMBINATIONS ARE ATTACKS COORDINATED BETWEEN THE SETTER AND THE ATTACKER.

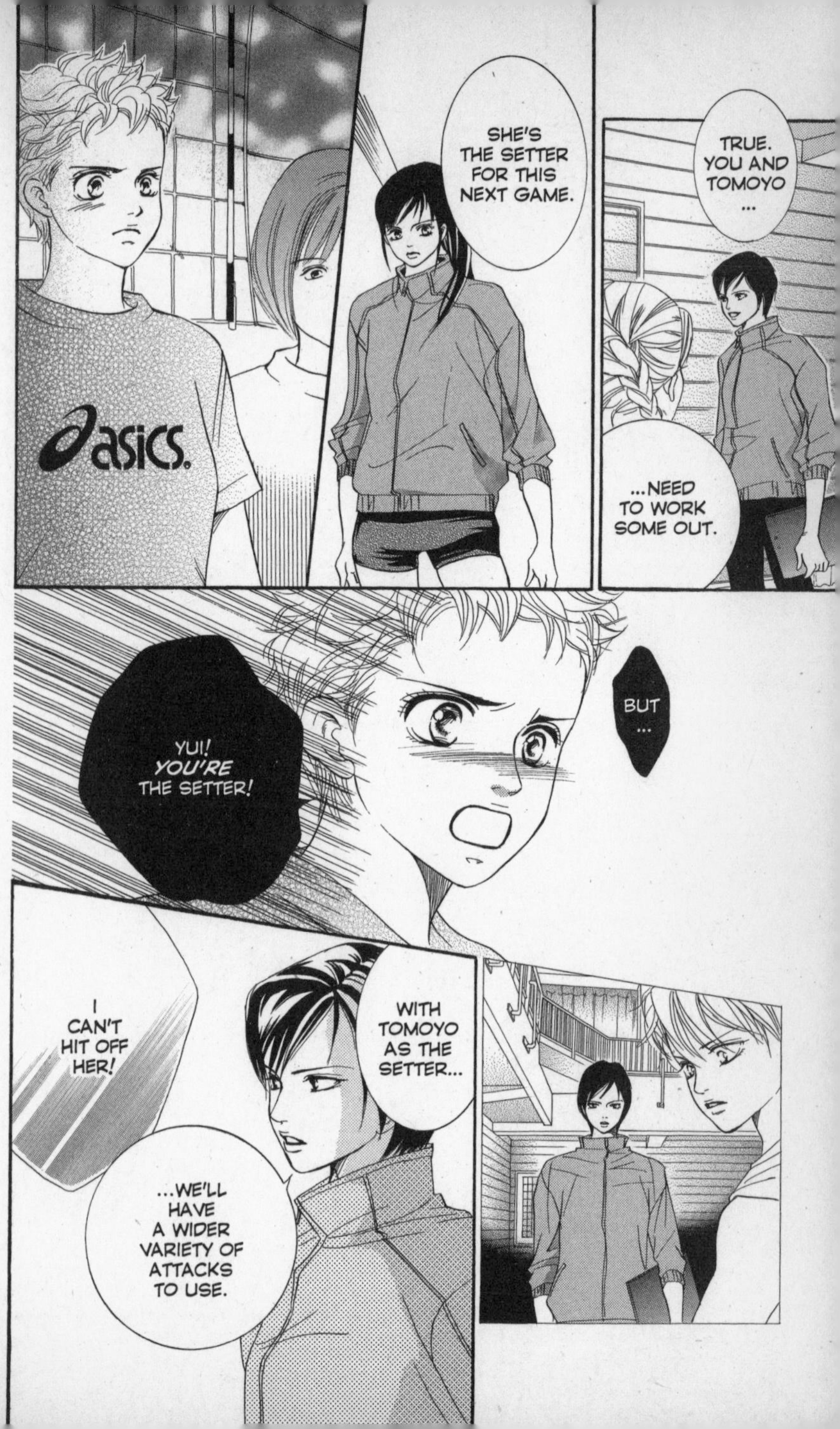
TRUE. YOU AND TOMOYO ...
...NEED TO WORK SOME OUT.
SHE'S THE SETTER FOR THIS NEXT GAME.
BUT ...
YUI! *YOU'RE* THE SETTER!
WITH TOMOYO AS THE SETTER...
...WE'LL HAVE A WIDER VARIETY OF ATTACKS TO USE.
I CAN'T HIT OFF HER!

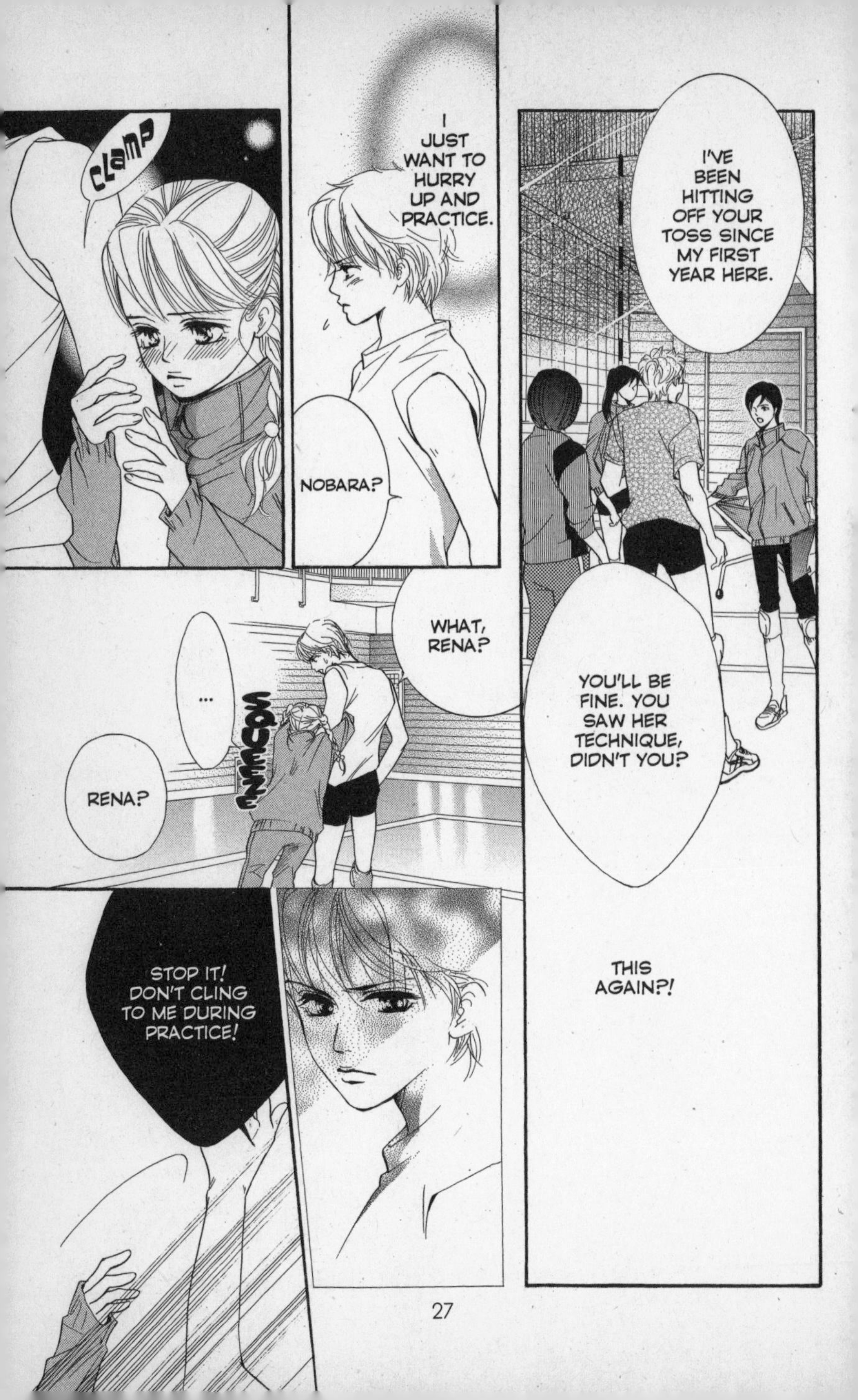
I'VE BEEN HITTING OFF YOUR TOSS SINCE MY FIRST YEAR HERE.
YOU'LL BE FINE. YOU SAW HER TECHNIQUE, DIDN'T YOU?
THIS AGAIN?!
I JUST WANT TO HURRY UP AND PRACTICE.
NOBARA?
CLAMP
WHAT, RENA?
...
SQUEEZE
RENA?
STOP IT! DON'T CLING TO ME DURING PRACTICE!

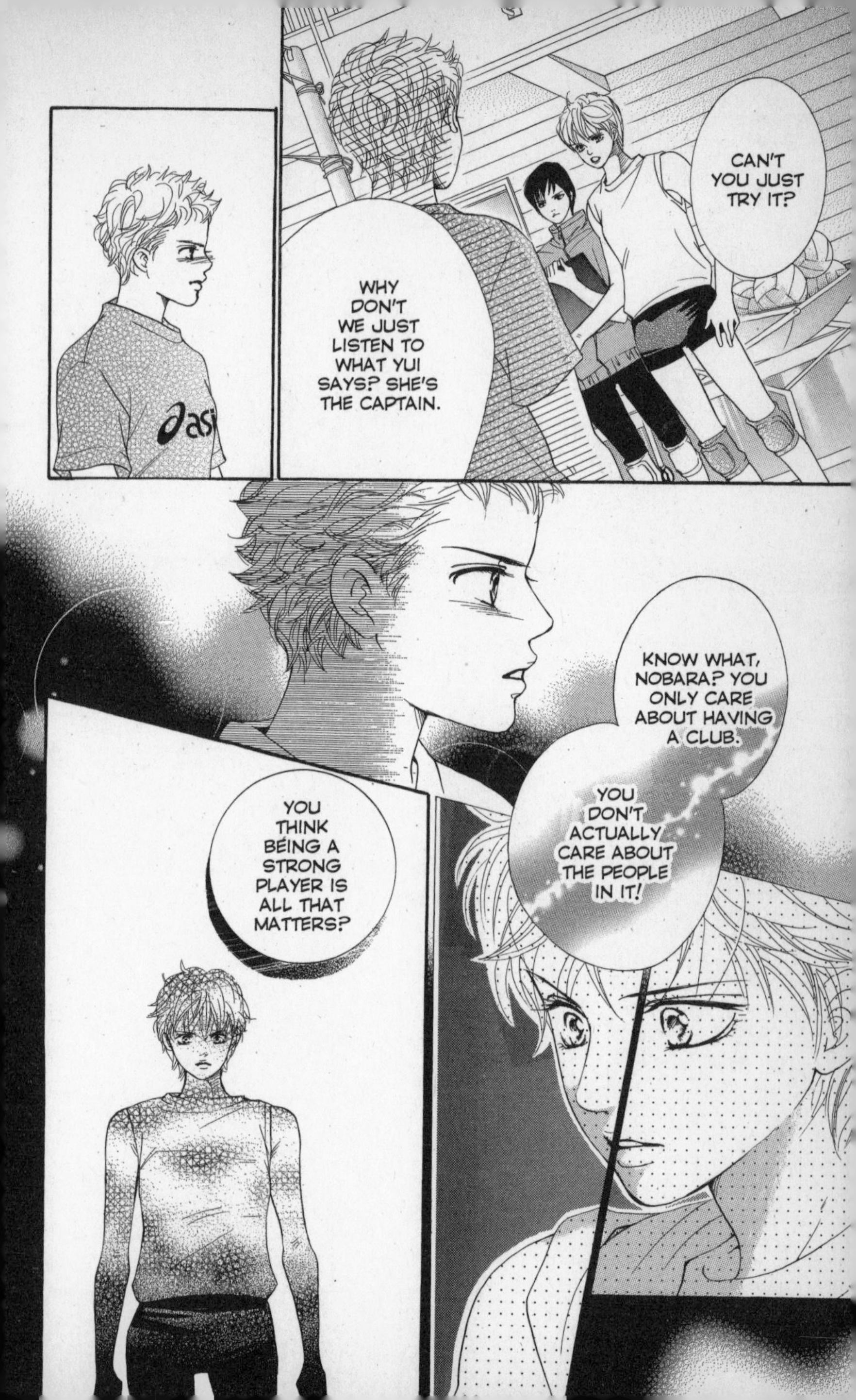
CAN'T YOU JUST TRY IT?
WHY DON'T WE JUST LISTEN TO WHAT YUI SAYS? SHE'S THE CAPTAIN.
KNOW WHAT, NOBARA? YOU ONLY CARE ABOUT HAVING A CLUB.
YOU DON'T ACTUALLY CARE ABOUT THE PEOPLE IN IT!
YOU THINK BEING A STRONG PLAYER IS ALL THAT MATTERS?

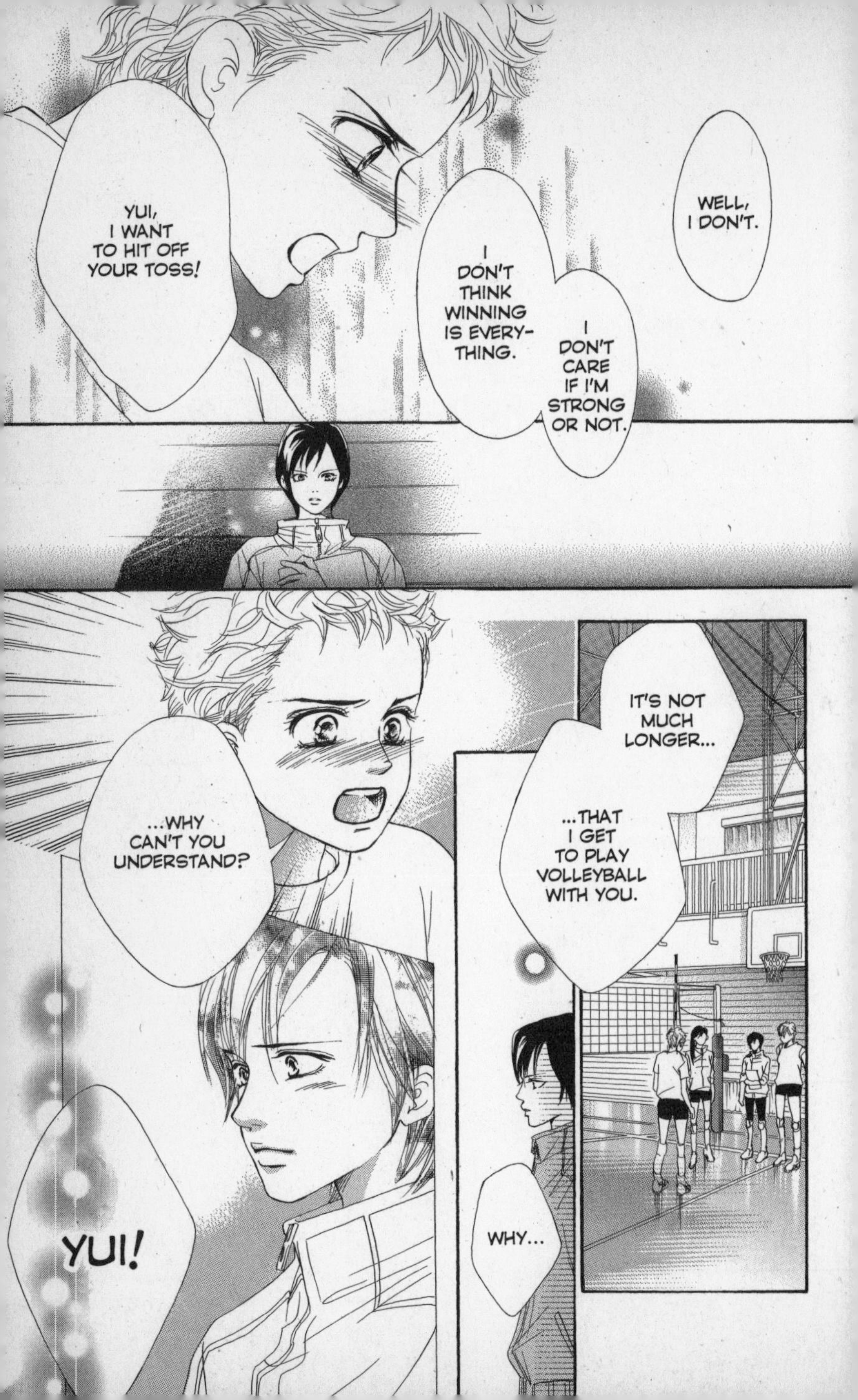
WELL, I DON'T.
I DON'T THINK WINNING IS EVERY-THING.
I DON'T CARE IF I'M STRONG OR NOT.
YUI, I WANT TO HIT OFF YOUR TOSS!
IT'S NOT MUCH LONGER...
...THAT I GET TO PLAY VOLLEYBALL WITH YOU.
WHY...
...WHY CAN'T YOU UNDERSTAND?
YUI!

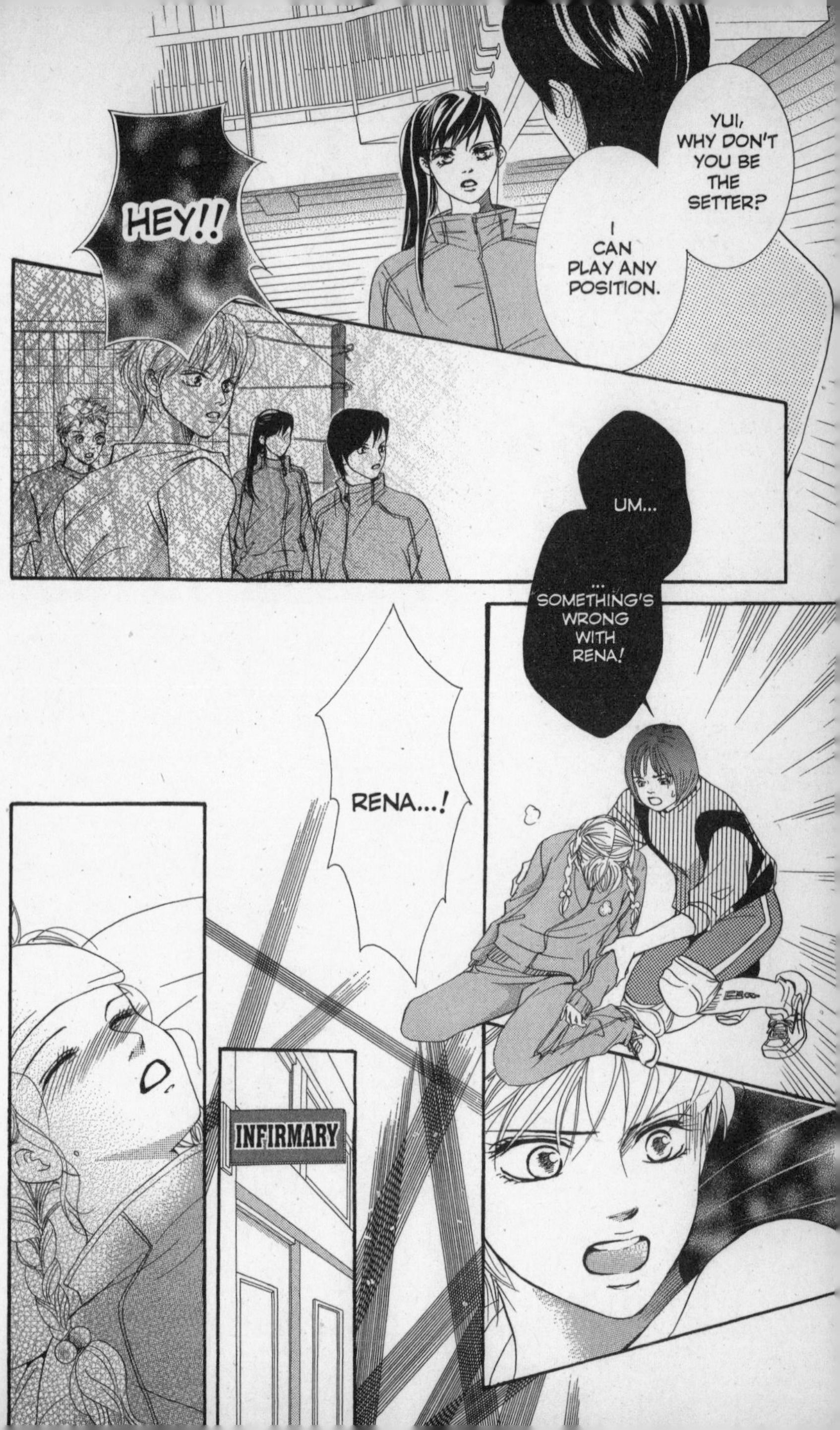
YUI, WHY DON'T YOU BE THE SETTER?
I CAN PLAY ANY POSITION.
HEY!!
UM...
...SOMETHING'S WRONG WITH RENA!
RENA...!
INFIRMARY

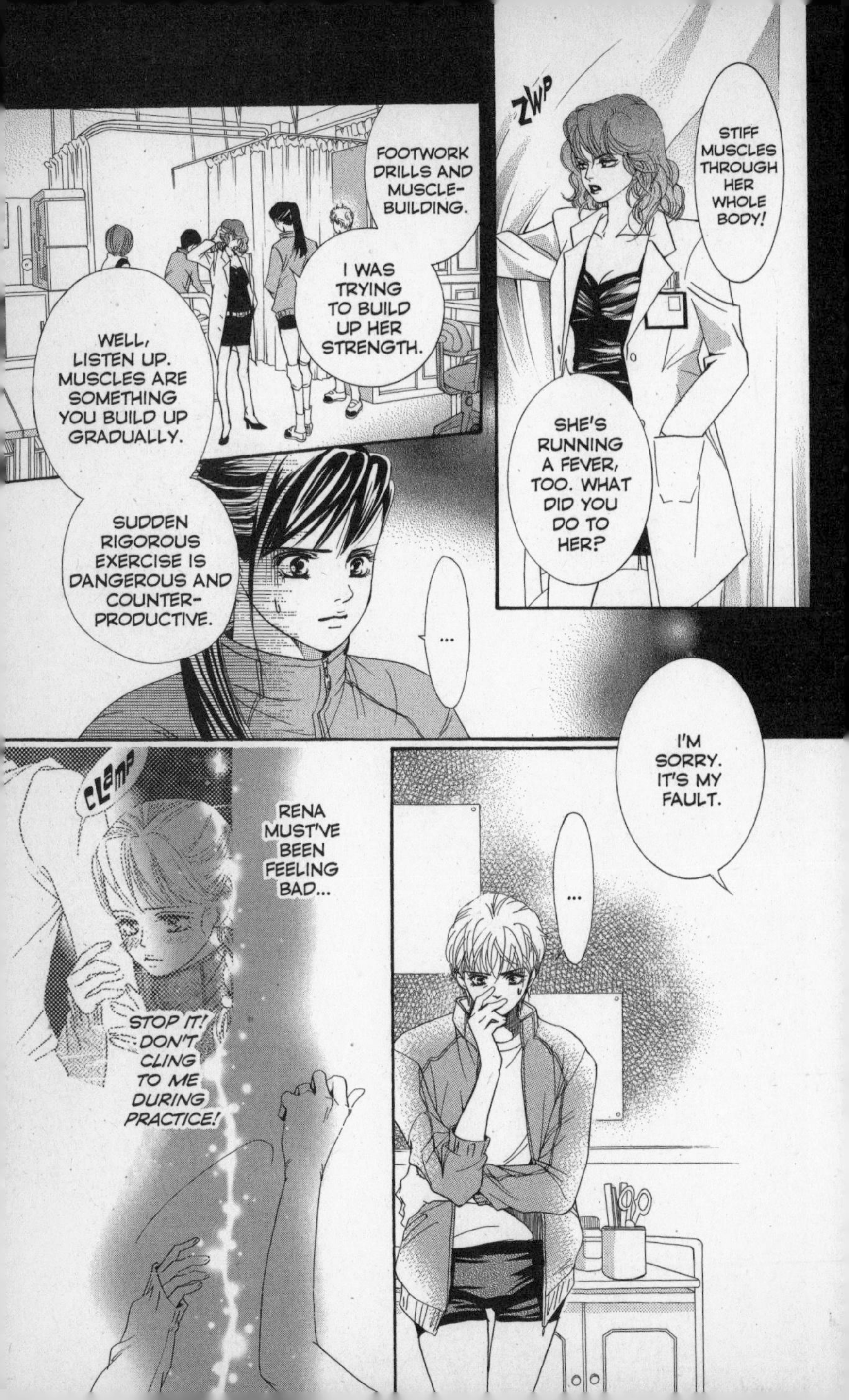
ZWP
STIFF MUSCLES THROUGH HER WHOLE BODY!
SHE'S RUNNING A FEVER, TOO. WHAT DID YOU DO TO HER?
FOOTWORK DRILLS AND MUSCLE-BUILDING.
I WAS TRYING TO BUILD UP HER STRENGTH.
WELL, LISTEN UP. MUSCLES ARE SOMETHING YOU BUILD UP GRADUALLY.
SUDDEN RIGOROUS EXERCISE IS DANGEROUS AND COUNTER-PRODUCTIVE.
...
I'M SORRY. IT'S MY FAULT.
...
RENA MUST'VE BEEN FEELING BAD...
CLAMP
STOP IT! DON'T CLING TO ME DURING PRACTICE!

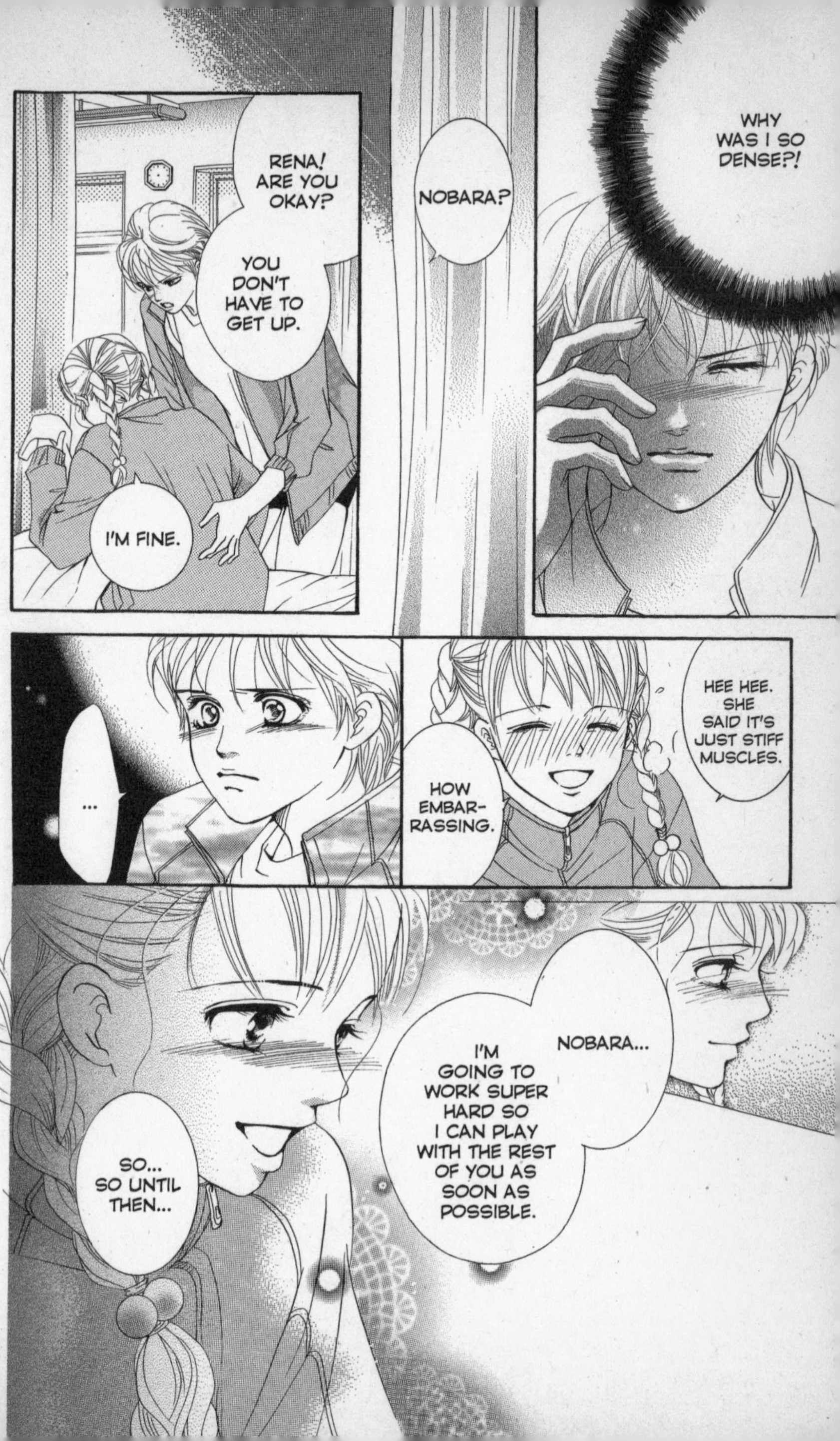
WHY WAS I SO DENSE?!
NOBARA?
RENA! ARE YOU OKAY?
YOU DON'T HAVE TO GET UP.
I'M FINE.
HEE HEE. SHE SAID IT'S JUST STIFF MUSCLES.
HOW EMBAR-RASSING.
...
NOBARA...
I'M GOING TO WORK SUPER HARD SO I CAN PLAY WITH THE REST OF YOU AS SOON AS POSSIBLE.
SO... SO UNTIL THEN...

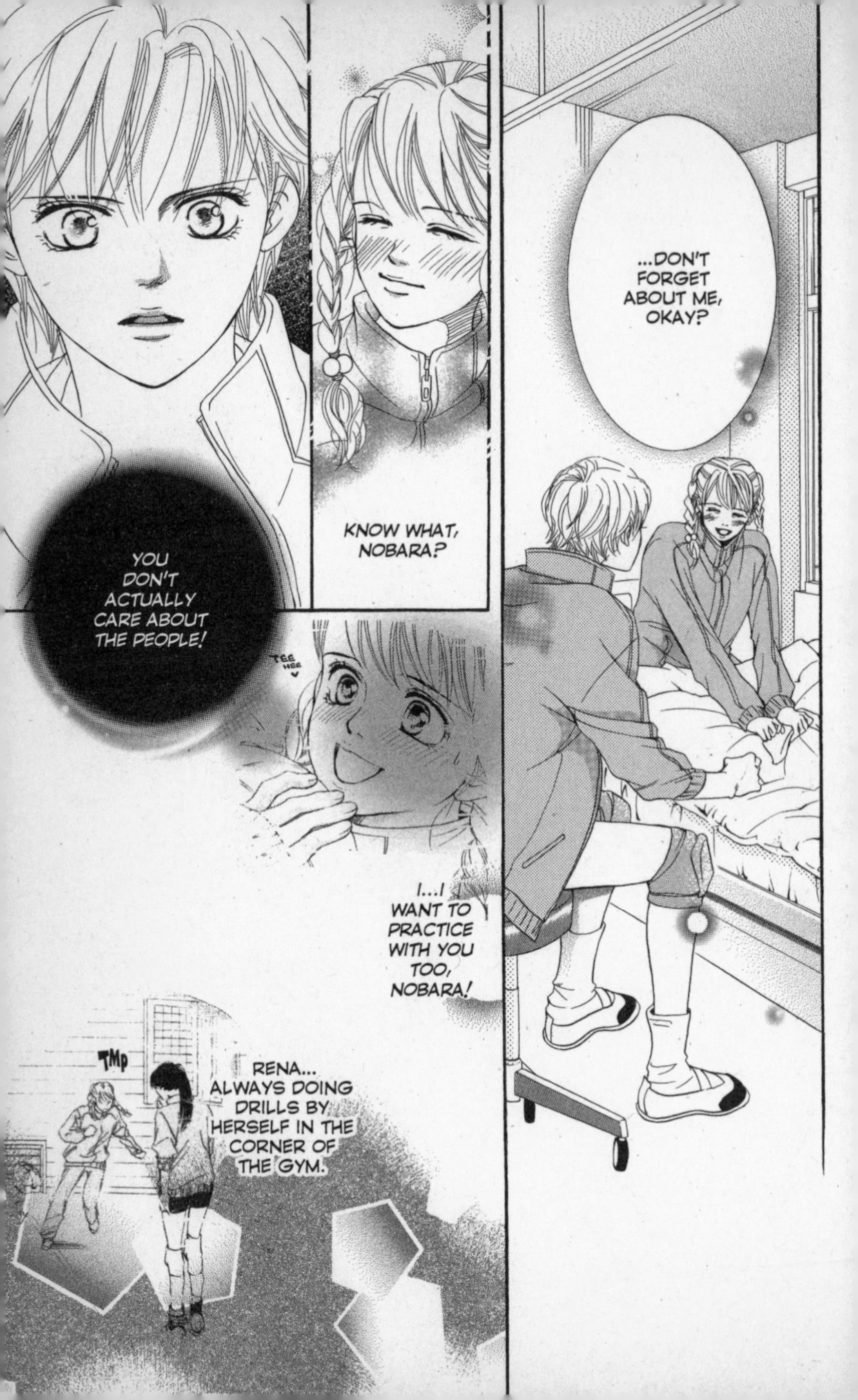
...DON'T FORGET ABOUT ME, OKAY?
KNOW WHAT, NOBARA?
YOU DON'T ACTUALLY CARE ABOUT THE PEOPLE!
TEE HEE
I...I WANT TO PRACTICE WITH YOU TOO, NOBARA!
TMP
RENA... ALWAYS DOING DRILLS BY HERSELF IN THE CORNER OF THE GYM.

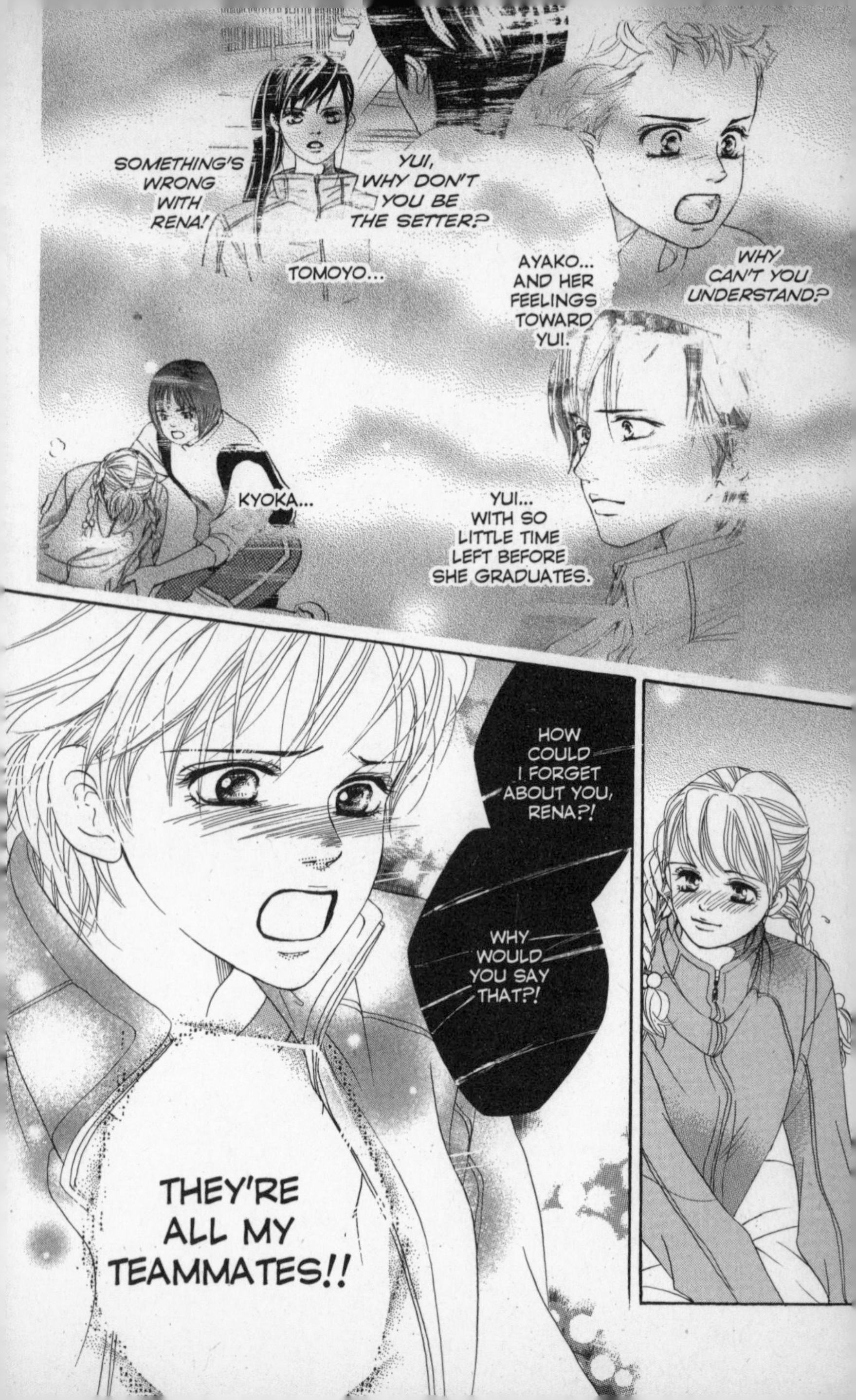
YUI, WHY DON'T YOU BE THE SETTER?
SOMETHING'S WRONG WITH RENA!
WHY CAN'T YOU UNDERSTAND?
AYAKO... AND HER FEELINGS TOWARD YUI.
TOMOYO...
YUI... WITH SO LITTLE TIME LEFT BEFORE SHE GRADUATES.
KYOKA...
HOW COULD I FORGET ABOUT YOU, RENA?!
WHY WOULD YOU SAY THAT?!
THEY'RE ALL MY TEAMMATES!!

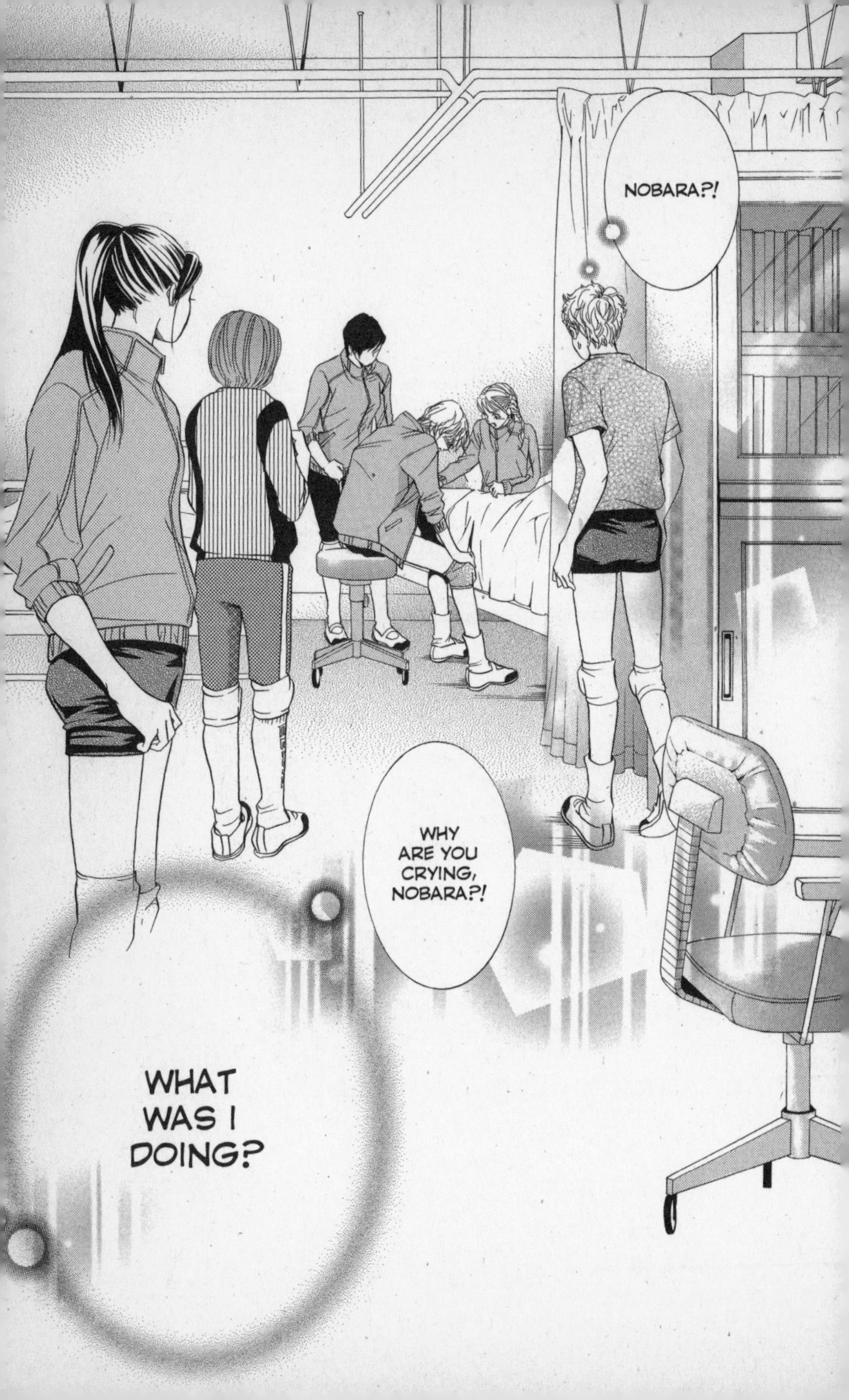
NOBARA?!
WHY ARE YOU CRYING, NOBARA?!
WHAT WAS I DOING?

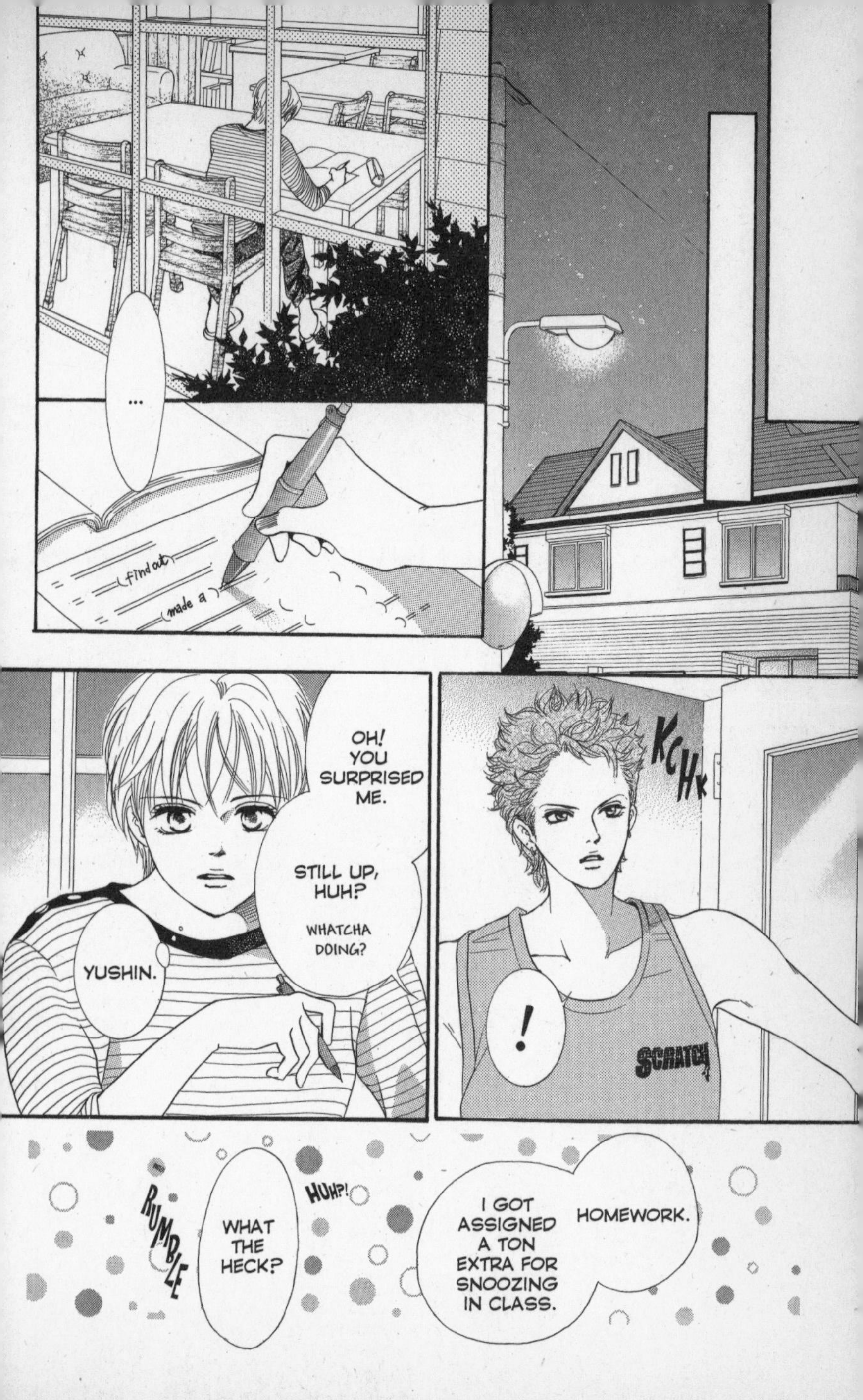
...
find out
made a
KCHK
!
OH! YOU SURPRISED ME.
STILL UP, HUH?
WHATCHA DOING?
YUSHIN.
HOMEWORK.
I GOT ASSIGNED A TON EXTRA FOR SNOOZING IN CLASS.
HUH?!
WHAT THE HECK?
RUMBLE

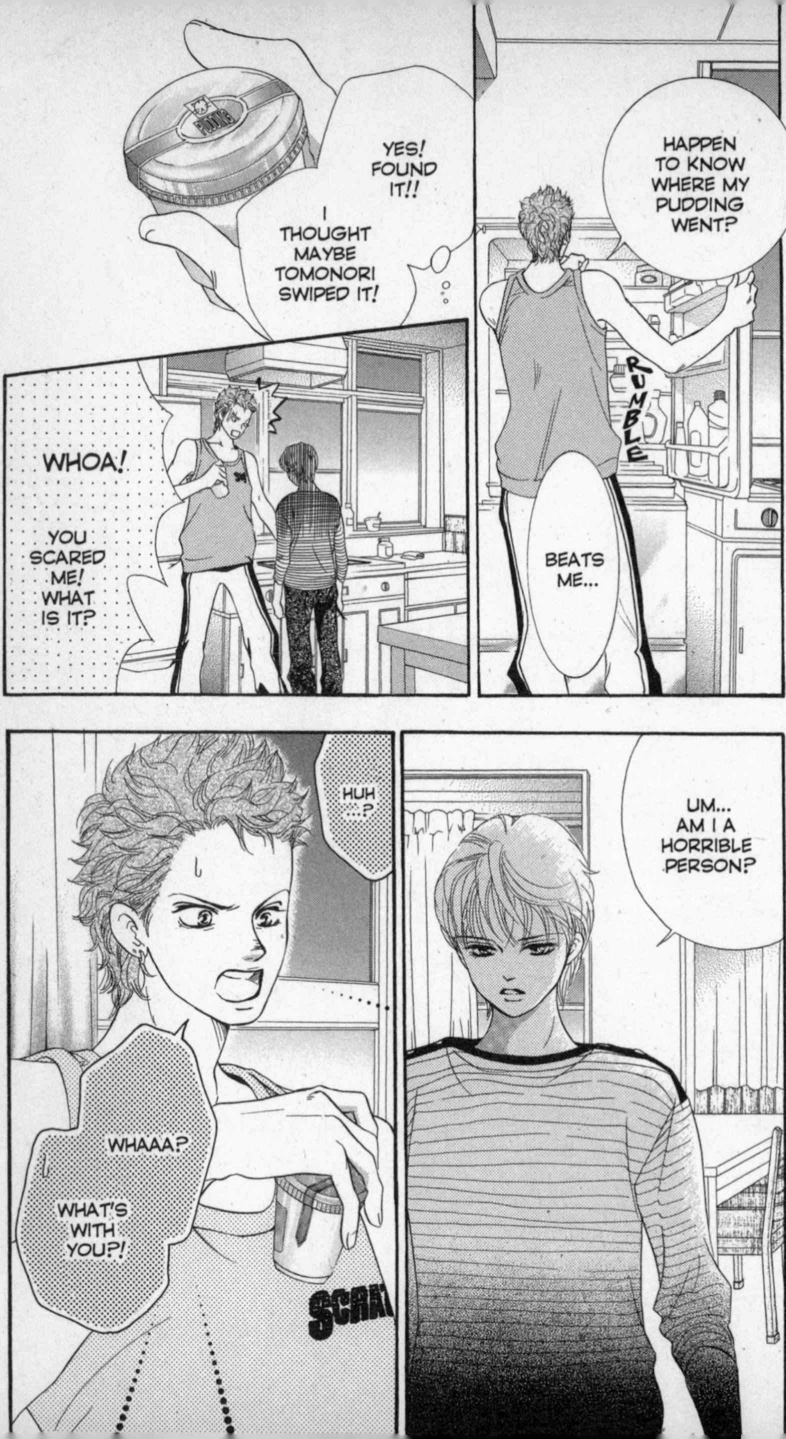
HAPPEN TO KNOW WHERE MY PUDDING WENT?
RUMBLE
BEATS ME...
PUDDING
YES! FOUND IT!!
I THOUGHT MAYBE TOMONORI SWIPED IT!
WHOA!
YOU SCARED ME! WHAT IS IT?
UM... AM I A HORRIBLE PERSON?
HUH ...?
WHAAA?
WHAT'S WITH YOU?!

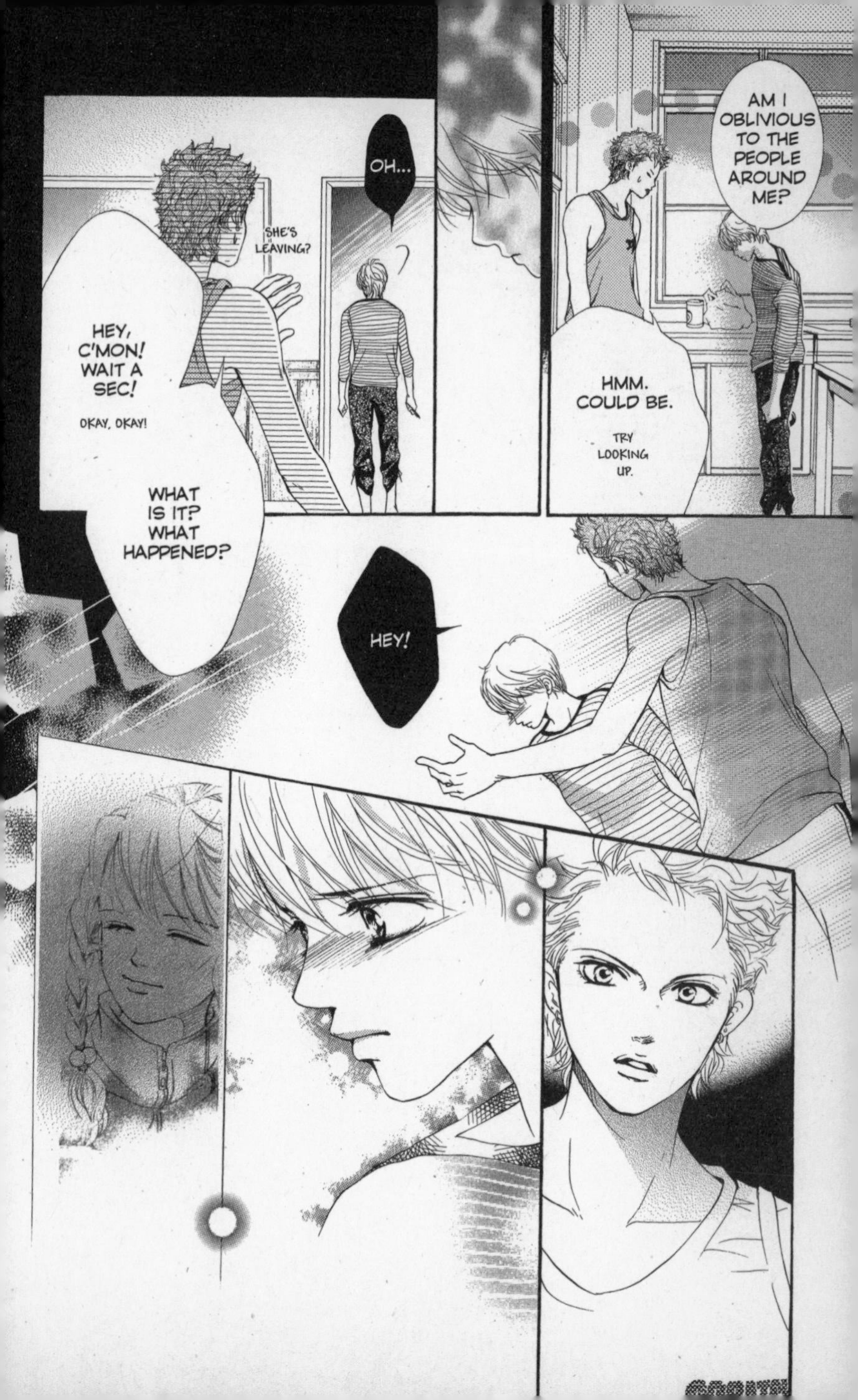
AM I OBLIVIOUS TO THE PEOPLE AROUND ME?
HMM. COULD BE.
TRY LOOKING UP.
OH...
SHE'S LEAVING?
HEY, C'MON! WAIT A SEC!
OKAY, OKAY!
HEY!
WHAT IS IT? WHAT HAPPENED?

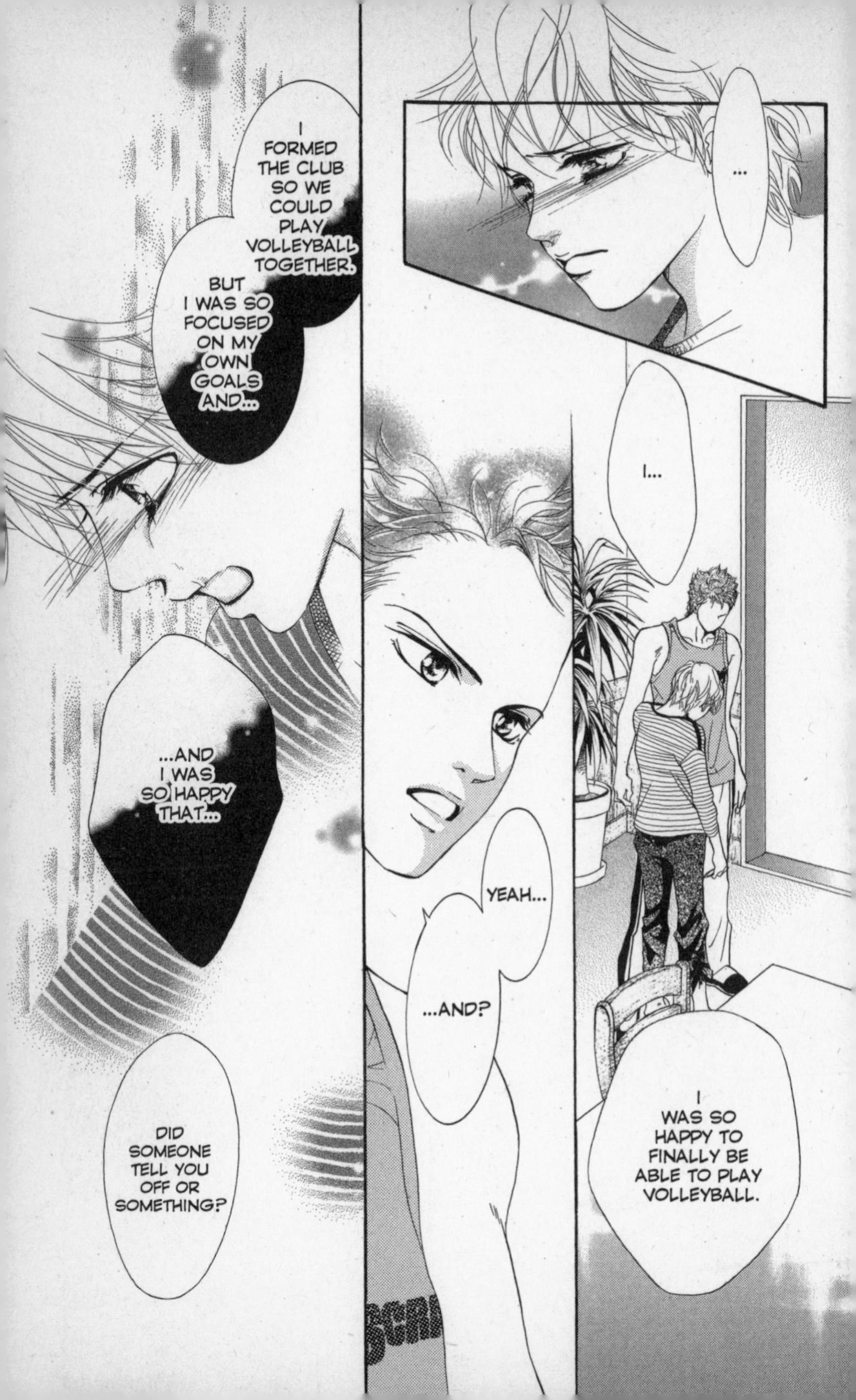
...
I...
I WAS SO HAPPY TO FINALLY BE ABLE TO PLAY VOLLEYBALL.
YEAH...
...AND?
I FORMED THE CLUB SO WE COULD PLAY VOLLEYBALL TOGETHER.
BUT I WAS SO FOCUSED ON MY OWN GOALS AND...
...AND I WAS SO HAPPY THAT...
DID SOMEONE TELL YOU OFF OR SOMETHING?

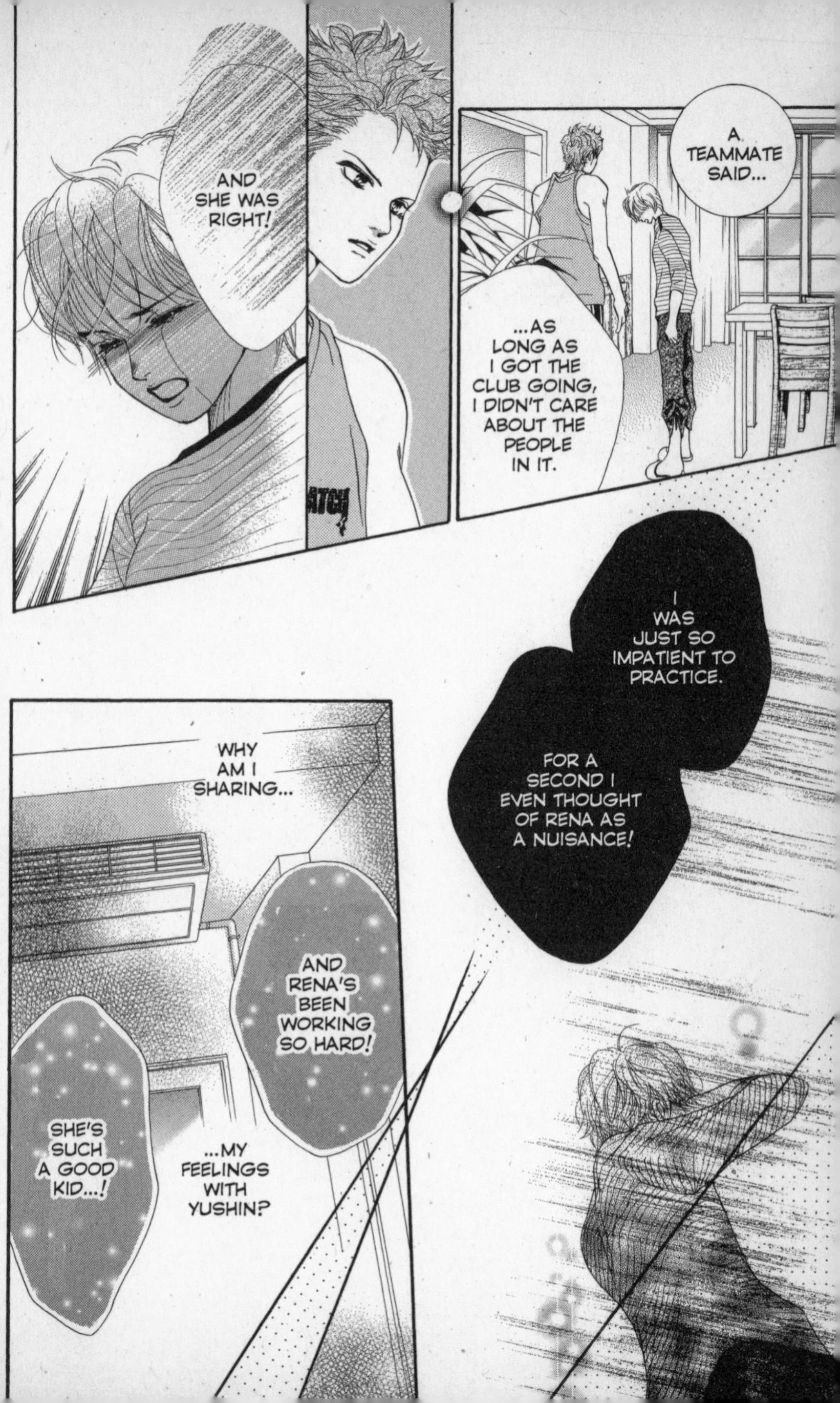
A TEAMMATE SAID...
...AS LONG AS I GOT THE CLUB GOING, I DIDN'T CARE ABOUT THE PEOPLE IN IT.
AND SHE WAS RIGHT!
I WAS JUST SO IMPATIENT TO PRACTICE.
FOR A SECOND I EVEN THOUGHT OF RENA AS A NUISANCE!
WHY AM I SHARING...
AND RENA'S BEEN WORKING SO HARD!
...MY FEELINGS WITH YUSHIN?
SHE'S SUCH A GOOD KID...!

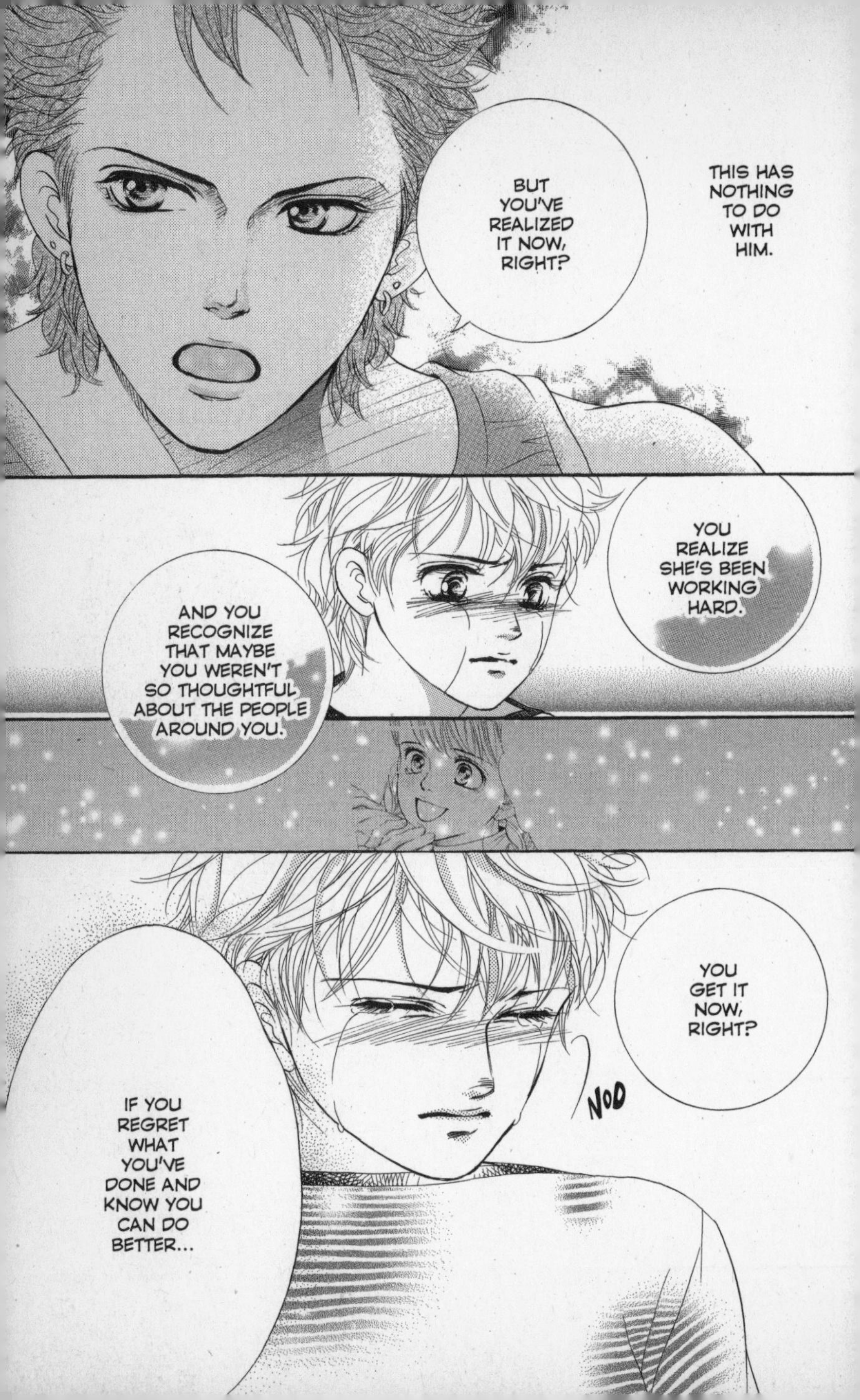
THIS HAS NOTHING TO DO WITH HIM.
BUT YOU'VE REALIZED IT NOW, RIGHT?
YOU REALIZE SHE'S BEEN WORKING HARD.
AND YOU RECOGNIZE THAT MAYBE YOU WEREN'T SO THOUGHTFUL ABOUT THE PEOPLE AROUND YOU.
YOU GET IT NOW, RIGHT?
NOD
IF YOU REGRET WHAT YOU'VE DONE AND KNOW YOU CAN DO BETTER...

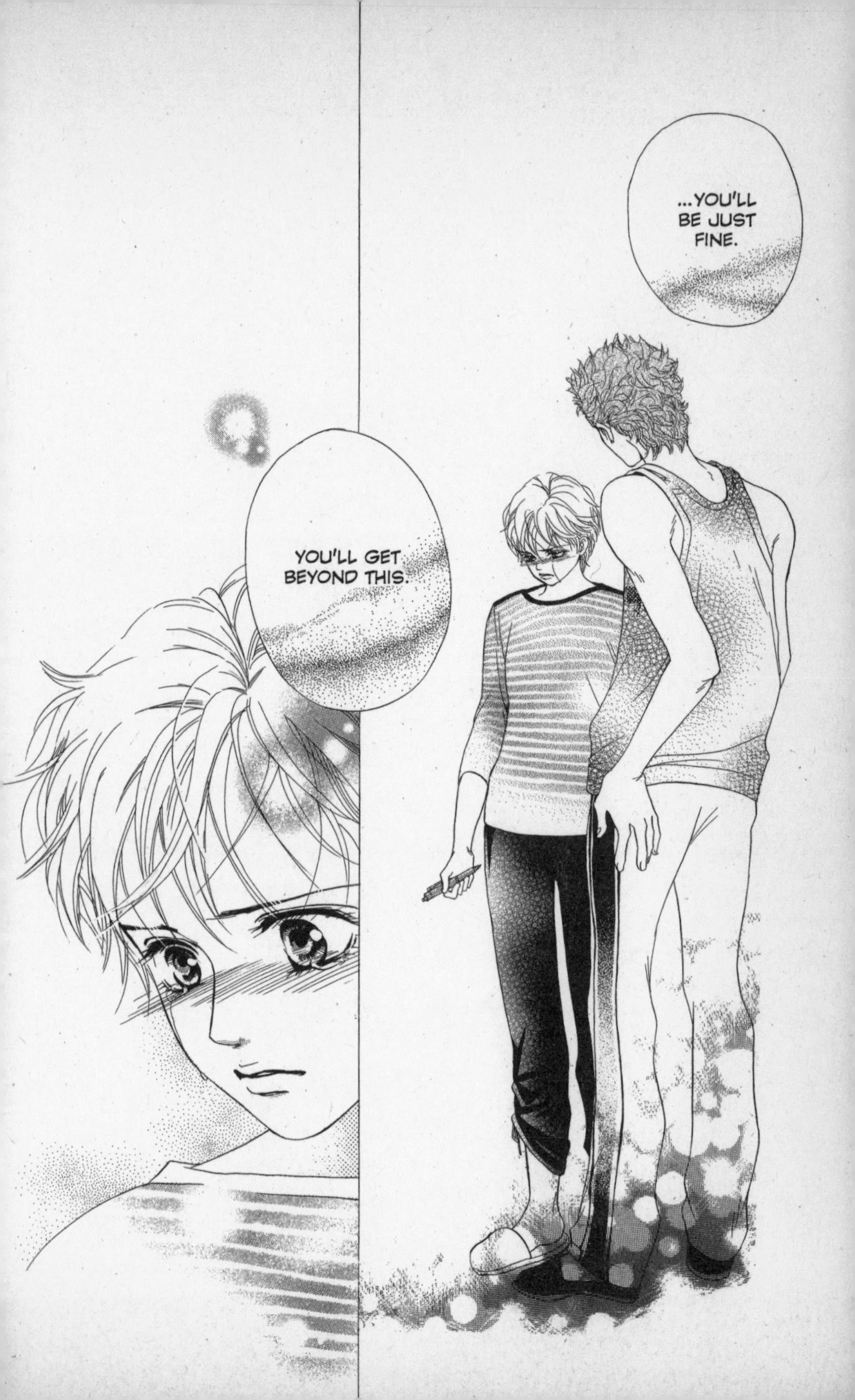
...YOU'LL BE JUST FINE.
YOU'LL GET BEYOND THIS.

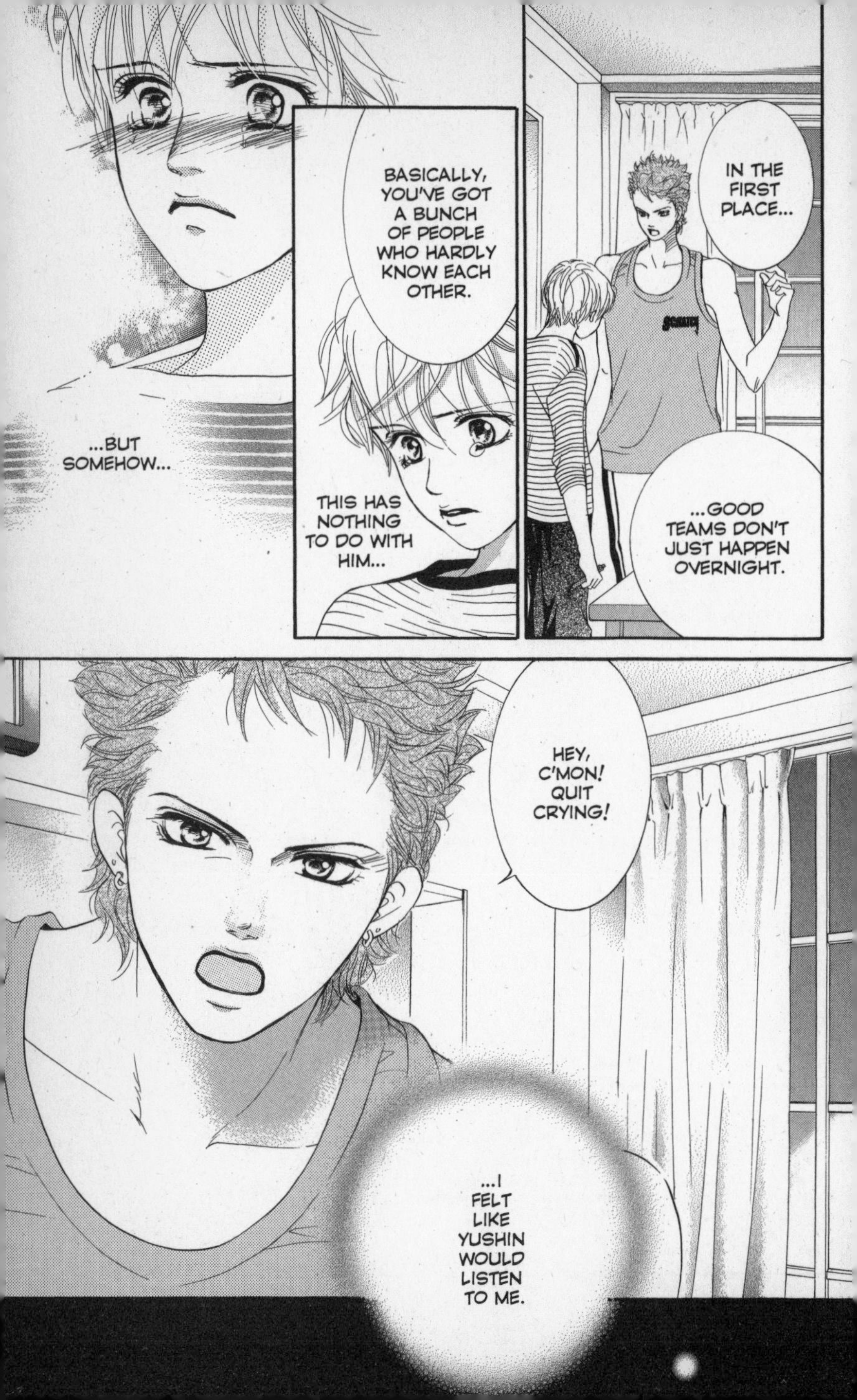
IN THE FIRST PLACE...
...GOOD TEAMS DON'T JUST HAPPEN OVERNIGHT.
BASICALLY, YOU'VE GOT A BUNCH OF PEOPLE WHO HARDLY KNOW EACH OTHER.
THIS HAS NOTHING TO DO WITH HIM...
...BUT SOMEHOW...
HEY, C'MON! QUIT CRYING!
...I FELT LIKE YUSHIN WOULD LISTEN TO ME.

Crimson Hero

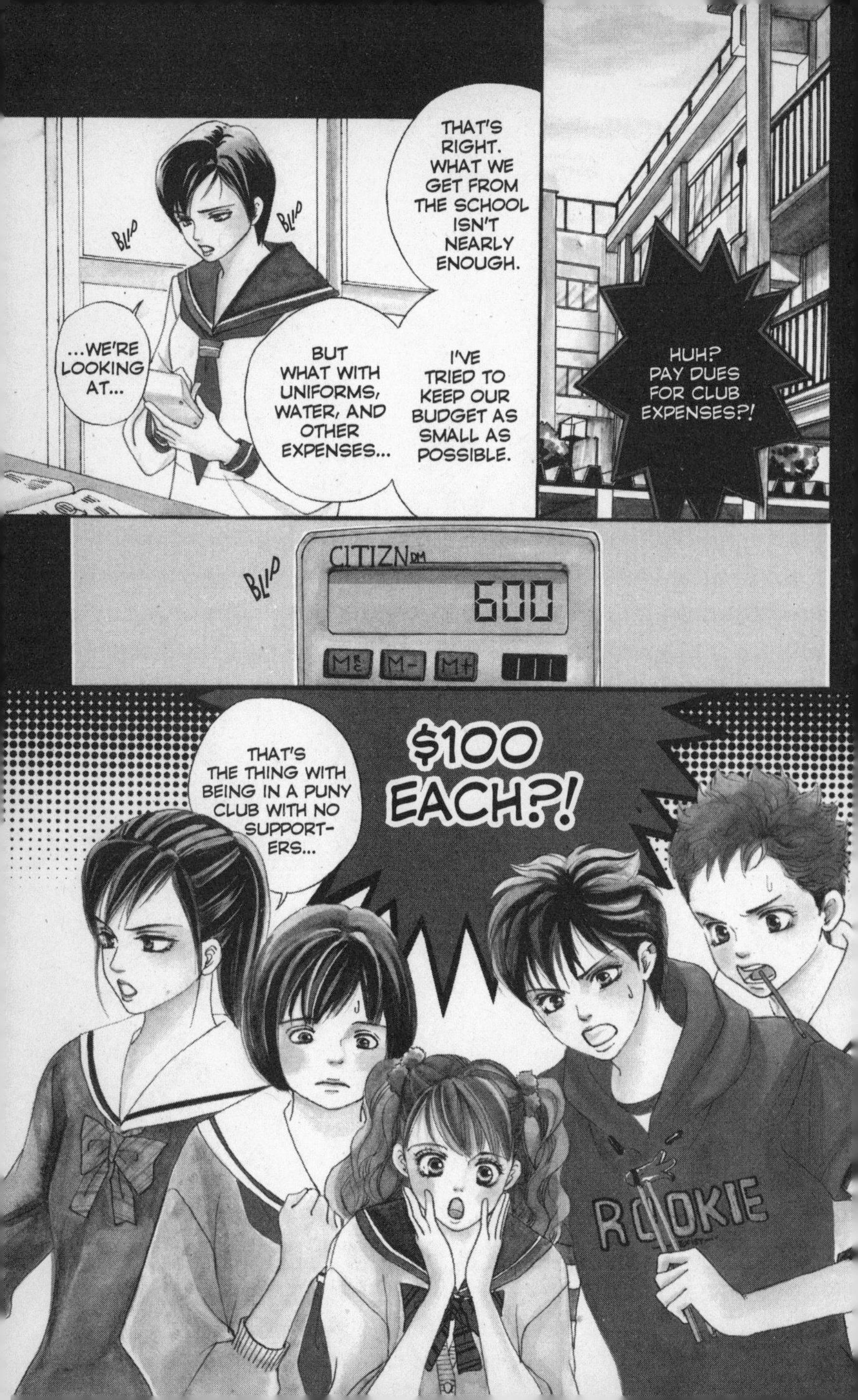
HUH? PAY DUES FOR CLUB EXPENSES?!
THAT'S RIGHT. WHAT WE GET FROM THE SCHOOL ISN'T NEARLY ENOUGH.
I'VE TRIED TO KEEP OUR BUDGET AS SMALL AS POSSIBLE.
BUT WHAT WITH UNIFORMS, WATER, AND OTHER EXPENSES...
BLIP
BLIP
...WE'RE LOOKING AT...
CITIZN
600
BLIP
$100 EACH?!
THAT'S THE THING WITH BEING IN A PUNY CLUB WITH NO SUPPORTERS...
ROOKIE

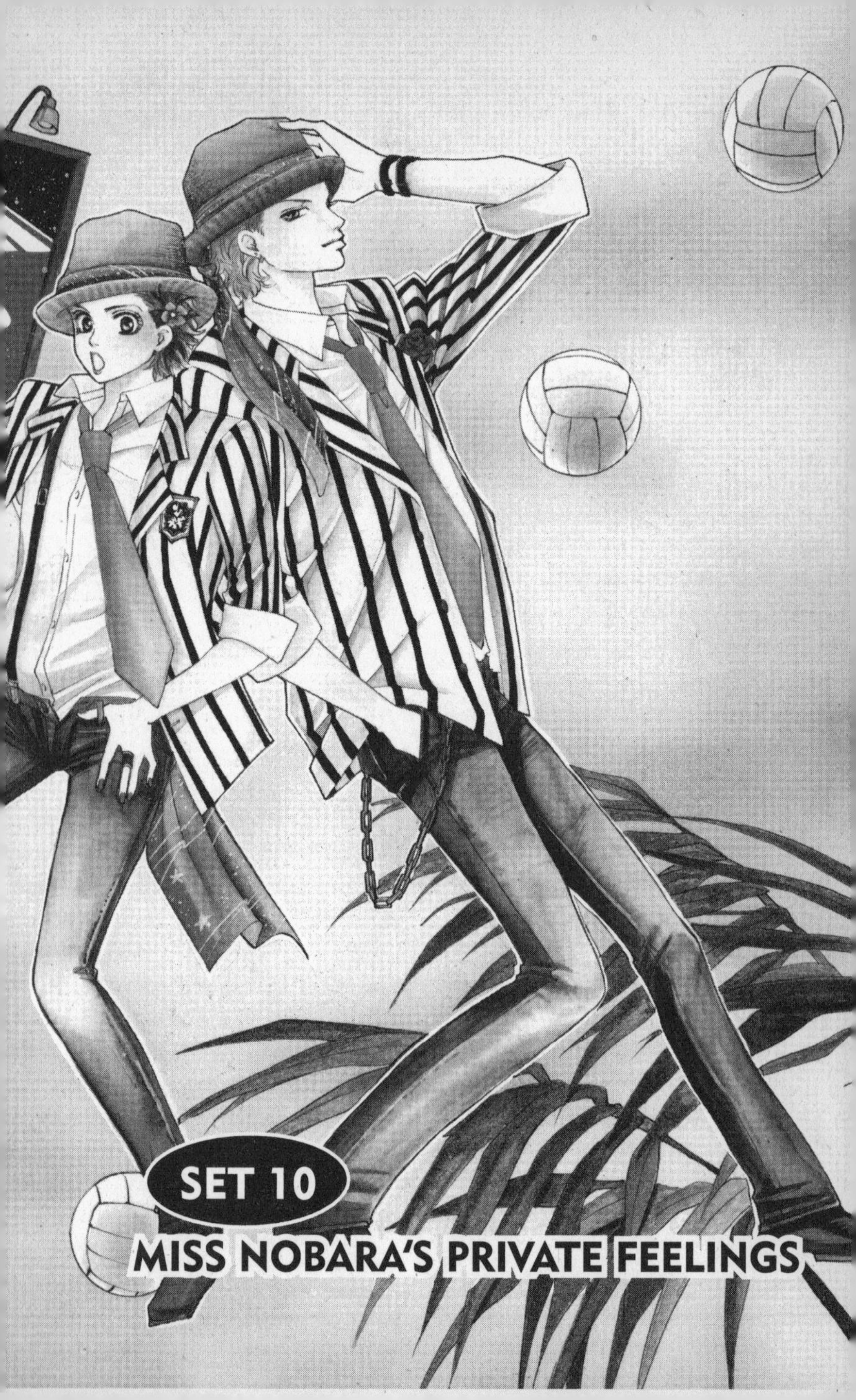
SET 10
MISS NOBARA'S PRIVATE FEELINGS

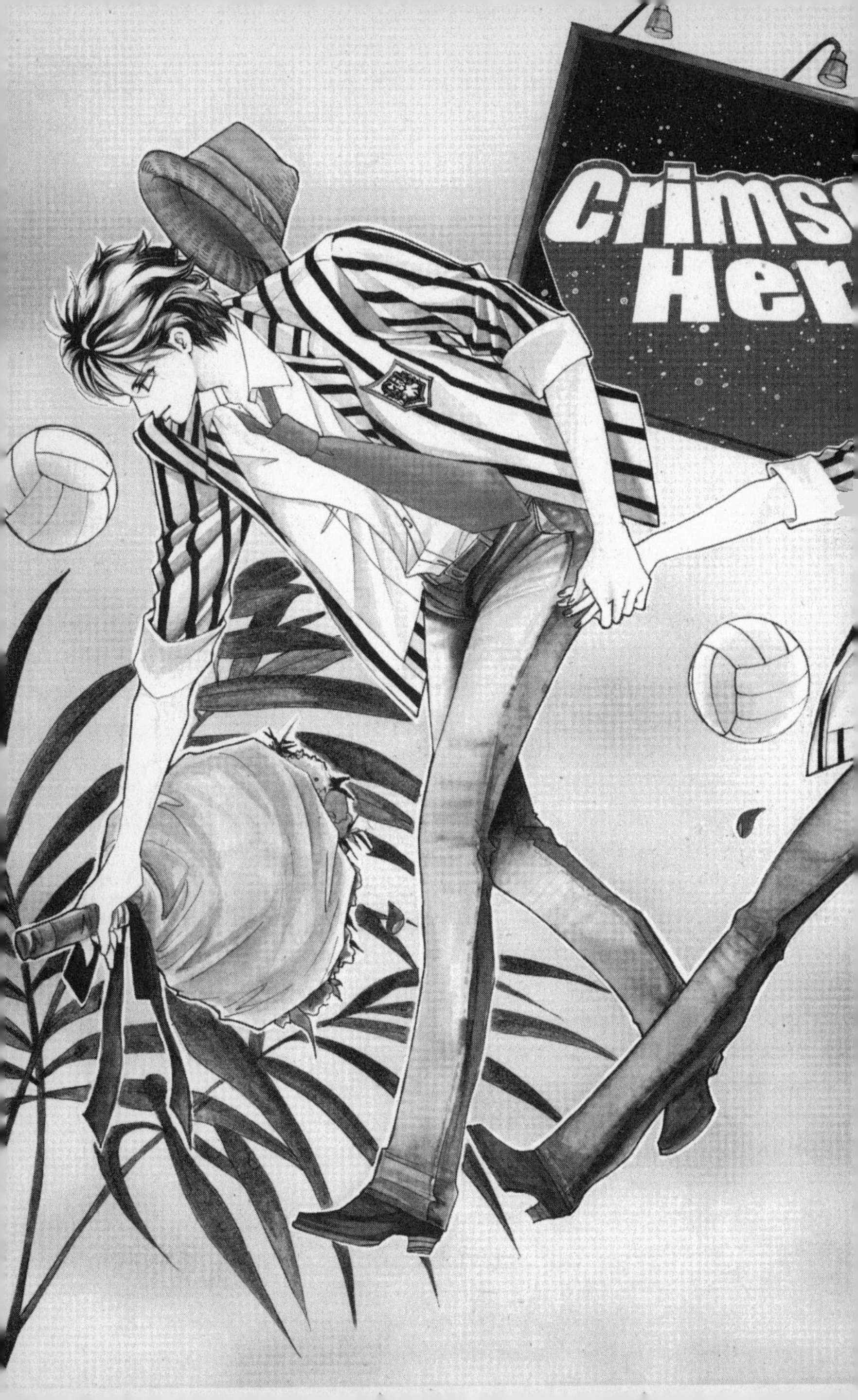
Crims
Her

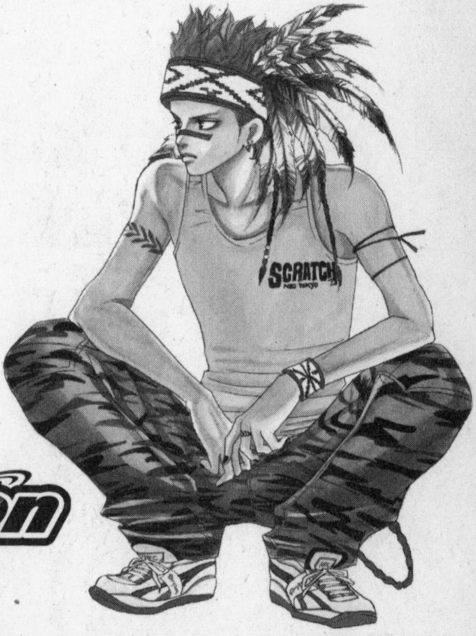
SCRATCH

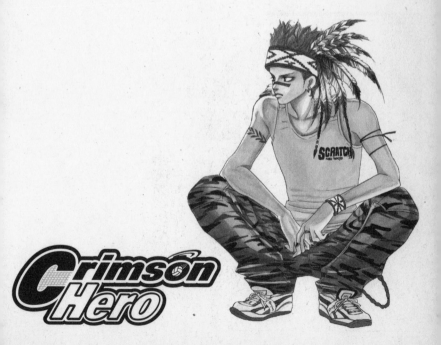

Crimson Hero

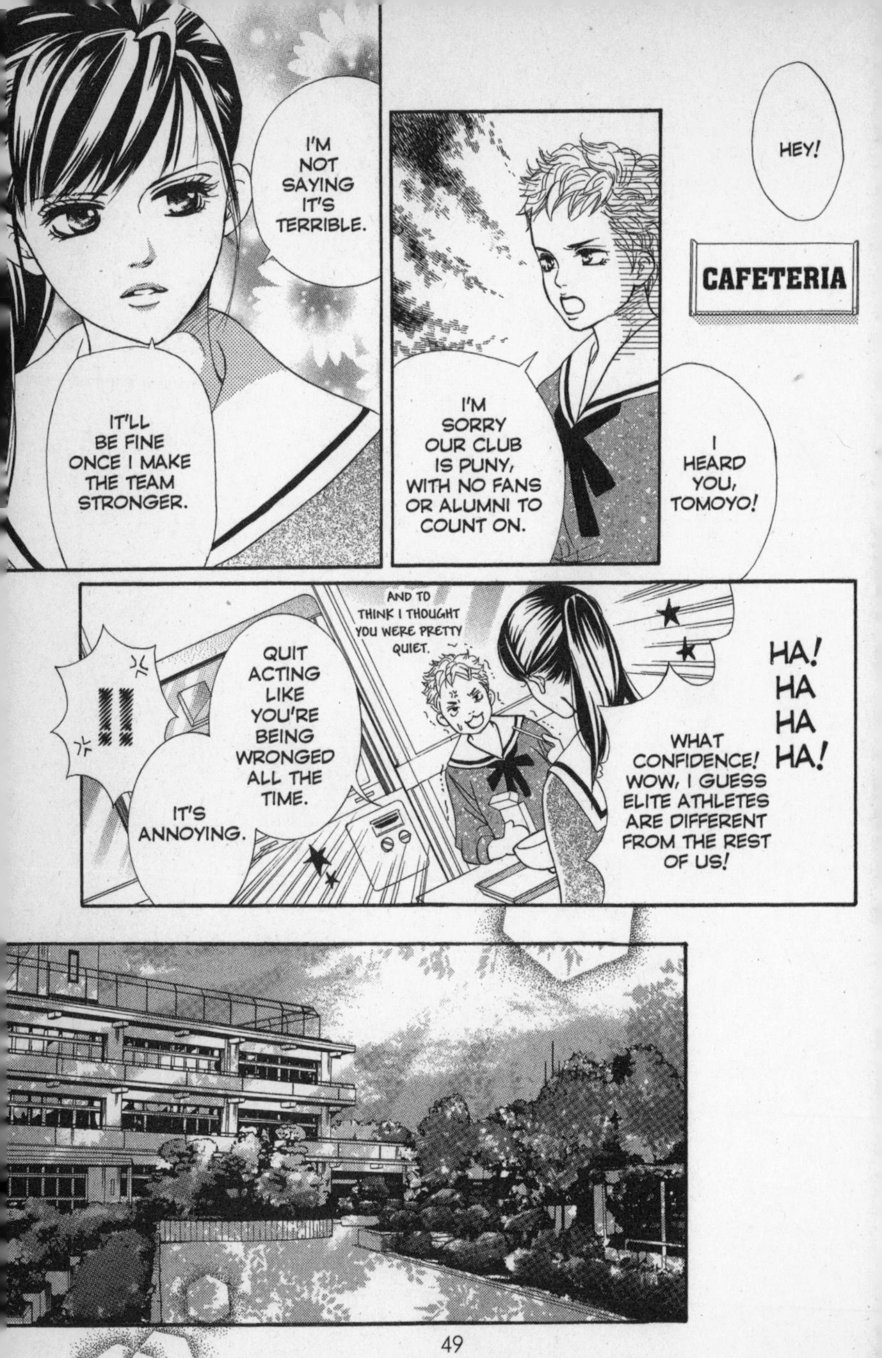
HEY!
CAFETERIA
I HEARD YOU, TOMOYO!
I'M SORRY OUR CLUB IS PUNY, WITH NO FANS OR ALUMNI TO COUNT ON.
I'M NOT SAYING IT'S TERRIBLE.
IT'LL BE FINE ONCE I MAKE THE TEAM STRONGER.
HA! HA HA HA!
WHAT CONFIDENCE! WOW, I GUESS ELITE ATHLETES ARE DIFFERENT FROM THE REST OF US!
AND TO THINK I THOUGHT YOU WERE PRETTY QUIET.
QUIT ACTING LIKE YOU'RE BEING WRONGED ALL THE TIME.
IT'S ANNOYING.
!!

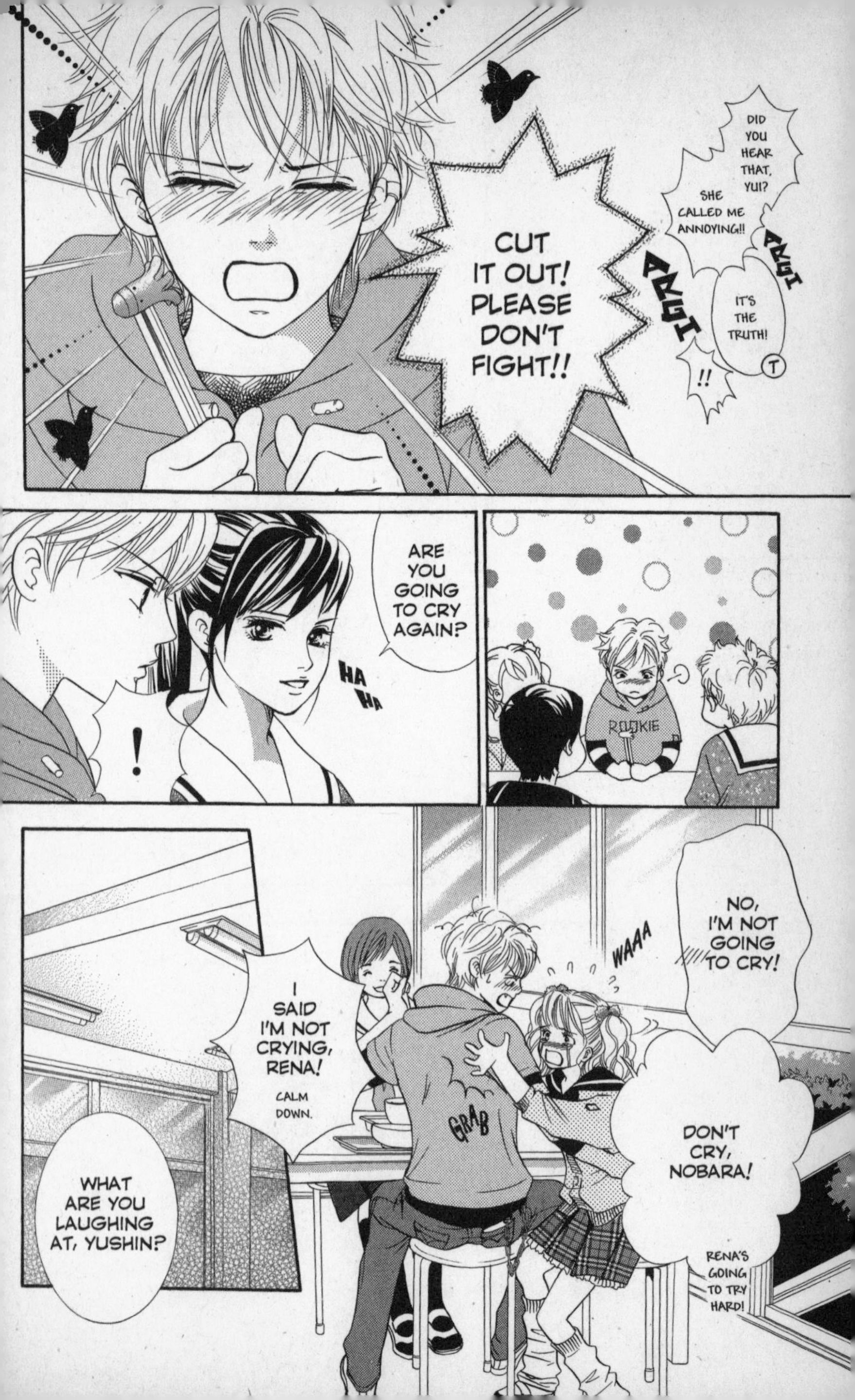
DID YOU HEAR THAT, YUI?
SHE CALLED ME ANNOYING!!
ARGI
ARGI
IT'S THE TRUTH!
T
!!
CUT IT OUT! PLEASE DON'T FIGHT!!
ROOKIE
ARE YOU GOING TO CRY AGAIN?
HA HA
!
NO, I'M NOT GOING TO CRY!
WAAA
DON'T CRY, NOBARA!
RENA'S GOING TO TRY HARD!
GRAB
I SAID I'M NOT CRYING, RENA!
CALM DOWN.
WHAT ARE YOU LAUGHING AT, YUSHIN?

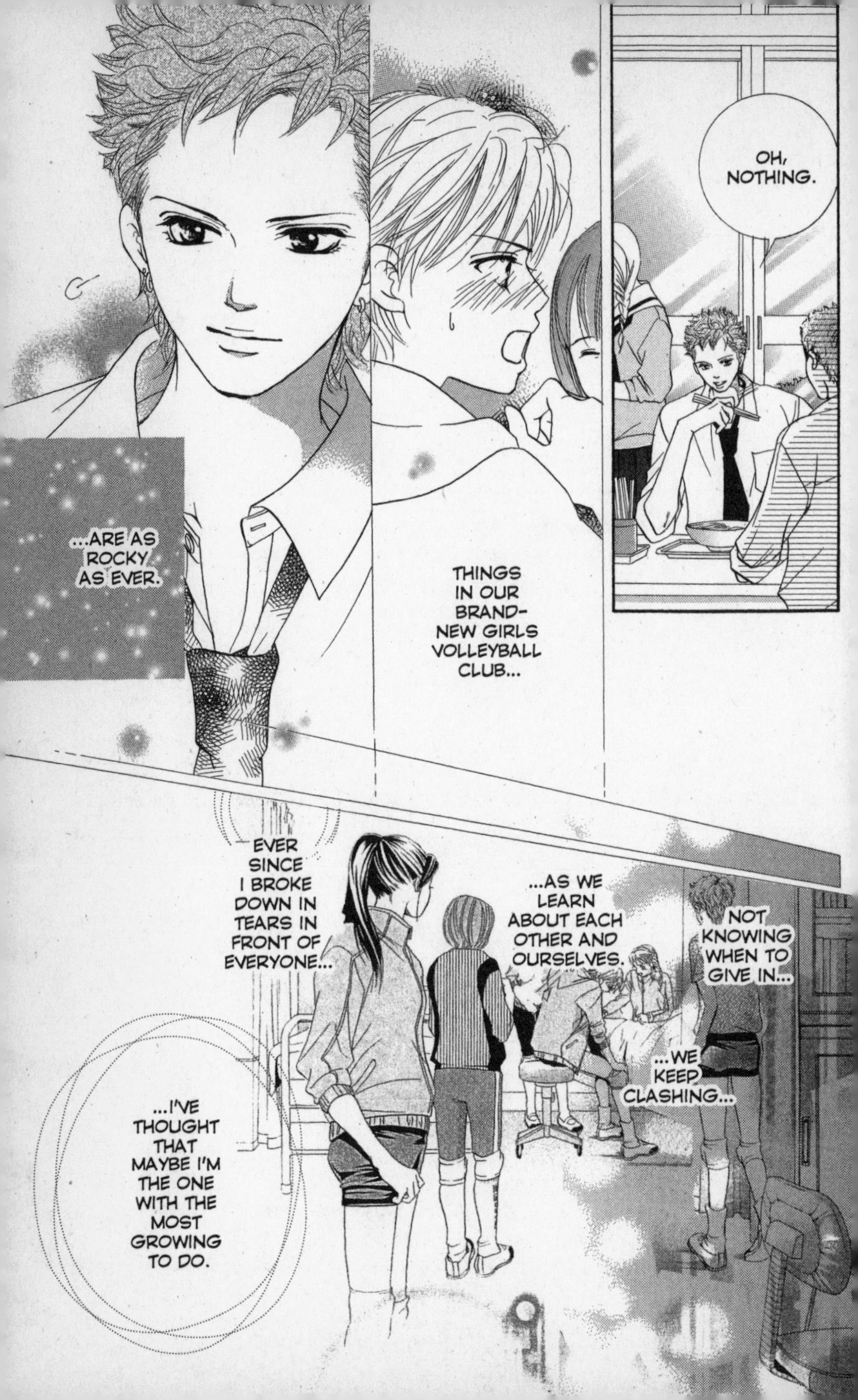
OH, NOTHING.
THINGS IN OUR BRAND-NEW GIRLS VOLLEYBALL CLUB...
...ARE AS ROCKY AS EVER.
NOT KNOWING WHEN TO GIVE IN...
...WE KEEP CLASHING...
...AS WE LEARN ABOUT EACH OTHER AND OURSELVES.
EVER SINCE I BROKE DOWN IN TEARS IN FRONT OF EVERYONE...
...I'VE THOUGHT THAT MAYBE I'M THE ONE WITH THE MOST GROWING TO DO.

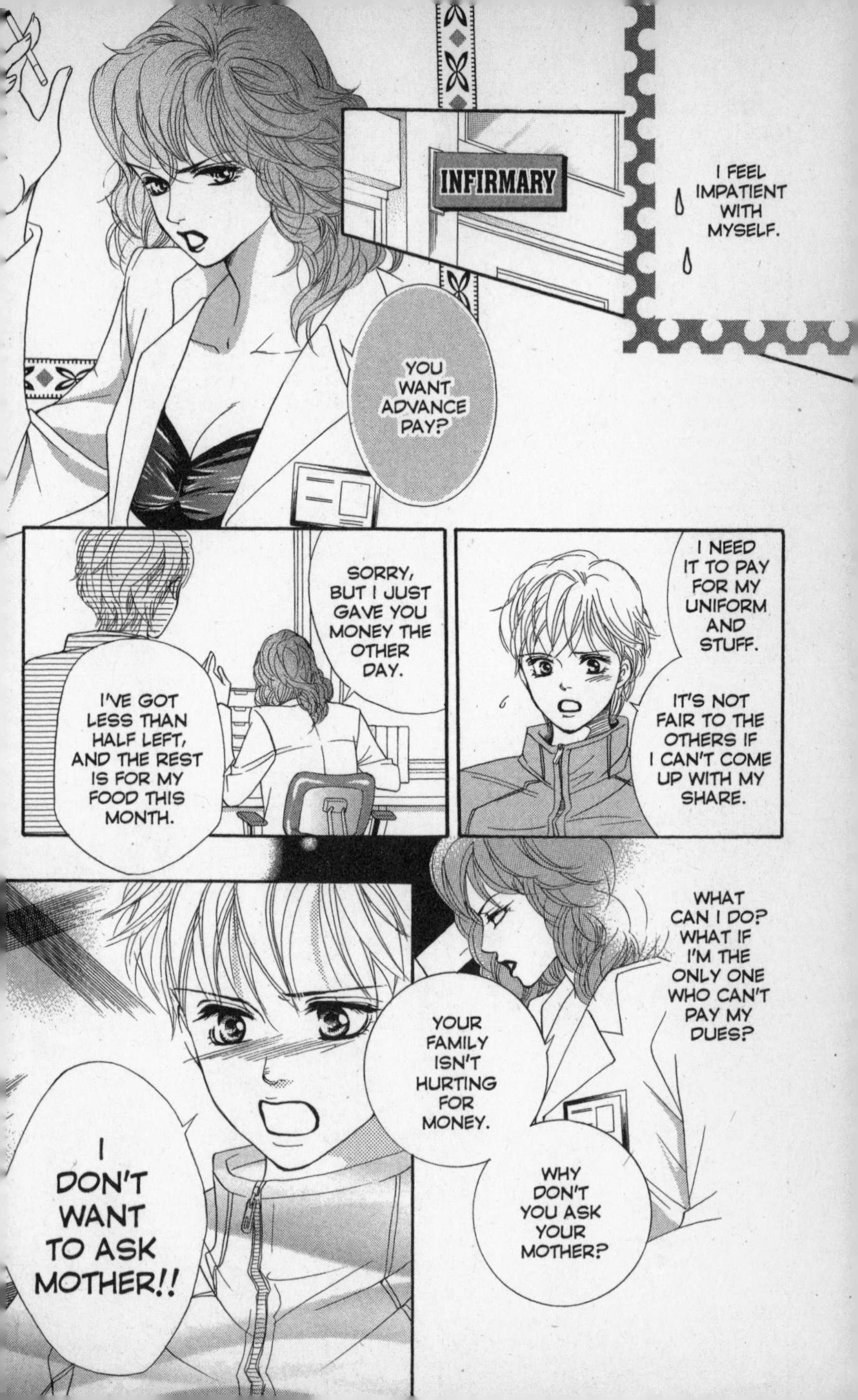
INFIRMARY
I FEEL IMPATIENT WITH MYSELF.
YOU WANT ADVANCE PAY?
I NEED IT TO PAY FOR MY UNIFORM AND STUFF.
IT'S NOT FAIR TO THE OTHERS IF I CAN'T COME UP WITH MY SHARE.
SORRY, BUT I JUST GAVE YOU MONEY THE OTHER DAY.
I'VE GOT LESS THAN HALF LEFT, AND THE REST IS FOR MY FOOD THIS MONTH.
WHAT CAN I DO? WHAT IF I'M THE ONLY ONE WHO CAN'T PAY MY DUES?
YOUR FAMILY ISN'T HURTING FOR MONEY.
WHY DON'T YOU ASK YOUR MOTHER?
I DON'T WANT TO ASK MOTHER!!

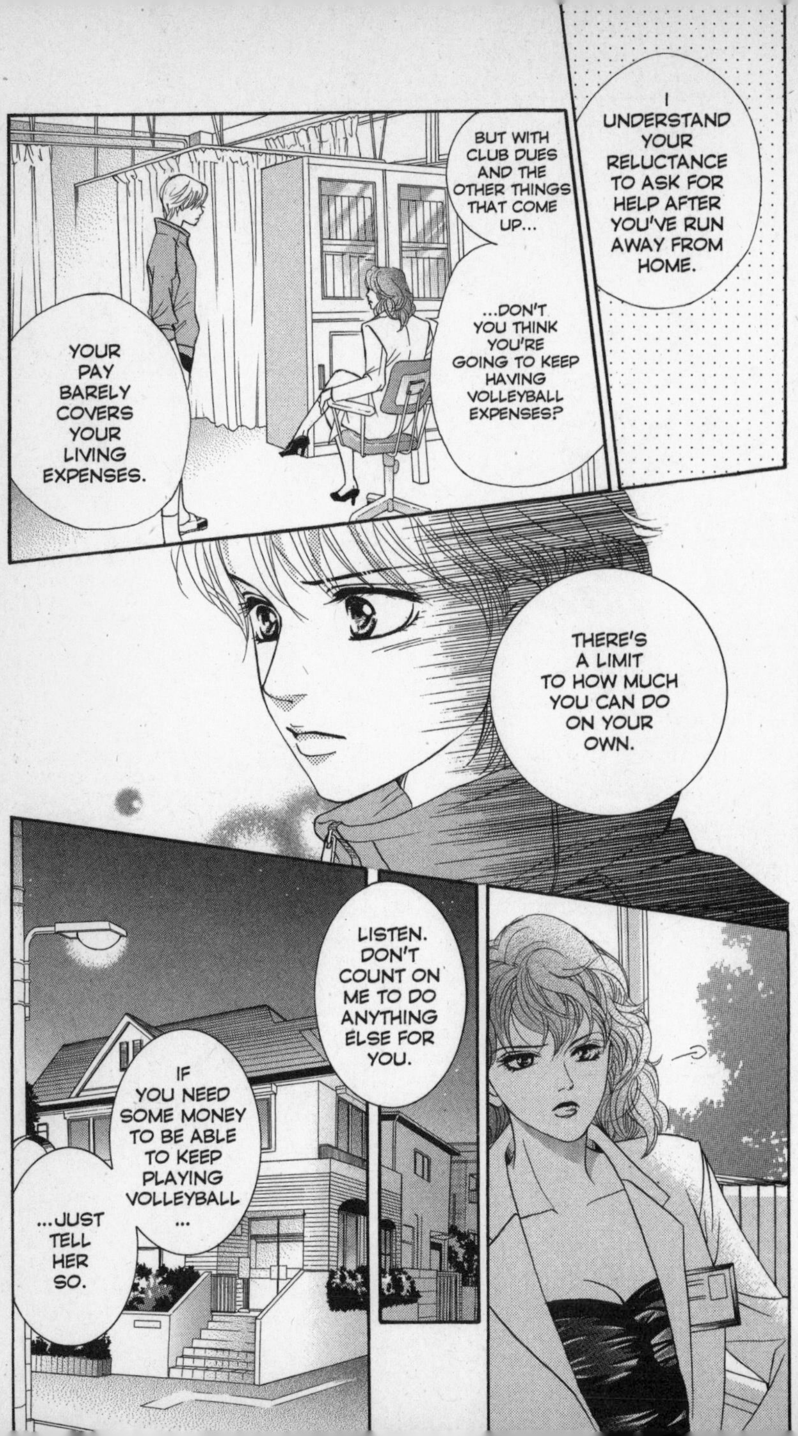
I UNDERSTAND YOUR RELUCTANCE TO ASK FOR HELP AFTER YOU'VE RUN AWAY FROM HOME.
BUT WITH CLUB DUES AND THE OTHER THINGS THAT COME UP...
...DON'T YOU THINK YOU'RE GOING TO KEEP HAVING VOLLEYBALL EXPENSES?
YOUR PAY BARELY COVERS YOUR LIVING EXPENSES.
THERE'S A LIMIT TO HOW MUCH YOU CAN DO ON YOUR OWN.
LISTEN. DON'T COUNT ON ME TO DO ANYTHING ELSE FOR YOU.
IF YOU NEED SOME MONEY TO BE ABLE TO KEEP PLAYING VOLLEYBALL ...
...JUST TELL HER SO.

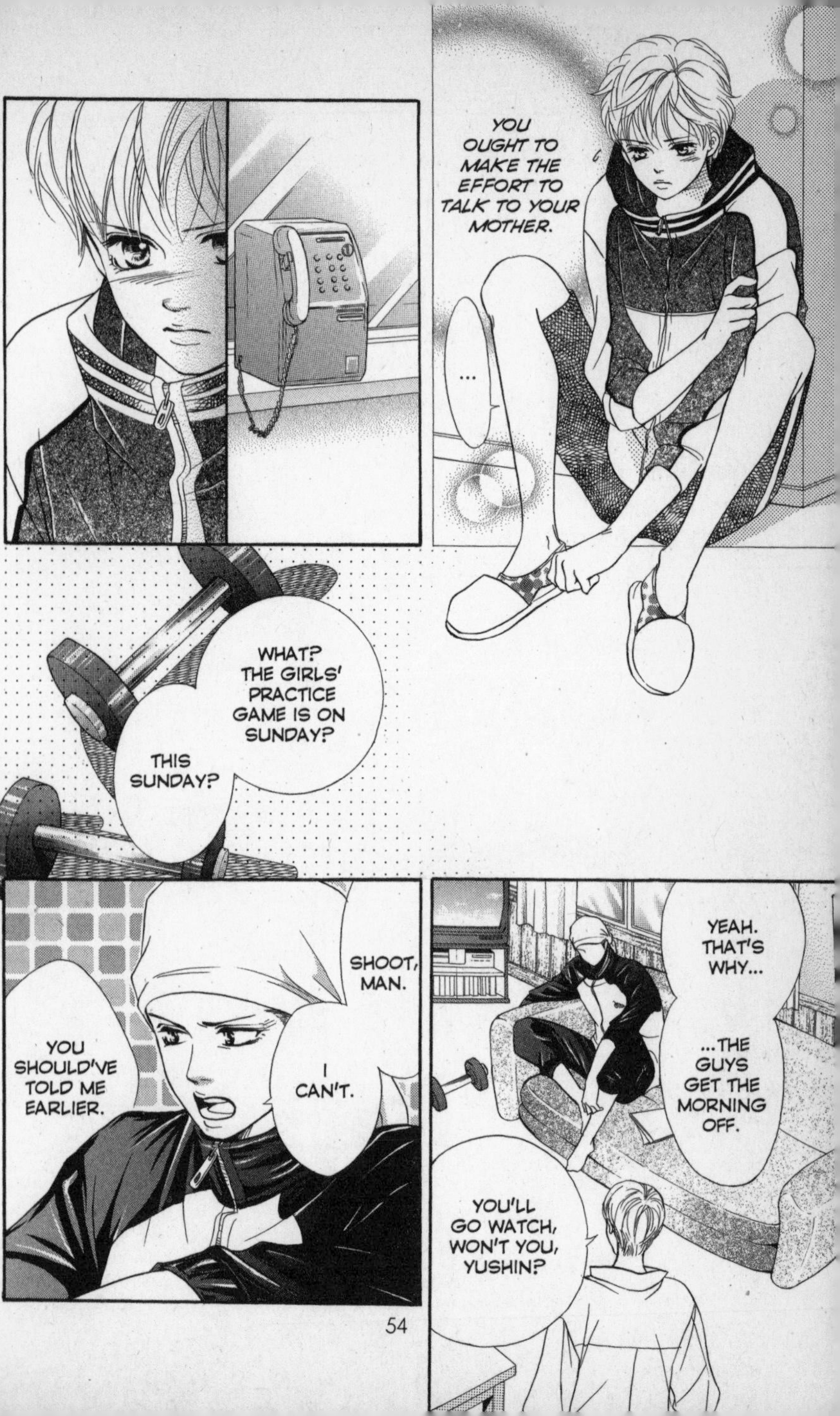
YOU OUGHT TO MAKE THE EFFORT TO TALK TO YOUR MOTHER.
...
WHAT? THE GIRLS' PRACTICE GAME IS ON SUNDAY?
THIS SUNDAY?
YEAH. THAT'S WHY...
...THE GUYS GET THE MORNING OFF.
YOU'LL GO WATCH, WON'T YOU, YUSHIN?
SHOOT, MAN.
I CAN'T.
YOU SHOULD'VE TOLD ME EARLIER.

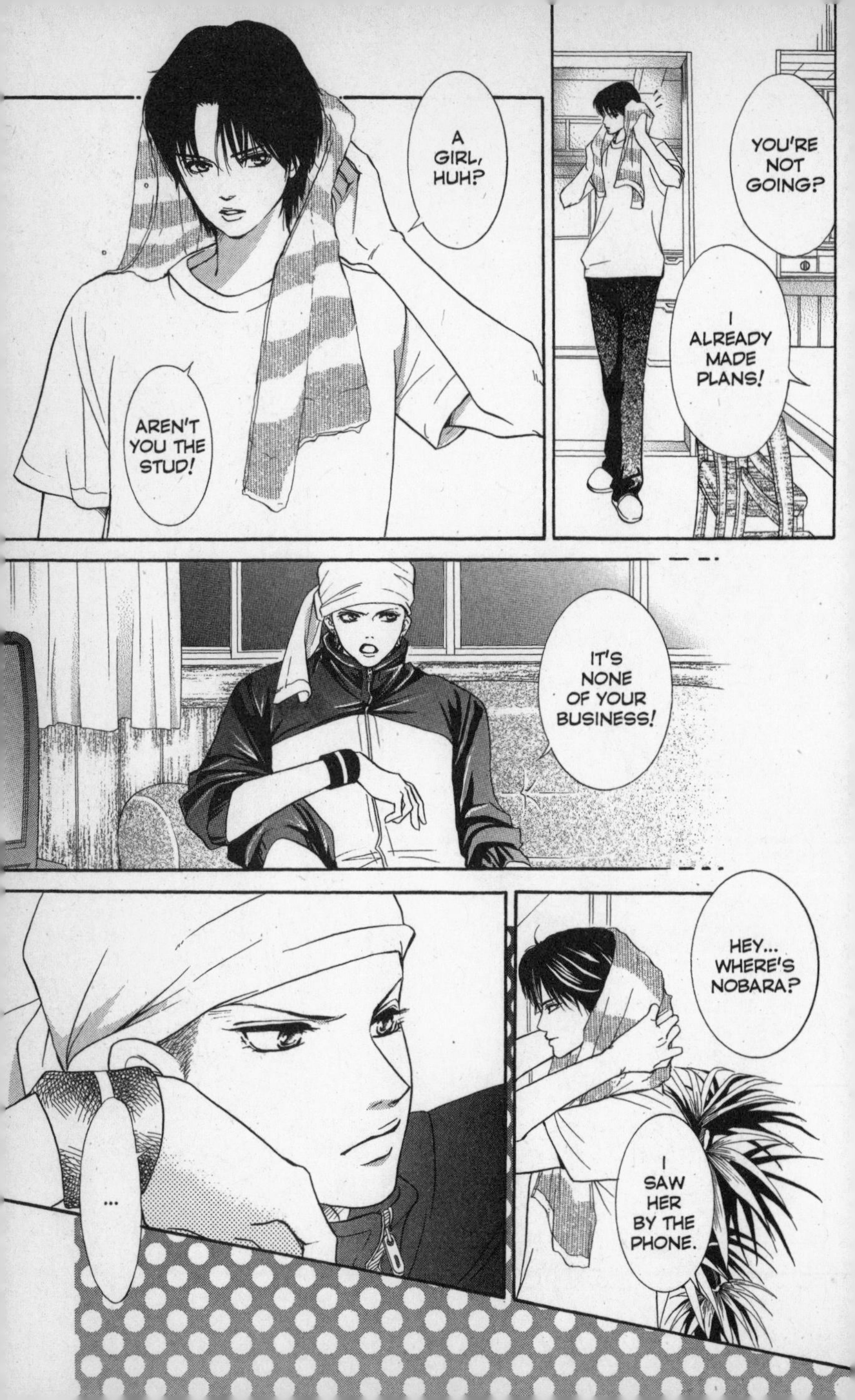
YOU'RE NOT GOING?
I ALREADY MADE PLANS!
A GIRL, HUH?
AREN'T YOU THE STUD!
IT'S NONE OF YOUR BUSINESS!
HEY... WHERE'S NOBARA?
I SAW HER BY THE PHONE.
...

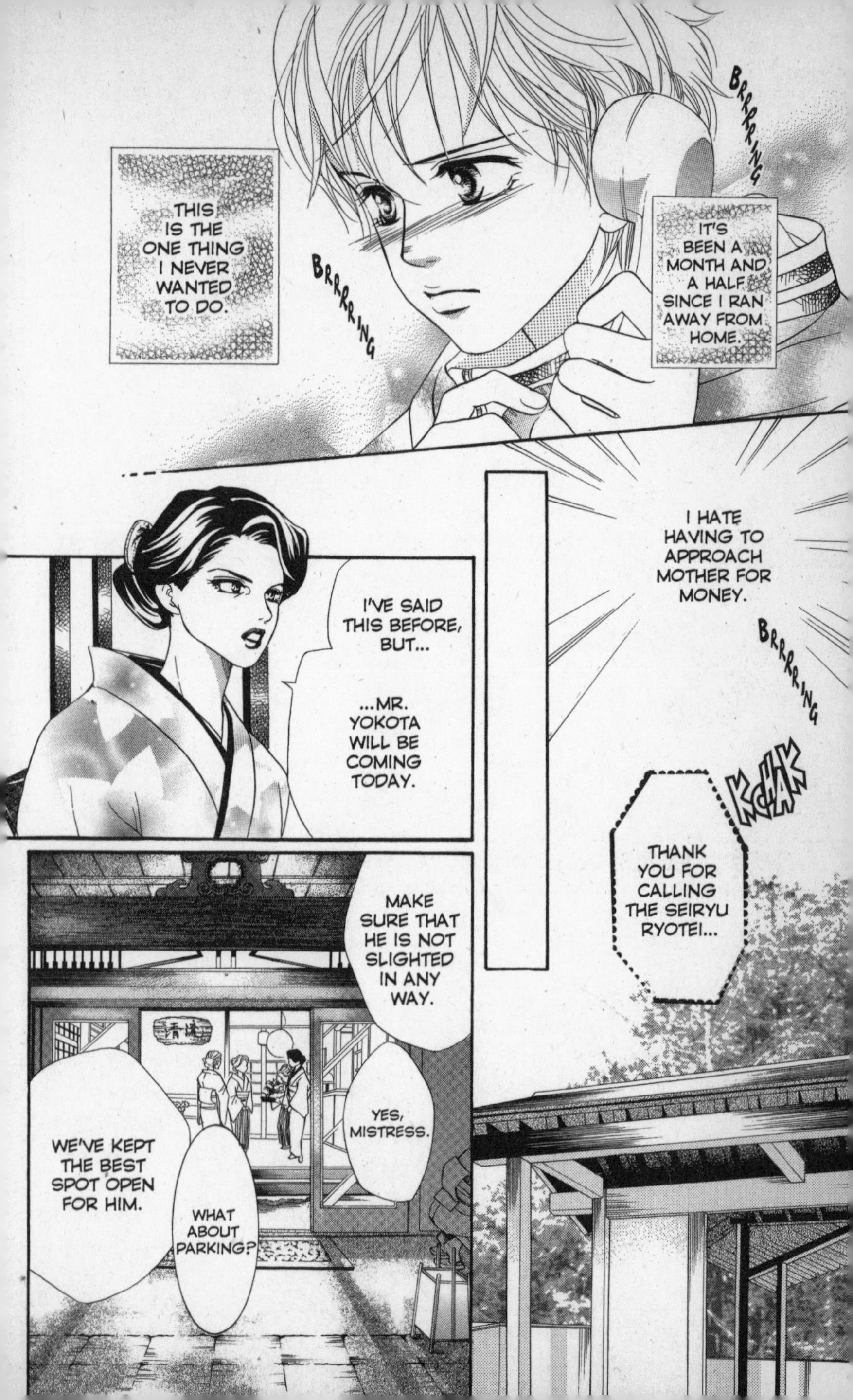

IT'S BEEN A MONTH AND A HALF SINCE I RAN AWAY FROM HOME.
BRRRRING
THIS IS THE ONE THING I NEVER WANTED TO DO.
BRRRRING
I HATE HAVING TO APPROACH MOTHER FOR MONEY.
BRRRRING
KCHAK
THANK YOU FOR CALLING THE SEIRYU RYOTEI...
I'VE SAID THIS BEFORE, BUT...
...MR. YOKOTA WILL BE COMING TODAY.
MAKE SURE THAT HE IS NOT SLIGHTED IN ANY WAY.
YES, MISTRESS.
WE'VE KEPT THE BEST SPOT OPEN FOR HIM.
WHAT ABOUT PARKING?

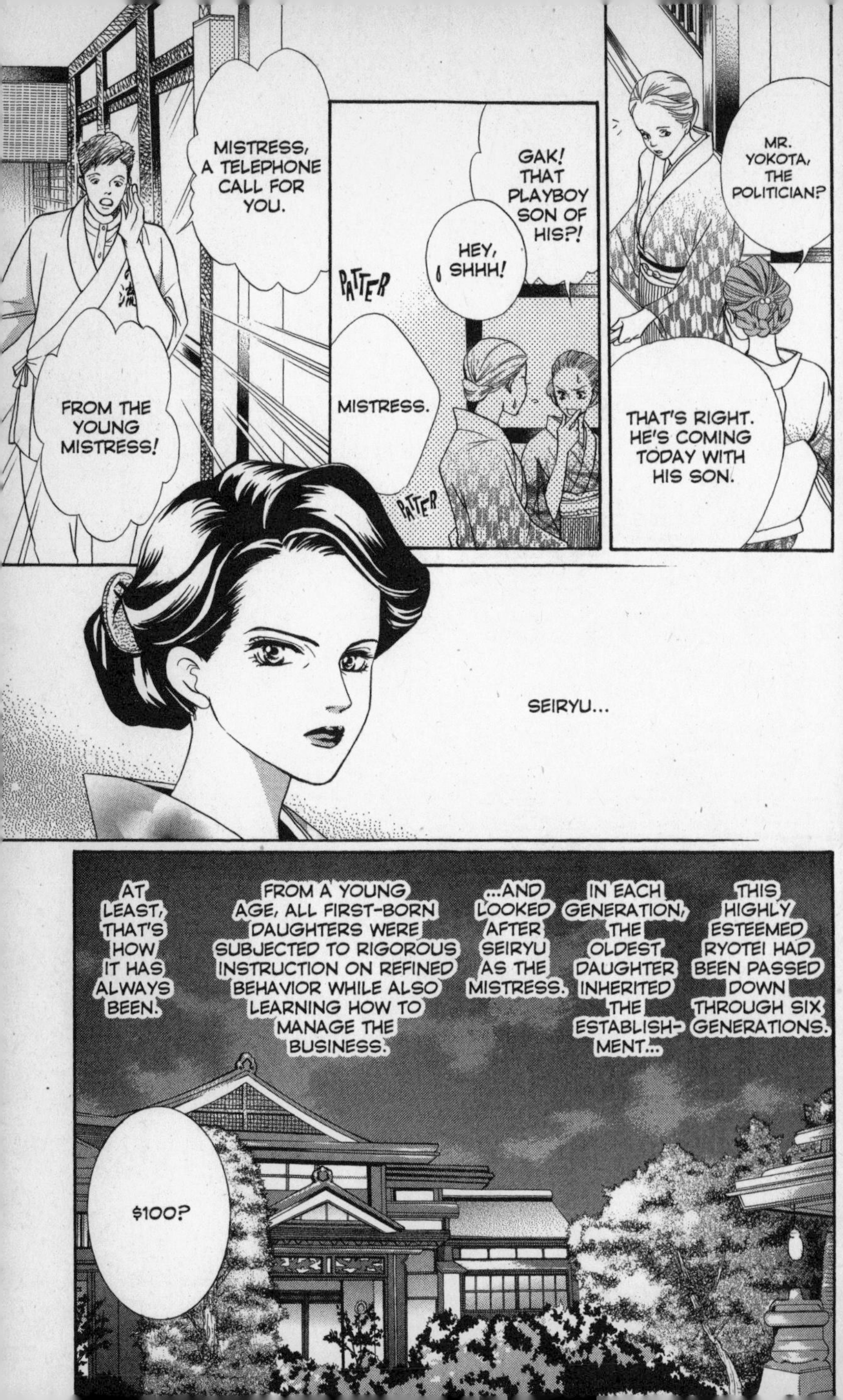
MR. YOKOTA, THE POLITICIAN?
THAT'S RIGHT. HE'S COMING TODAY WITH HIS SON.
GAK! THAT PLAYBOY SON OF HIS?!
HEY, SHHH!
PATTER
MISTRESS.
PATTER
MISTRESS, A TELEPHONE CALL FOR YOU.
FROM THE YOUNG MISTRESS!
SEIRYU...
THIS HIGHLY ESTEEMED RYOTEI HAD BEEN PASSED DOWN THROUGH SIX GENERATIONS.
IN EACH GENERATION, THE OLDEST DAUGHTER INHERITED THE ESTABLISHMENT...
...AND LOOKED AFTER SEIRYU AS THE MISTRESS.
FROM A YOUNG AGE, ALL FIRST-BORN DAUGHTERS WERE SUBJECTED TO RIGOROUS INSTRUCTION ON REFINED BEHAVIOR WHILE ALSO LEARNING HOW TO MANAGE THE BUSINESS.
AT LEAST, THAT'S HOW IT HAS ALWAYS BEEN.
$100?

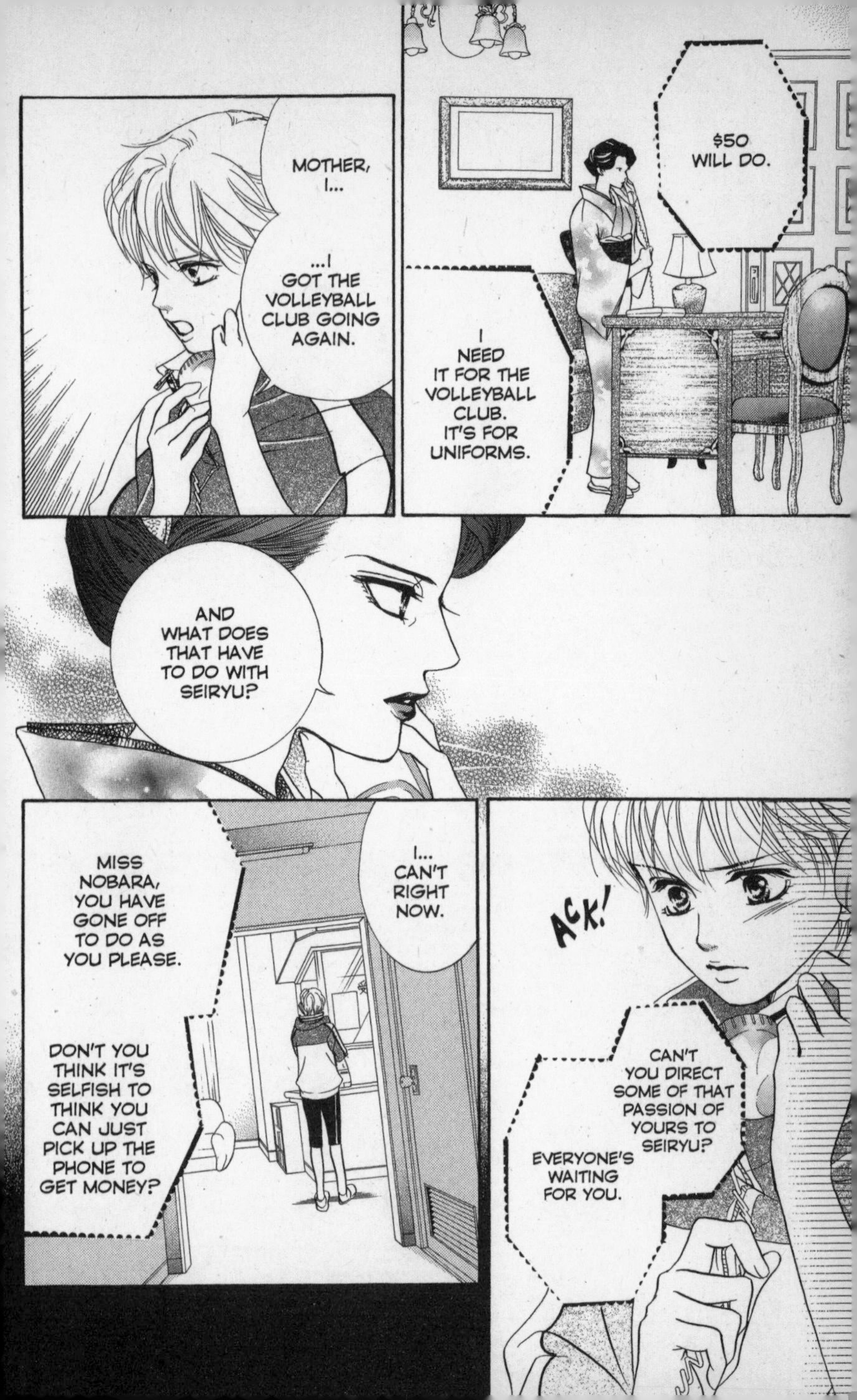
$50 WILL DO.
I NEED IT FOR THE VOLLEYBALL CLUB. IT'S FOR UNIFORMS.
MOTHER, I...
...I GOT THE VOLLEYBALL CLUB GOING AGAIN.
AND WHAT DOES THAT HAVE TO DO WITH SEIRYU?
ACK!
CAN'T YOU DIRECT SOME OF THAT PASSION OF YOURS TO SEIRYU?
EVERYONE'S WAITING FOR YOU.
I... CAN'T RIGHT NOW.
MISS NOBARA, YOU HAVE GONE OFF TO DO AS YOU PLEASE.
DON'T YOU THINK IT'S SELFISH TO THINK YOU CAN JUST PICK UP THE PHONE TO GET MONEY?

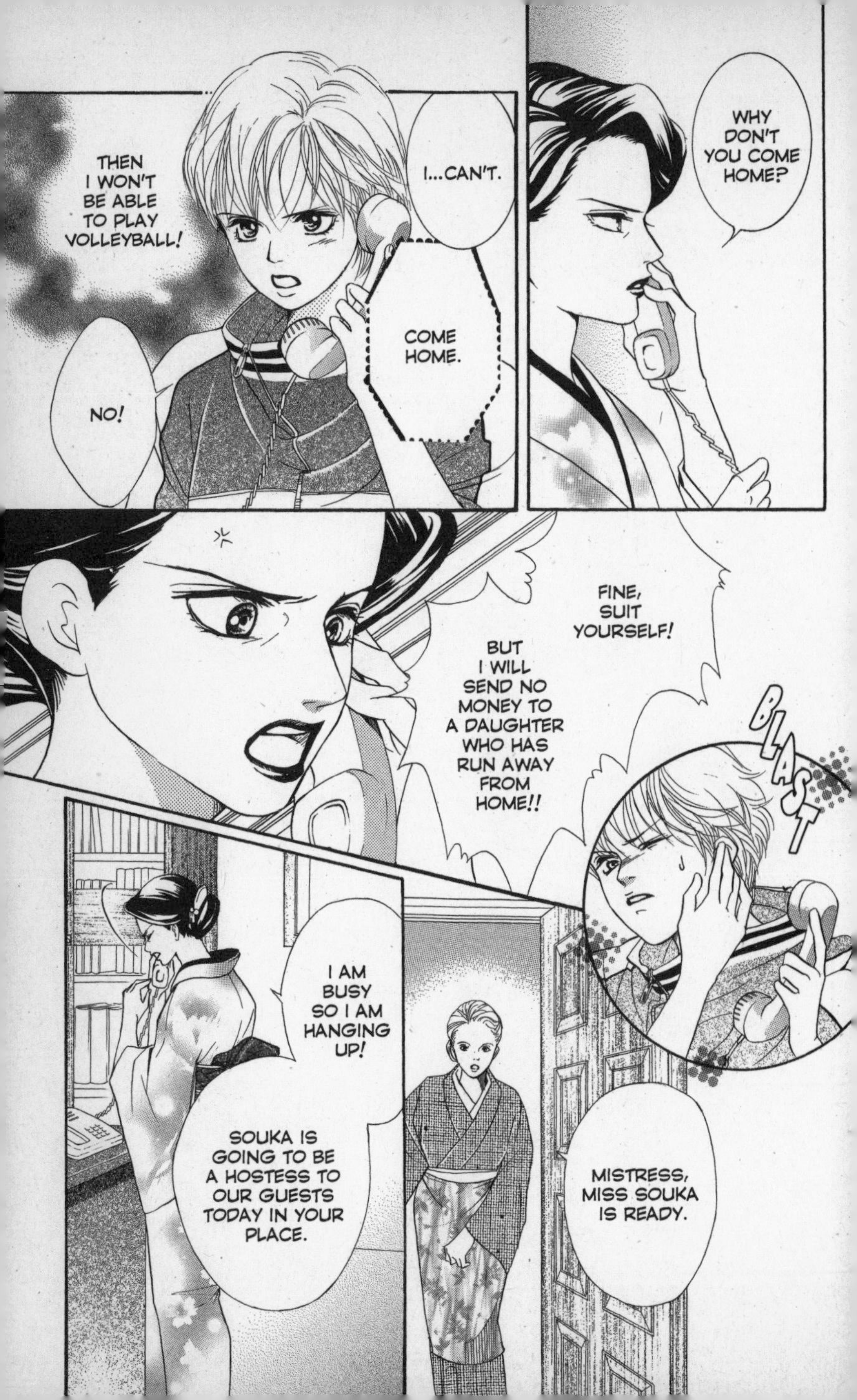
WHY DON'T YOU COME HOME?
I...CAN'T.
COME HOME.
THEN I WON'T BE ABLE TO PLAY VOLLEYBALL!
NO!
FINE, SUIT YOURSELF!
BUT I WILL SEND NO MONEY TO A DAUGHTER WHO HAS RUN AWAY FROM HOME!!
BLAST
MISTRESS, MISS SOUKA IS READY.
I AM BUSY SO I AM HANGING UP!
SOUKA IS GOING TO BE A HOSTESS TO OUR GUESTS TODAY IN YOUR PLACE.

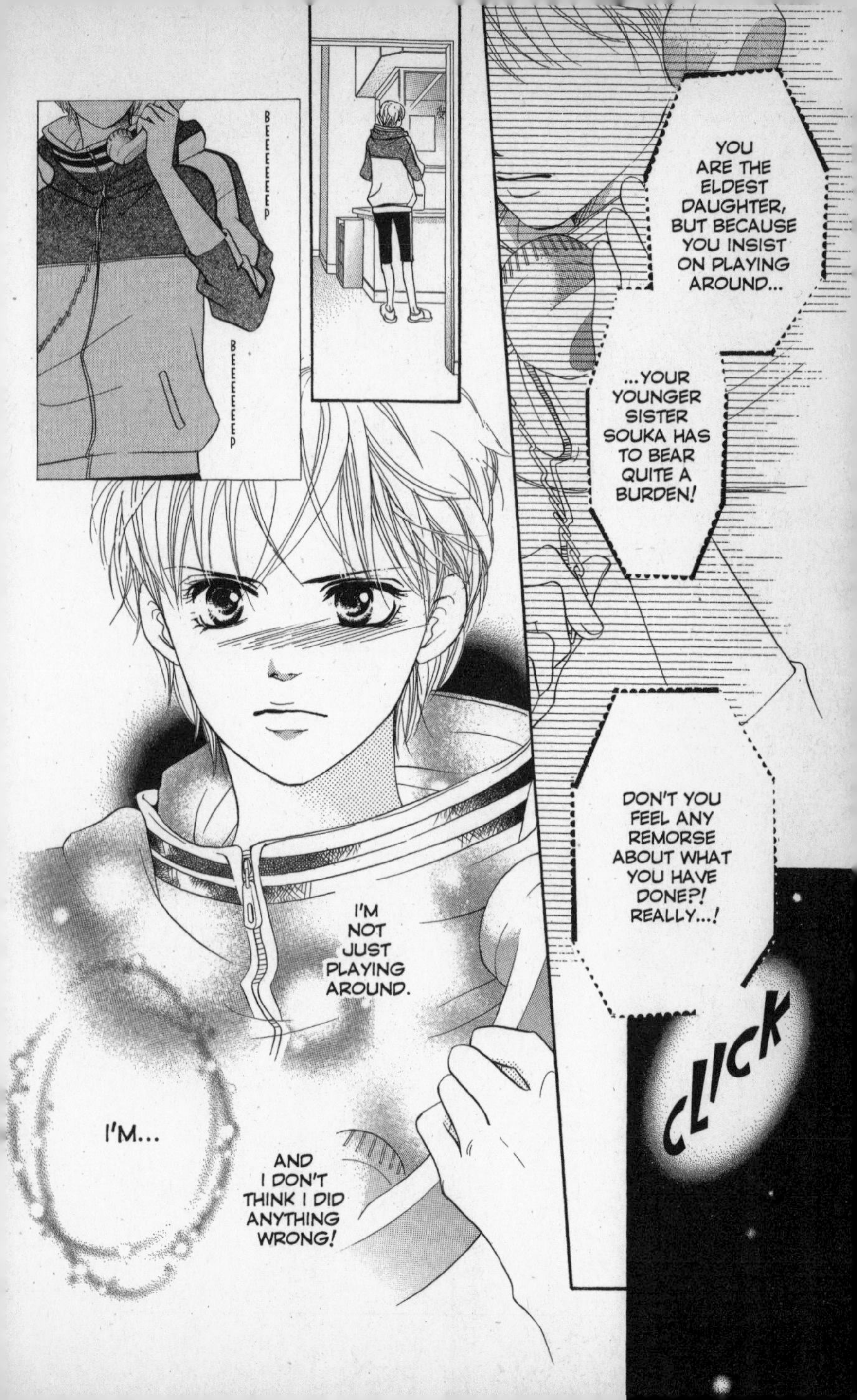
YOU ARE THE ELDEST DAUGHTER, BUT BECAUSE YOU INSIST ON PLAYING AROUND...
...YOUR YOUNGER SISTER SOUKA HAS TO BEAR QUITE A BURDEN!
DON'T YOU FEEL ANY REMORSE ABOUT WHAT YOU HAVE DONE?! REALLY...!
CLICK
BEEEEEEEP
BEEEEEEEP
I'M NOT JUST PLAYING AROUND.
AND I DON'T THINK I DID ANYTHING WRONG!
I'M...

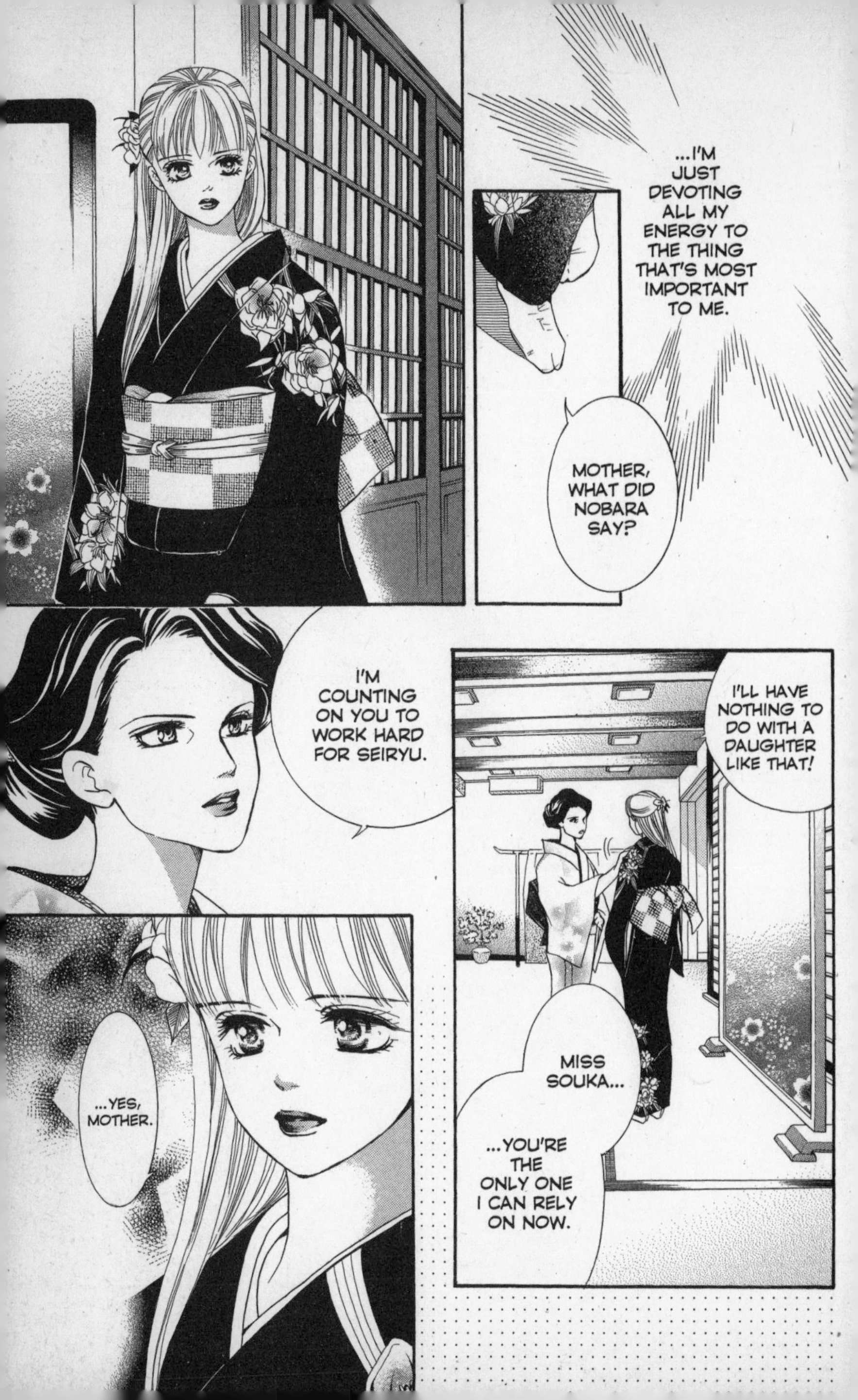
...I'M JUST DEVOTING ALL MY ENERGY TO THE THING THAT'S MOST IMPORTANT TO ME.
MOTHER, WHAT DID NOBARA SAY?
I'LL HAVE NOTHING TO DO WITH A DAUGHTER LIKE THAT!
MISS SOUKA...
...YOU'RE THE ONLY ONE I CAN RELY ON NOW.
I'M COUNTING ON YOU TO WORK HARD FOR SEIRYU.
...YES, MOTHER.

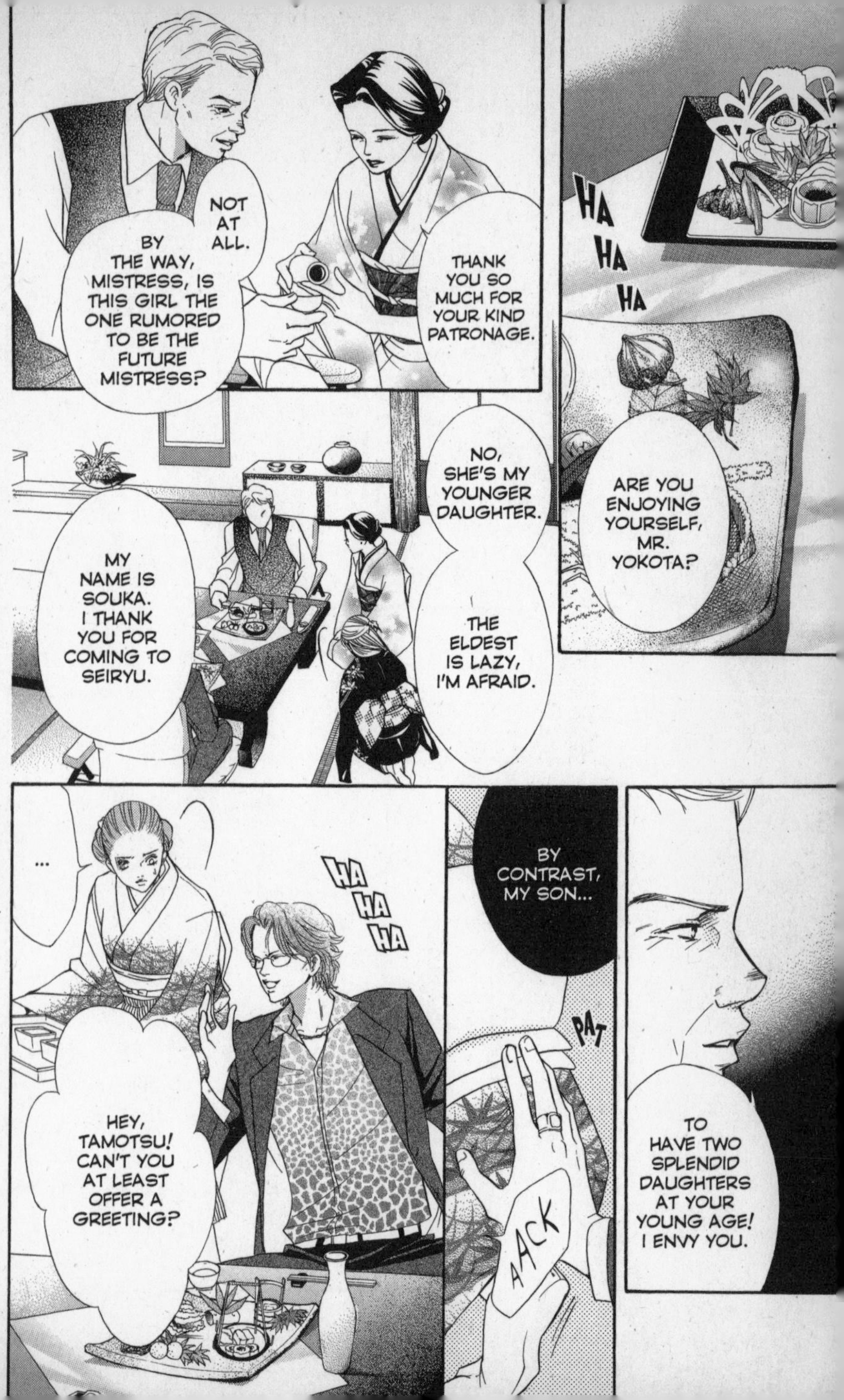
HA HA HA
ARE YOU ENJOYING YOURSELF, MR. YOKOTA?
THANK YOU SO MUCH FOR YOUR KIND PATRONAGE.
NOT AT ALL.
BY THE WAY, MISTRESS, IS THIS GIRL THE ONE RUMORED TO BE THE FUTURE MISTRESS?
NO, SHE'S MY YOUNGER DAUGHTER.
THE ELDEST IS LAZY, I'M AFRAID.
MY NAME IS SOUKA. I THANK YOU FOR COMING TO SEIRYU.
TO HAVE TWO SPLENDID DAUGHTERS AT YOUR YOUNG AGE! I ENVY YOU.
BY CONTRAST, MY SON...
PAT
AACK
HA HA HA
...
HEY, TAMOTSU! CAN'T YOU AT LEAST OFFER A GREETING?

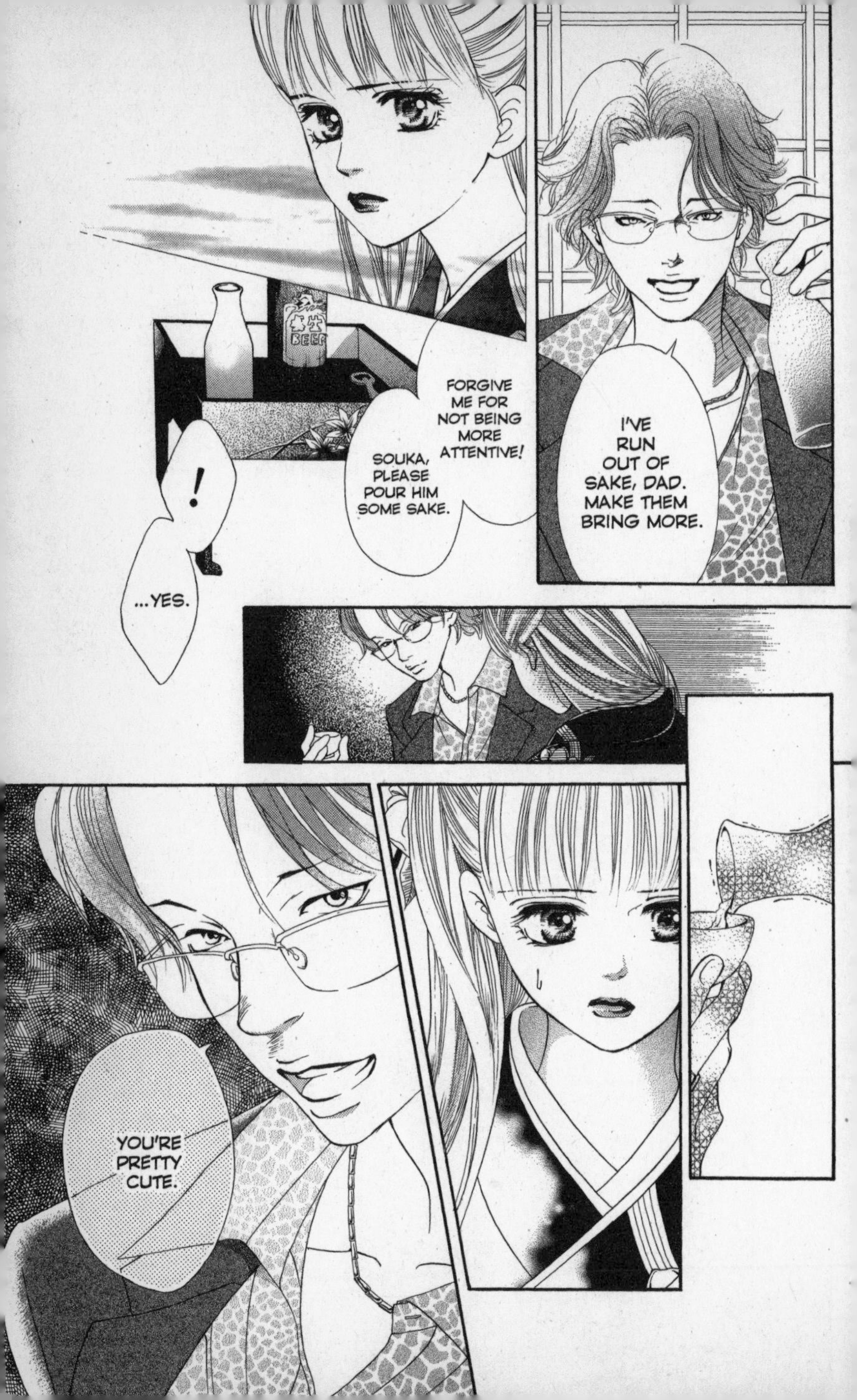
I'VE RUN OUT OF SAKE, DAD. MAKE THEM BRING MORE.
FORGIVE ME FOR NOT BEING MORE ATTENTIVE!
SOUKA, PLEASE POUR HIM SOME SAKE.
!
...YES.
YOU'RE PRETTY CUTE.

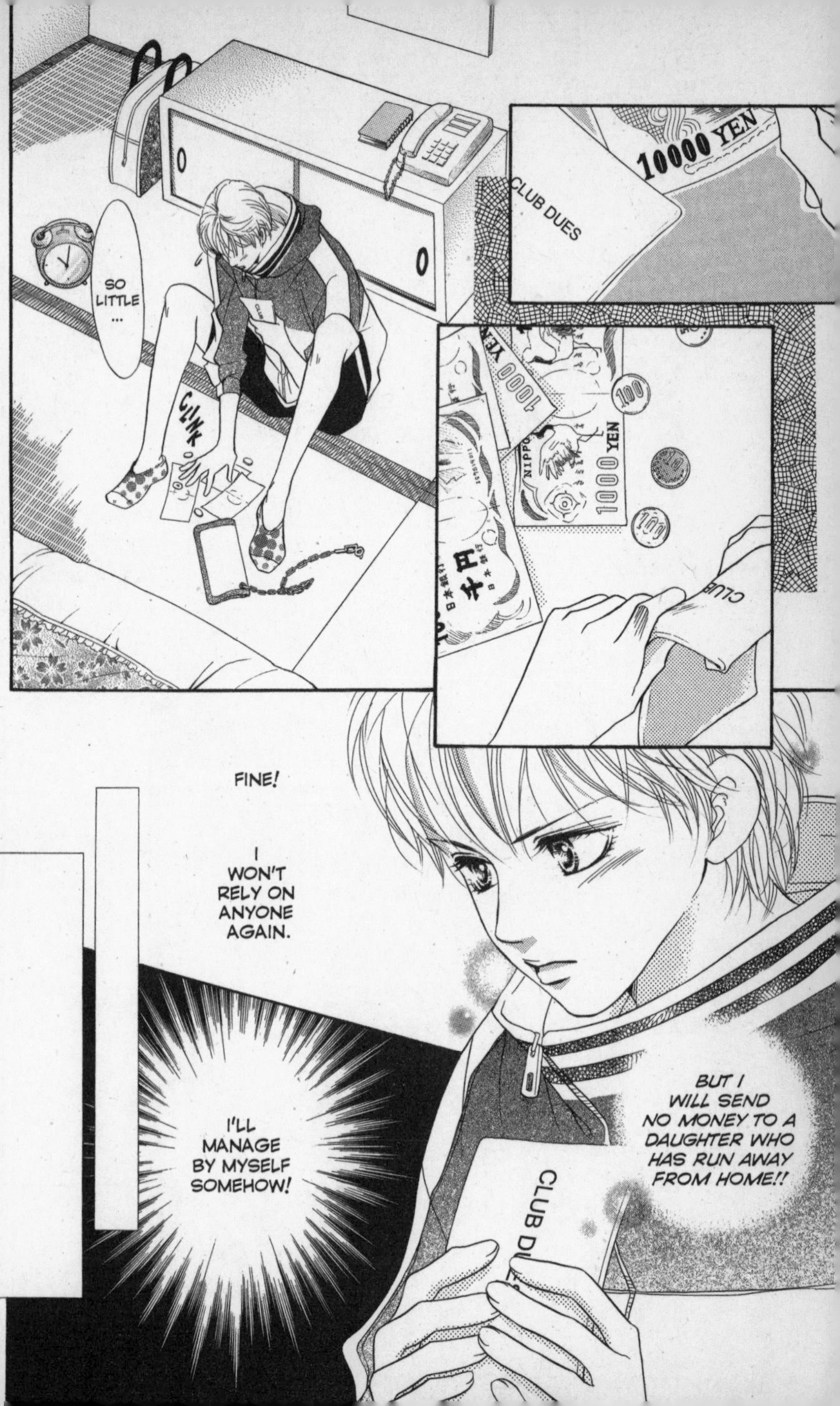
10000 YEN
CLUB DUES
1000 YEN
SO LITTLE ...
CLINK
BUT I WILL SEND NO MONEY TO A DAUGHTER WHO HAS RUN AWAY FROM HOME!!
FINE!
I WON'T RELY ON ANYONE AGAIN.
I'LL MANAGE BY MYSELF SOMEHOW!

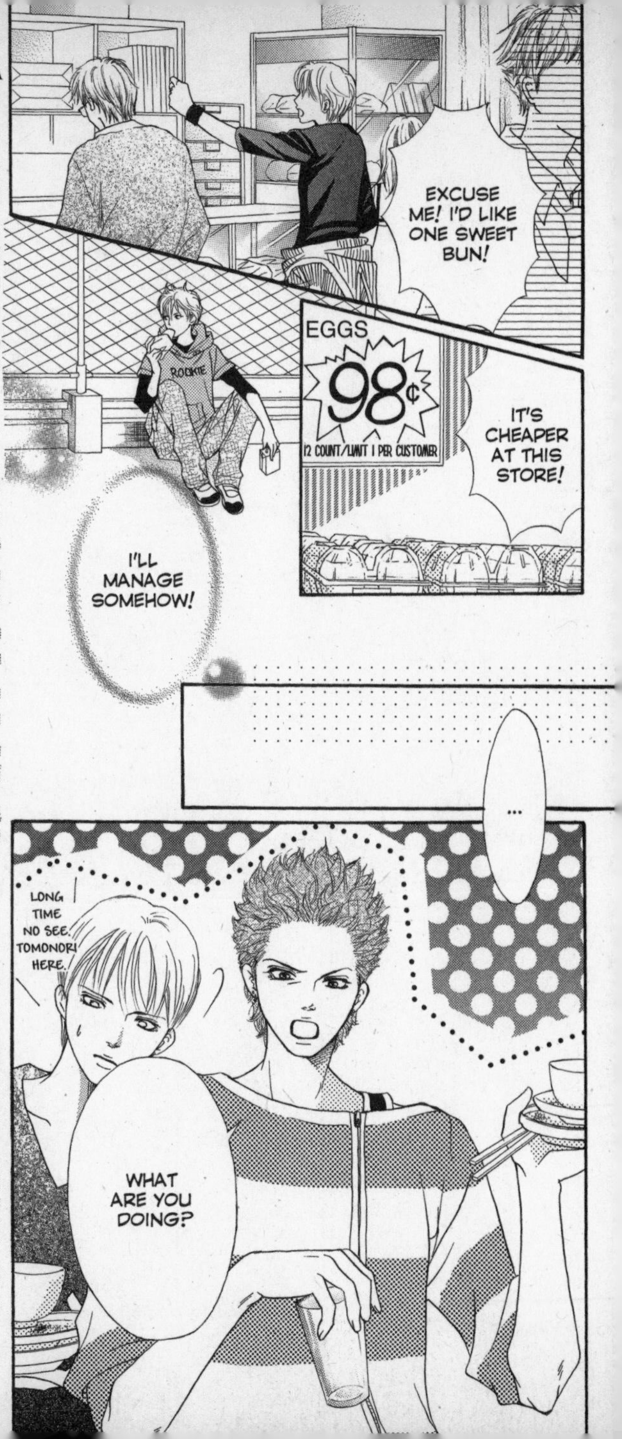
EXCUSE ME! I'D LIKE ONE SWEET BUN!
EGGS
98¢
12 COUNT/LIMIT 1 PER CUSTOMER
IT'S CHEAPER AT THIS STORE!
ROOKIE
I'LL MANAGE SOMEHOW!
...
LONG TIME NO SEE. TOMONORI HERE.
WHAT ARE YOU DOING?

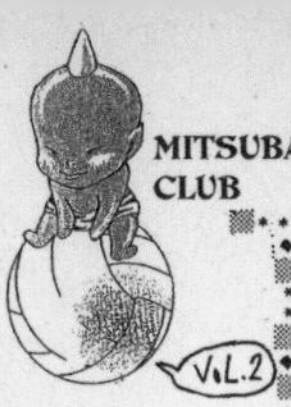
MITSUBA CLUB
VOL.2

WE HAVE FOUR TO FIVE ASSISTANTS COME IN EVERY MONTH. THEY'RE ALWAYS SUCH CHARACTERS SO IT'S A LOT OF FUN FOR ME. SOMETIMES WE'RE ON SUCH A TIGHT DEADLINE THAT EVERYBODY IS SHORT ON SLEEP, SO WE PLAY WORD GAMES TO KEEP OURSELVES AWAKE.

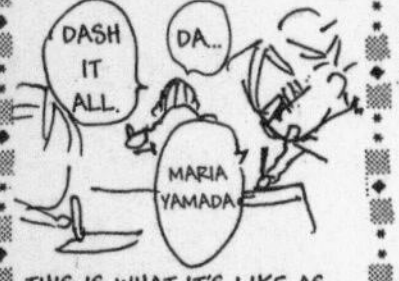
DASH IT ALL.
DA...
MARIA YAMADA

THIS IS WHAT IT'S LIKE AS WE WORK ON THE MANGA.

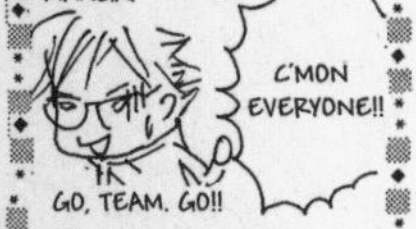
C'MON EVERYONE!!
GO, TEAM. GO!!

RECENTLY I'VE NOTICED THAT I START WORKING REALLY FERVENTLY WHEN THINGS GET TIGHT. I GOT ONLY FIVE HOURS OF SLEEP IN THREE DAYS!!

AND CHIRO LIKES TO CHEW ON THE STUFF THAT I'VE WORKED ON SO FURIOUSLY.

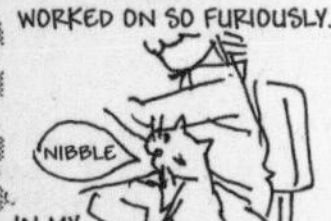
NIBBLE
IN MY LAP →
OH! NO!!

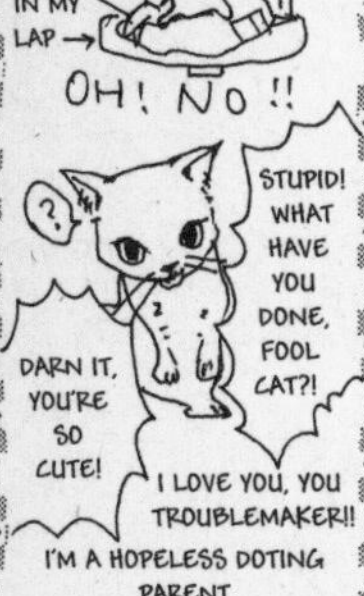
?
STUPID! WHAT HAVE YOU DONE, FOOL CAT?!
DARN IT, YOU'RE SO CUTE!
I LOVE YOU, YOU TROUBLEMAKER!!

I'M A HOPELESS DOTING PARENT.

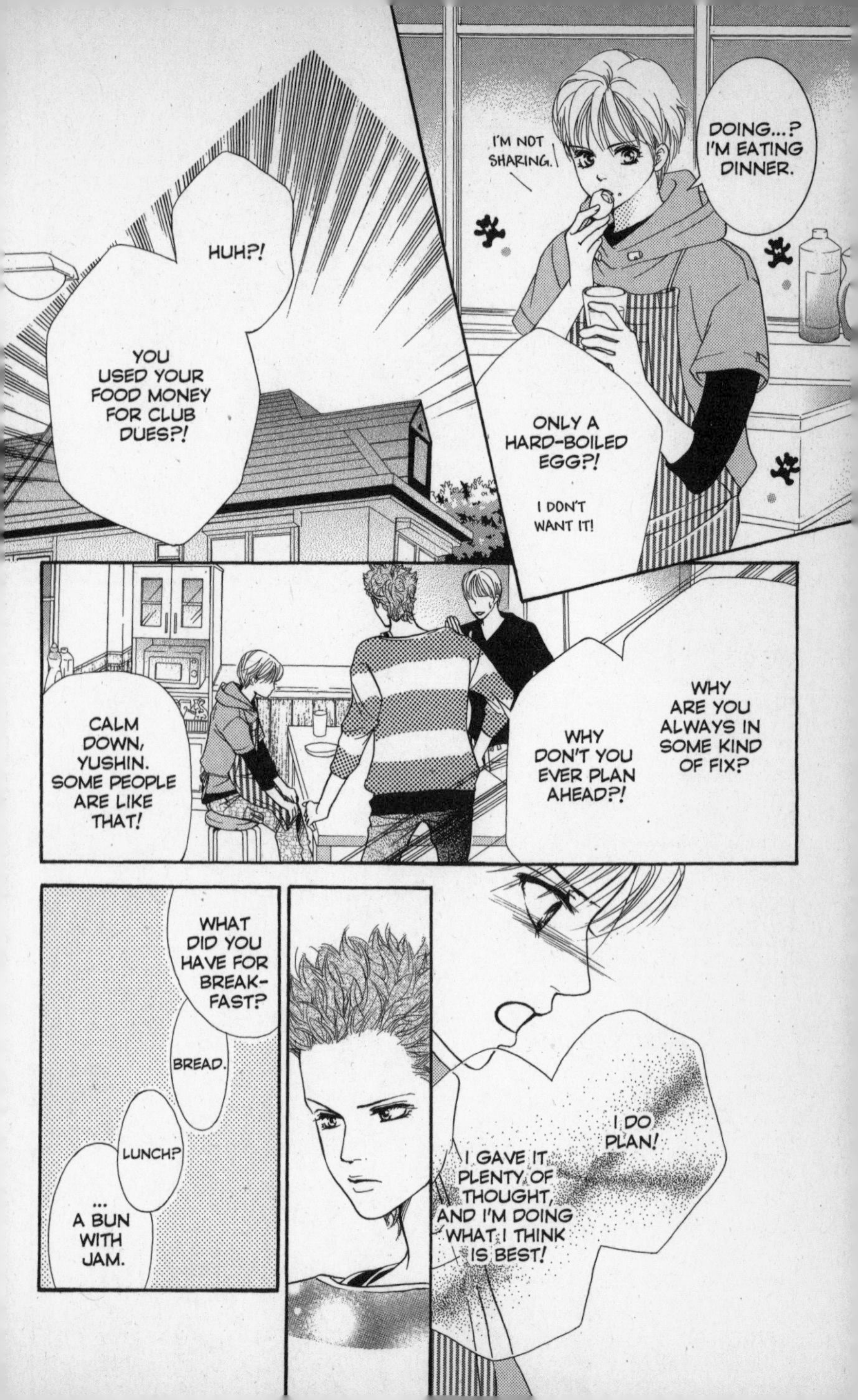
DOING...? I'M EATING DINNER.
I'M NOT SHARING.
ONLY A HARD-BOILED EGG?!
I DON'T WANT IT!
HUH?!
YOU USED YOUR FOOD MONEY FOR CLUB DUES?!
WHY ARE YOU ALWAYS IN SOME KIND OF FIX?
WHY DON'T YOU EVER PLAN AHEAD?!
CALM DOWN, YUSHIN. SOME PEOPLE ARE LIKE THAT!
I DO PLAN!
I GAVE IT PLENTY OF THOUGHT, AND I'M DOING WHAT I THINK IS BEST!
WHAT DID YOU HAVE FOR BREAK-FAST?
BREAD.
LUNCH?
... A BUN WITH JAM.

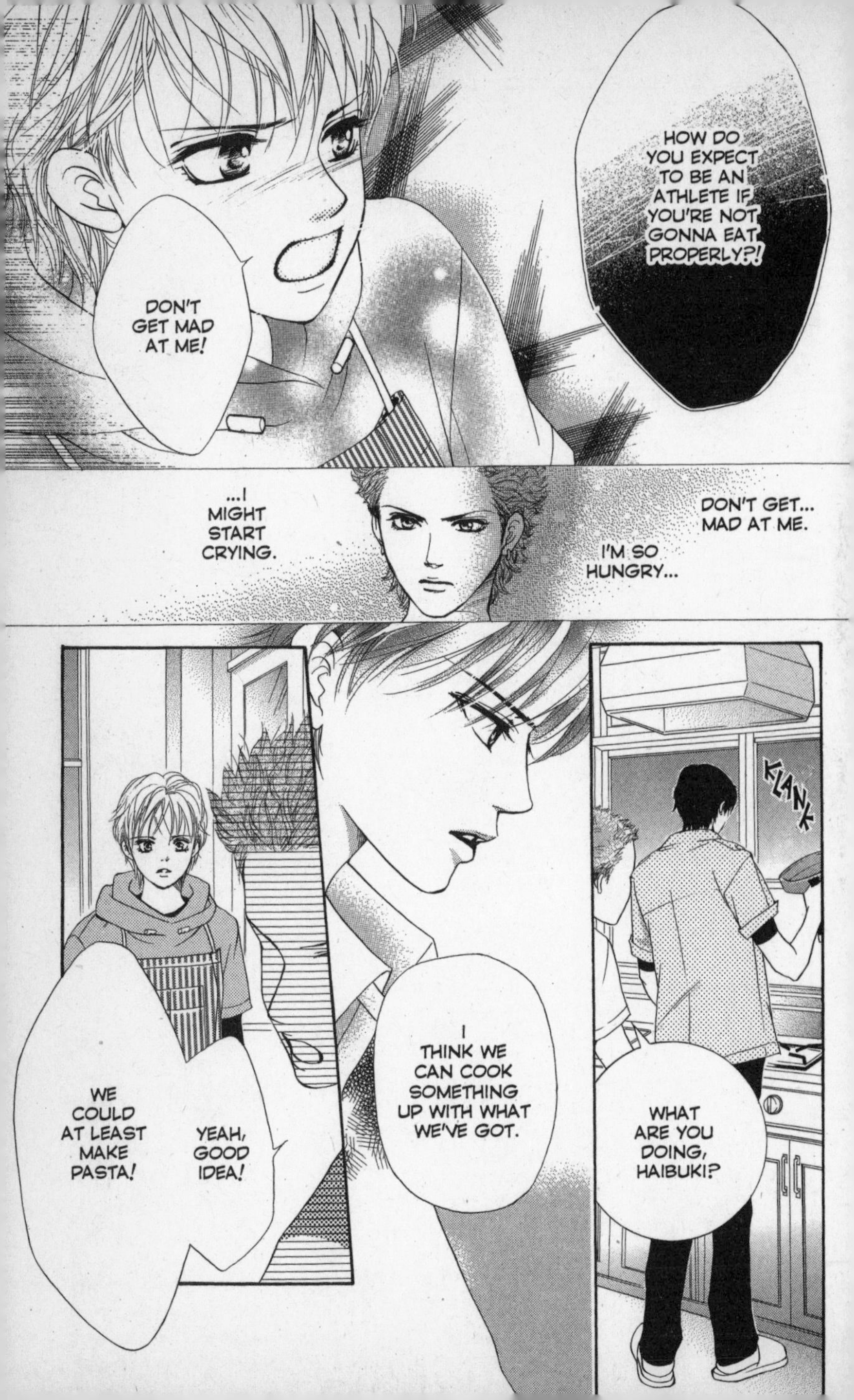
HOW DO YOU EXPECT TO BE AN ATHLETE IF YOU'RE NOT GONNA EAT PROPERLY?!
DON'T GET MAD AT ME!
DON'T GET... MAD AT ME.
I'M SO HUNGRY...
...I MIGHT START CRYING.
KLANK
WHAT ARE YOU DOING, HAIBUKI?
I THINK WE CAN COOK SOMETHING UP WITH WHAT WE'VE GOT.
WE COULD AT LEAST MAKE PASTA!
YEAH, GOOD IDEA!

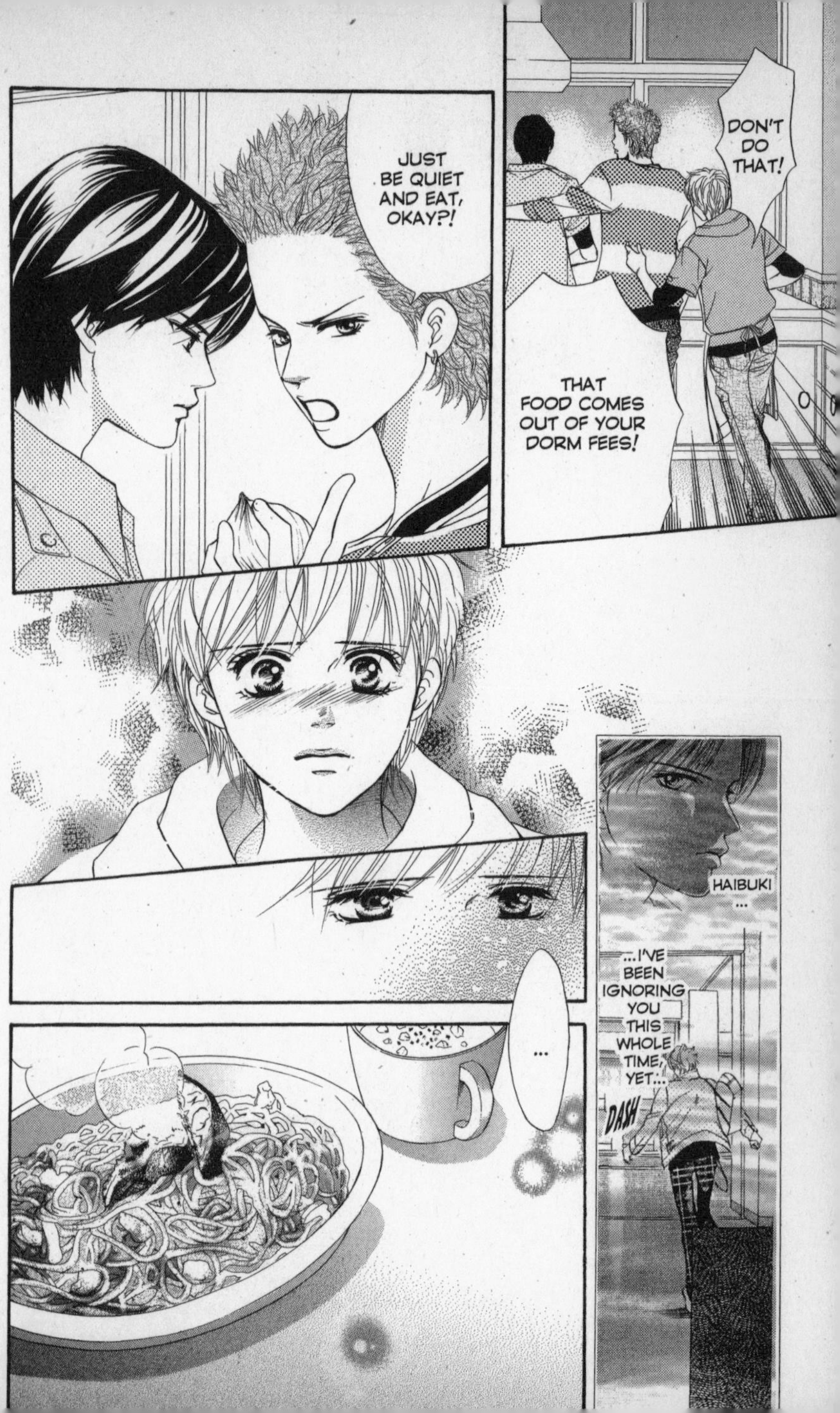
DON'T DO THAT!
THAT FOOD COMES OUT OF YOUR DORM FEES!
JUST BE QUIET AND EAT, OKAY?!
HAIBUKI ...
...I'VE BEEN IGNORING YOU THIS WHOLE TIME, YET...
DASH
...

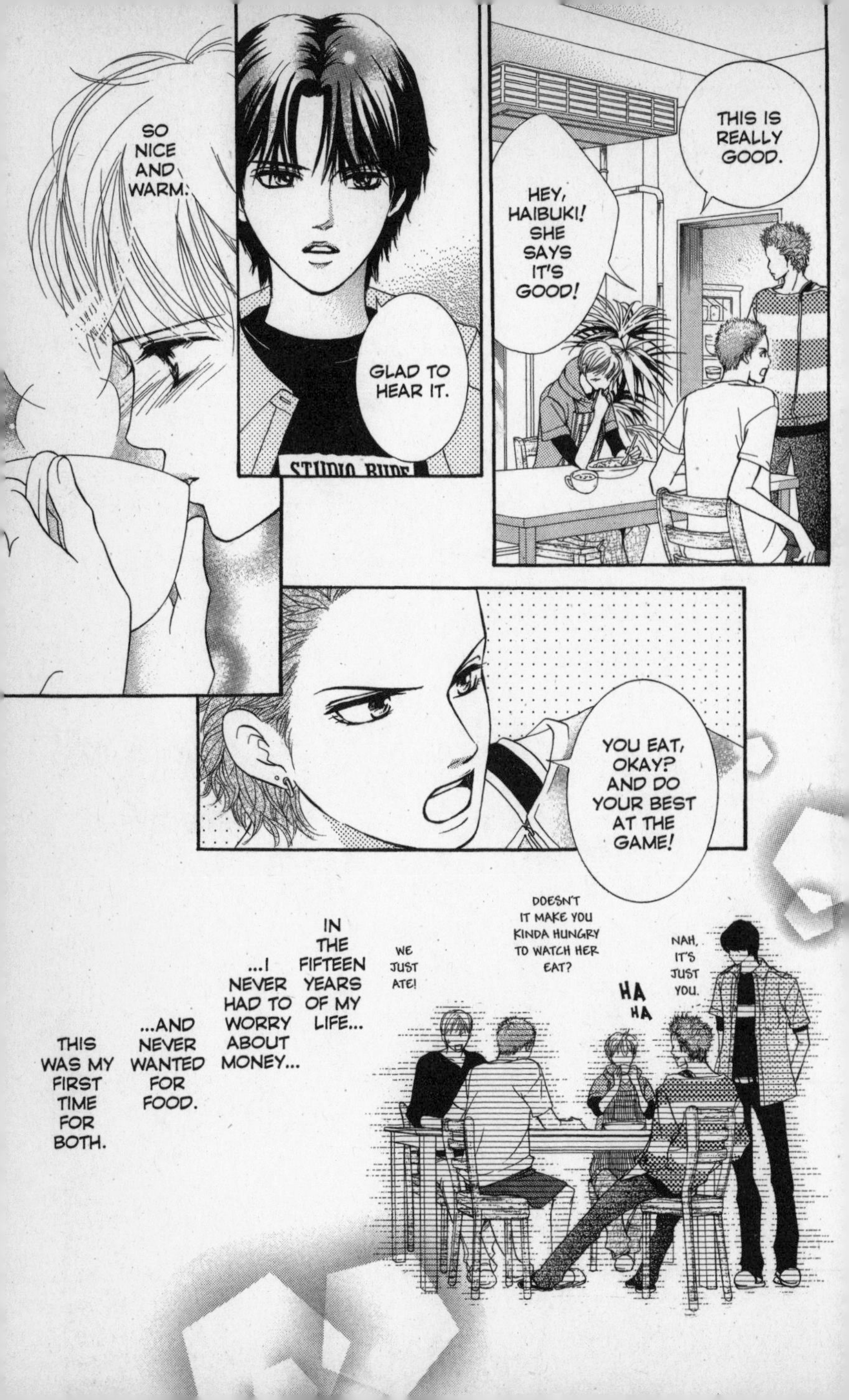
THIS IS REALLY GOOD.
HEY, HAIBUKI! SHE SAYS IT'S GOOD!
GLAD TO HEAR IT.
SO NICE AND WARM.
YOU EAT, OKAY? AND DO YOUR BEST AT THE GAME!
DOESN'T IT MAKE YOU KINDA HUNGRY TO WATCH HER EAT?
NAH, IT'S JUST YOU.
HA HA
WE JUST ATE!
IN THE FIFTEEN YEARS OF MY LIFE...
...I NEVER HAD TO WORRY ABOUT MONEY...
...AND NEVER WANTED FOR FOOD.
THIS WAS MY FIRST TIME FOR BOTH.

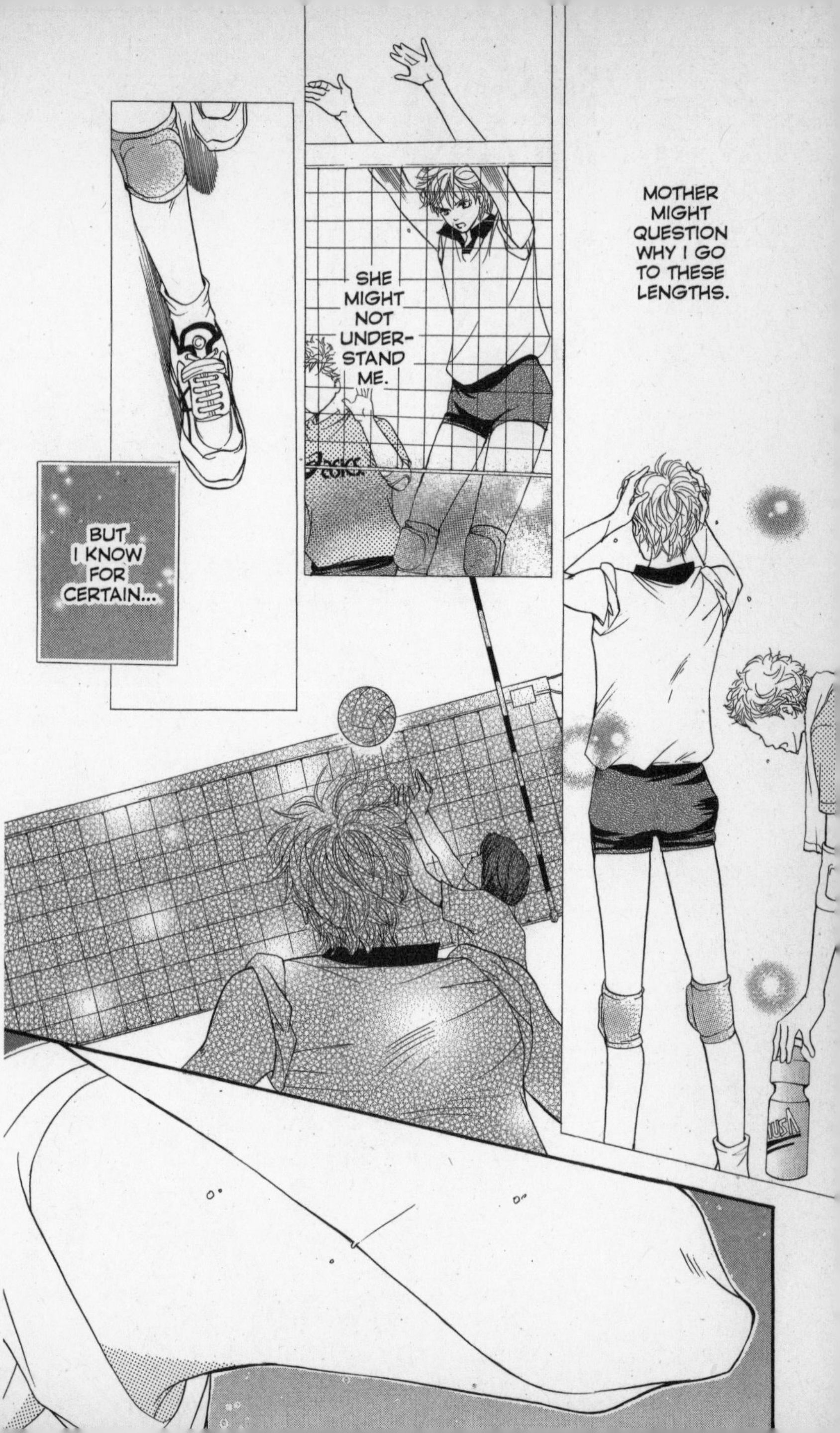
MOTHER MIGHT QUESTION WHY I GO TO THESE LENGTHS.
SHE MIGHT NOT UNDER-STAND ME.
BUT I KNOW FOR CERTAIN...

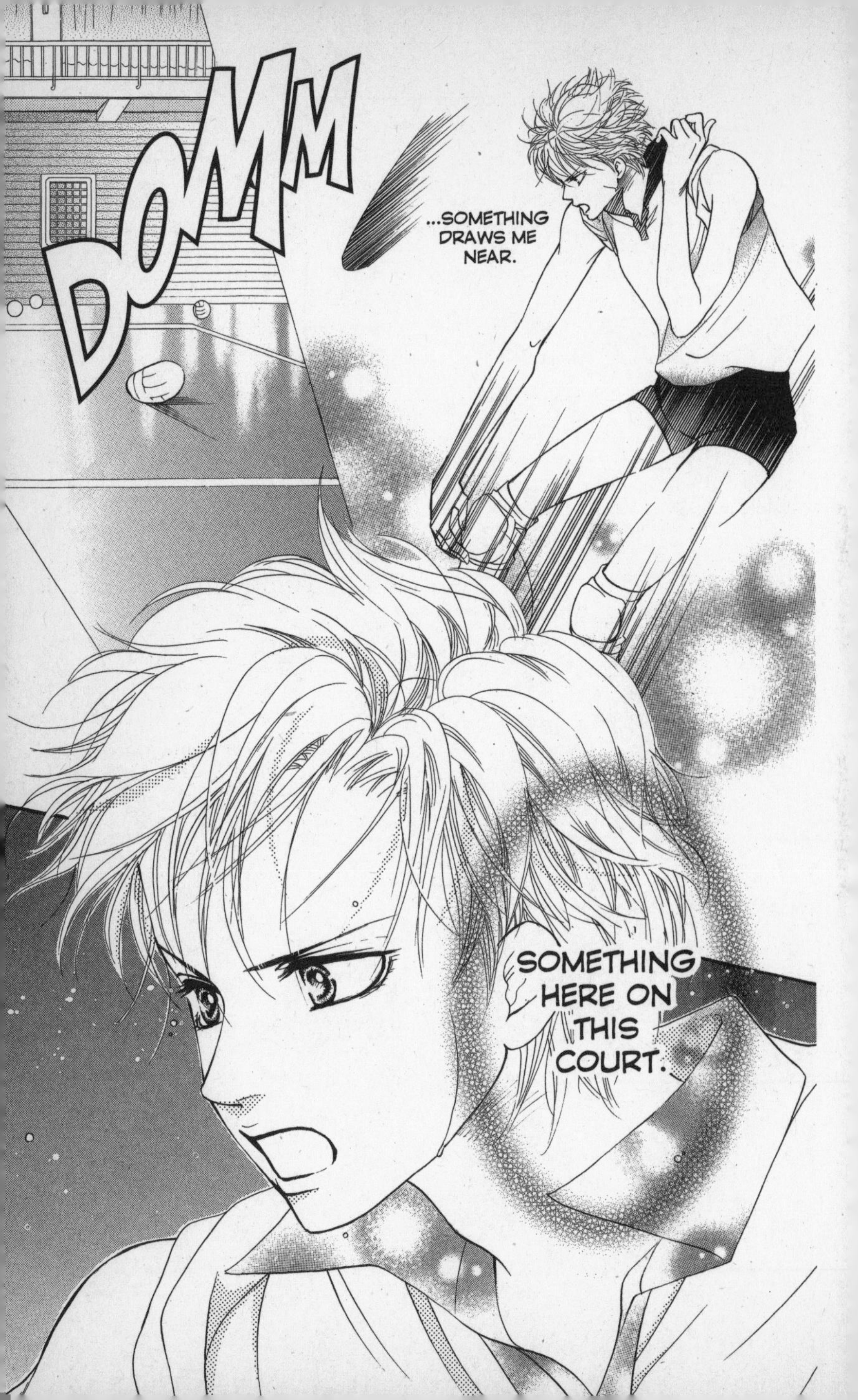
DOMM
...SOMETHING DRAWS ME NEAR.
SOMETHING HERE ON THIS COURT.

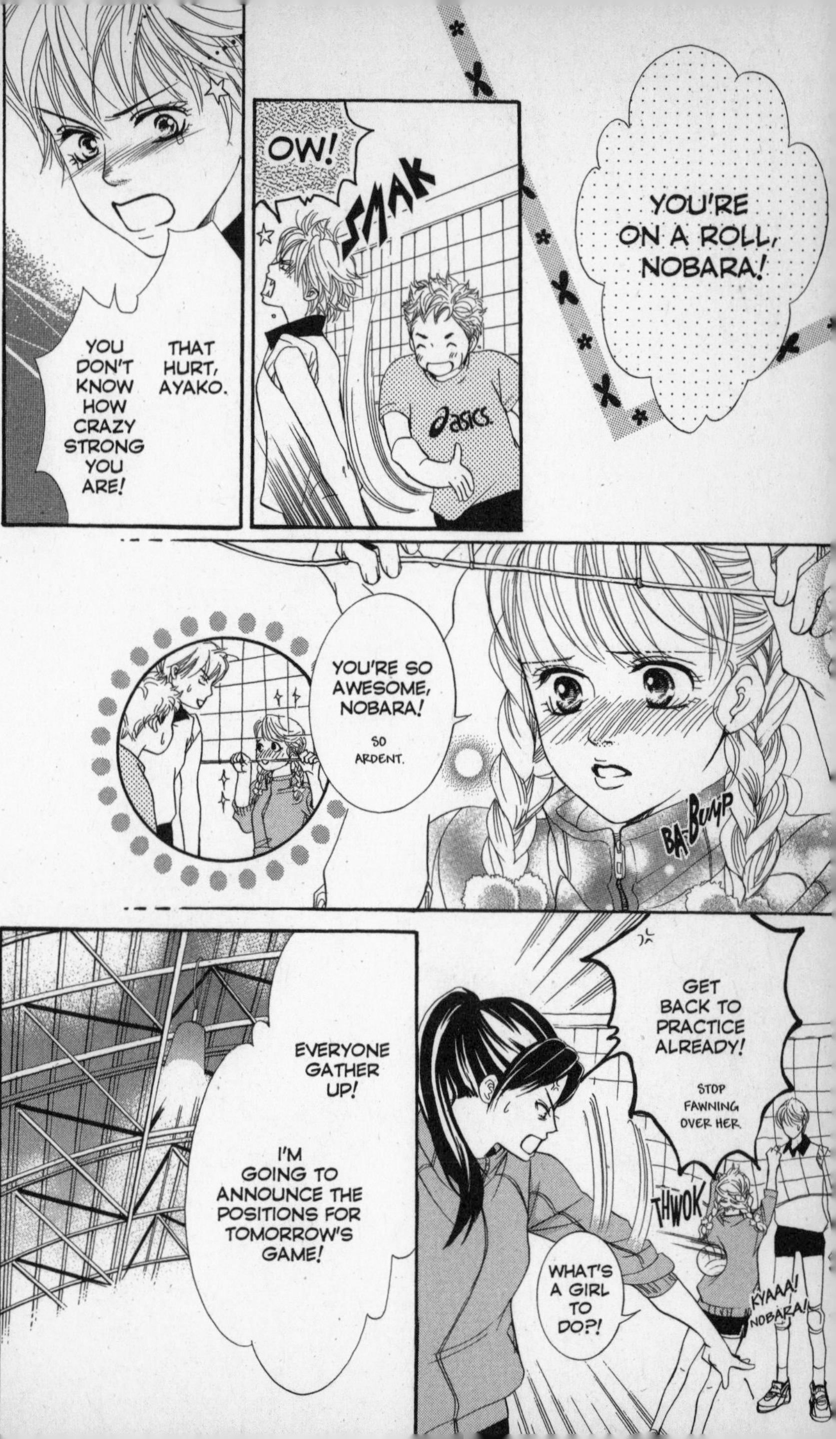
YOU'RE ON A ROLL, NOBARA!
OW!
SMAK
THAT HURT, AYAKO.
YOU DON'T KNOW HOW CRAZY STRONG YOU ARE!
YOU'RE SO AWESOME, NOBARA!
SO ARDENT.
BA-BUMP
GET BACK TO PRACTICE ALREADY!
STOP FAWNING OVER HER.
THWOK
KYAAA! NOBARA!
WHAT'S A GIRL TO DO?!
EVERYONE GATHER UP!
I'M GOING TO ANNOUNCE THE POSITIONS FOR TOMORROW'S GAME!

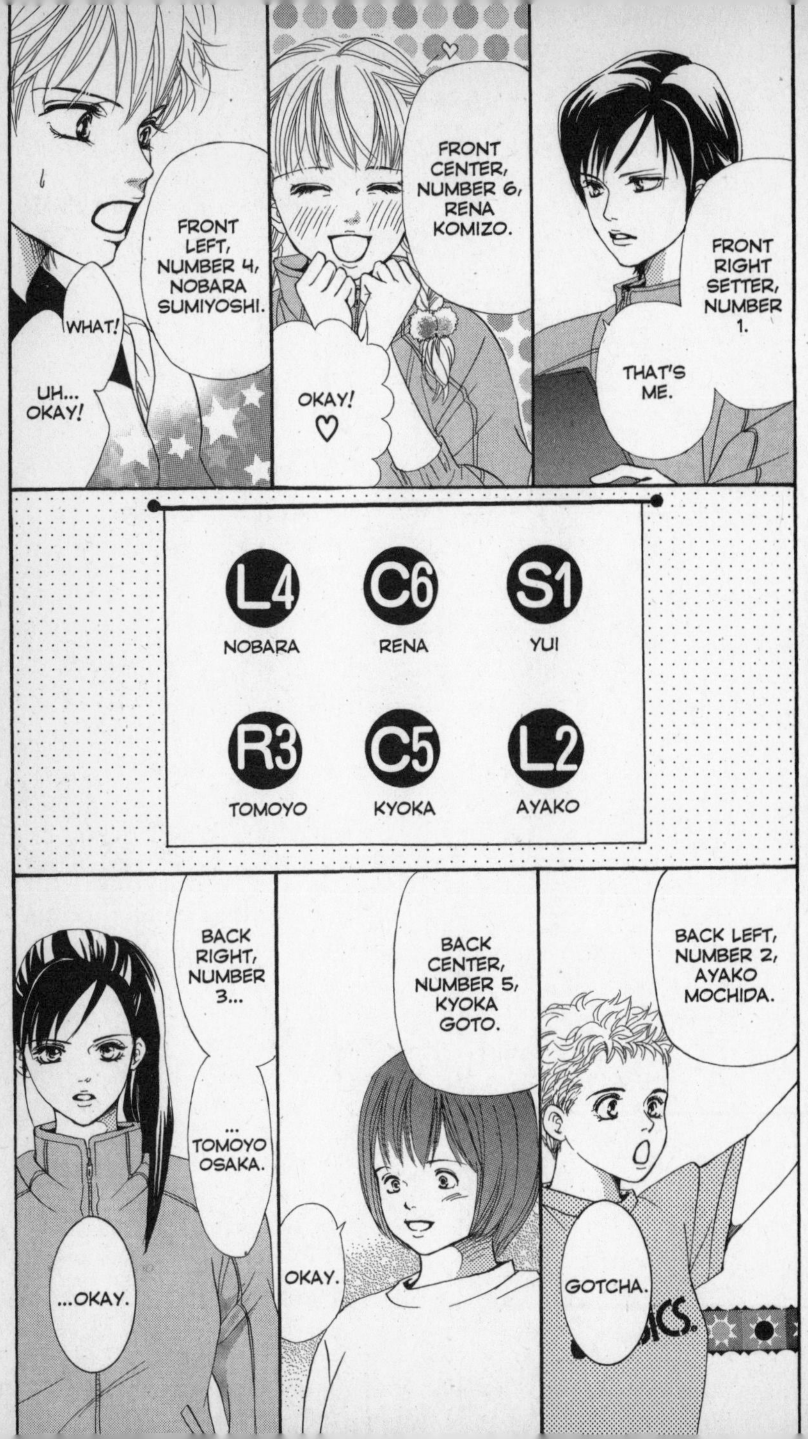
FRONT RIGHT SETTER, NUMBER 1.
THAT'S ME.
FRONT CENTER, NUMBER 6, RENA KOMIZO.
OKAY! ♡
FRONT LEFT, NUMBER 4, NOBARA SUMIYOSHI.
WHAT!
UH... OKAY!
L4 NOBARA
C6 RENA
S1 YUI
R3 TOMOYO
C5 KYOKA
L2 AYAKO
BACK LEFT, NUMBER 2, AYAKO MOCHIDA.
GOTCHA.
BACK CENTER, NUMBER 5, KYOKA GOTO.
OKAY.
BACK RIGHT, NUMBER 3...
...TOMOYO OSAKA.
...OKAY.

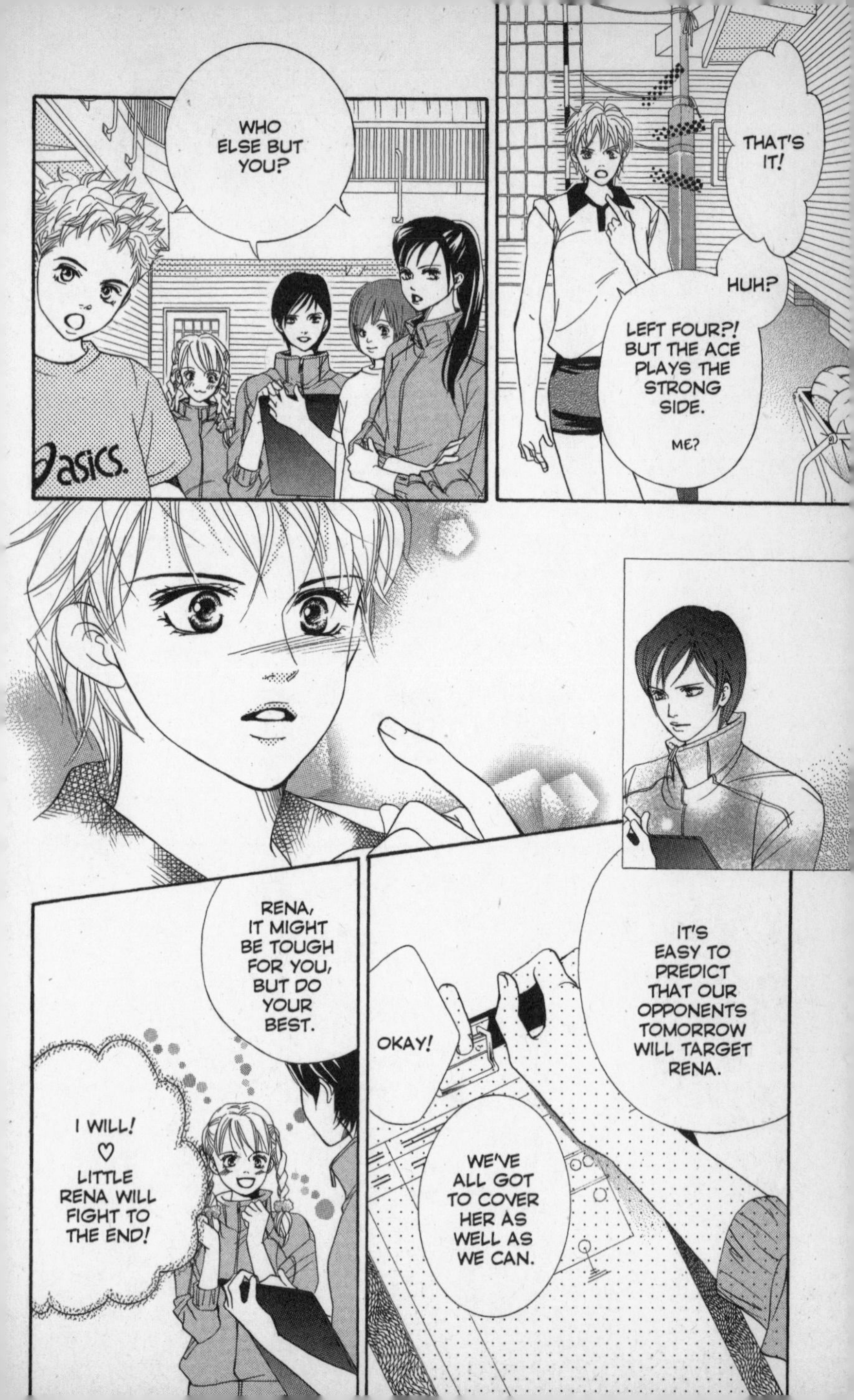
THAT'S IT!
HUH?
LEFT FOUR?! BUT THE ACE PLAYS THE STRONG SIDE.
ME?
WHO ELSE BUT YOU?
IT'S EASY TO PREDICT THAT OUR OPPONENTS TOMORROW WILL TARGET RENA.
OKAY!
WE'VE ALL GOT TO COVER HER AS WELL AS WE CAN.
RENA, IT MIGHT BE TOUGH FOR YOU, BUT DO YOUR BEST.
I WILL! ♡ LITTLE RENA WILL FIGHT TO THE END!

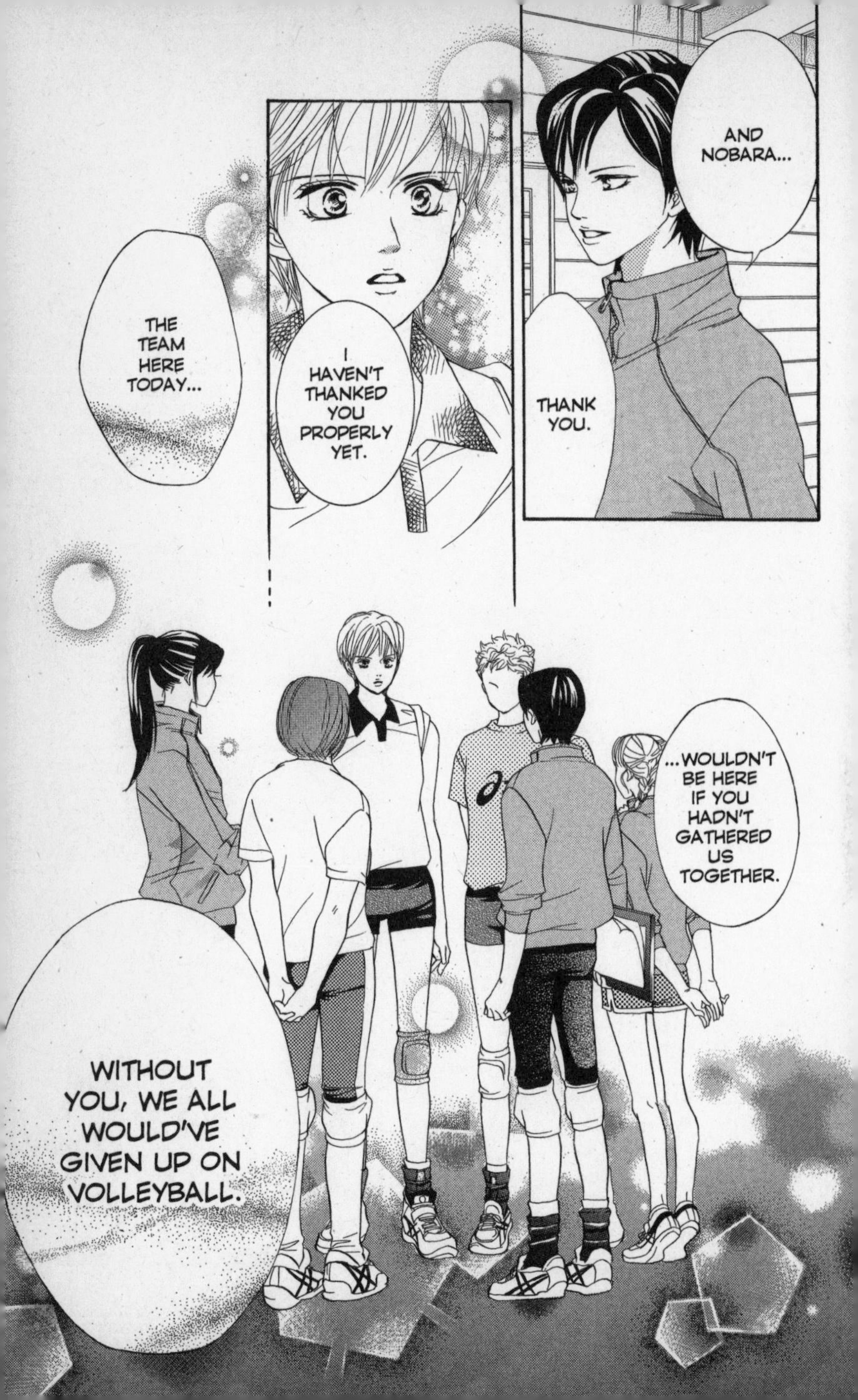
AND NOBARA...
THANK YOU.
I HAVEN'T THANKED YOU PROPERLY YET.
THE TEAM HERE TODAY...
...WOULDN'T BE HERE IF YOU HADN'T GATHERED US TOGETHER.
WITHOUT YOU, WE ALL WOULD'VE GIVEN UP ON VOLLEYBALL.

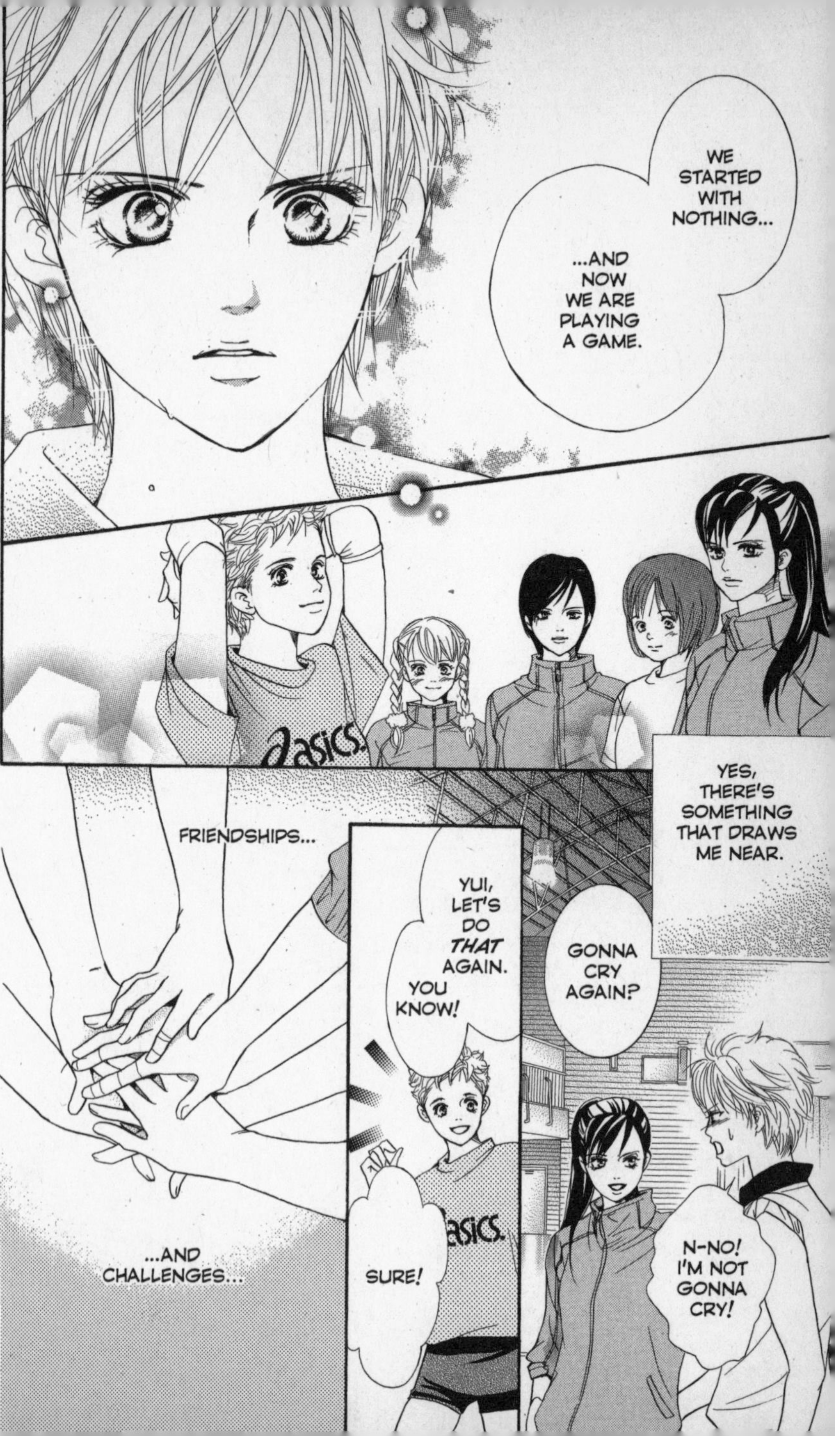
WE STARTED WITH NOTHING...
...AND NOW WE ARE PLAYING A GAME.
asics
YES, THERE'S SOMETHING THAT DRAWS ME NEAR.
GONNA CRY AGAIN?
N-NO! I'M NOT GONNA CRY!
YUI, LET'S DO *THAT* AGAIN. YOU KNOW!
SURE!
asics
FRIENDSHIPS...
...AND CHALLENGES...

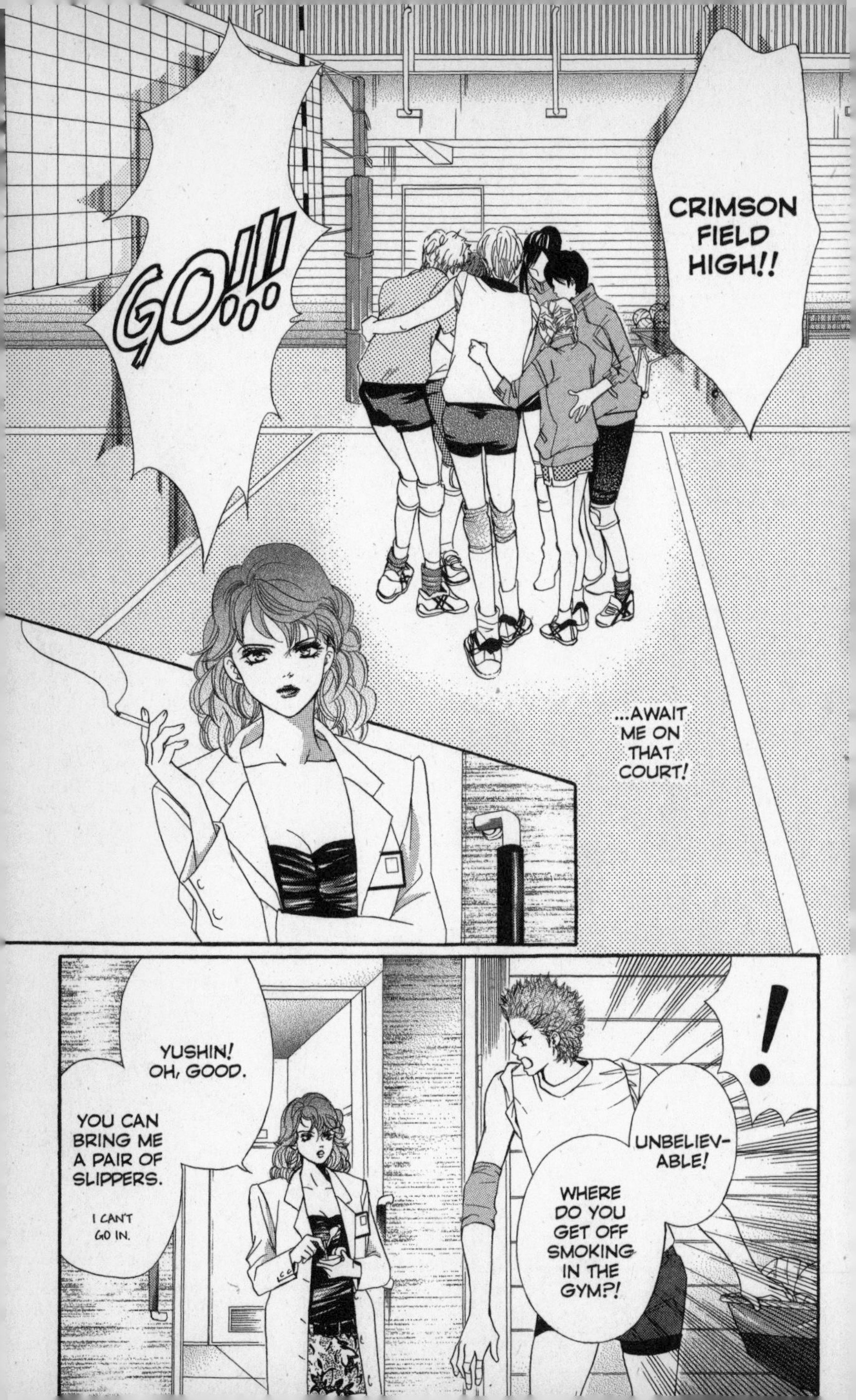
CRIMSON FIELD HIGH!!
GO!!!
...AWAIT ME ON THAT COURT!
!
UNBELIEV-ABLE!
WHERE DO YOU GET OFF SMOKING IN THE GYM?!
YUSHIN! OH, GOOD.
YOU CAN BRING ME A PAIR OF SLIPPERS.
I CAN'T GO IN.

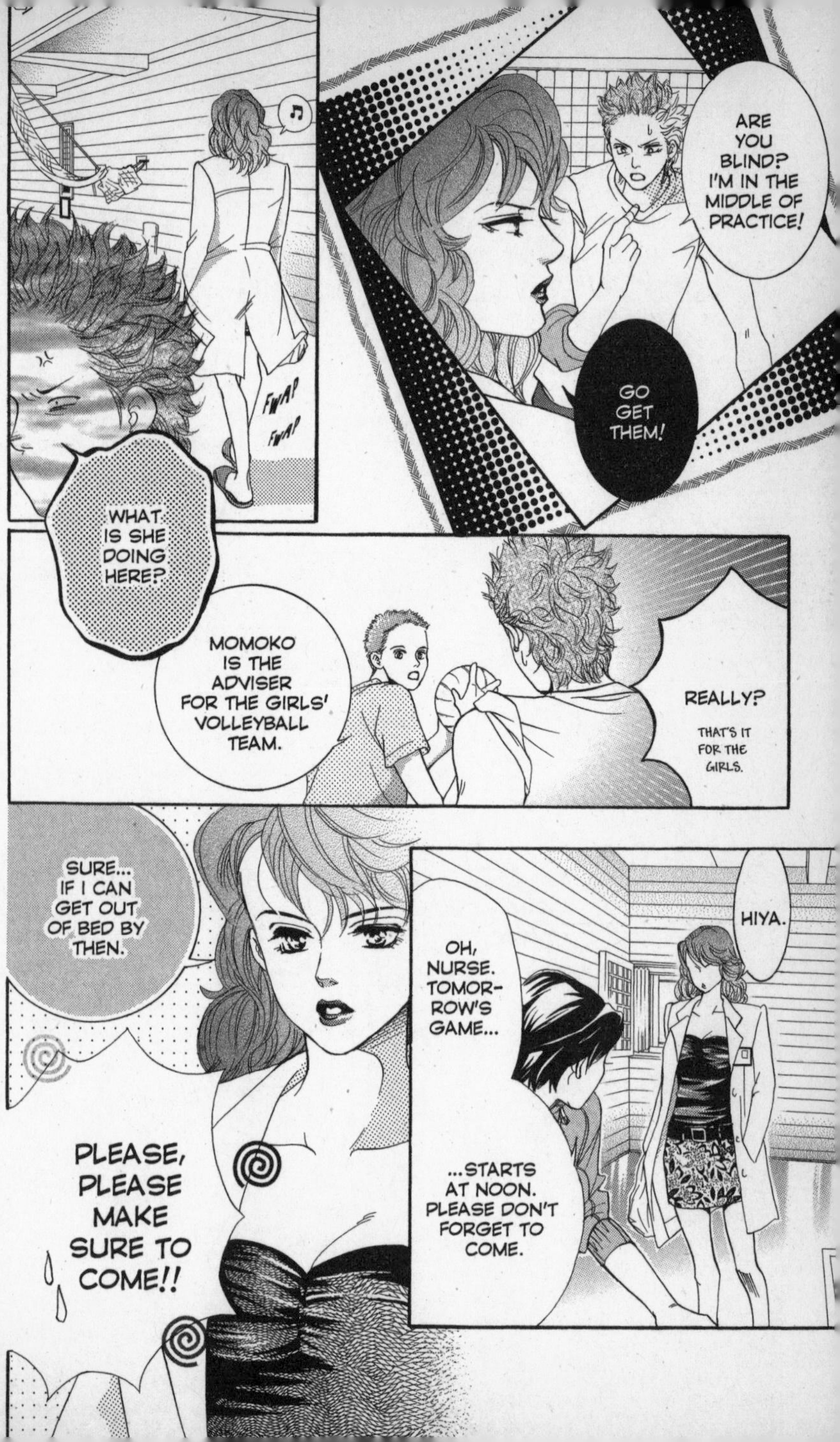
ARE YOU BLIND? I'M IN THE MIDDLE OF PRACTICE!
GO GET THEM!
♪
FWAP FWAP
WHAT IS SHE DOING HERE?
MOMOKO IS THE ADVISER FOR THE GIRLS' VOLLEYBALL TEAM.
REALLY?
THAT'S IT FOR THE GIRLS.
HIYA.
OH, NURSE. TOMOR-ROW'S GAME...
...STARTS AT NOON. PLEASE DON'T FORGET TO COME.
SURE... IF I CAN GET OUT OF BED BY THEN.
PLEASE, PLEASE MAKE SURE TO COME!!

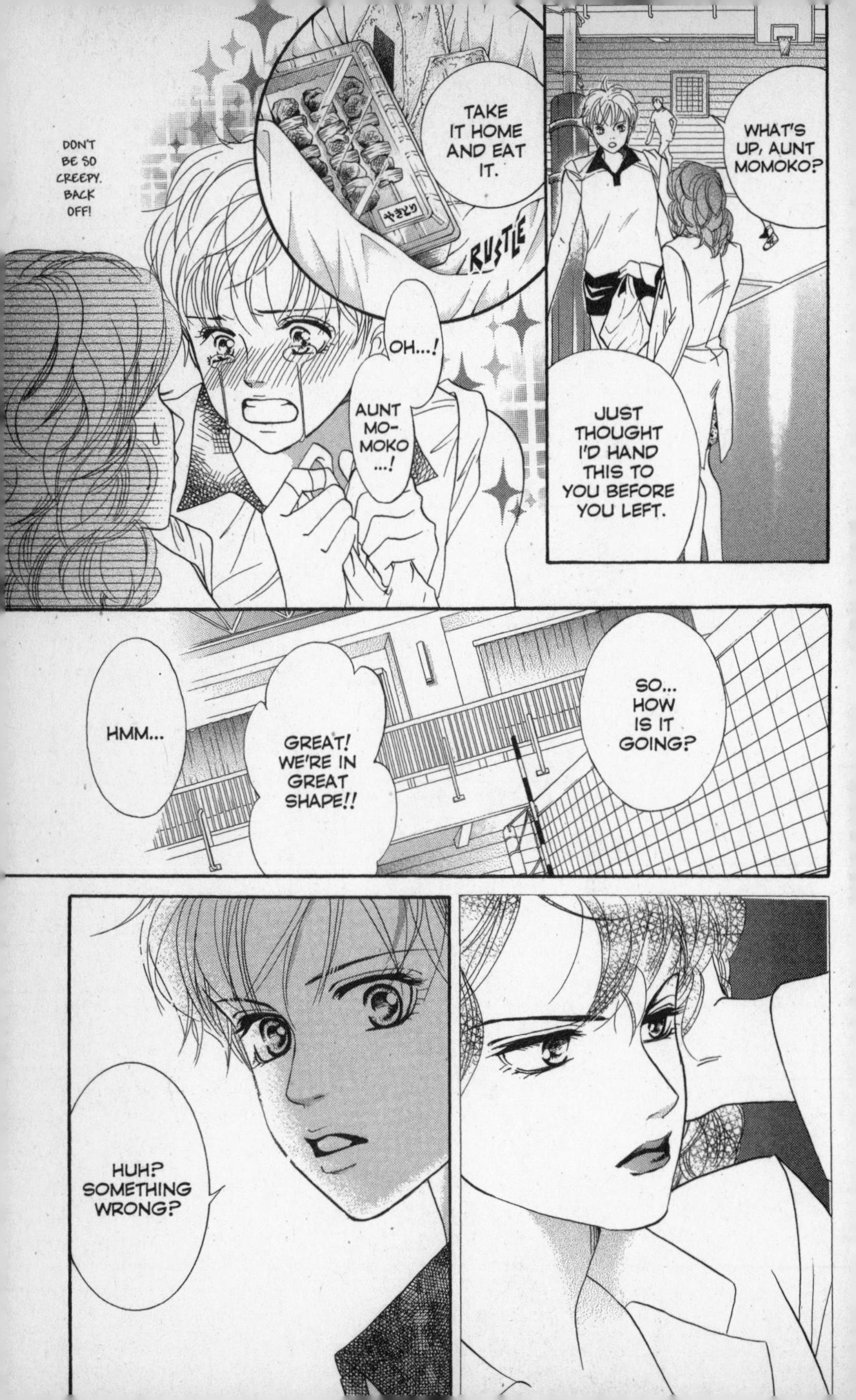
WHAT'S UP, AUNT MOMOKO?
JUST THOUGHT I'D HAND THIS TO YOU BEFORE YOU LEFT.
TAKE IT HOME AND EAT IT.
やきとり
RUSTLE
OH...!
AUNT MO-MOKO...!
DON'T BE SO CREEPY. BACK OFF!
SO... HOW IS IT GOING?
GREAT! WE'RE IN GREAT SHAPE!!
HMM...
HUH? SOMETHING WRONG?

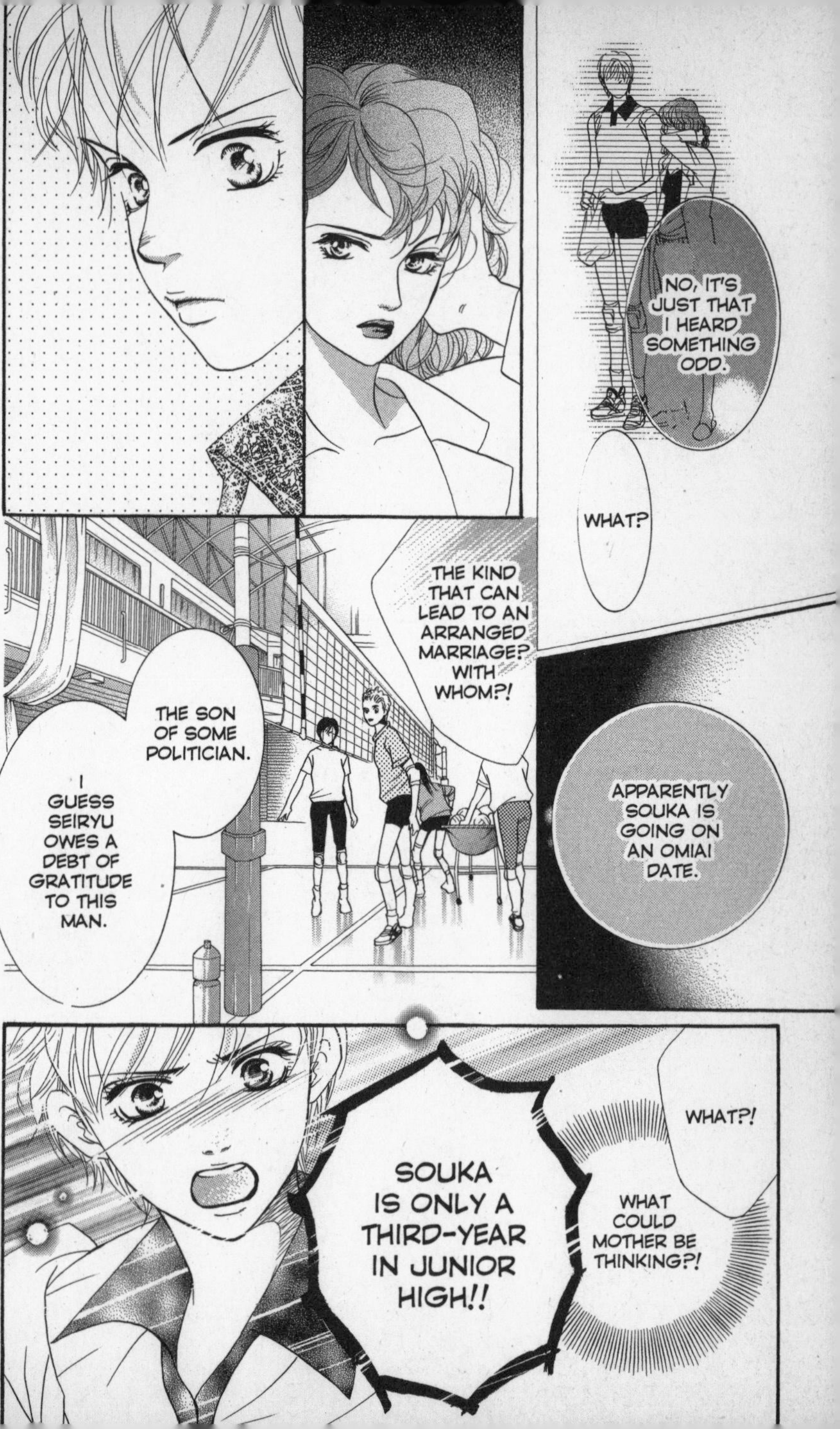
NO, IT'S JUST THAT I HEARD SOMETHING ODD.
WHAT?
APPARENTLY SOUKA IS GOING ON AN OMIAI DATE.
THE KIND THAT CAN LEAD TO AN ARRANGED MARRIAGE? WITH WHOM?!
THE SON OF SOME POLITICIAN.
I GUESS SEIRYU OWES A DEBT OF GRATITUDE TO THIS MAN.
WHAT?!
WHAT COULD MOTHER BE THINKING?!
SOUKA IS ONLY A THIRD-YEAR IN JUNIOR HIGH!!

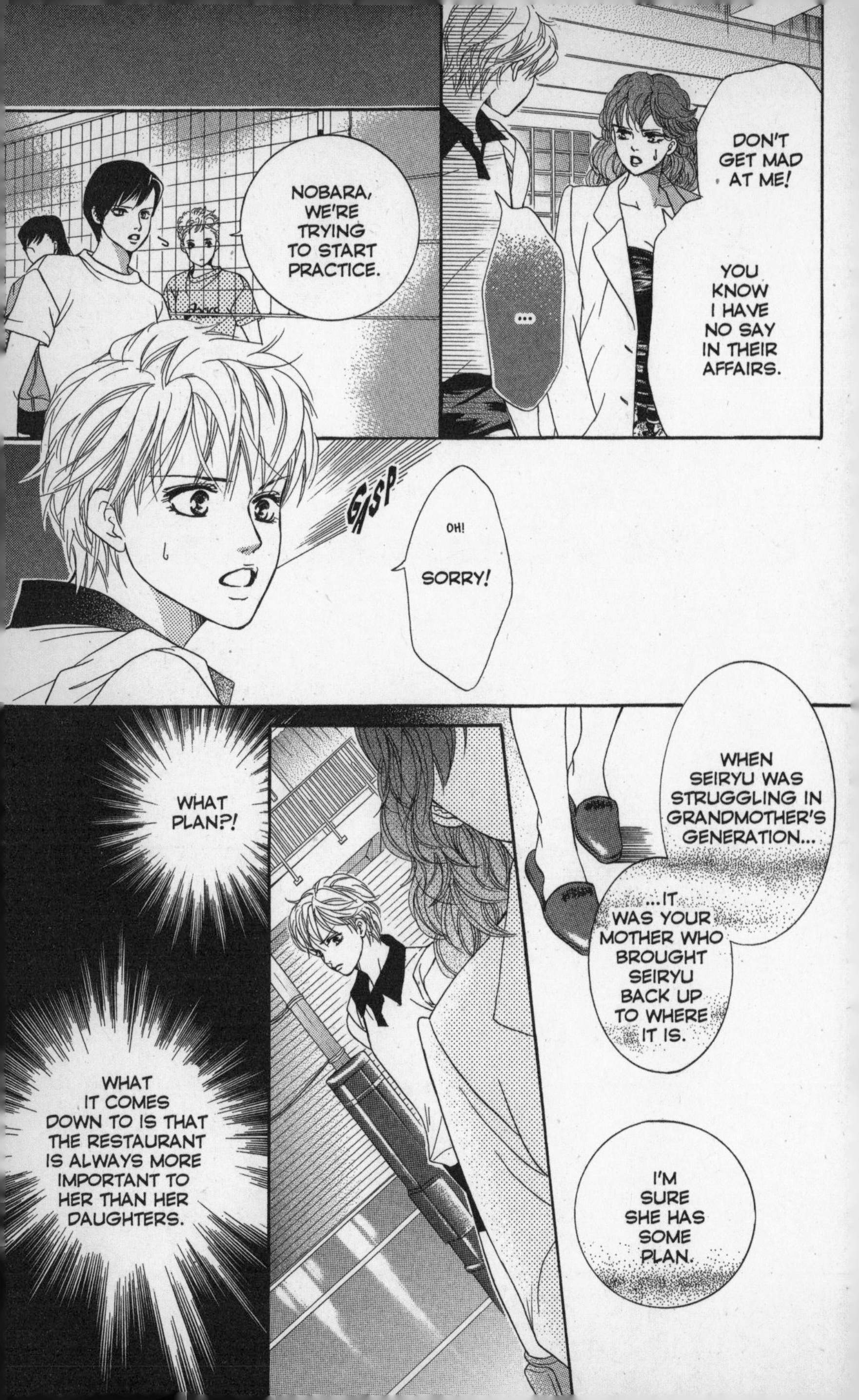
DON'T GET MAD AT ME!
YOU KNOW I HAVE NO SAY IN THEIR AFFAIRS.
...
NOBARA, WE'RE TRYING TO START PRACTICE.
GASP
OH!
SORRY!
WHEN SEIRYU WAS STRUGGLING IN GRANDMOTHER'S GENERATION...
...IT WAS YOUR MOTHER WHO BROUGHT SEIRYU BACK UP TO WHERE IT IS.
I'M SURE SHE HAS SOME PLAN.
WHAT PLAN?!
WHAT IT COMES DOWN TO IS THAT THE RESTAURANT IS ALWAYS MORE IMPORTANT TO HER THAN HER DAUGHTERS.

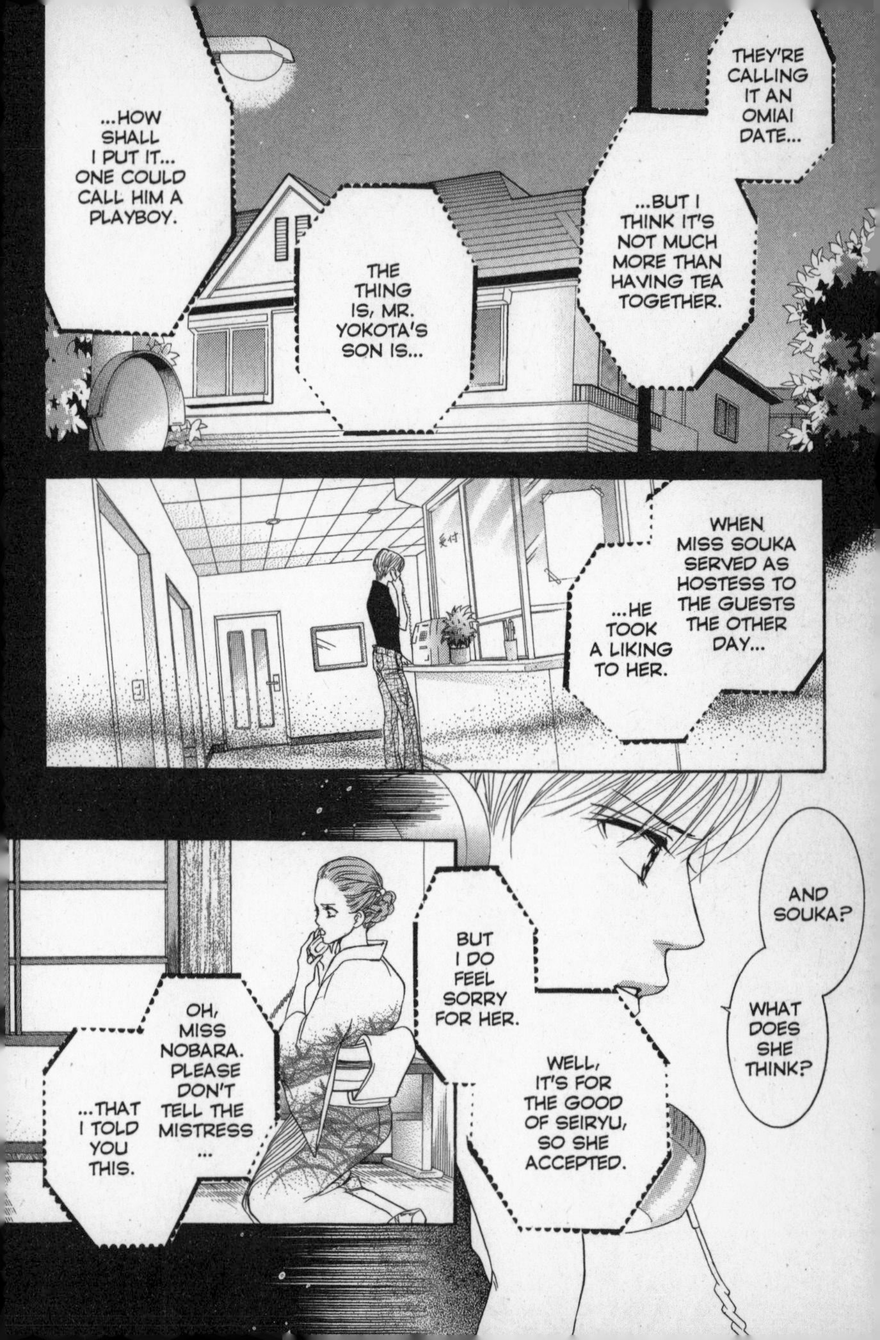
THEY'RE CALLING IT AN OMIAI DATE...
...BUT I THINK IT'S NOT MUCH MORE THAN HAVING TEA TOGETHER.
THE THING IS, MR. YOKOTA'S SON IS...
...HOW SHALL I PUT IT... ONE COULD CALL HIM A PLAYBOY.
WHEN MISS SOUKA SERVED AS HOSTESS TO THE GUESTS THE OTHER DAY...
...HE TOOK A LIKING TO HER.
AND SOUKA?
WHAT DOES SHE THINK?
WELL, IT'S FOR THE GOOD OF SEIRYU, SO SHE ACCEPTED.
BUT I DO FEEL SORRY FOR HER.
OH, MISS NOBARA. PLEASE DON'T TELL THE MISTRESS...
...THAT I TOLD YOU THIS.

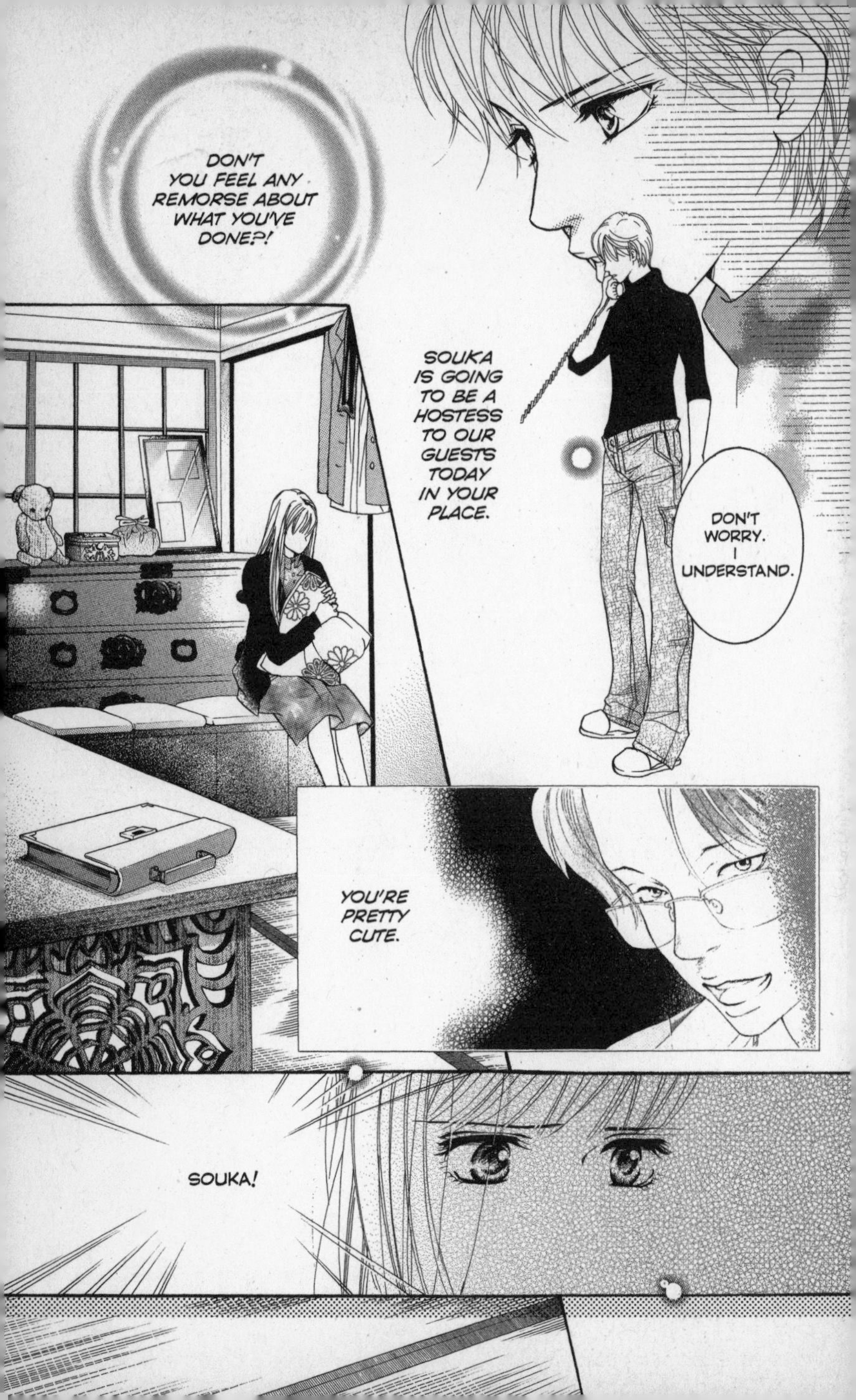
DON'T YOU FEEL ANY REMORSE ABOUT WHAT YOU'VE DONE?!
DON'T WORRY. I UNDERSTAND.
SOUKA IS GOING TO BE A HOSTESS TO OUR GUESTS TODAY IN YOUR PLACE.
YOU'RE PRETTY CUTE.
SOUKA!

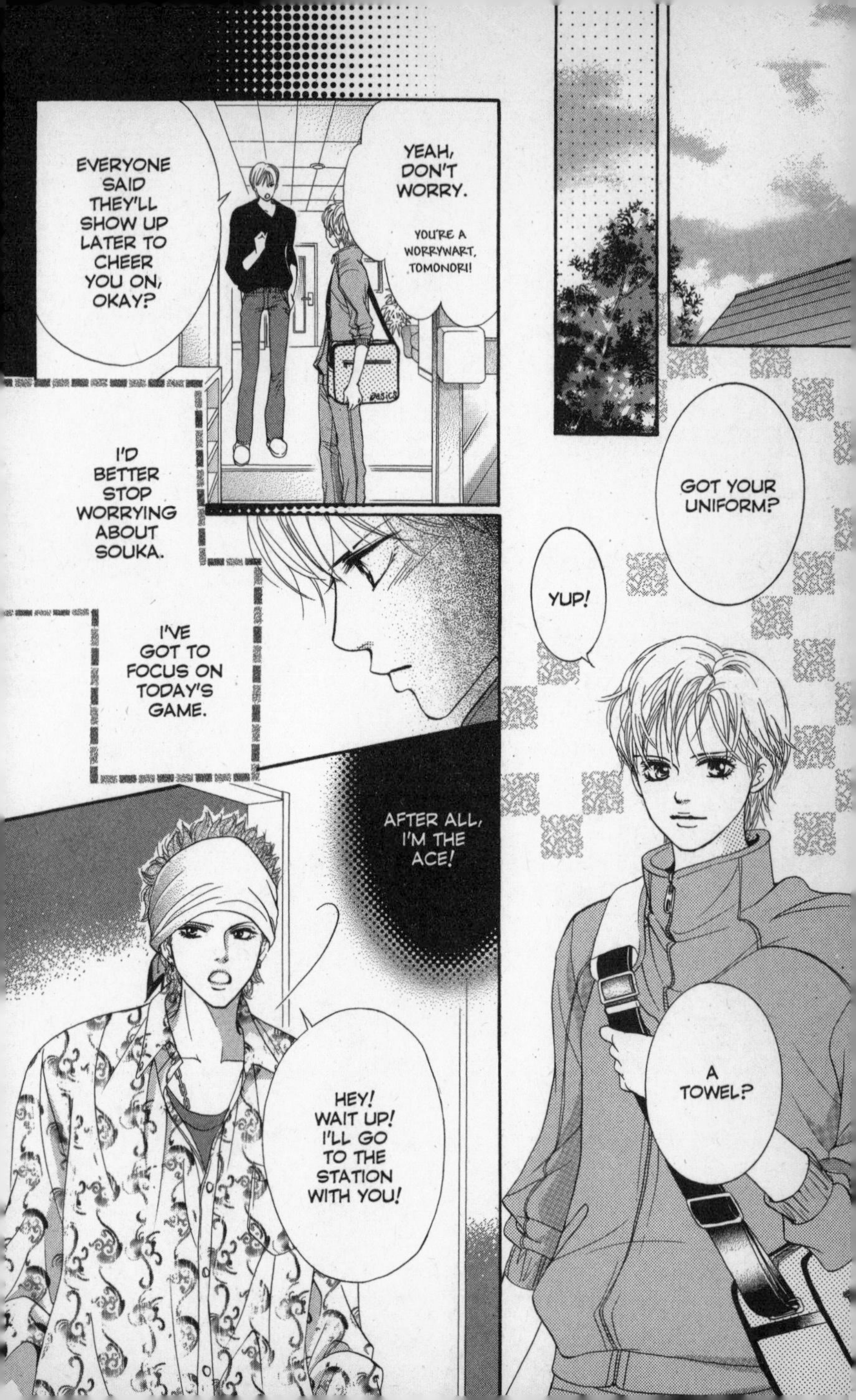
GOT YOUR UNIFORM?
YUP!
A TOWEL?
YEAH, DON'T WORRY.
YOU'RE A WORRYWART, TOMONORI!
EVERYONE SAID THEY'LL SHOW UP LATER TO CHEER YOU ON, OKAY?
I'D BETTER STOP WORRYING ABOUT SOUKA.
I'VE GOT TO FOCUS ON TODAY'S GAME.
AFTER ALL, I'M THE ACE!
HEY! WAIT UP! I'LL GO TO THE STATION WITH YOU!

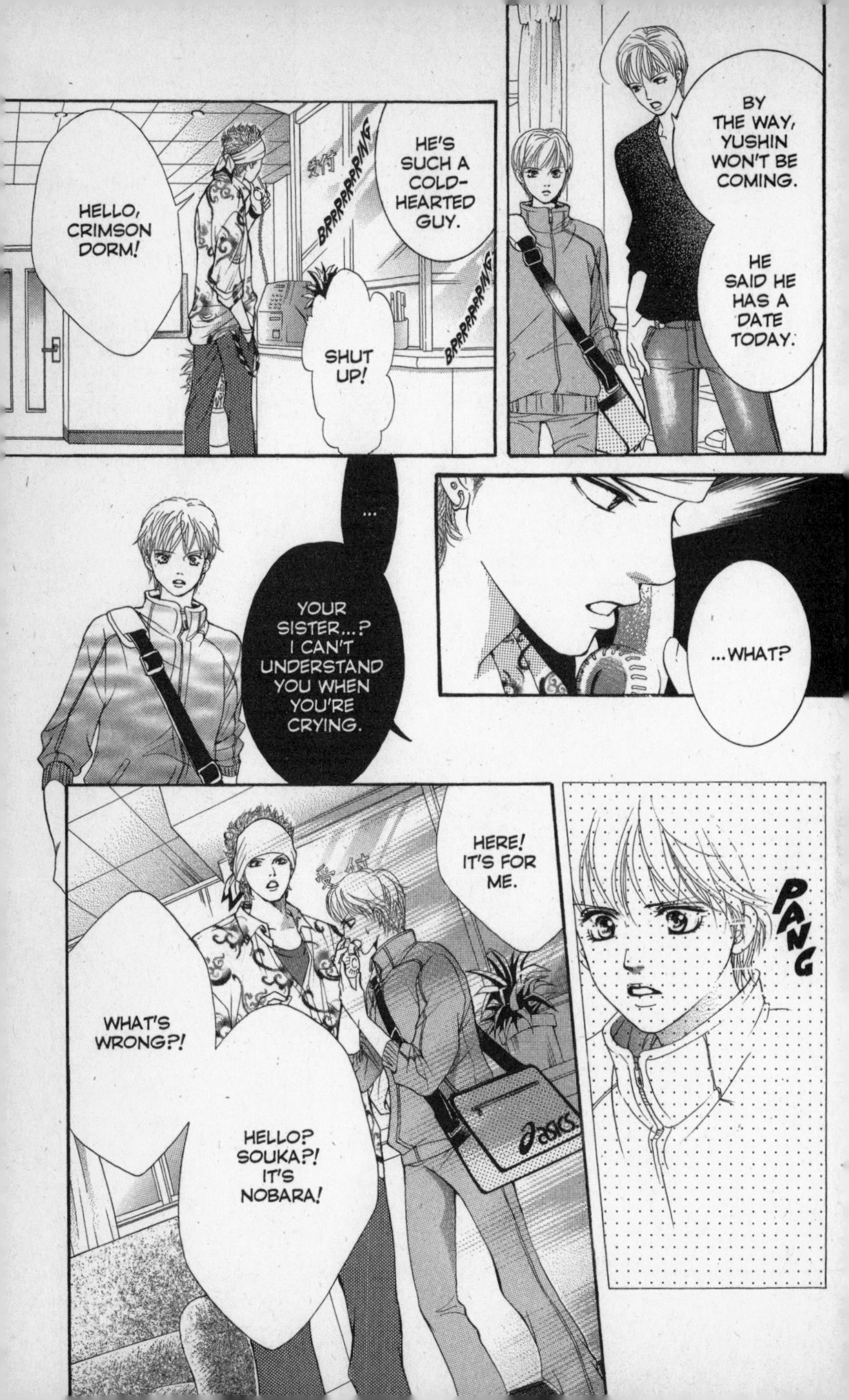
BY THE WAY, YUSHIN WON'T BE COMING.
HE SAID HE HAS A DATE TODAY.
HE'S SUCH A COLD-HEARTED GUY.
受付
BRRRRRRRING
SHUT UP!
BRRRRRRRING
BRRRRRRRING
HELLO, CRIMSON DORM!
...WHAT?
...
YOUR SISTER...? I CAN'T UNDERSTAND YOU WHEN YOU'RE CRYING.
PANG
HERE! IT'S FOR ME.
受付
WHAT'S WRONG?!
HELLO? SOUKA?! IT'S NOBARA!
asics

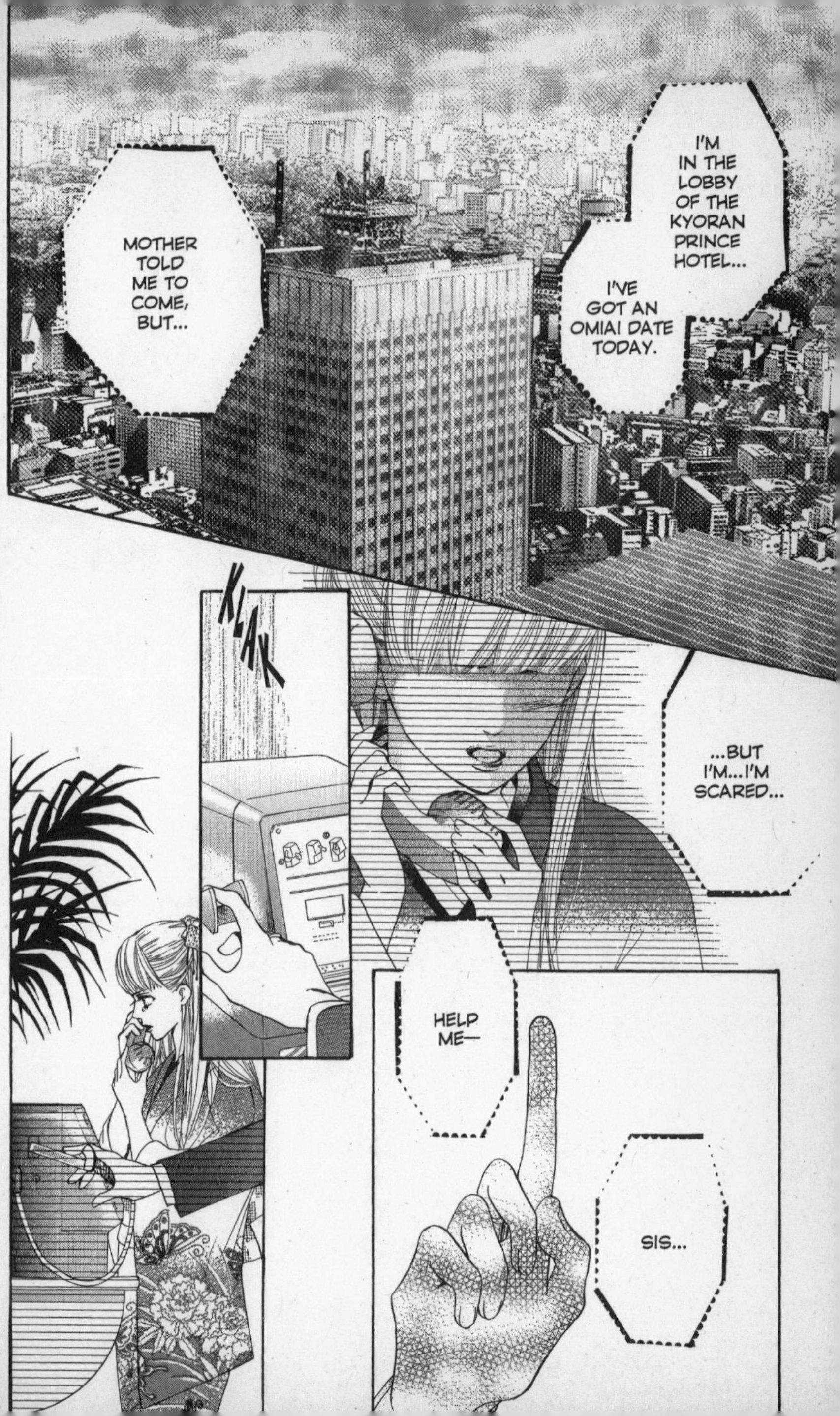
I'M IN THE LOBBY OF THE KYORAN PRINCE HOTEL...
I'VE GOT AN OMIAI DATE TODAY.
MOTHER TOLD ME TO COME, BUT...
...BUT I'M...I'M SCARED...
KLAK
HELP ME—
SIS...

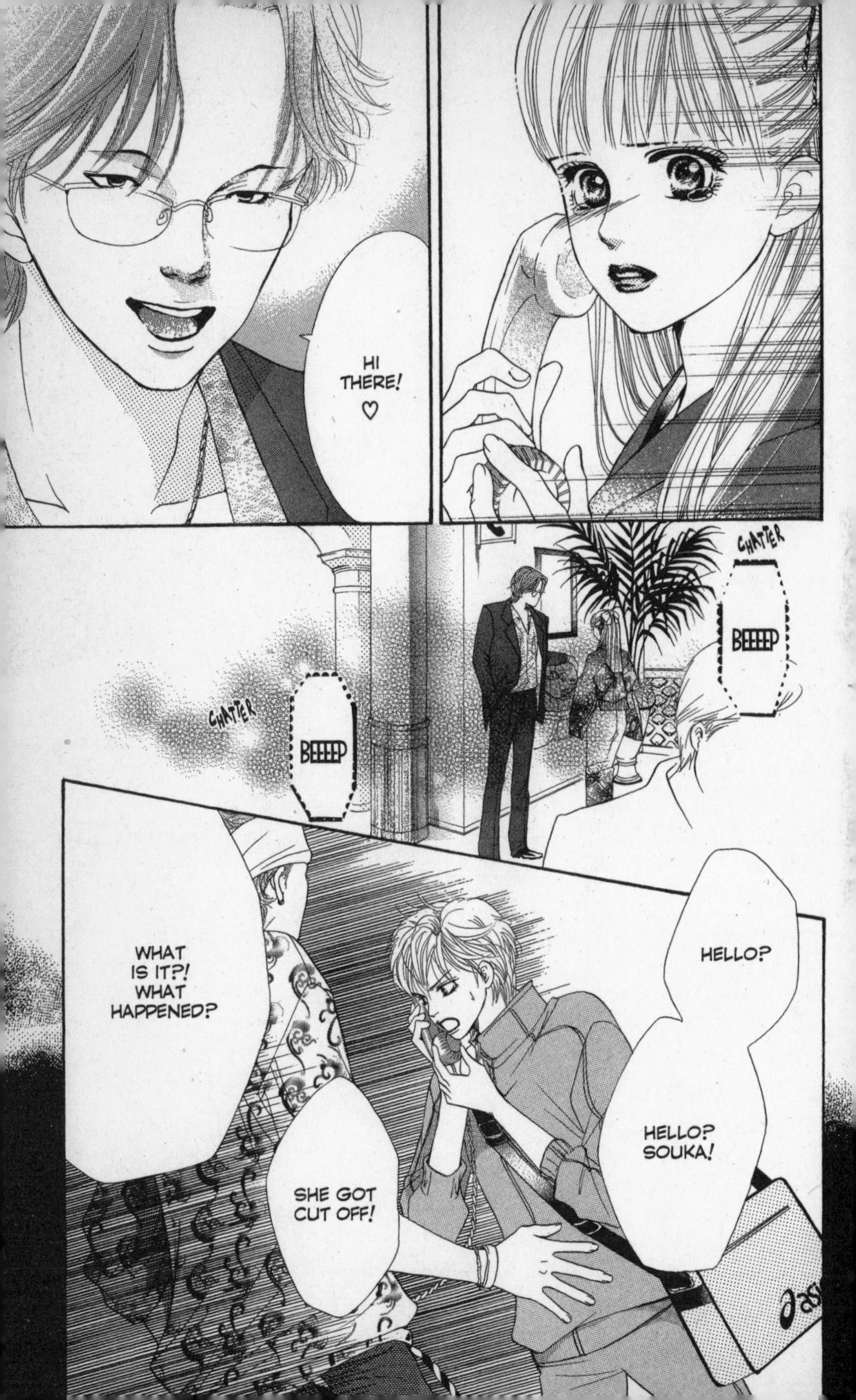
HI THERE! ♡
CHATTER
BEEEEP
CHATTER
BEEEEP
HELLO?
HELLO? SOUKA!
WHAT IS IT?! WHAT HAPPENED?
SHE GOT CUT OFF!

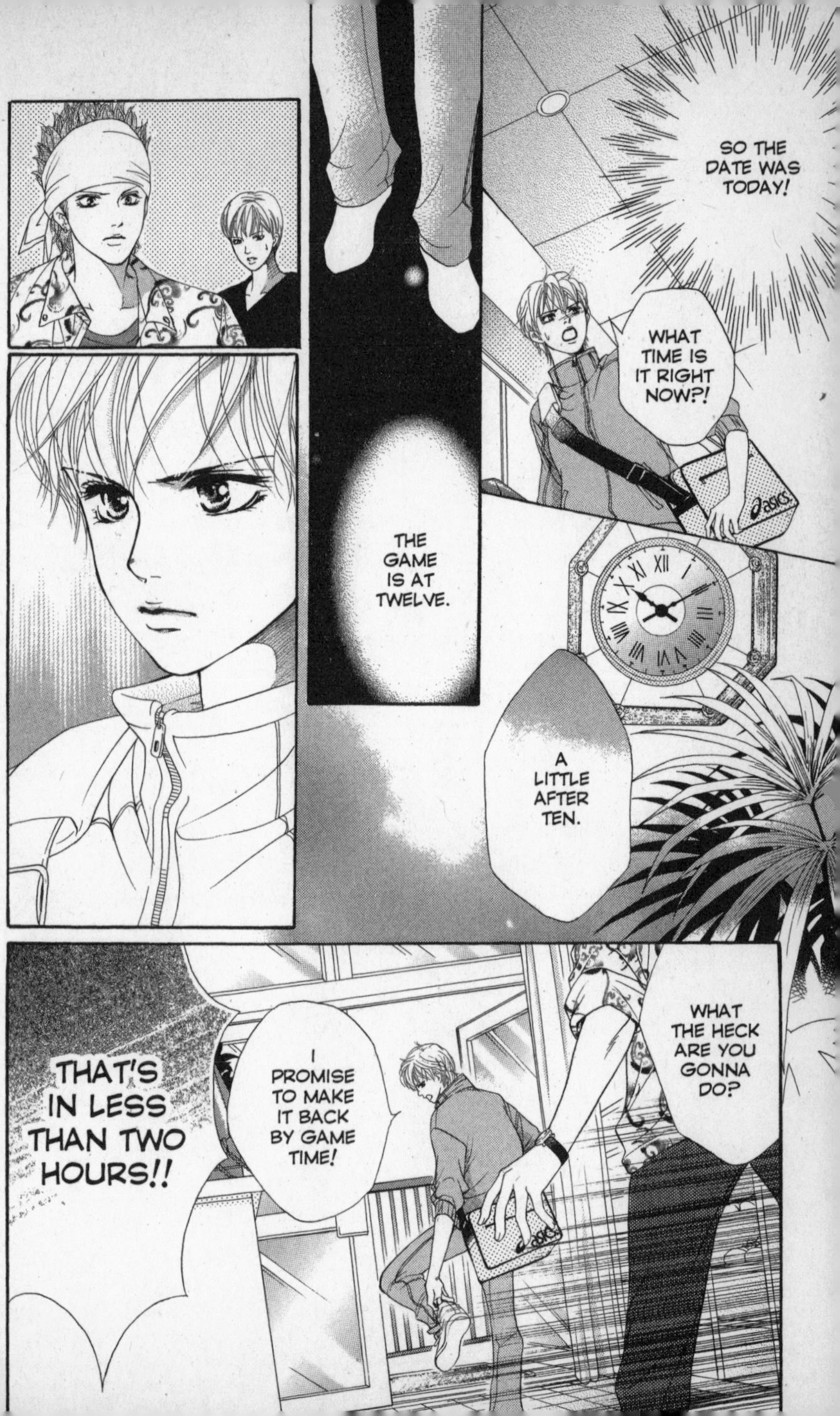
SO THE DATE WAS TODAY!
WHAT TIME IS IT RIGHT NOW?!
A LITTLE AFTER TEN.
THE GAME IS AT TWELVE.
WHAT THE HECK ARE YOU GONNA DO?
I PROMISE TO MAKE IT BACK BY GAME TIME!
THAT'S IN LESS THAN TWO HOURS!!

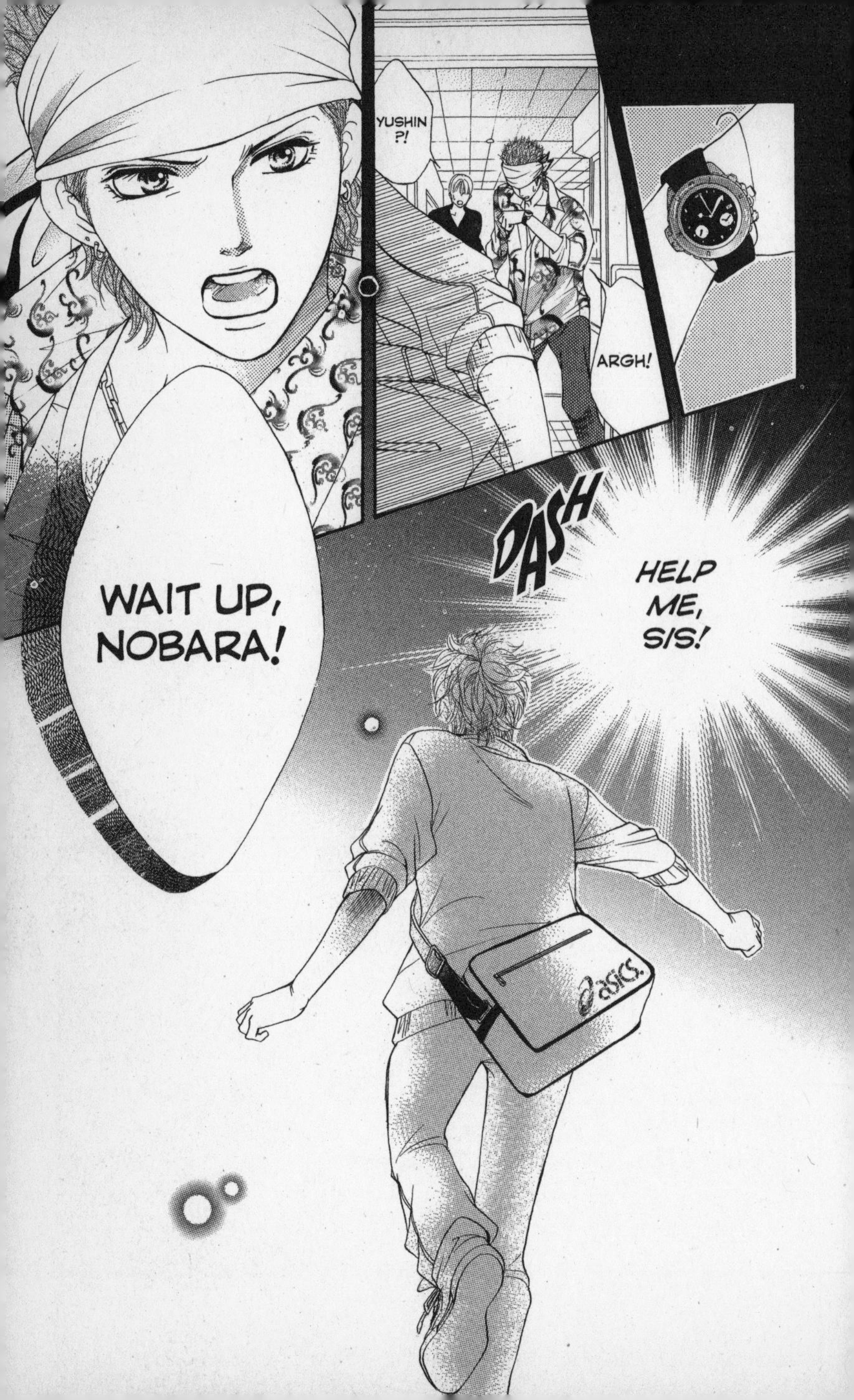
YUSHIN ?!
ARGH!
WAIT UP, NOBARA!
DASH
HELP ME, SIS!

Crimson Hero

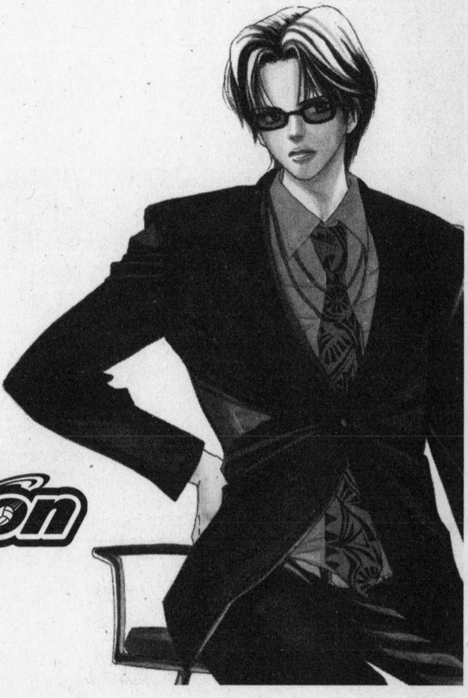

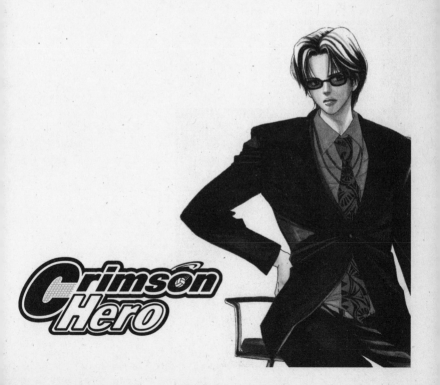

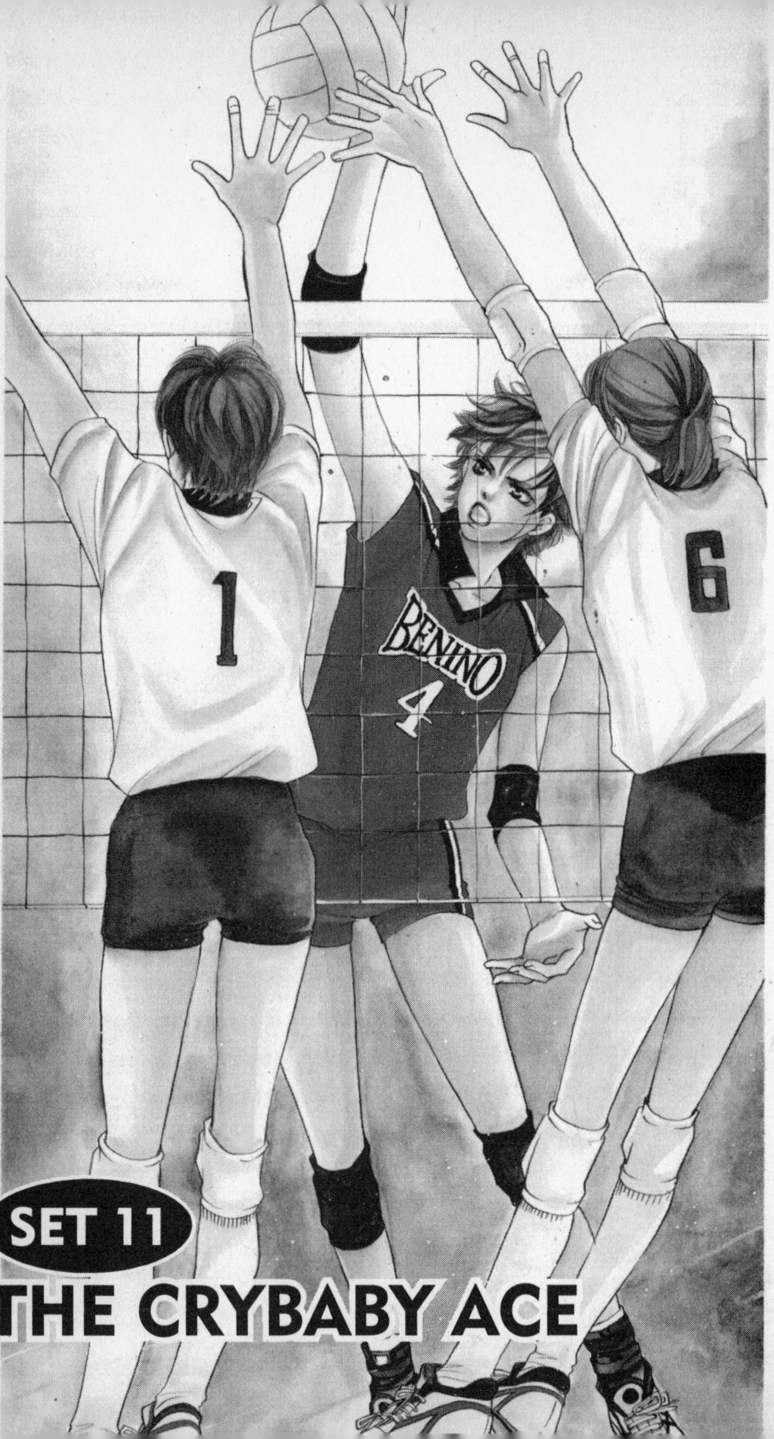
1
BENINO
4
6

SET 11

THE CRYBABY ACE

Crimson Hero

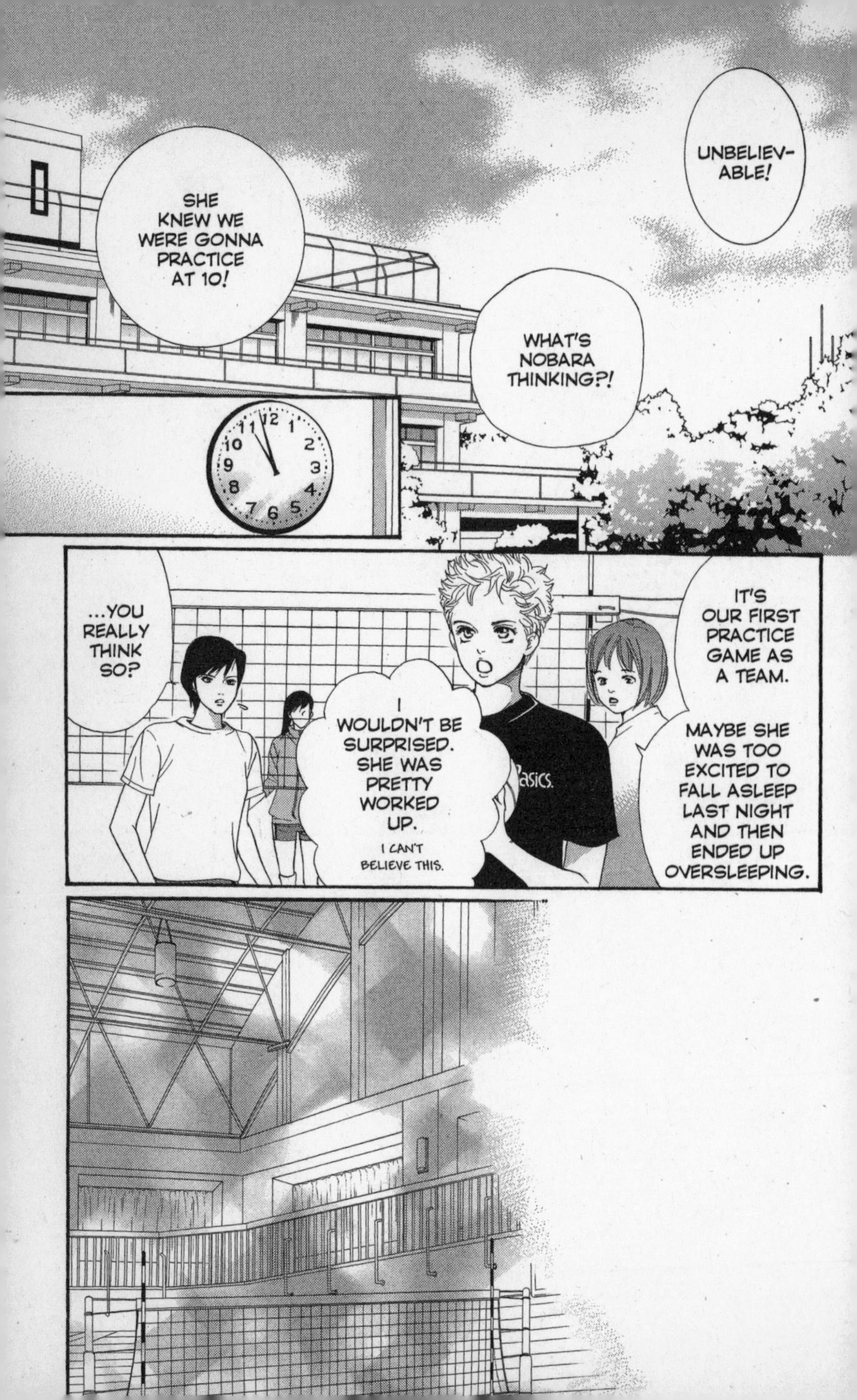
UNBELIEVABLE!
WHAT'S NOBARA THINKING?!
SHE KNEW WE WERE GONNA PRACTICE AT 10!
IT'S OUR FIRST PRACTICE GAME AS A TEAM.
MAYBE SHE WAS TOO EXCITED TO FALL ASLEEP LAST NIGHT AND THEN ENDED UP OVERSLEEPING.
I WOULDN'T BE SURPRISED. SHE WAS PRETTY WORKED UP.
I CAN'T BELIEVE THIS.
...YOU REALLY THINK SO?

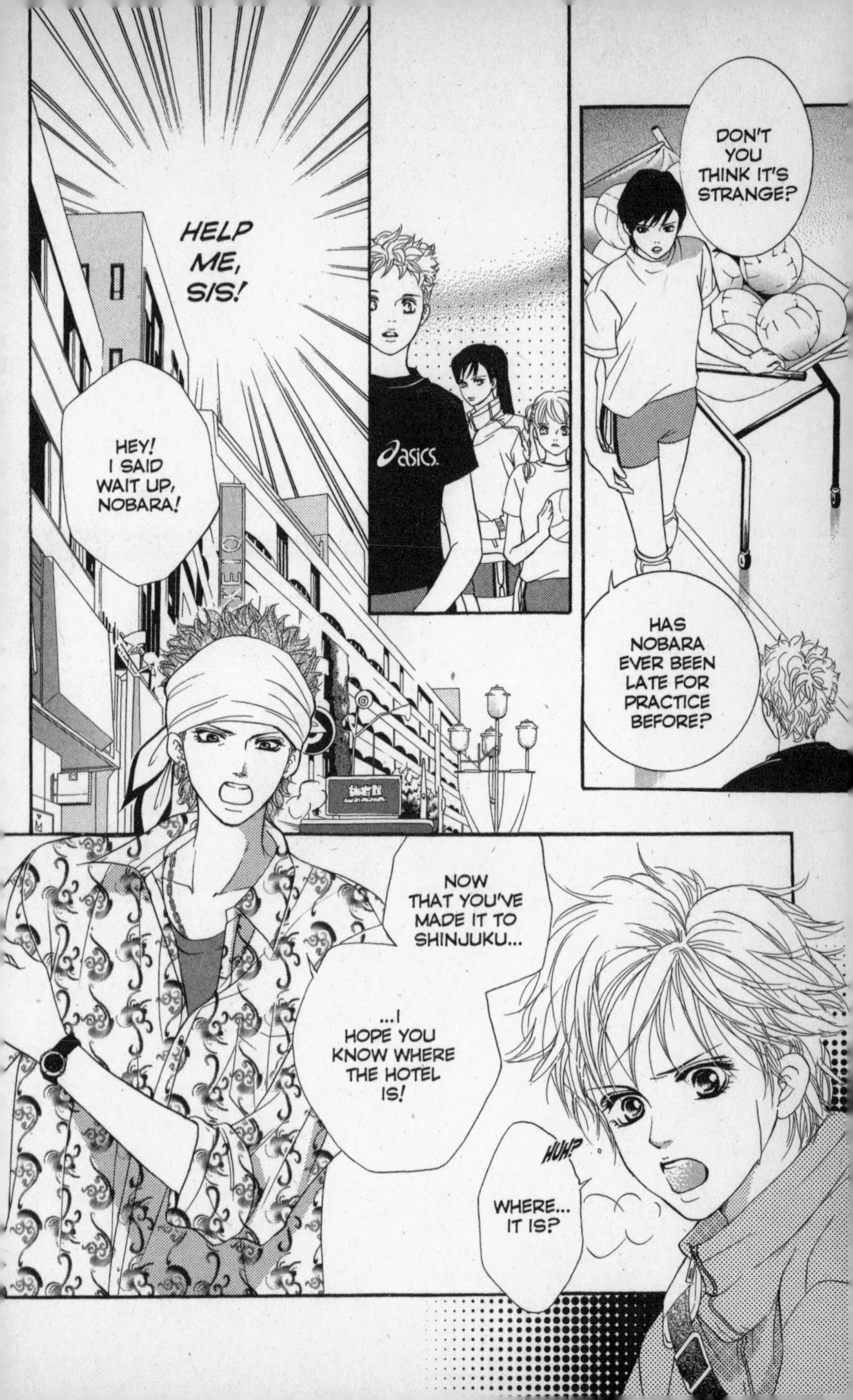
DON'T YOU THINK IT'S STRANGE?
HAS NOBARA EVER BEEN LATE FOR PRACTICE BEFORE?
HELP ME, SIS!
HEY! I SAID WAIT UP, NOBARA!
NOW THAT YOU'VE MADE IT TO SHINJUKU...
...I HOPE YOU KNOW WHERE THE HOTEL IS!
HUH?
WHERE... IT IS?

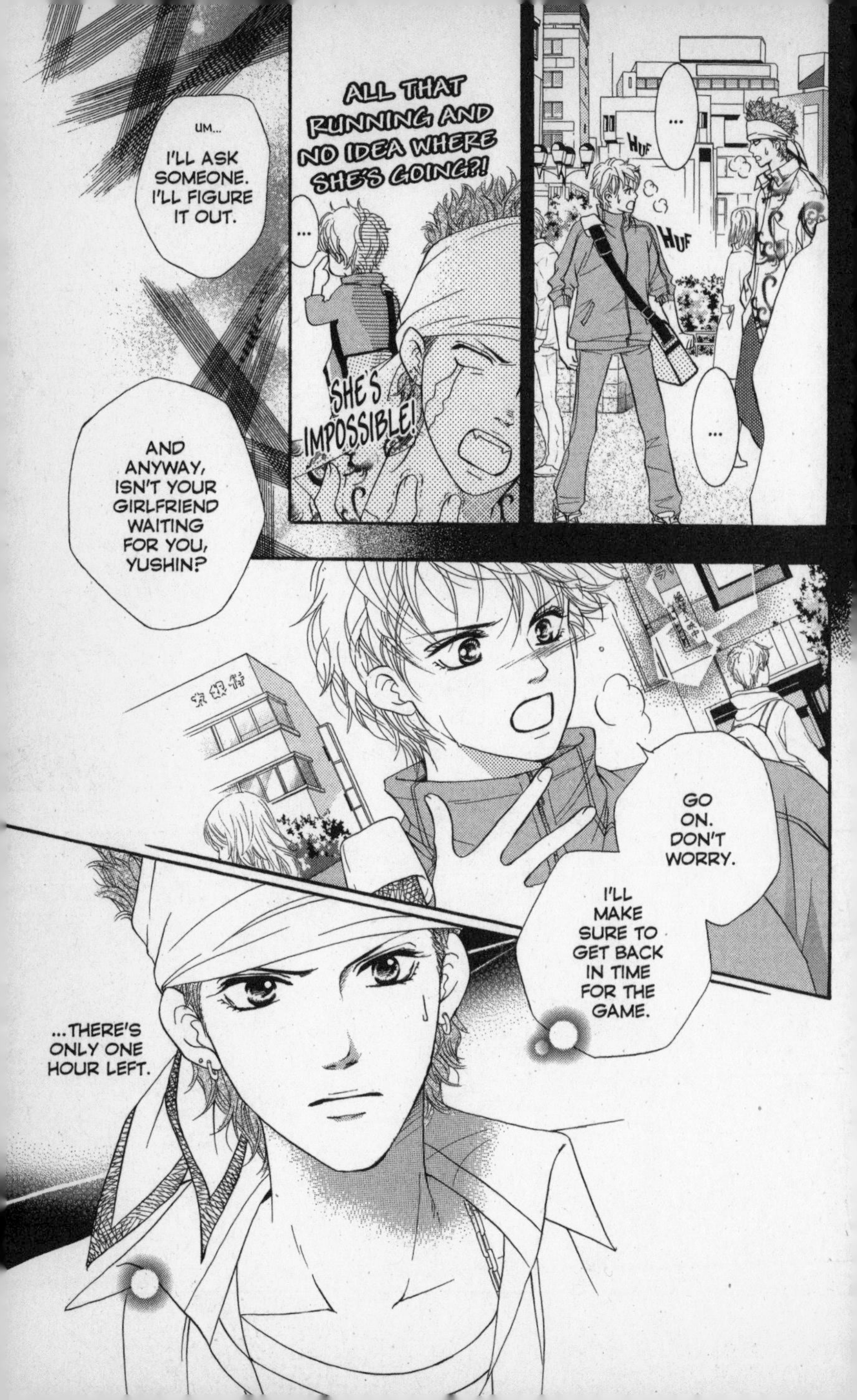
...
HUF
HUF
...
ALL THAT RUNNING AND NO IDEA WHERE SHE'S GOING?!
...
SHE'S IMPOSSIBLE!
UM... I'LL ASK SOMEONE. I'LL FIGURE IT OUT.
AND ANYWAY, ISN'T YOUR GIRLFRIEND WAITING FOR YOU, YUSHIN?
GO ON. DON'T WORRY.
I'LL MAKE SURE TO GET BACK IN TIME FOR THE GAME.
...THERE'S ONLY ONE HOUR LEFT.

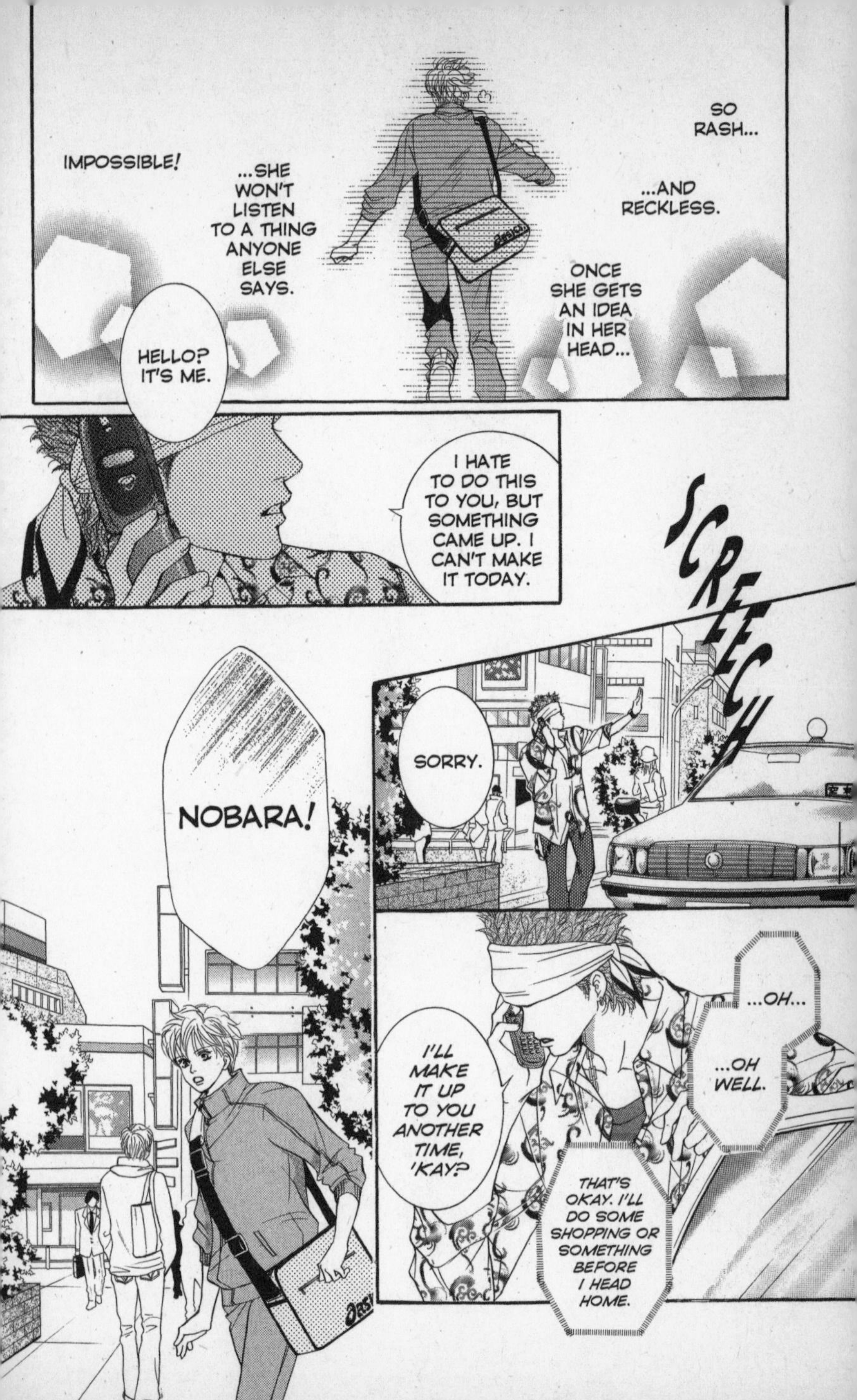
SO RASH...
...AND RECKLESS.
ONCE SHE GETS AN IDEA IN HER HEAD...
...SHE WON'T LISTEN TO A THING ANYONE ELSE SAYS.
IMPOSSIBLE!
HELLO? IT'S ME.
I HATE TO DO THIS TO YOU, BUT SOMETHING CAME UP. I CAN'T MAKE IT TODAY.
SCREECH
SORRY.
...OH...
...OH WELL.
THAT'S OKAY. I'LL DO SOME SHOPPING OR SOMETHING BEFORE I HEAD HOME.
I'LL MAKE IT UP TO YOU ANOTHER TIME, 'KAY?
NOBARA!

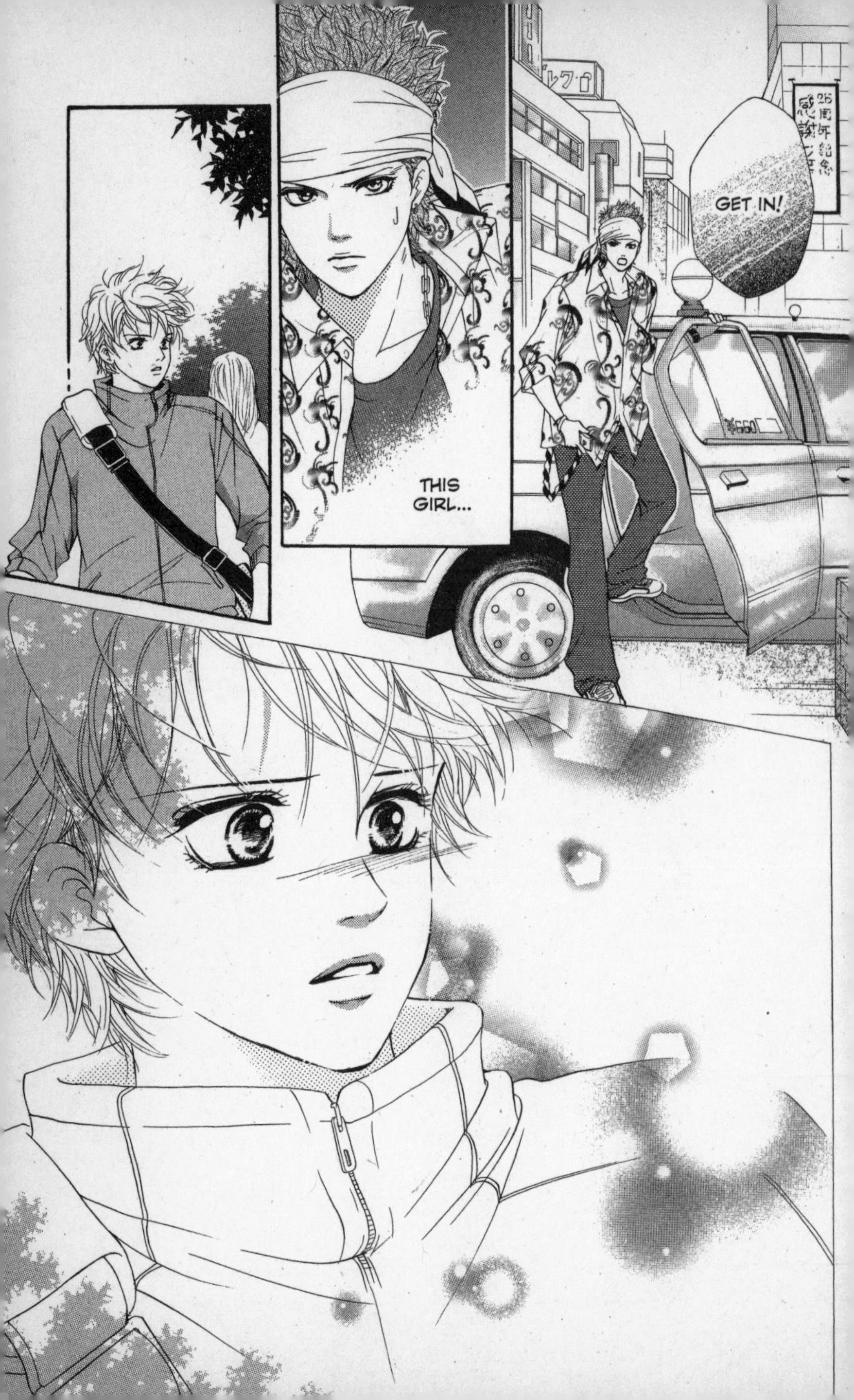
GET IN!
THIS GIRL...

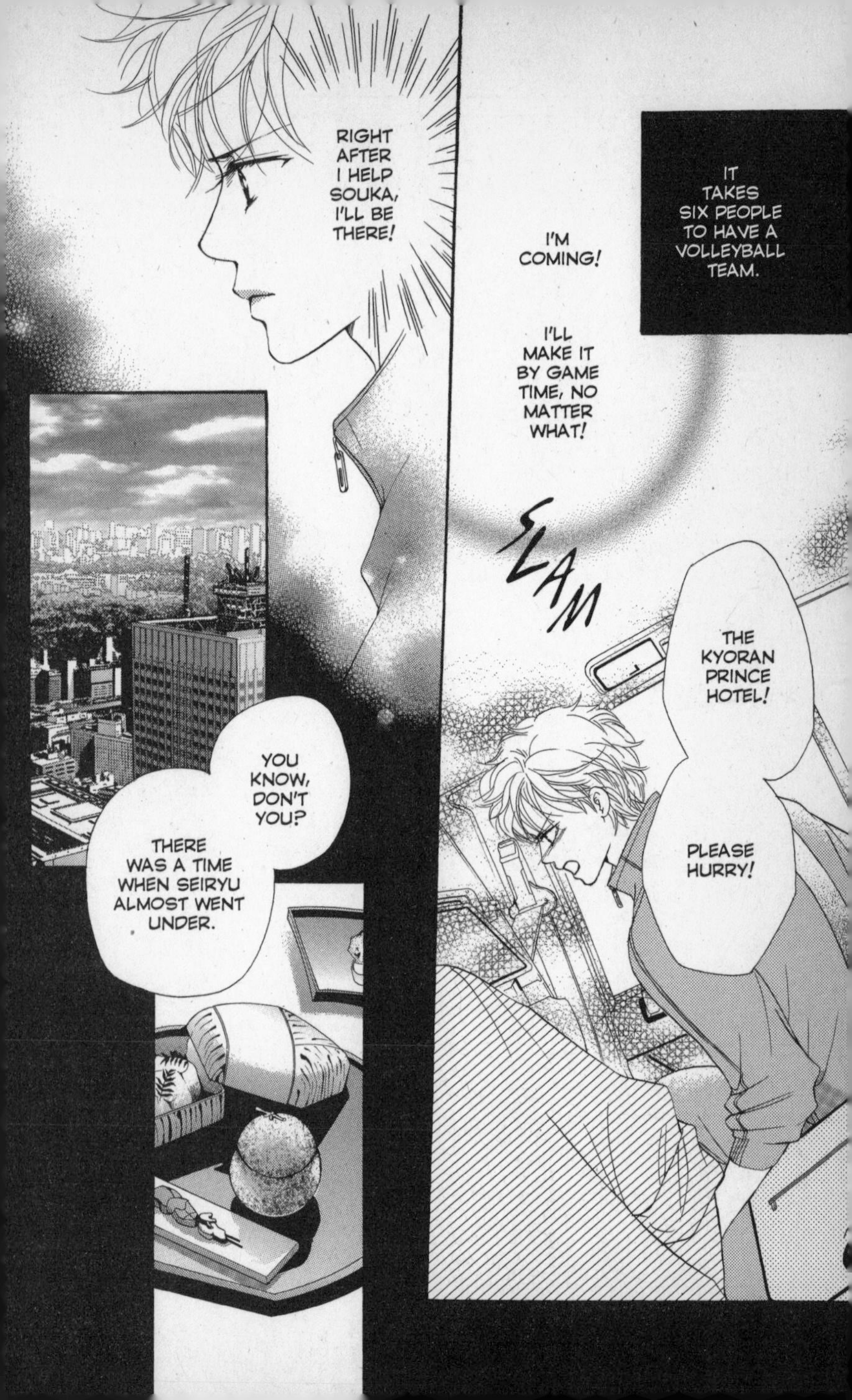
IT TAKES SIX PEOPLE TO HAVE A VOLLEYBALL TEAM.
I'M COMING!
I'LL MAKE IT BY GAME TIME, NO MATTER WHAT!
SLAM
THE KYORAN PRINCE HOTEL!
PLEASE HURRY!
RIGHT AFTER I HELP SOUKA, I'LL BE THERE!
YOU KNOW, DON'T YOU?
THERE WAS A TIME WHEN SEIRYU ALMOST WENT UNDER.

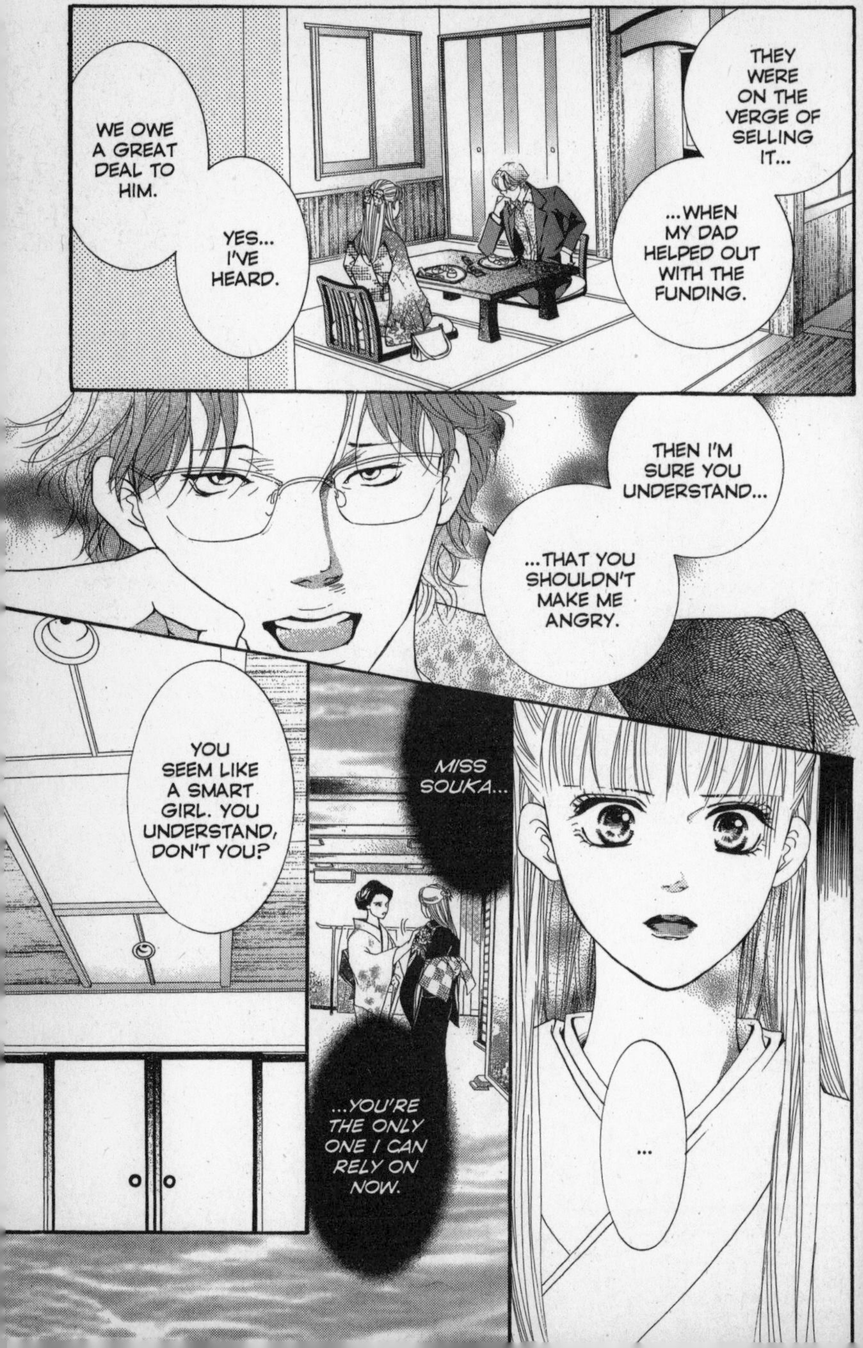
THEY WERE ON THE VERGE OF SELLING IT...
...WHEN MY DAD HELPED OUT WITH THE FUNDING.
WE OWE A GREAT DEAL TO HIM.
YES... I'VE HEARD.
THEN I'M SURE YOU UNDERSTAND...
...THAT YOU SHOULDN'T MAKE ME ANGRY.
YOU SEEM LIKE A SMART GIRL. YOU UNDERSTAND, DON'T YOU?
MISS SOUKA...
...YOU'RE THE ONLY ONE I CAN RELY ON NOW.
...

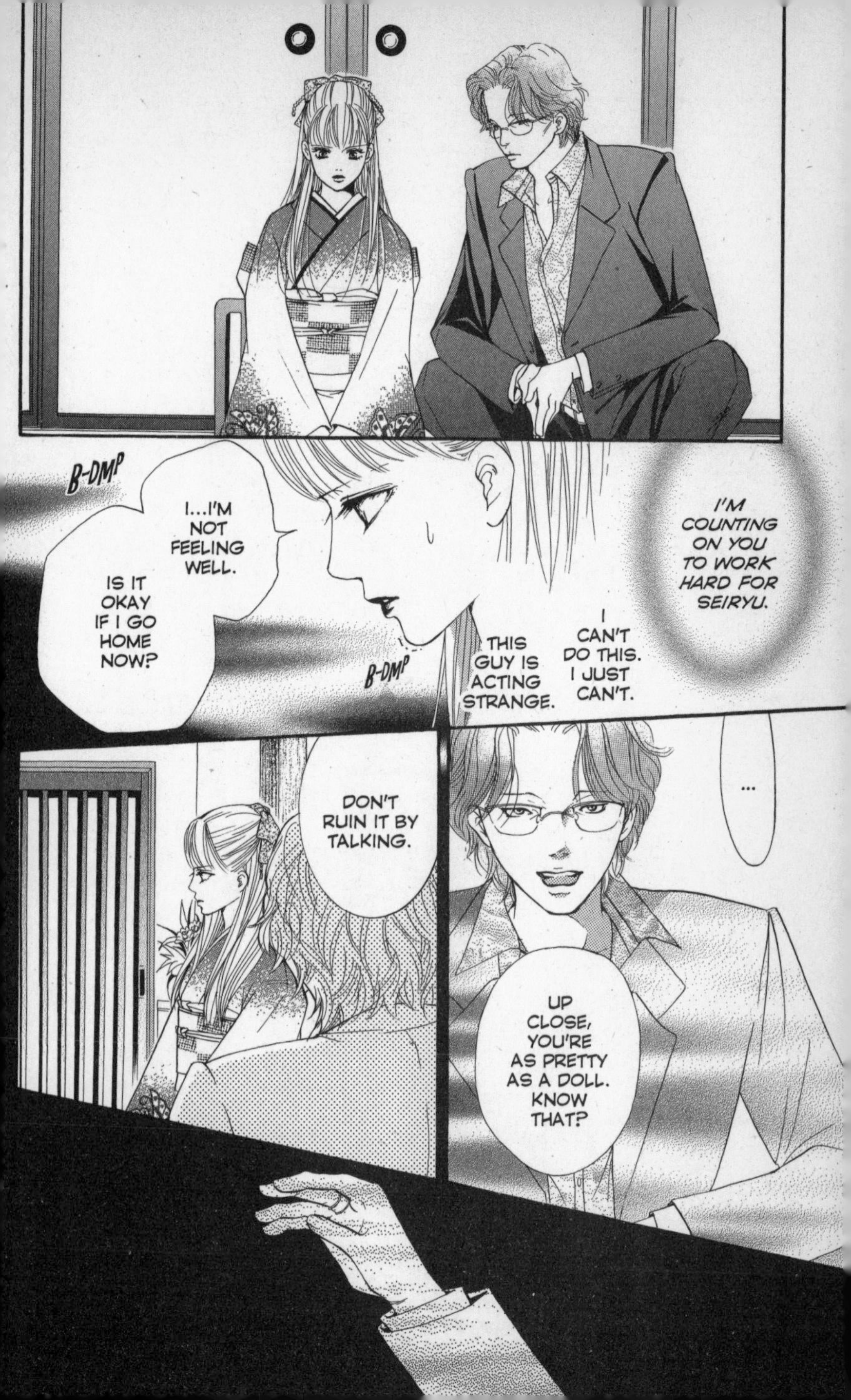
I'M COUNTING ON YOU TO WORK HARD FOR SEIRYU.
I CAN'T DO THIS. I JUST CAN'T.
THIS GUY IS ACTING STRANGE.
B-DMP
B-DMP
I...I'M NOT FEELING WELL.
IS IT OKAY IF I GO HOME NOW?
...
UP CLOSE, YOU'RE AS PRETTY AS A DOLL. KNOW THAT?
DON'T RUIN IT BY TALKING.

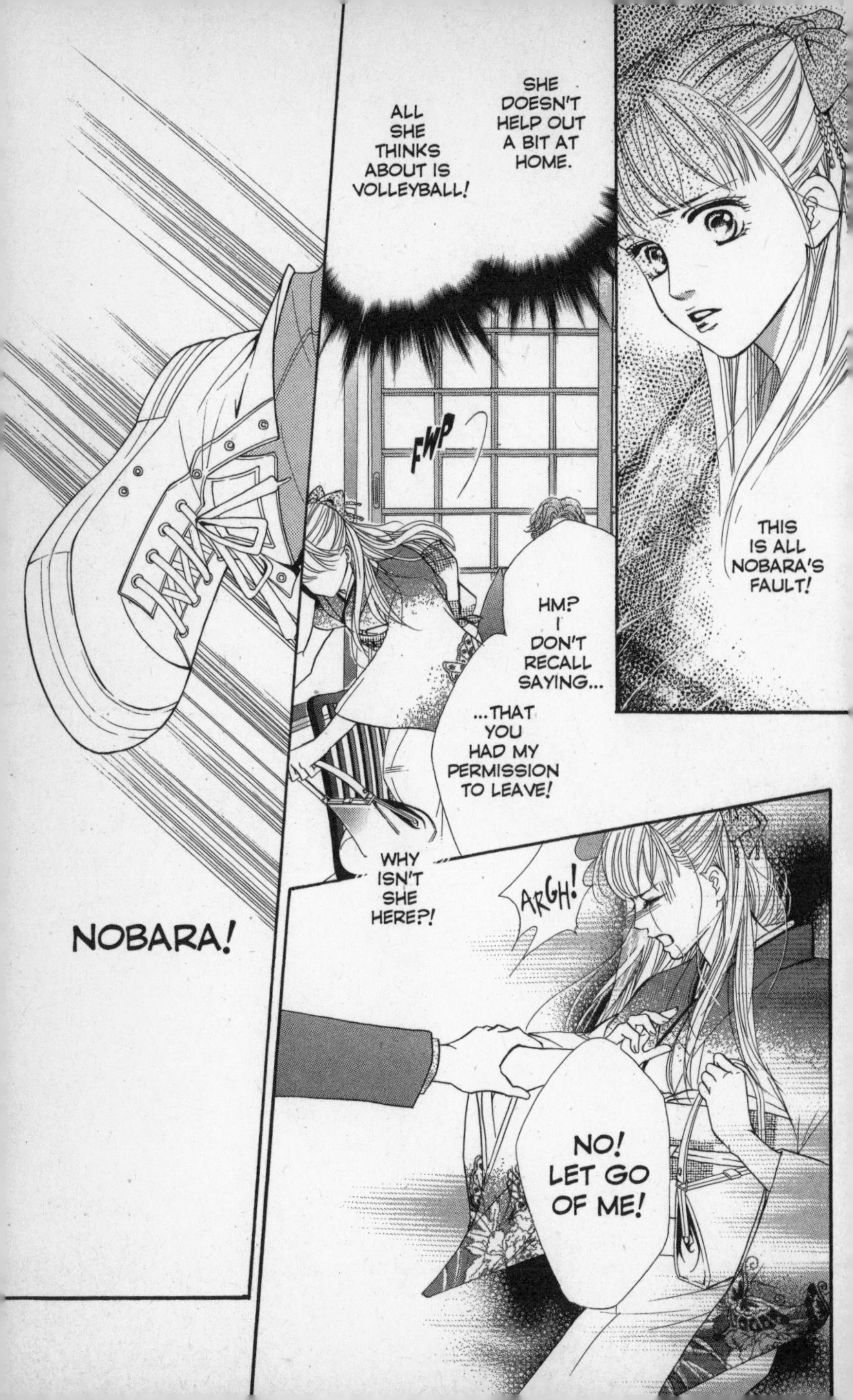
THIS IS ALL NOBARA'S FAULT!
SHE DOESN'T HELP OUT A BIT AT HOME.
ALL SHE THINKS ABOUT IS VOLLEYBALL!
FWP
HM? I DON'T RECALL SAYING...
...THAT YOU HAD MY PERMISSION TO LEAVE!
WHY ISN'T SHE HERE?!
ARGH!
NO! LET GO OF ME!
NOBARA!

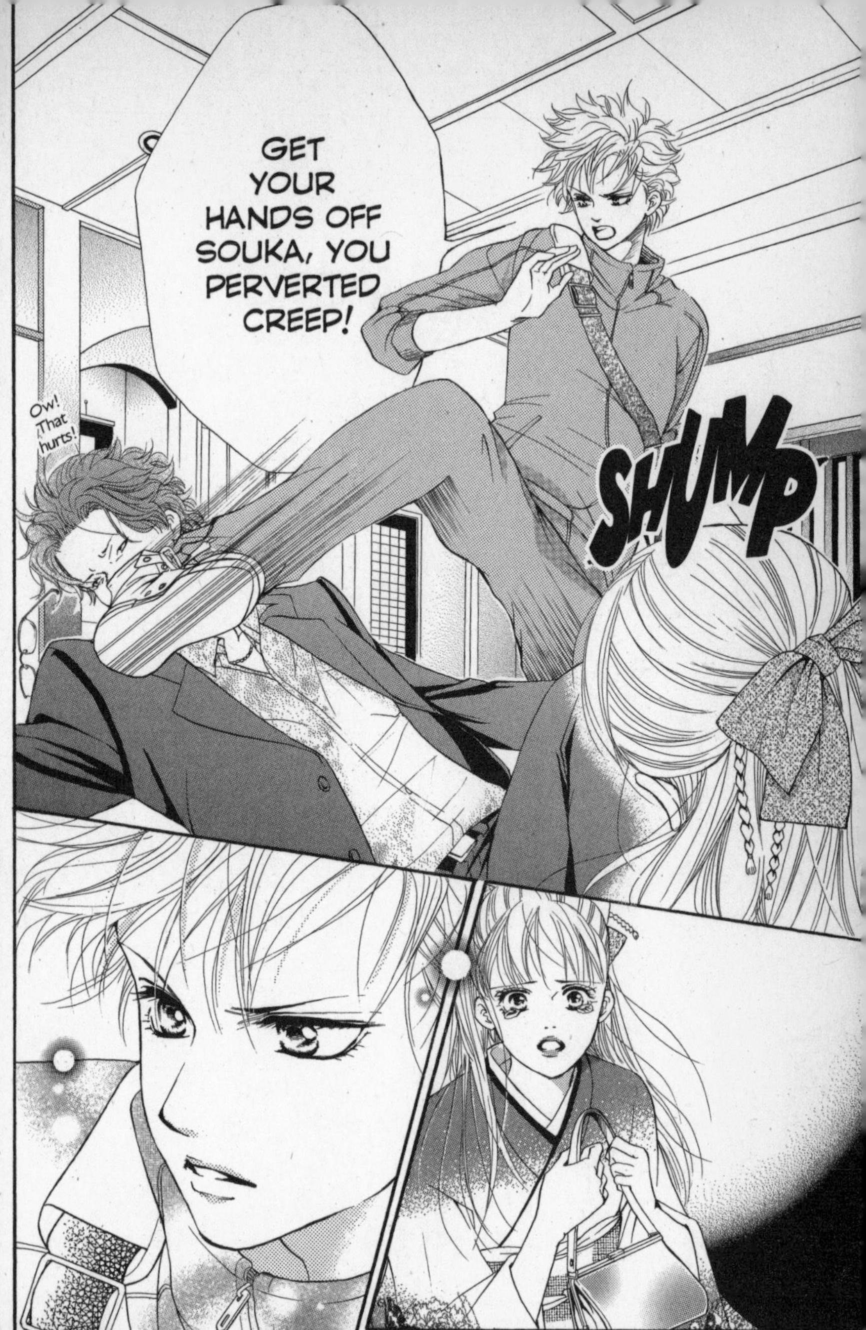
GET YOUR HANDS OFF SOUKA, YOU PERVERTED CREEP!
SHUMP
Ow! That hurts!

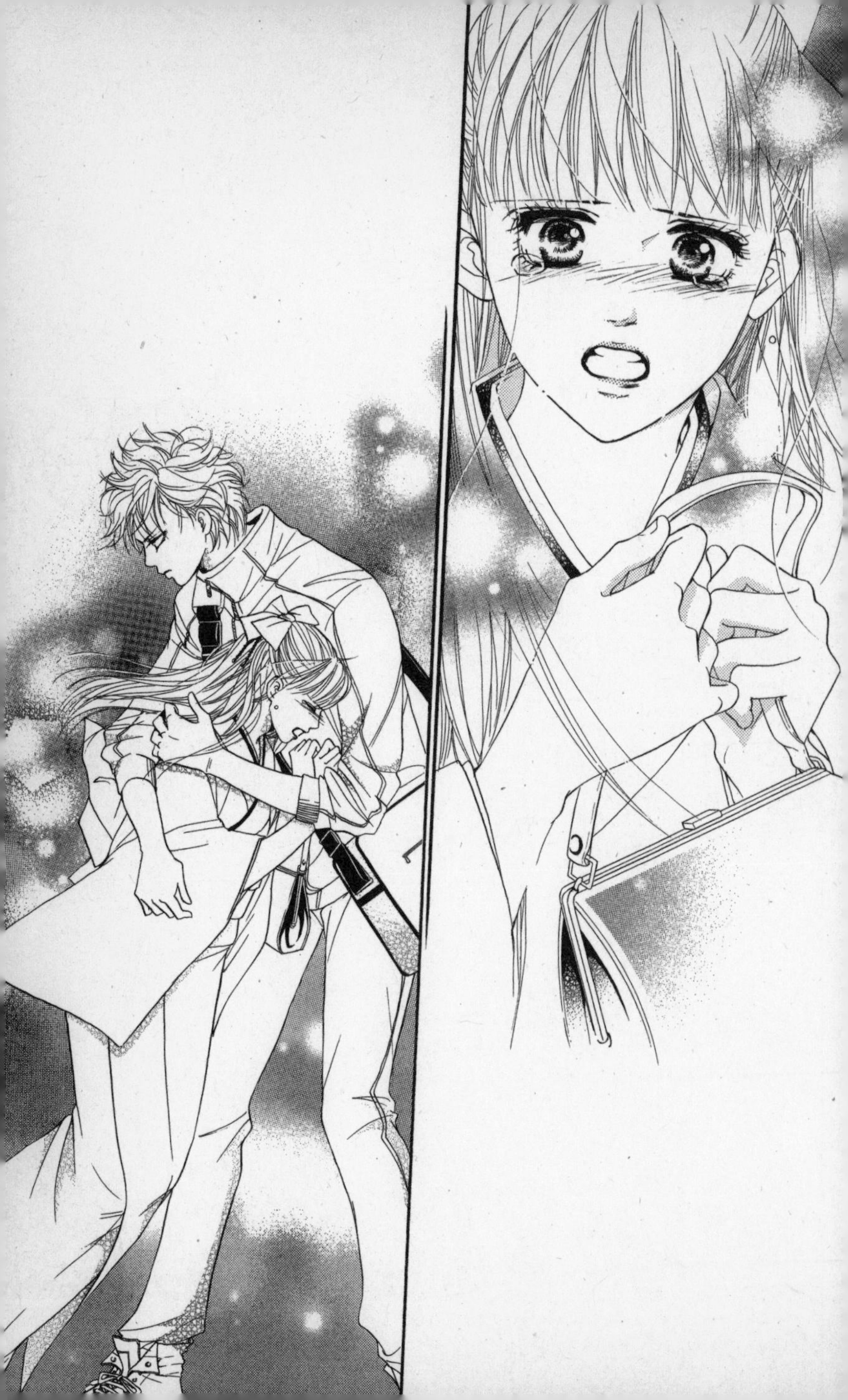

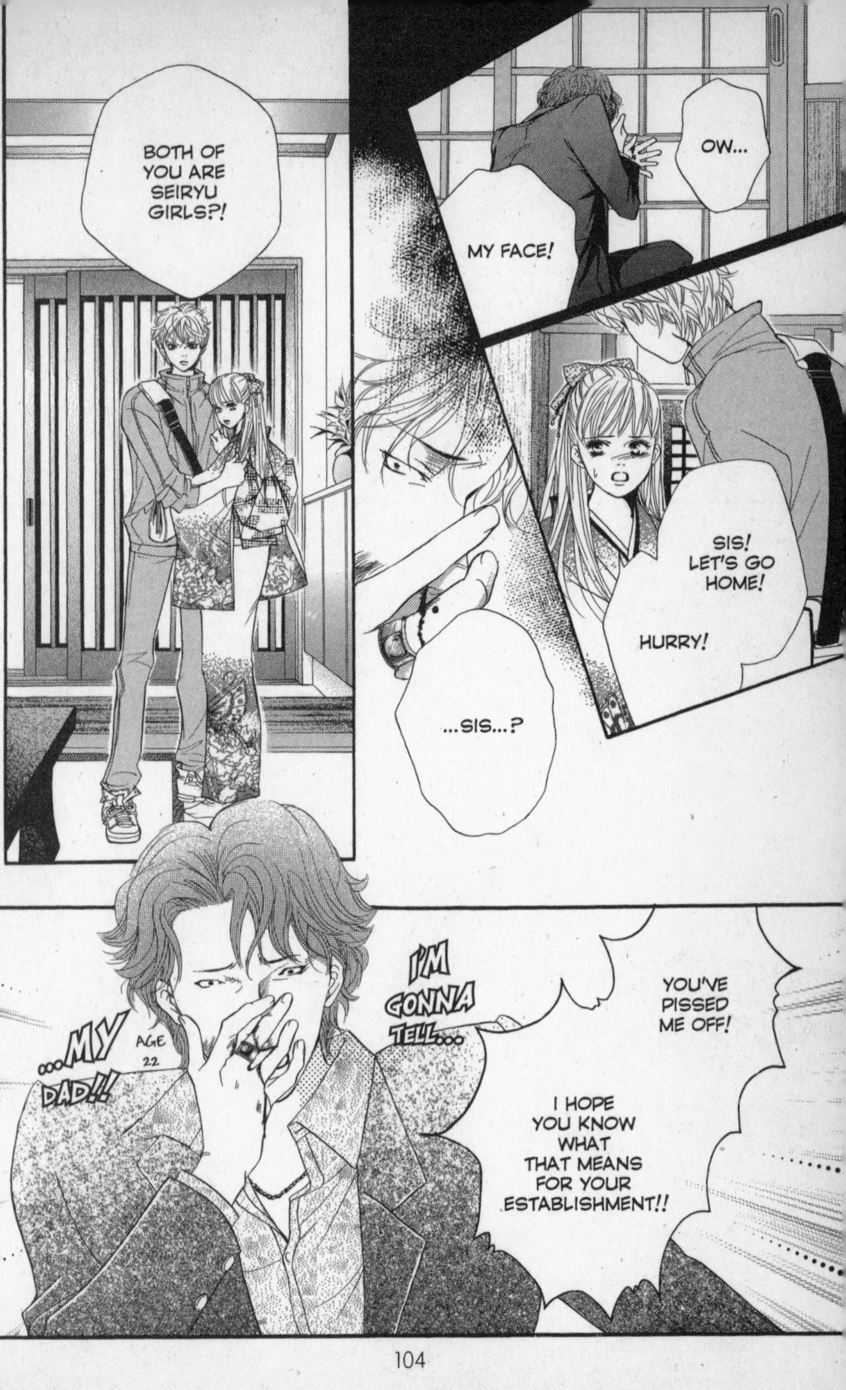
OW...
MY FACE!
SIS! LET'S GO HOME!
HURRY!
...SIS...?
BOTH OF YOU ARE SEIRYU GIRLS?!
YOU'VE PISSED ME OFF!
I HOPE YOU KNOW WHAT THAT MEANS FOR YOUR ESTABLISHMENT!!
I'M GONNA TELL...
AGE 22
...MY DAD!!

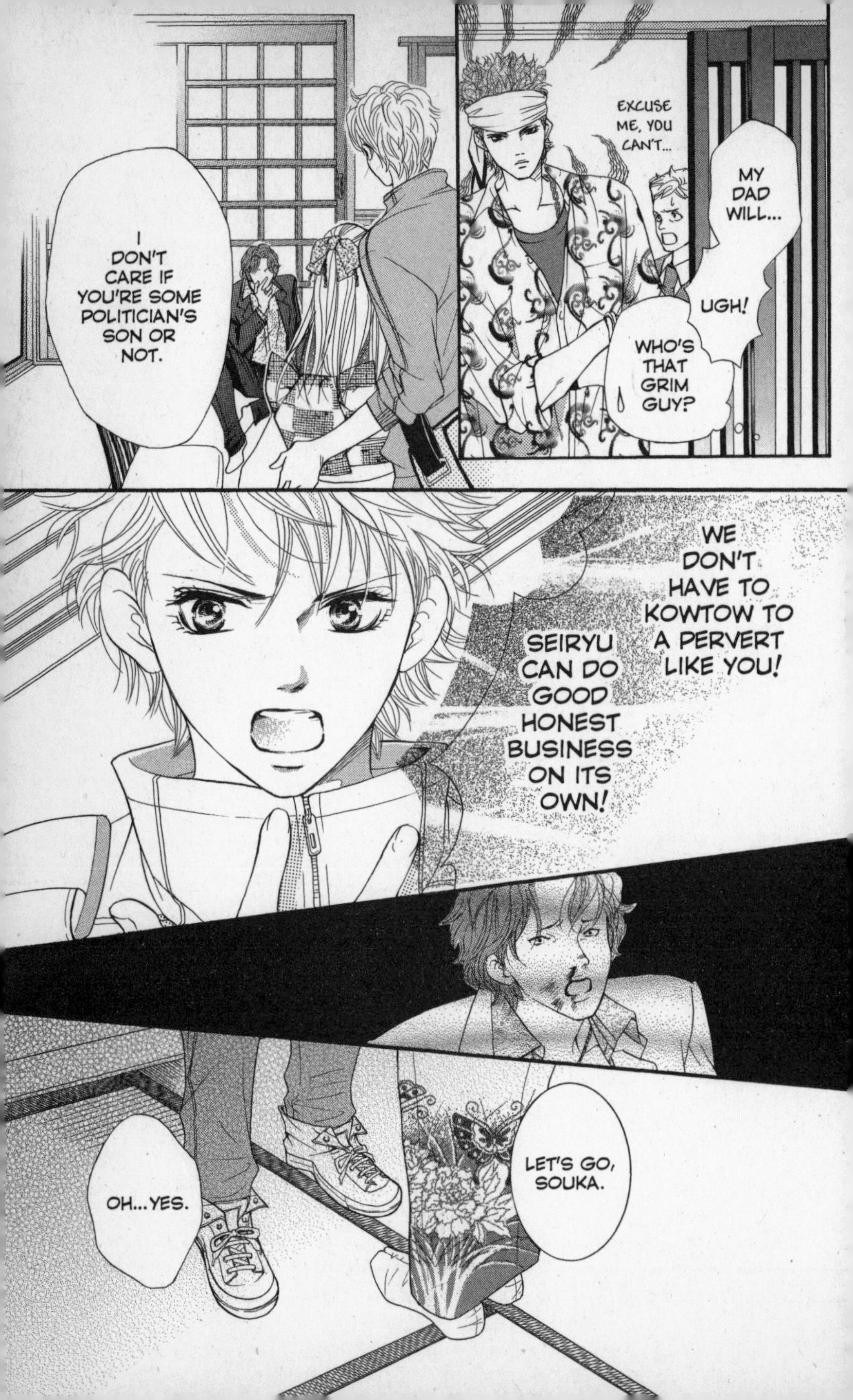
EXCUSE ME, YOU CAN'T...
MY DAD WILL...
UGH!
WHO'S THAT GRIM GUY?
I DON'T CARE IF YOU'RE SOME POLITICIAN'S SON OR NOT.
WE DON'T HAVE TO KOWTOW TO A PERVERT LIKE YOU!
SEIRYU CAN DO GOOD HONEST BUSINESS ON ITS OWN!
LET'S GO, SOUKA.
OH...YES.

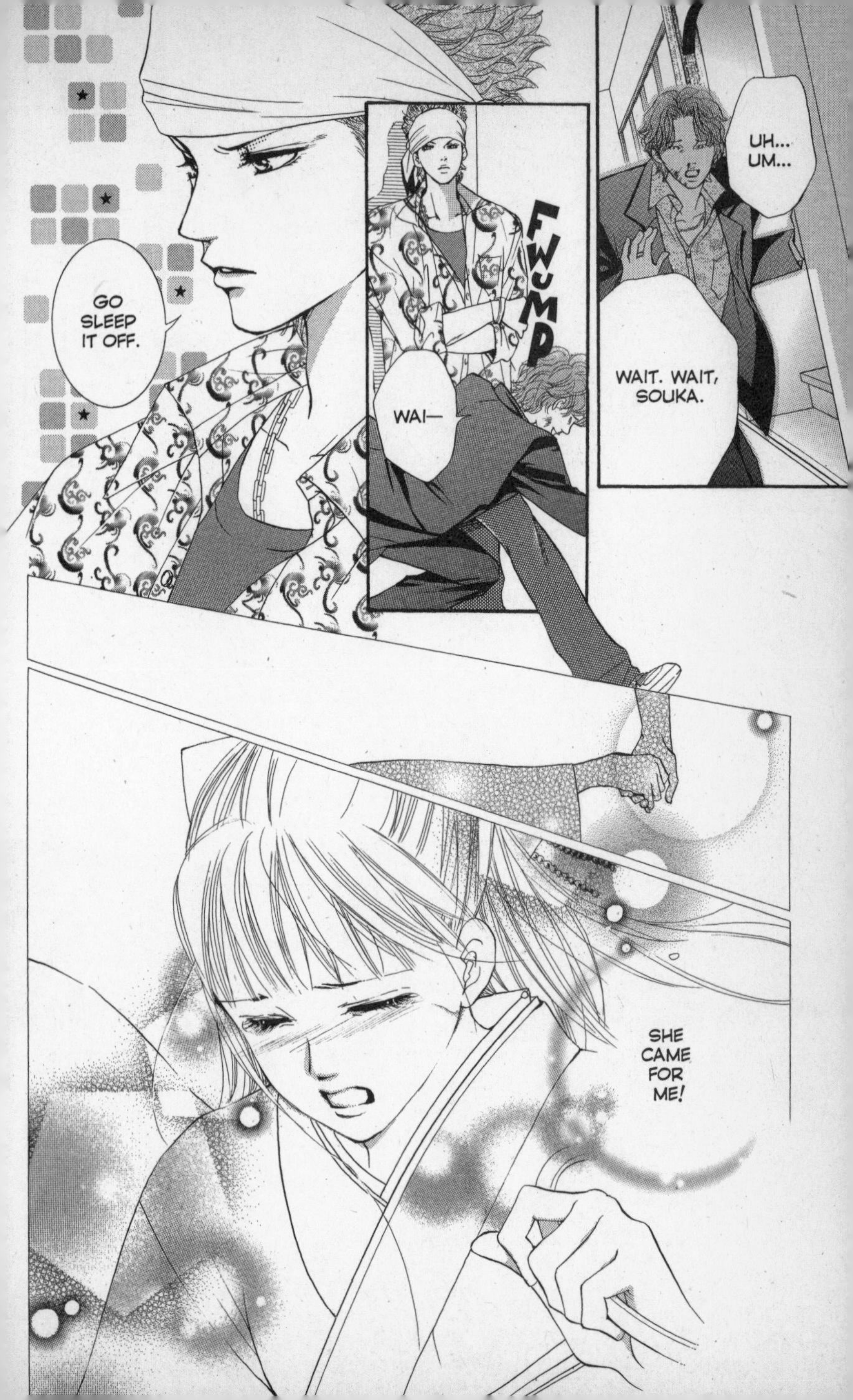
UH... UM...
WAIT. WAIT, SOUKA.
FWUMP
WAI—
GO SLEEP IT OFF.
SHE CAME FOR ME!

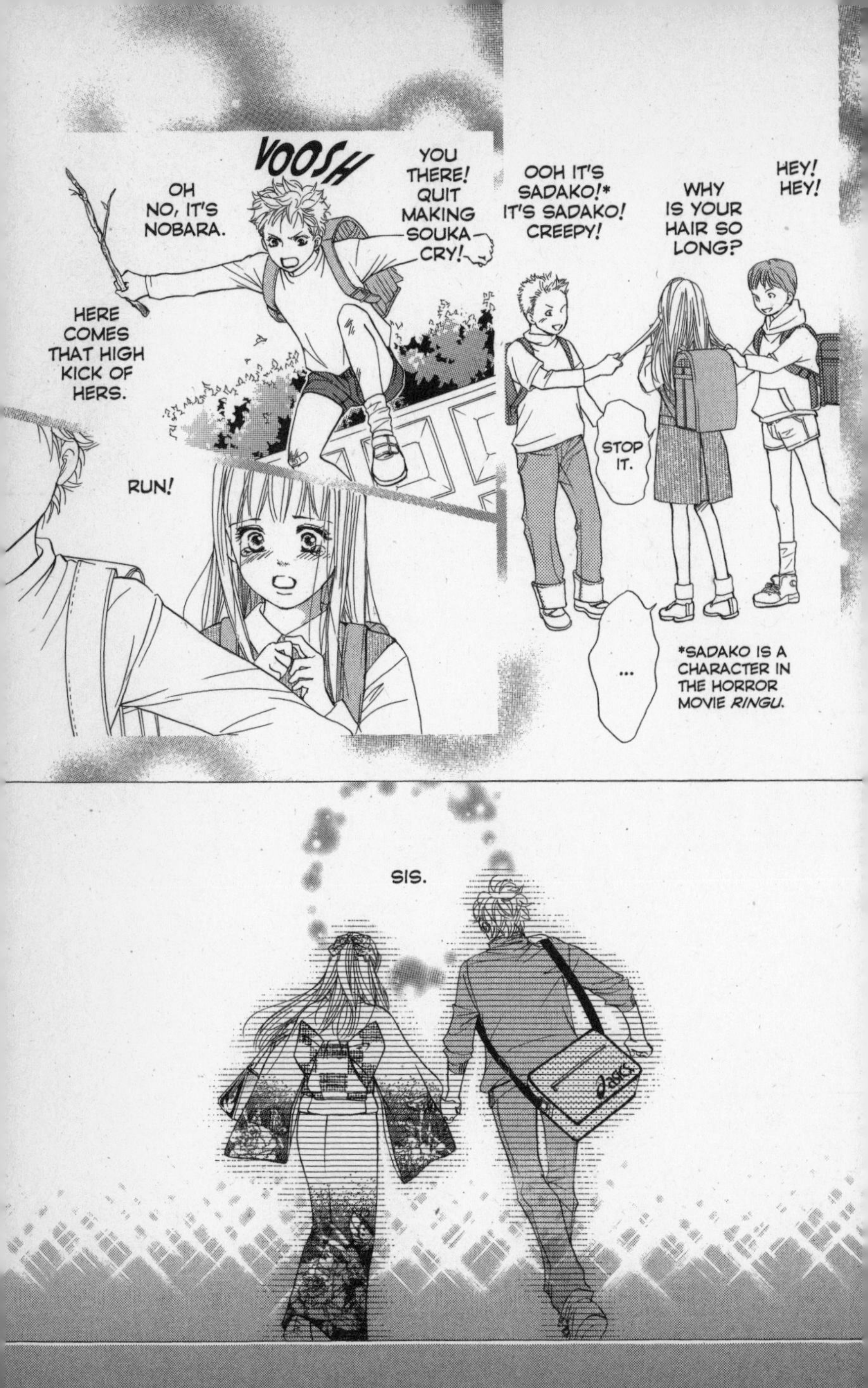
HEY! HEY!
WHY IS YOUR HAIR SO LONG?
OOH IT'S SADAKO!* IT'S SADAKO! CREEPY!
STOP IT.
...
*SADAKO IS A CHARACTER IN THE HORROR MOVIE *RINGU*.
YOU THERE! QUIT MAKING SOUKA CRY!
VOOSH
OH NO, IT'S NOBARA.
HERE COMES THAT HIGH KICK OF HERS.
RUN!
SIS.

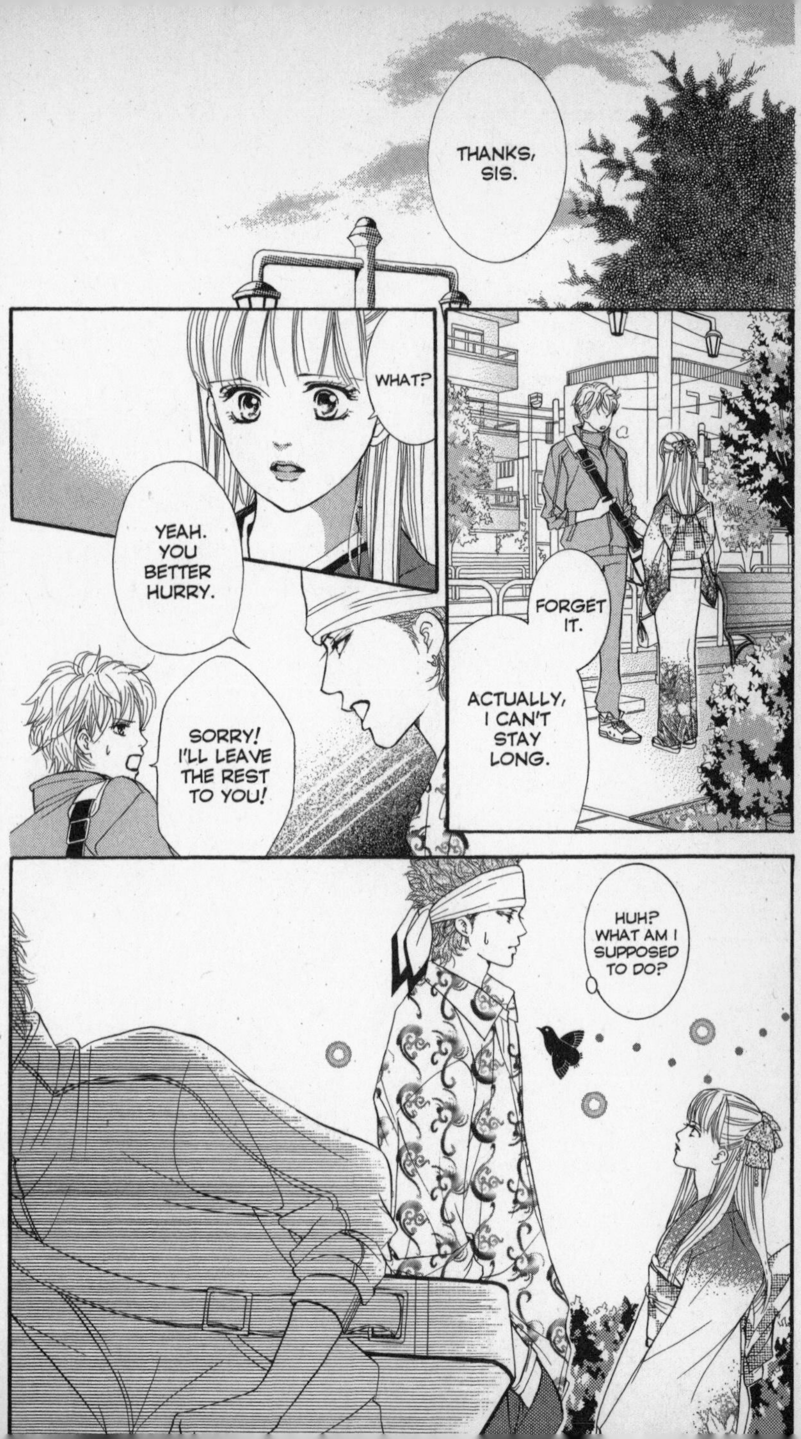
THANKS, SIS.
FORGET IT.
ACTUALLY, I CAN'T STAY LONG.
WHAT?
YEAH. YOU BETTER HURRY.
SORRY! I'LL LEAVE THE REST TO YOU!
HUH? WHAT AM I SUPPOSED TO DO?

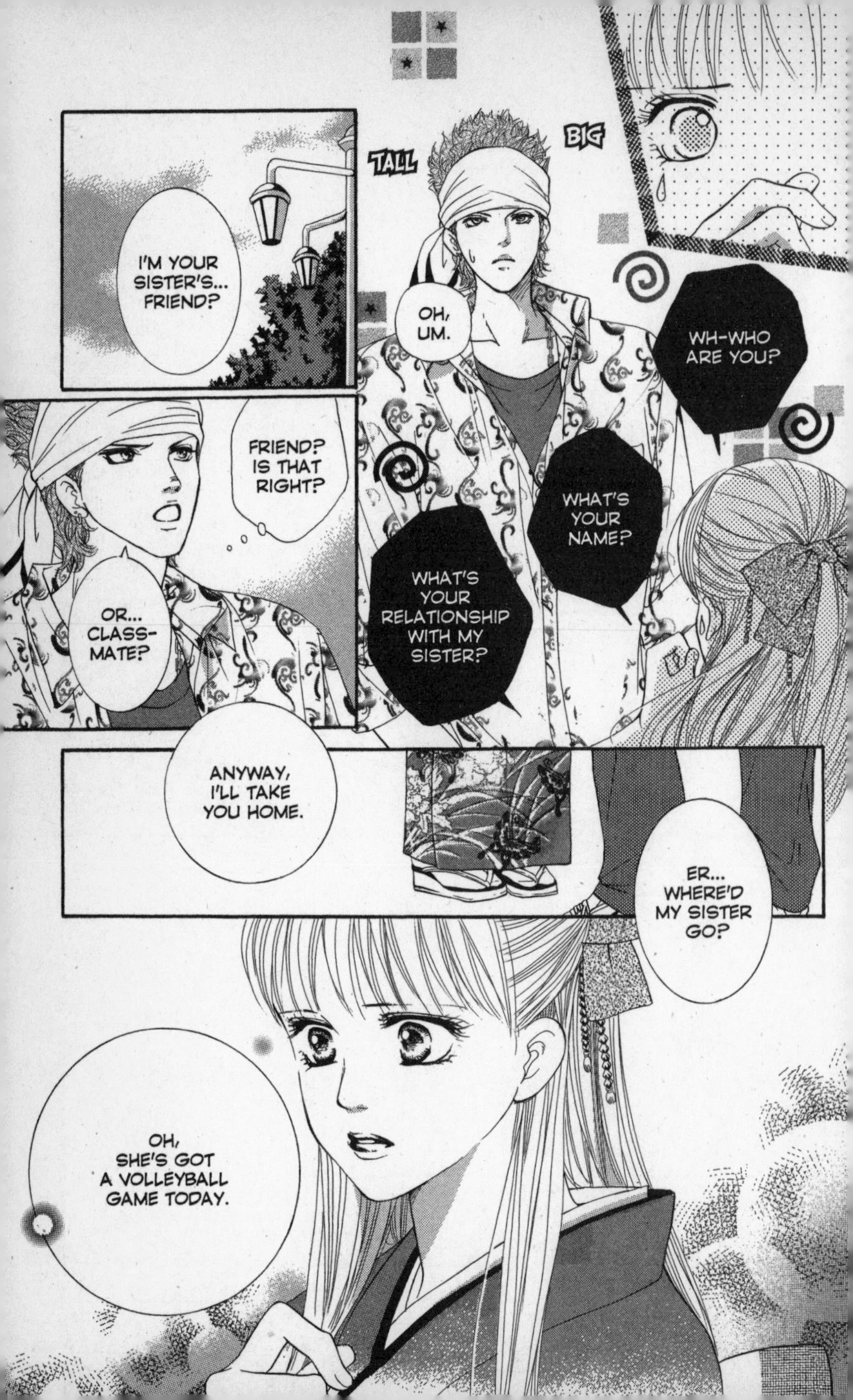
BIG
TALL
WH-WHO ARE YOU?
WHAT'S YOUR NAME?
WHAT'S YOUR RELATIONSHIP WITH MY SISTER?
OH, UM.
I'M YOUR SISTER'S... FRIEND?
FRIEND? IS THAT RIGHT?
OR... CLASS-MATE?
ANYWAY, I'LL TAKE YOU HOME.
ER... WHERE'D MY SISTER GO?
OH, SHE'S GOT A VOLLEYBALL GAME TODAY.

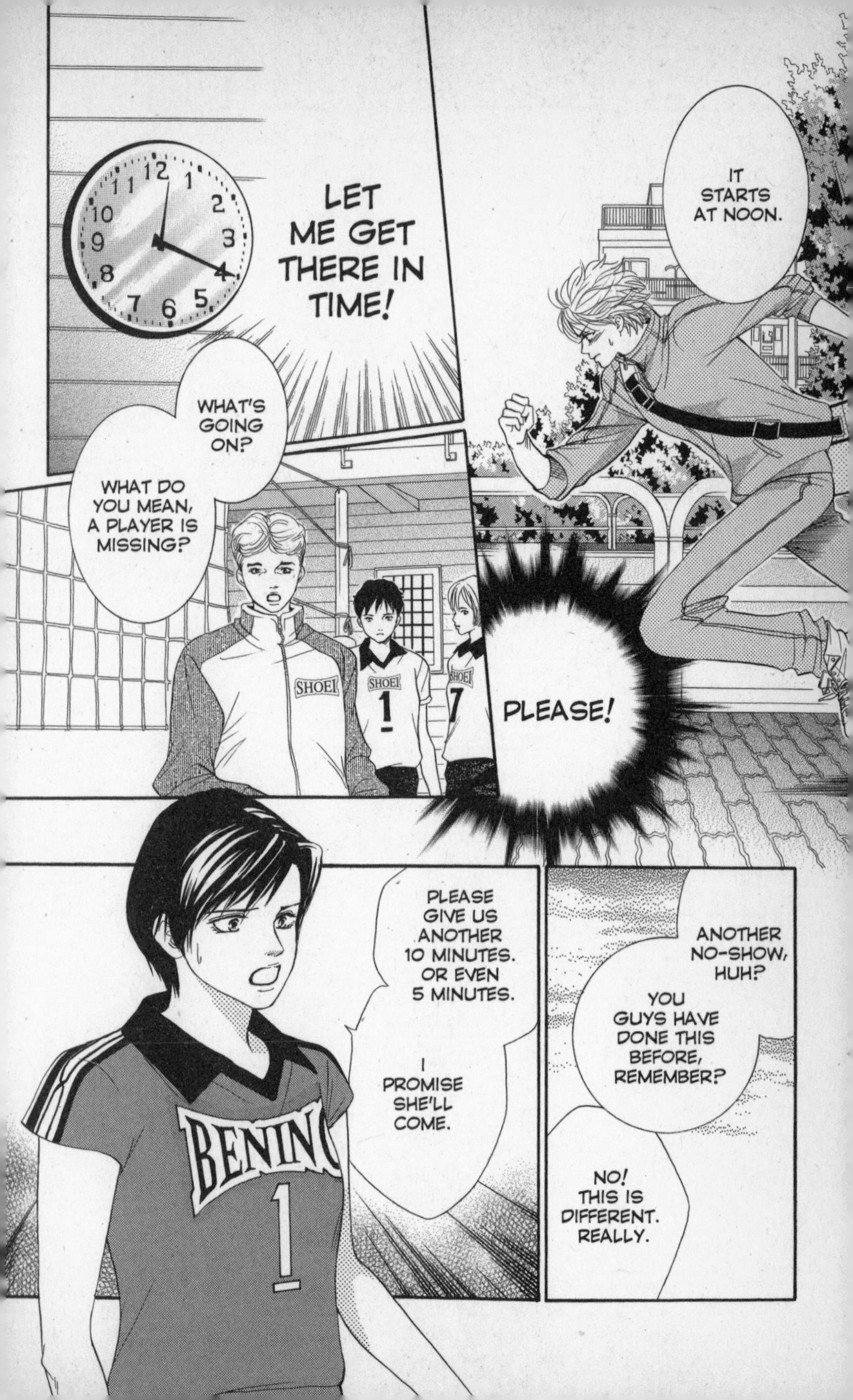
IT STARTS AT NOON.
PLEASE!
LET ME GET THERE IN TIME!
WHAT'S GOING ON?
WHAT DO YOU MEAN, A PLAYER IS MISSING?
SHOEI
SHOEI 1
SHOEI 7
ANOTHER NO-SHOW, HUH?
YOU GUYS HAVE DONE THIS BEFORE, REMEMBER?
NO! THIS IS DIFFERENT. REALLY.
PLEASE GIVE US ANOTHER 10 MINUTES. OR EVEN 5 MINUTES.
I PROMISE SHE'LL COME.
BENIN 1

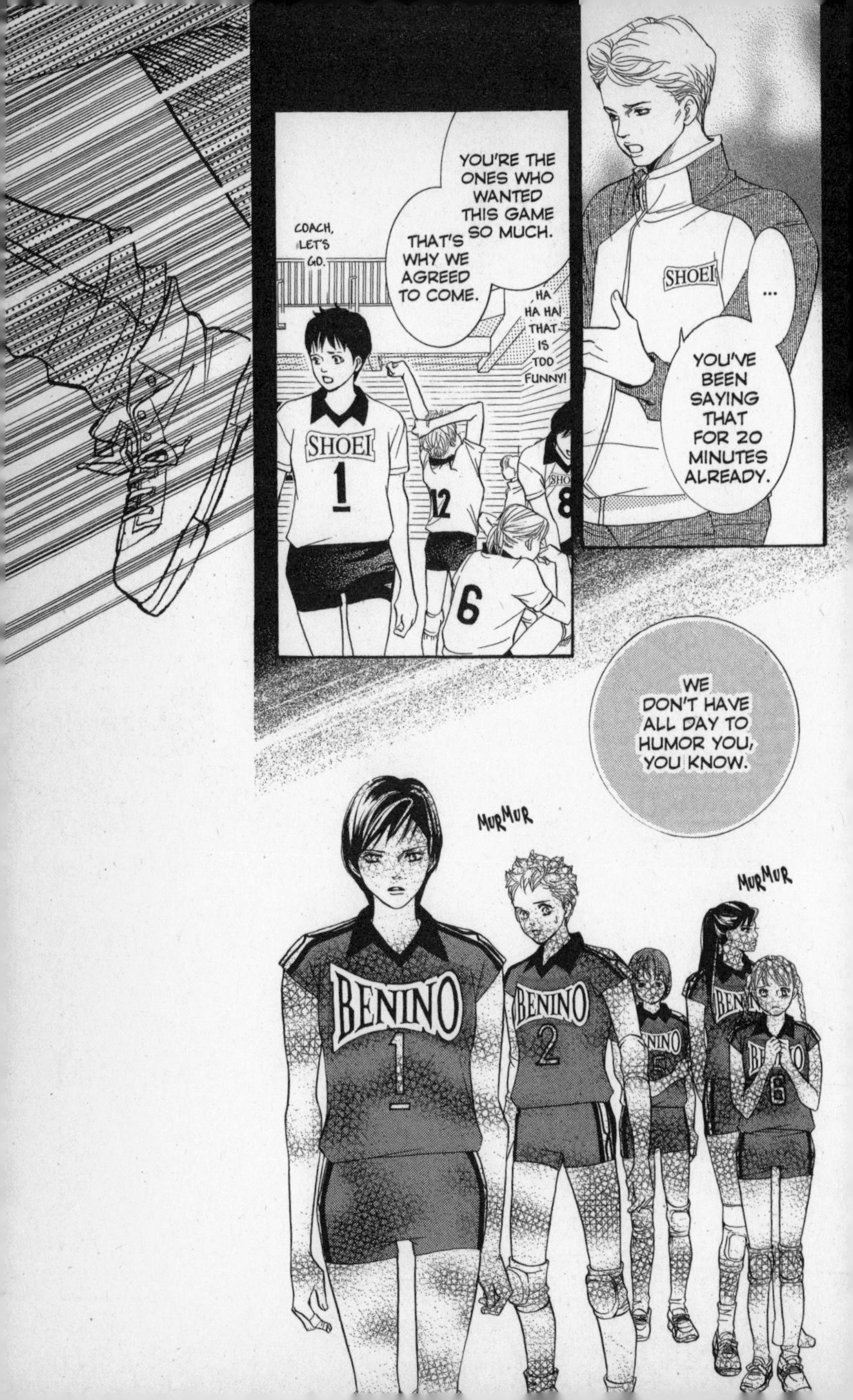
...
YOU'VE BEEN SAYING THAT FOR 20 MINUTES ALREADY.
YOU'RE THE ONES WHO WANTED THIS GAME SO MUCH.
THAT'S WHY WE AGREED TO COME.
HA HA HA! THAT IS TOO FUNNY!
COACH, LET'S GO.
WE DON'T HAVE ALL DAY TO HUMOR YOU, YOU KNOW.
MURMUR
MURMUR

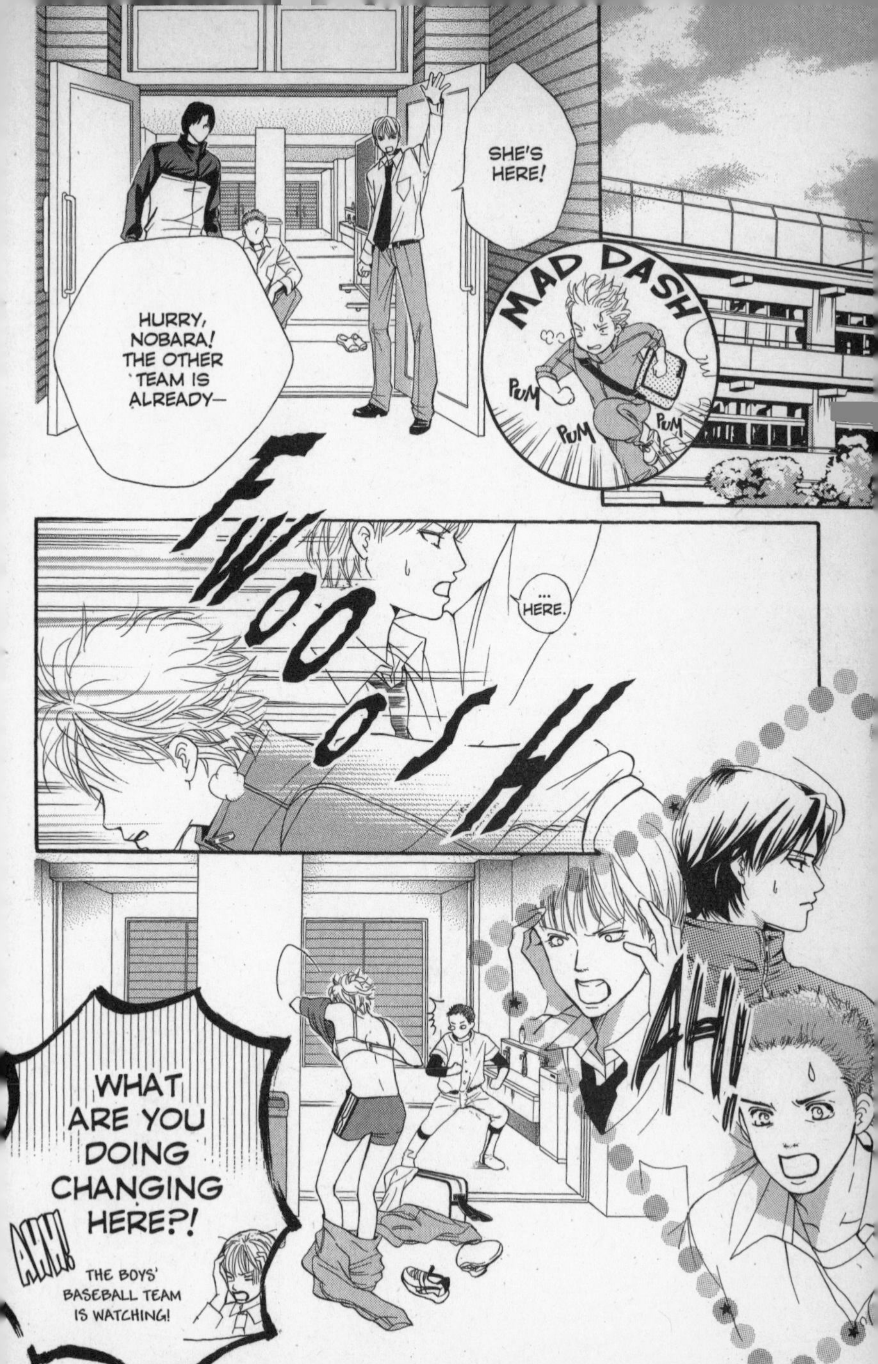
MAD DASH
PUM PUM PUM
SHE'S HERE!
HURRY, NOBARA! THE OTHER TEAM IS ALREADY—
FWOOSH
... HERE.
AH!
WHAT ARE YOU DOING CHANGING HERE?!
AHH!
THE BOYS' BASEBALL TEAM IS WATCHING!

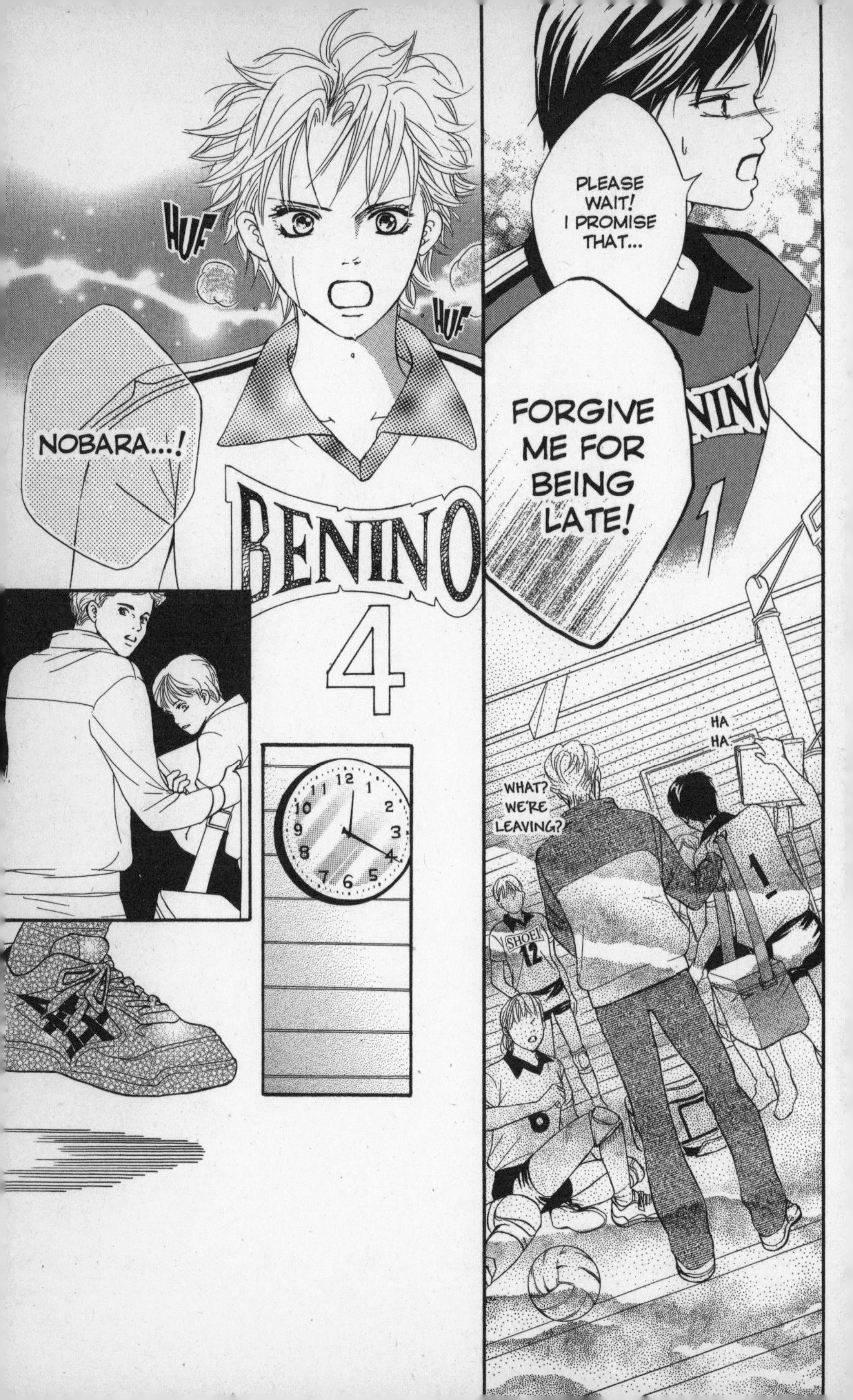
PLEASE WAIT! I PROMISE THAT...
FORGIVE ME FOR BEING LATE!
HA HA
WHAT? WE'RE LEAVING?
HUF
HUF
NOBARA...!

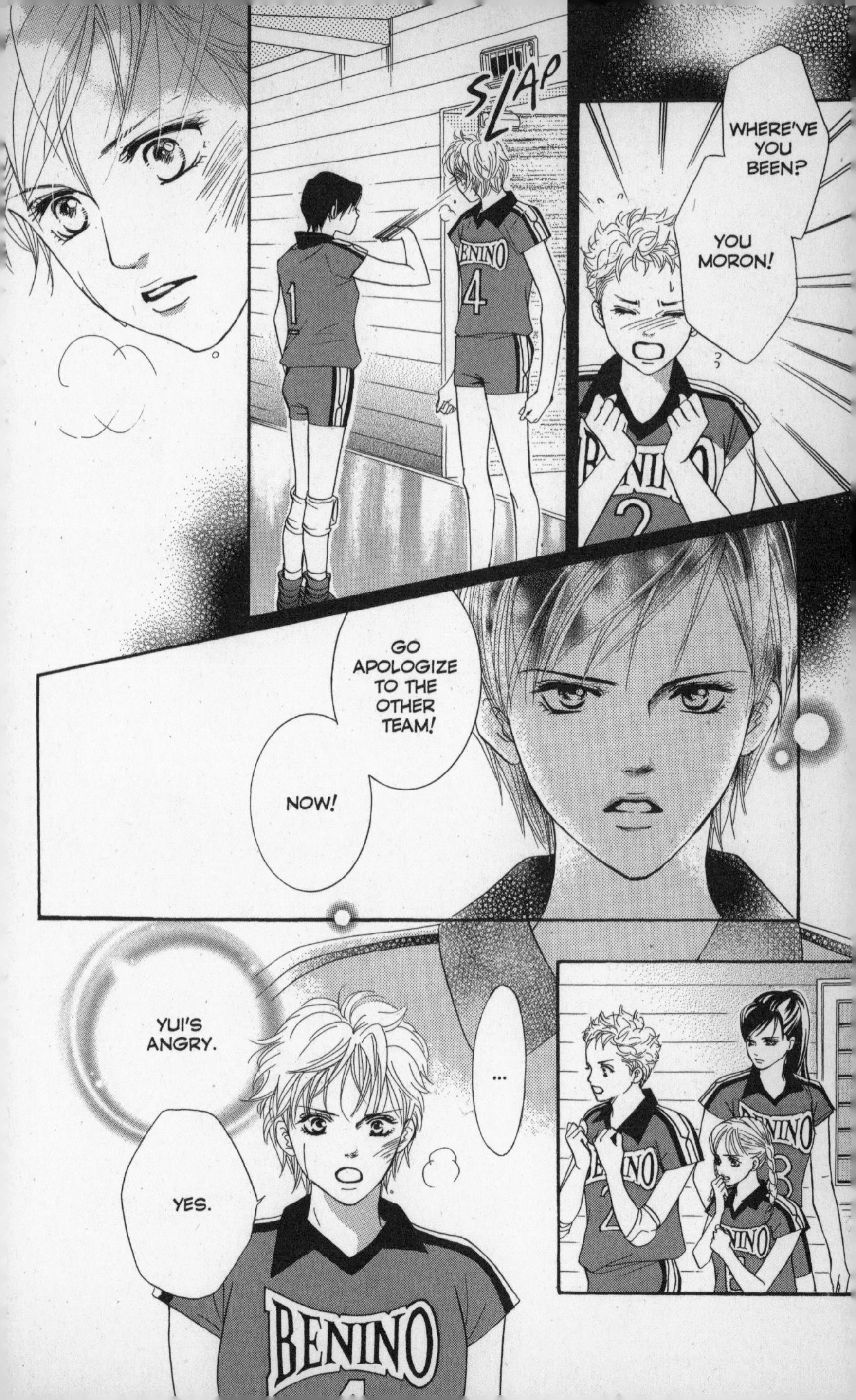

WHERE'VE YOU BEEN?
YOU MORON!
SLAP
BENINO
GO APOLOGIZE TO THE OTHER TEAM!
NOW!
...
YUI'S ANGRY.
YES.
BENINO

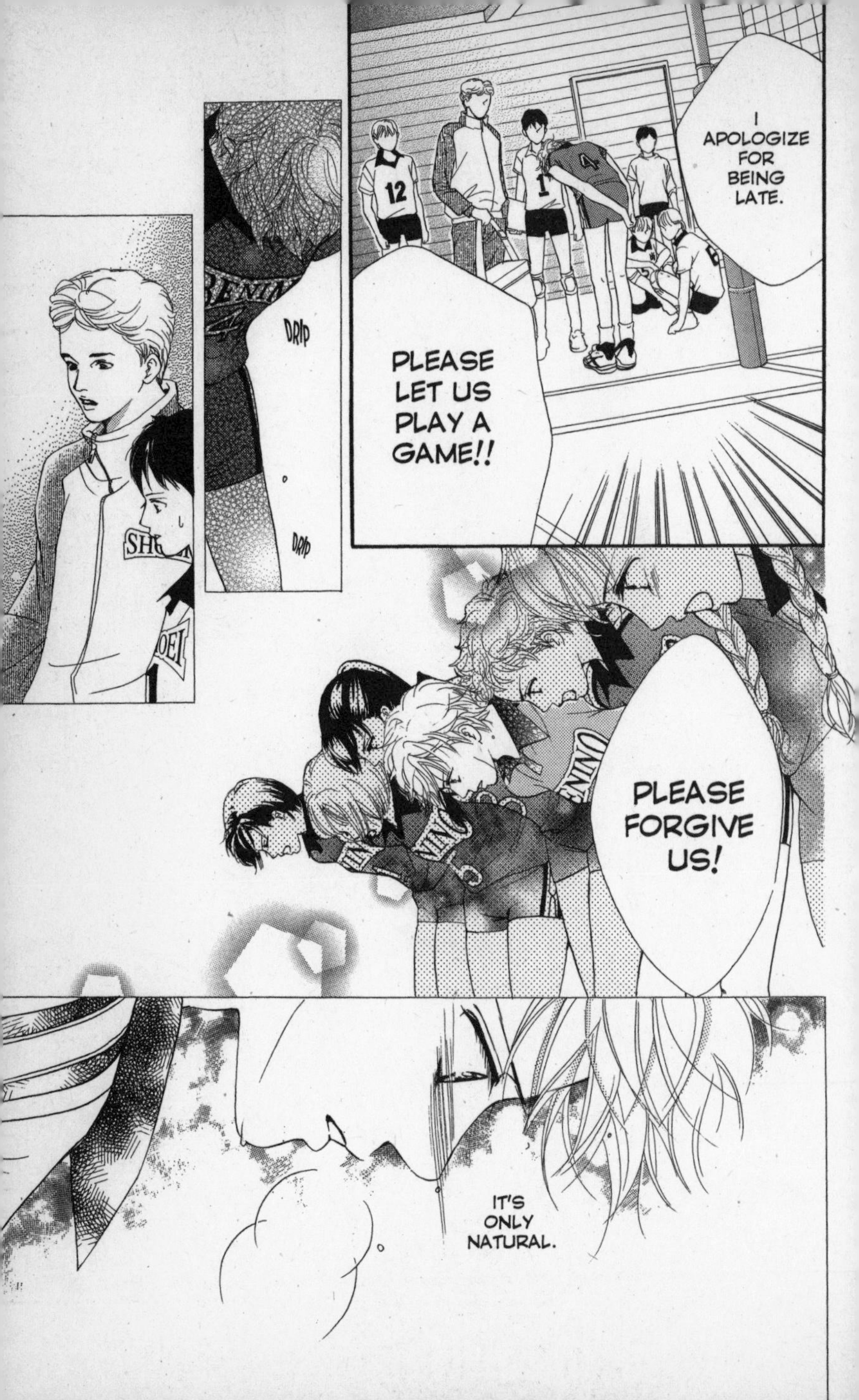
I APOLOGIZE FOR BEING LATE.
PLEASE LET US PLAY A GAME!!
DRIP
DRIP
PLEASE FORGIVE US!
IT'S ONLY NATURAL.

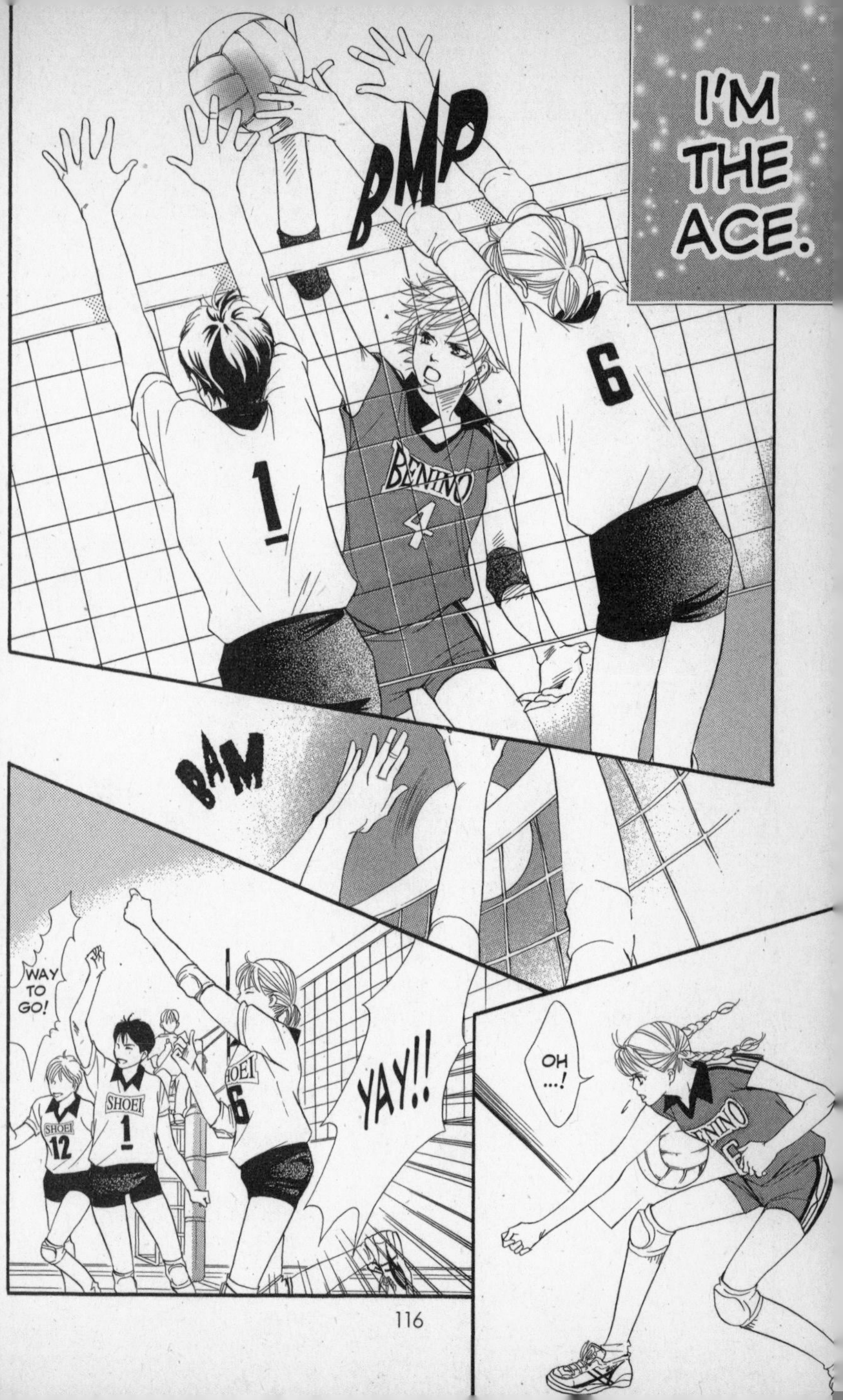
I'M THE ACE.
BMP
BAM
OH ...!
YAY!!
WAY TO GO!

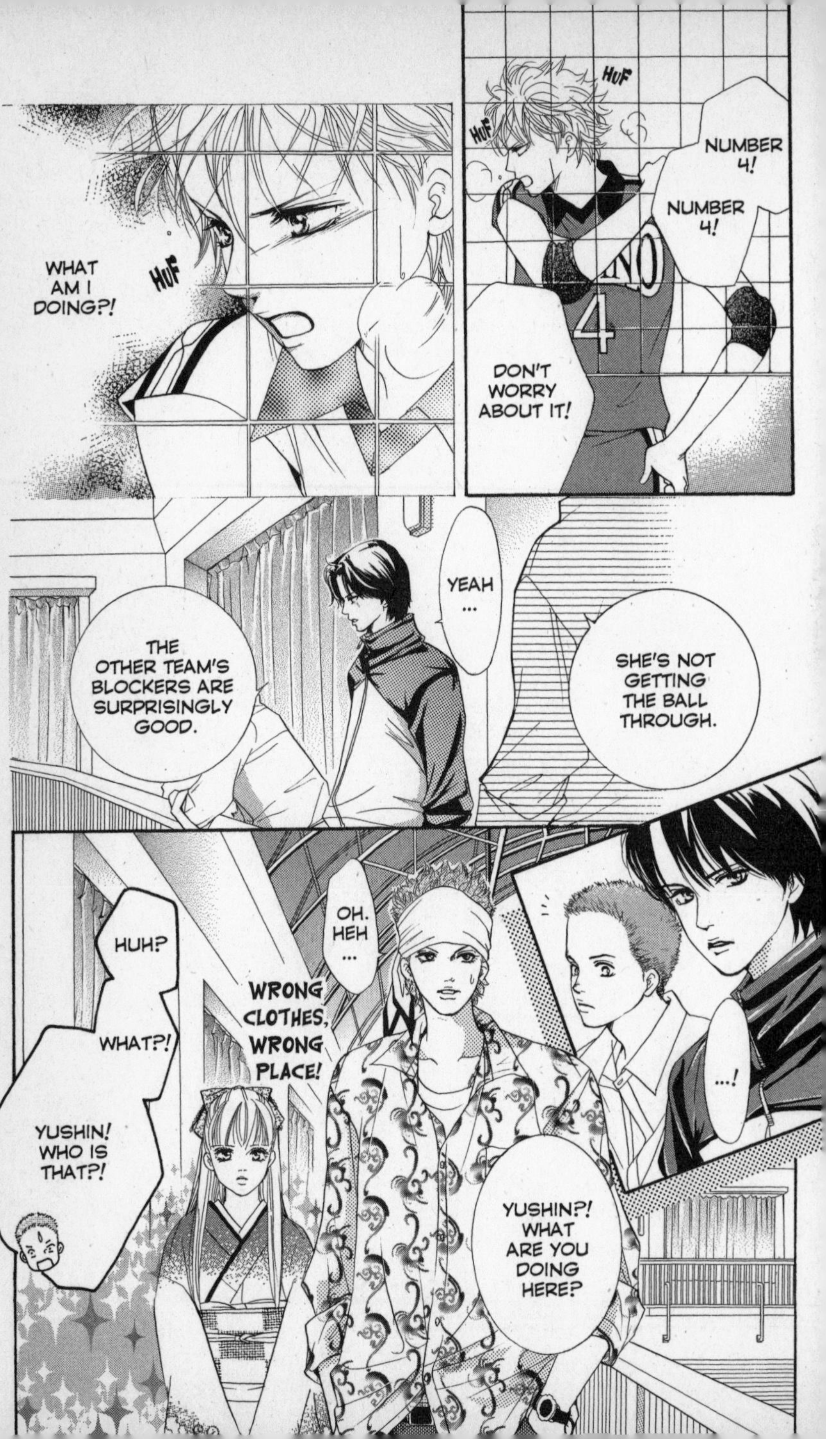
HUF
HUF
NUMBER 4!
NUMBER 4!
DON'T WORRY ABOUT IT!
HUF
WHAT AM I DOING?!
SHE'S NOT GETTING THE BALL THROUGH.
YEAH...
THE OTHER TEAM'S BLOCKERS ARE SURPRISINGLY GOOD.
...!
YUSHIN?! WHAT ARE YOU DOING HERE?
OH. HEH...
WRONG CLOTHES, WRONG PLACE!
HUH?
WHAT?!
YUSHIN! WHO IS THAT?!

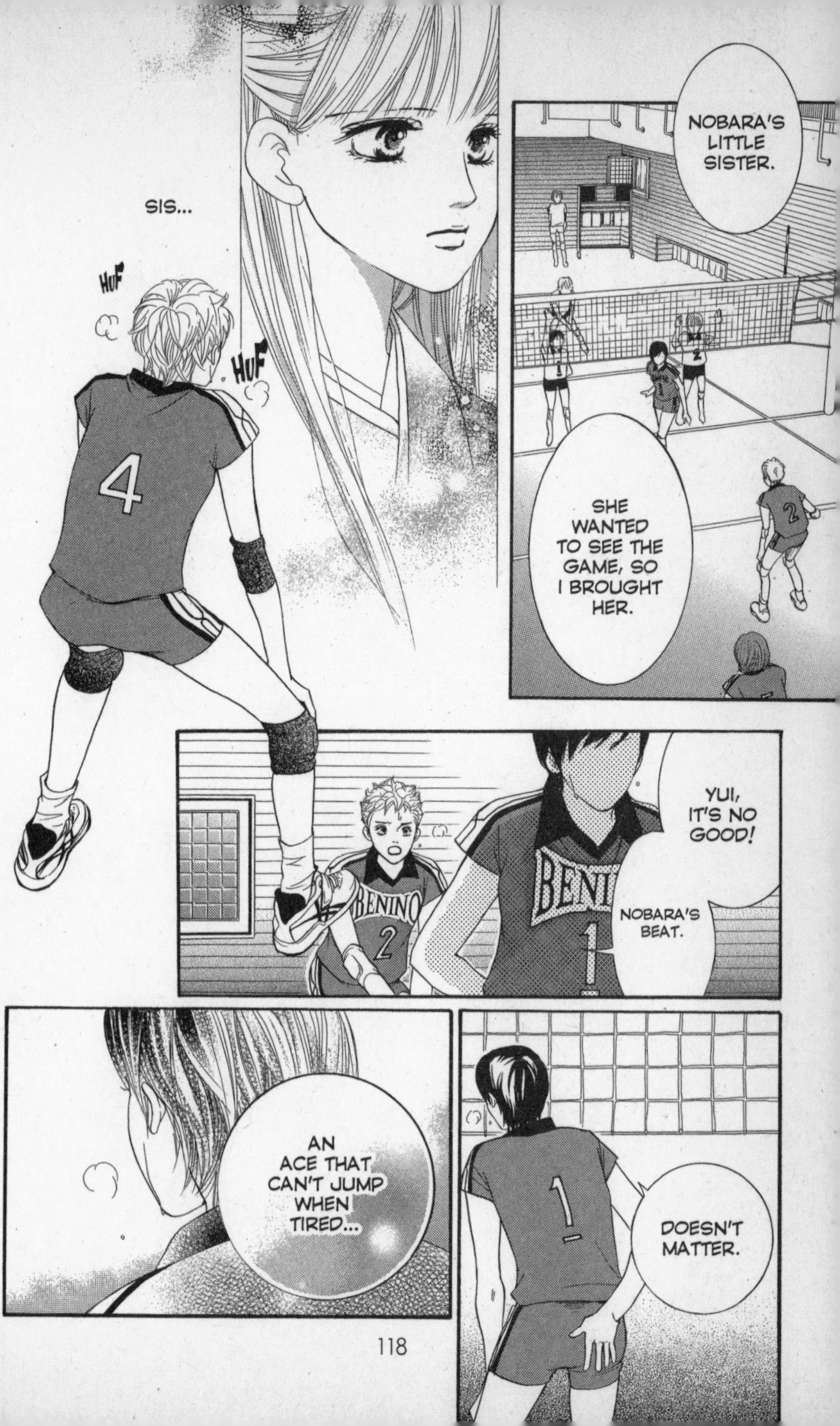
NOBARA'S LITTLE SISTER.
SHE WANTED TO SEE THE GAME, SO I BROUGHT HER.
SIS...
HUF
HUF
YUI, IT'S NO GOOD!
NOBARA'S BEAT.
DOESN'T MATTER.
AN ACE THAT CAN'T JUMP WHEN TIRED...

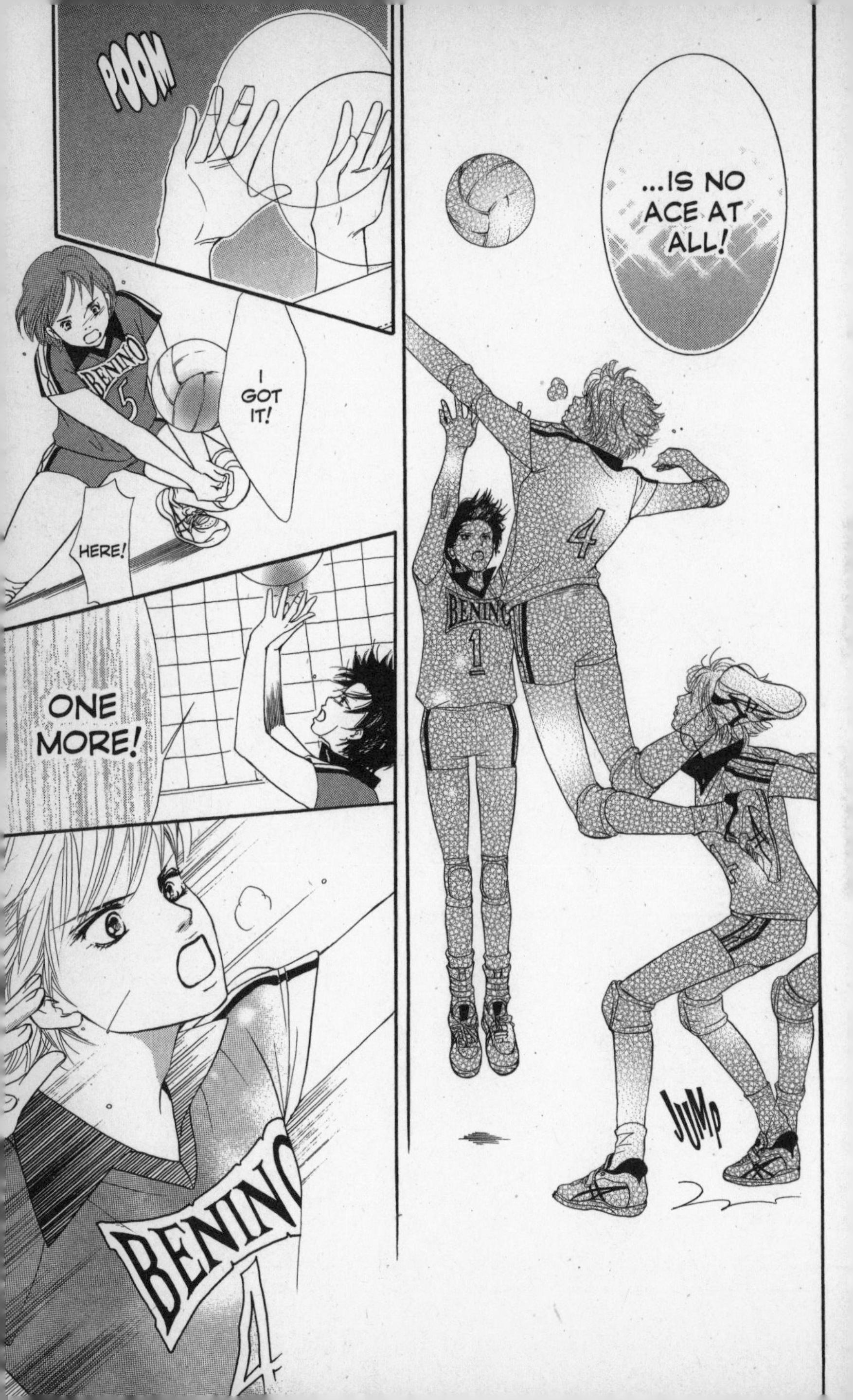
...IS NO ACE AT ALL!
JUMP
POOM
I GOT IT!
HERE!
ONE MORE!

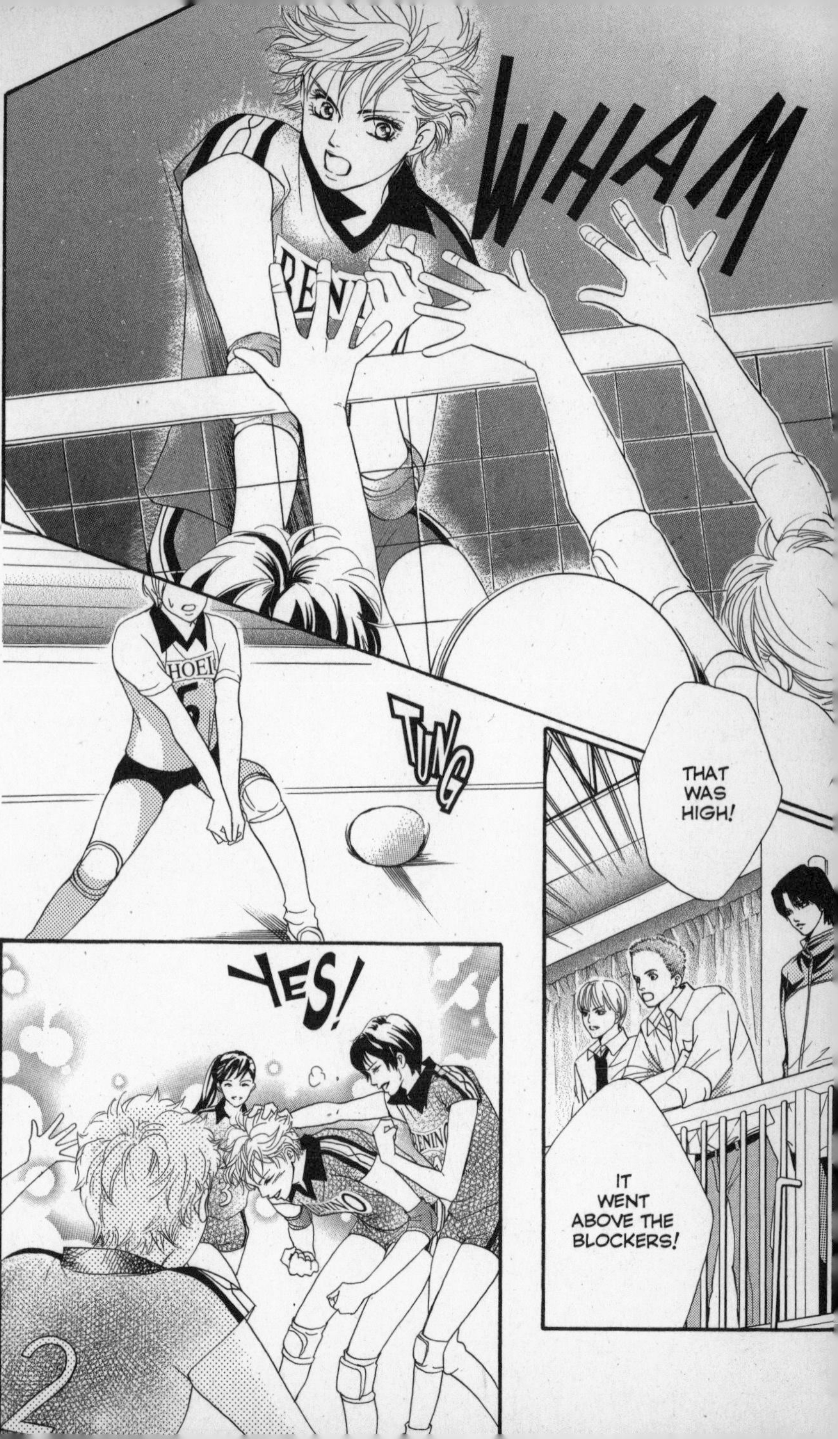
WHAM
THAT WAS HIGH!
IT WENT ABOVE THE BLOCKERS!
TUNG
YES!

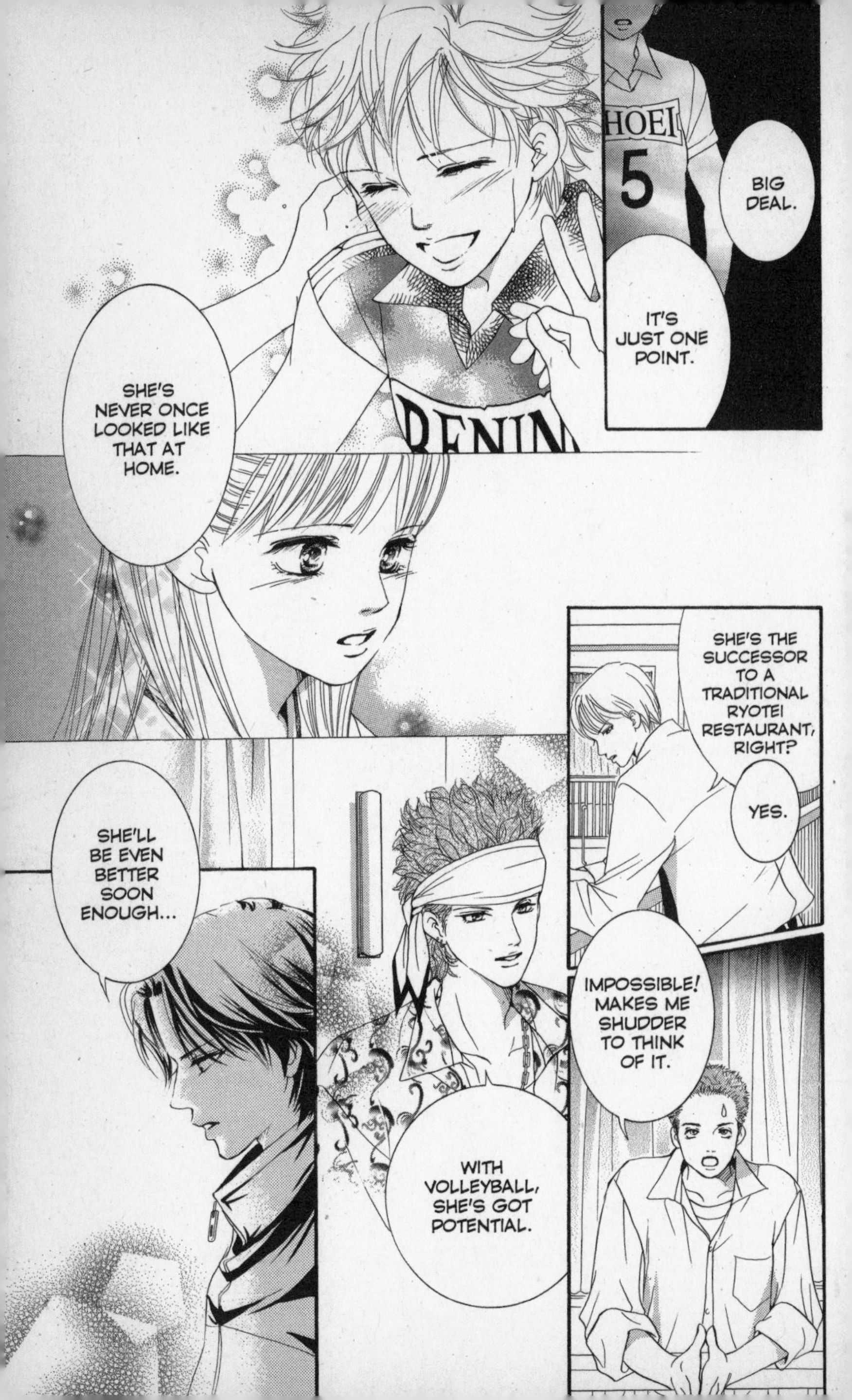
BIG DEAL.
IT'S JUST ONE POINT.
SHE'S NEVER ONCE LOOKED LIKE THAT AT HOME.
SHE'S THE SUCCESSOR TO A TRADITIONAL RYOTEI RESTAURANT, RIGHT?
YES.
IMPOSSIBLE! MAKES ME SHUDDER TO THINK OF IT.
WITH VOLLEYBALL, SHE'S GOT POTENTIAL.
SHE'LL BE EVEN BETTER SOON ENOUGH...

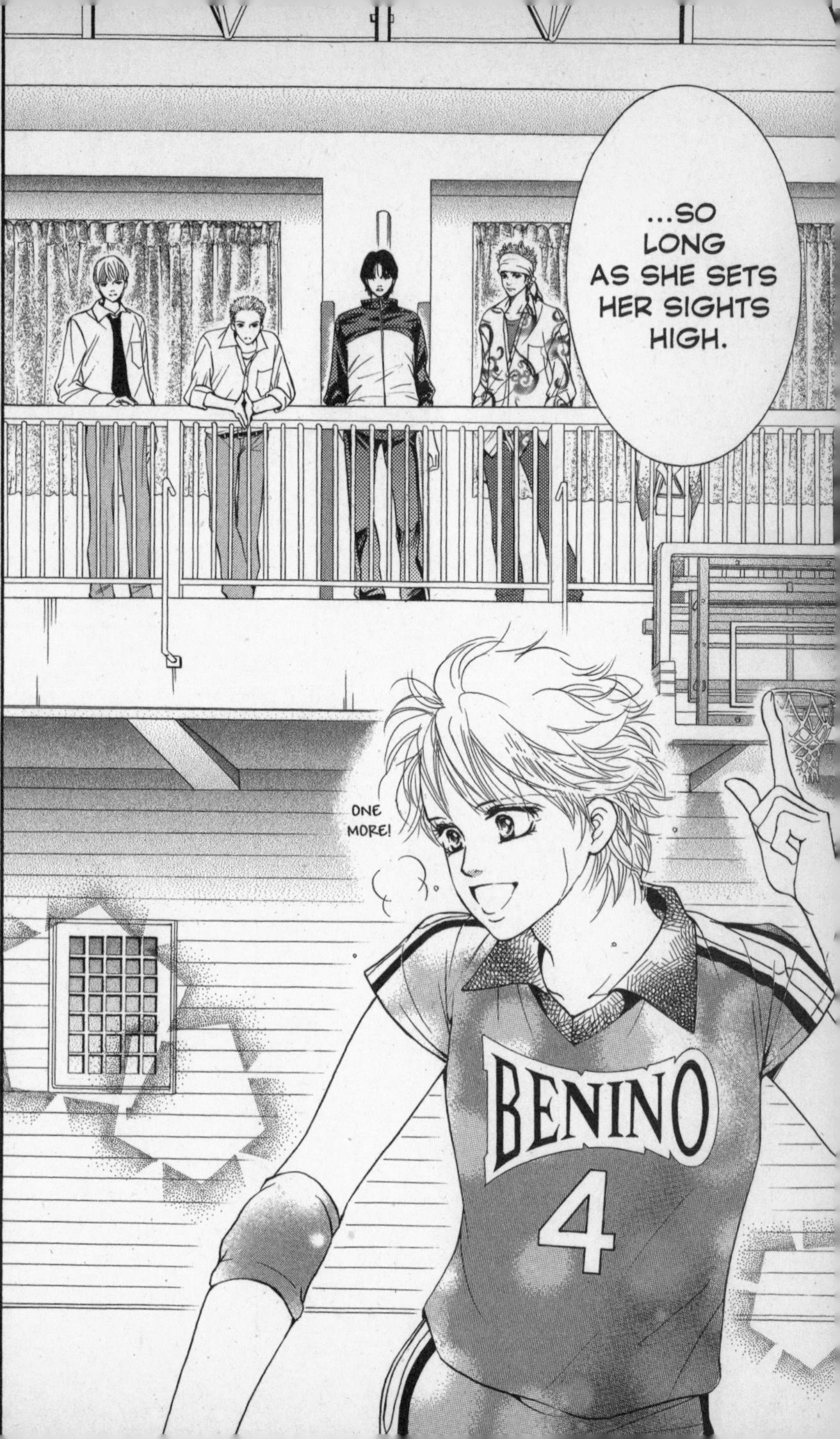
...SO LONG AS SHE SETS HER SIGHTS HIGH.
ONE MORE!
BENINO
4

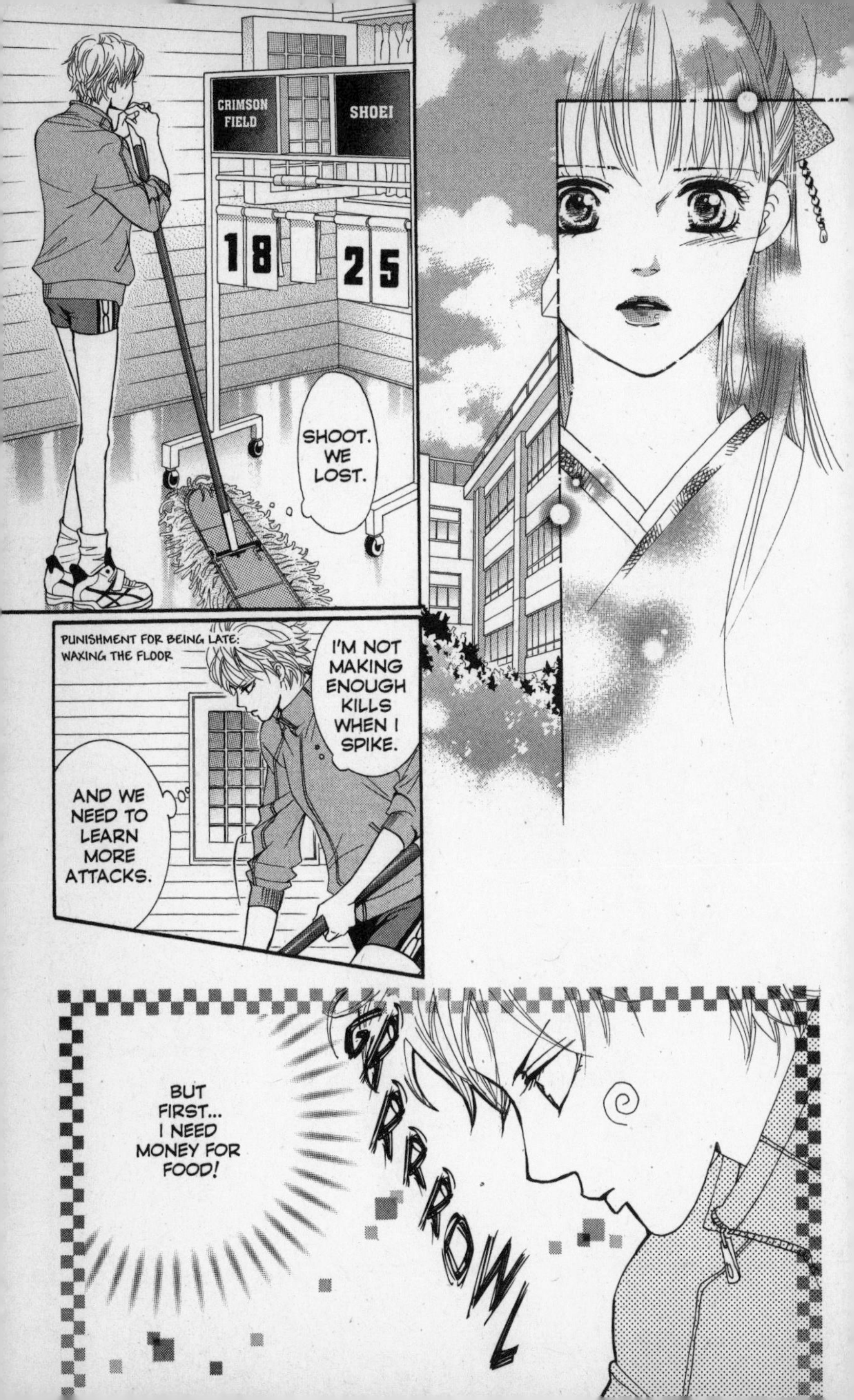
CRIMSON FIELD
SHOEI
18
25
SHOOT. WE LOST.
PUNISHMENT FOR BEING LATE: WAXING THE FLOOR
I'M NOT MAKING ENOUGH KILLS WHEN I SPIKE.
AND WE NEED TO LEARN MORE ATTACKS.
GRRRROWL
BUT FIRST... I NEED MONEY FOR FOOD!

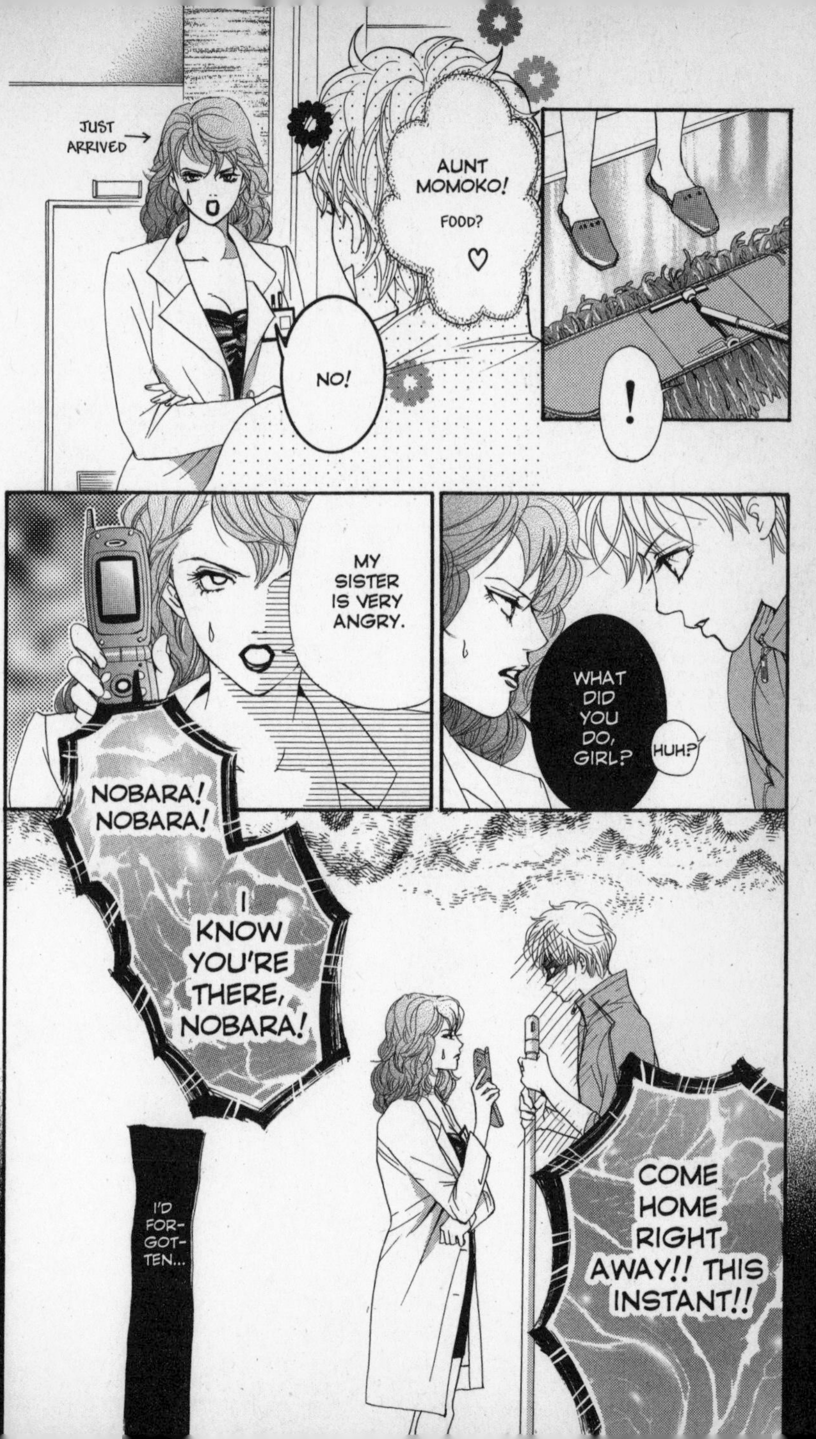
!
AUNT MOMOKO! FOOD? ♡
JUST ARRIVED
NO!
WHAT DID YOU DO, GIRL?
HUH?
MY SISTER IS VERY ANGRY.
NOBARA! NOBARA!
I KNOW YOU'RE THERE, NOBARA!
COME HOME RIGHT AWAY!! THIS INSTANT!!
I'D FORGOTTEN...

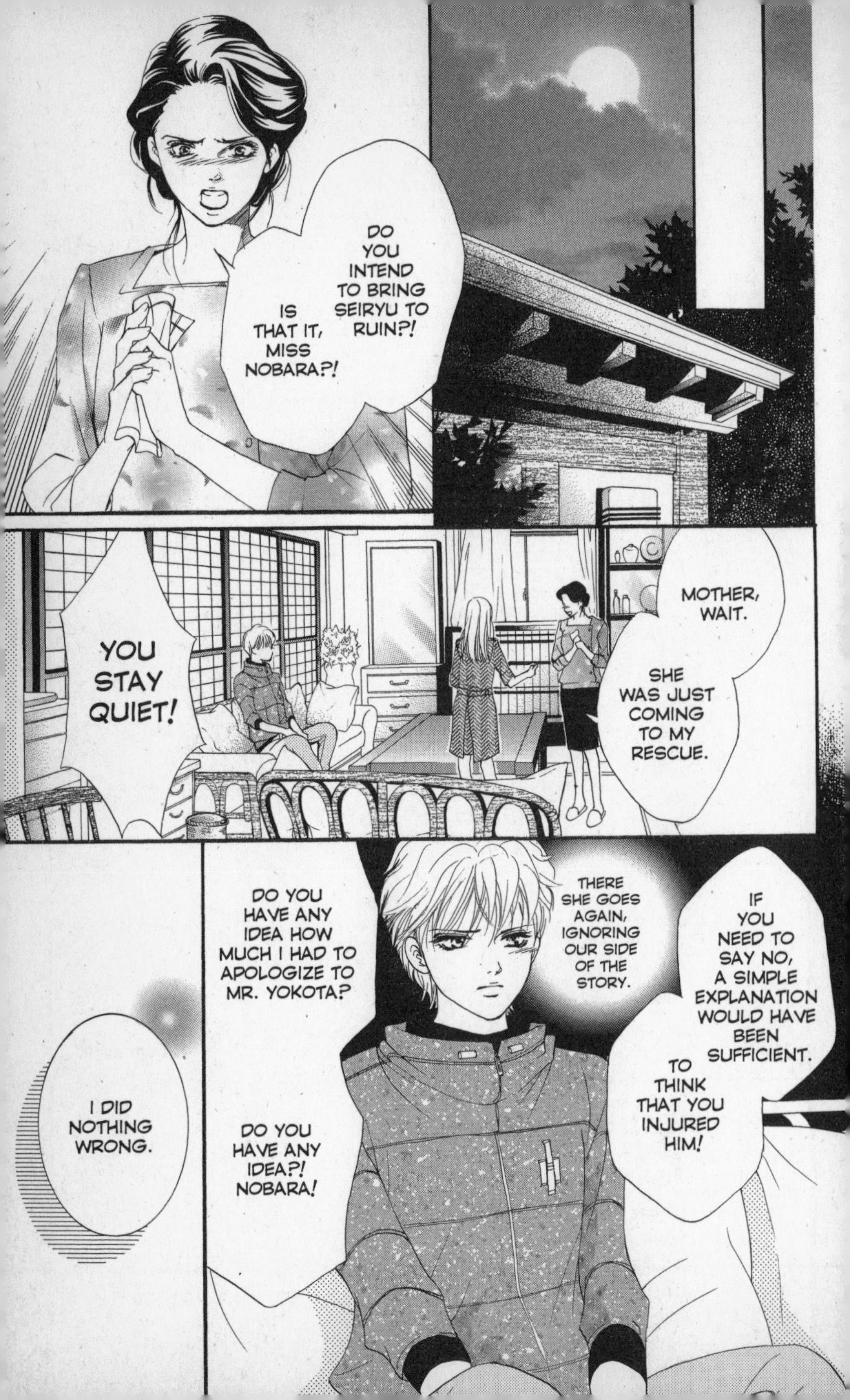
DO YOU INTEND TO BRING SEIRYU TO RUIN?!
IS THAT IT, MISS NOBARA?!
MOTHER, WAIT.
SHE WAS JUST COMING TO MY RESCUE.
YOU STAY QUIET!
IF YOU NEED TO SAY NO, A SIMPLE EXPLANATION WOULD HAVE BEEN SUFFICIENT.
THERE SHE GOES AGAIN, IGNORING OUR SIDE OF THE STORY.
DO YOU HAVE ANY IDEA HOW MUCH I HAD TO APOLOGIZE TO MR. YOKOTA?
TO THINK THAT YOU INJURED HIM!
DO YOU HAVE ANY IDEA?! NOBARA!
I DID NOTHING WRONG.

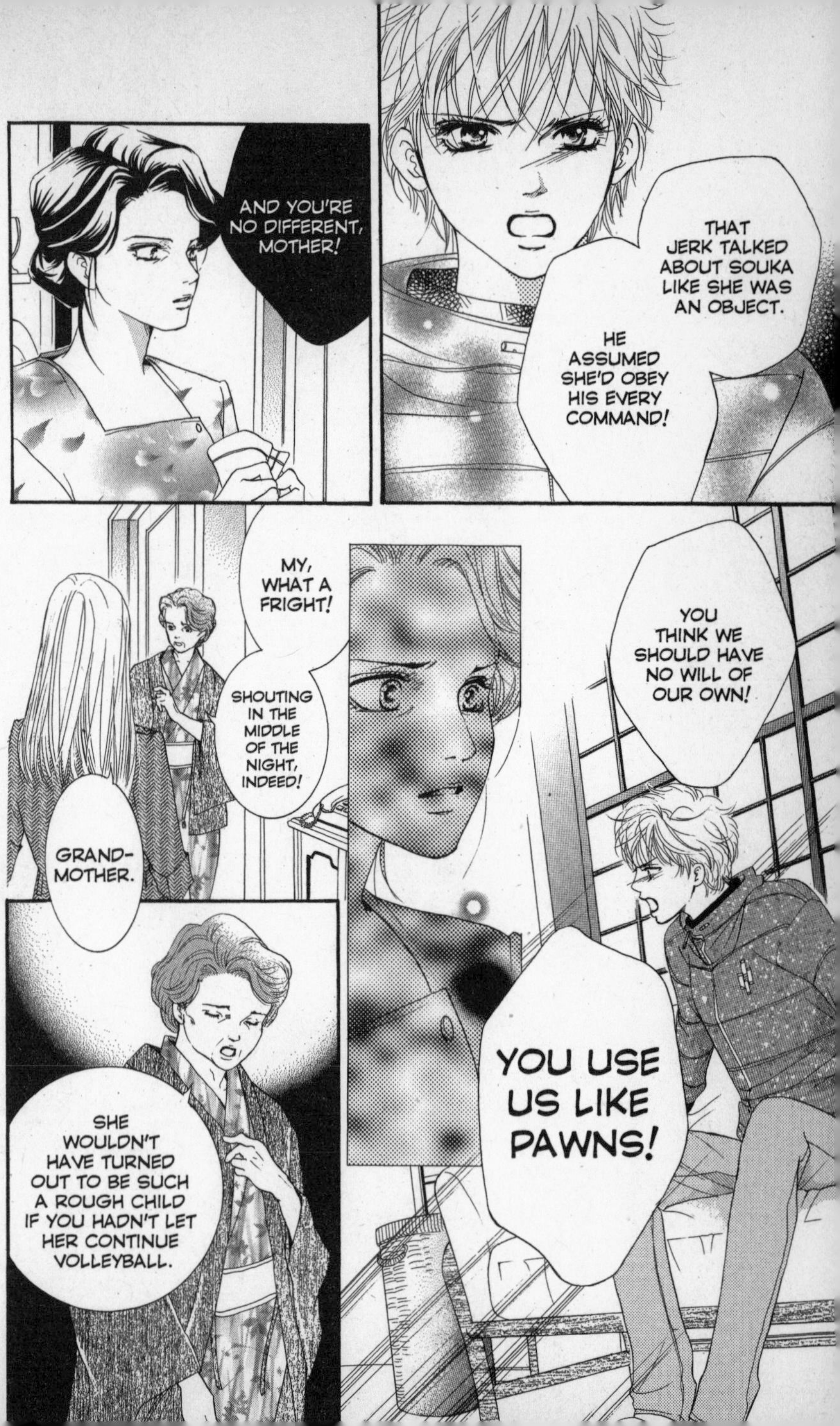
THAT JERK TALKED ABOUT SOUKA LIKE SHE WAS AN OBJECT.
HE ASSUMED SHE'D OBEY HIS EVERY COMMAND!
AND YOU'RE NO DIFFERENT, MOTHER!
YOU THINK WE SHOULD HAVE NO WILL OF OUR OWN!
YOU USE US LIKE PAWNS!
MY, WHAT A FRIGHT!
SHOUTING IN THE MIDDLE OF THE NIGHT, INDEED!
GRAND-MOTHER.
SHE WOULDN'T HAVE TURNED OUT TO BE SUCH A ROUGH CHILD IF YOU HADN'T LET HER CONTINUE VOLLEYBALL.

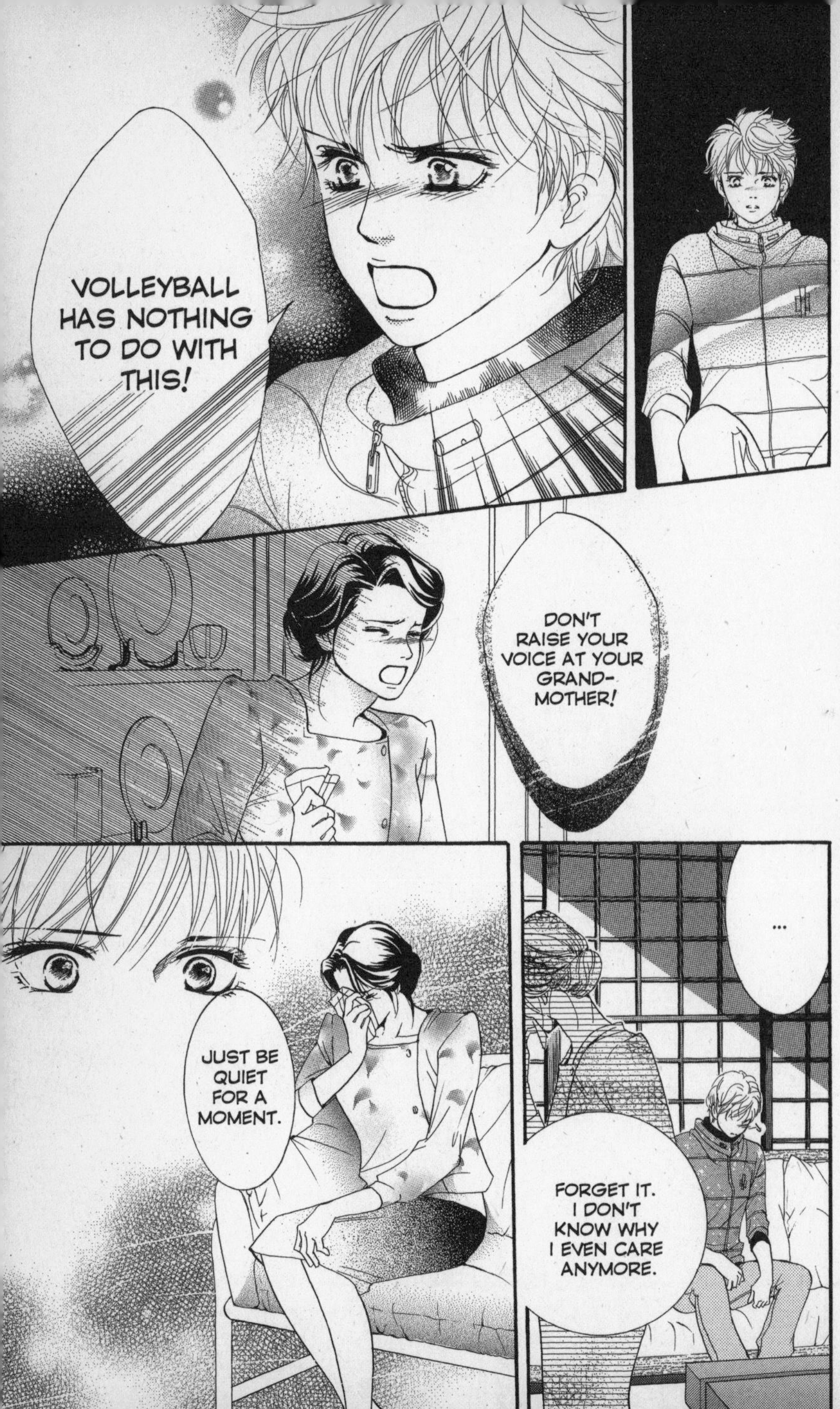
VOLLEYBALL HAS NOTHING TO DO WITH THIS!
DON'T RAISE YOUR VOICE AT YOUR GRAND-MOTHER!
...
FORGET IT. I DON'T KNOW WHY I EVEN CARE ANYMORE.
JUST BE QUIET FOR A MOMENT.

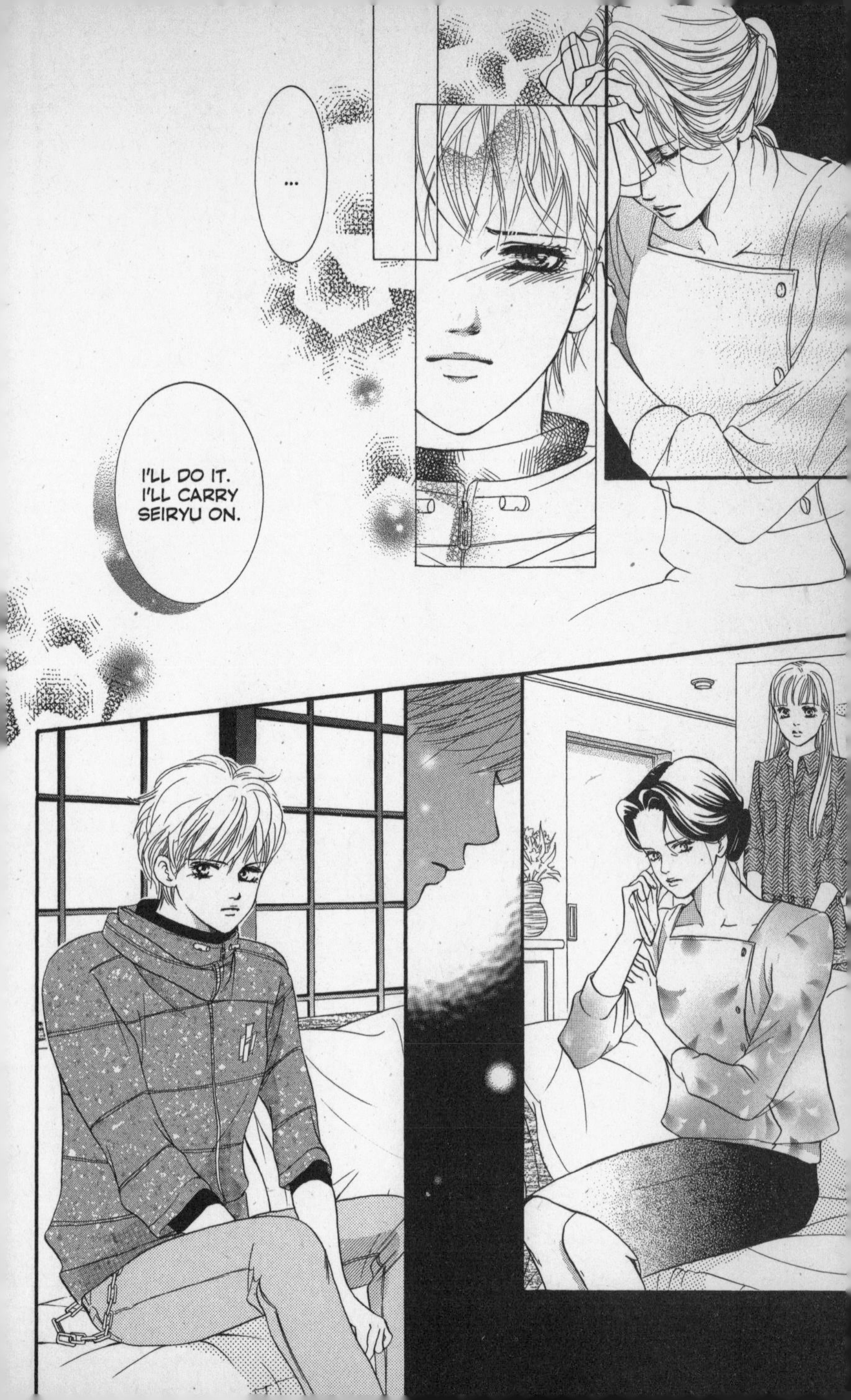
...
I'LL DO IT. I'LL CARRY SEIRYU ON.

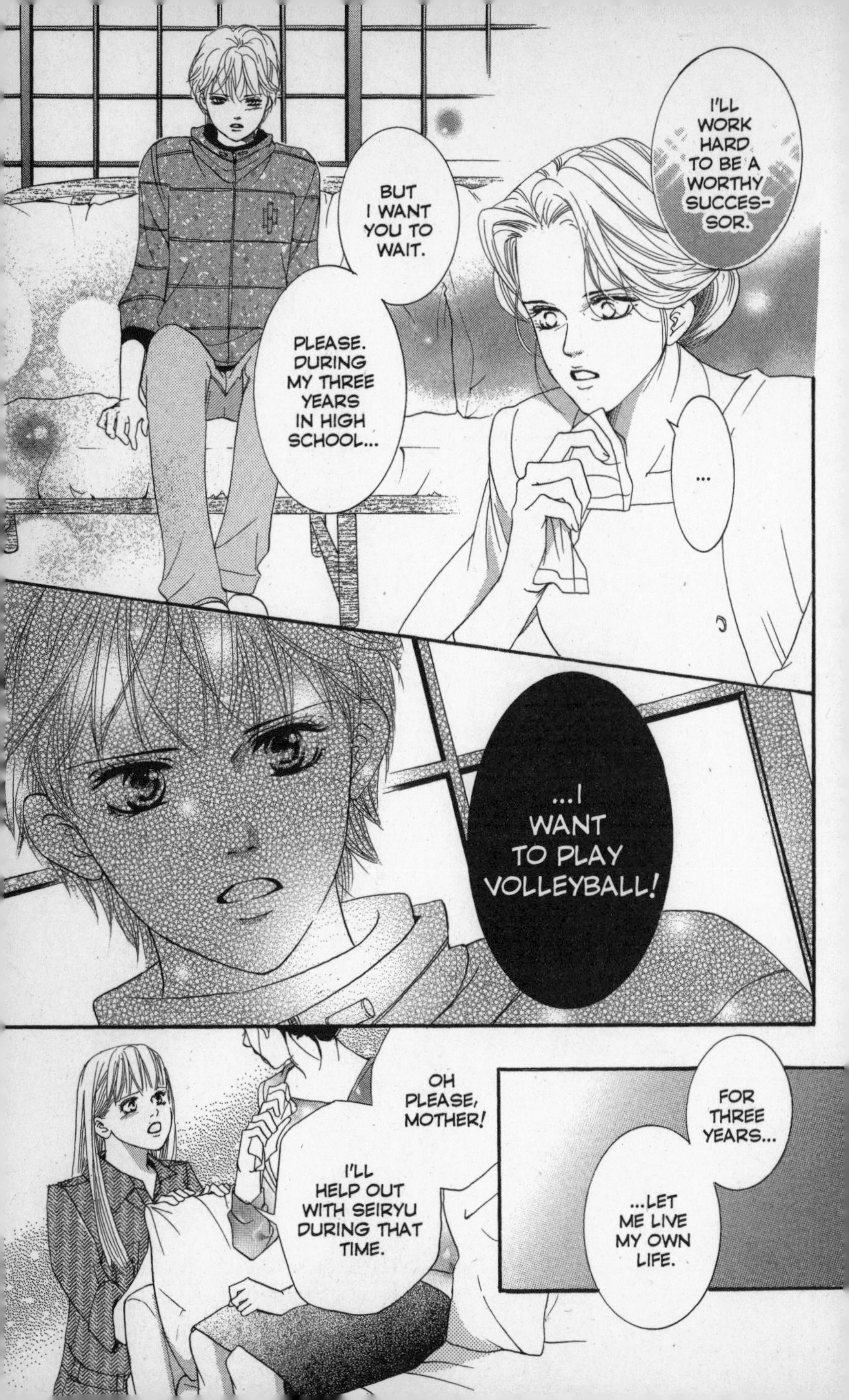
I'LL WORK HARD TO BE A WORTHY SUCCES-SOR.
BUT I WANT YOU TO WAIT.
PLEASE. DURING MY THREE YEARS IN HIGH SCHOOL...
...
...I WANT TO PLAY VOLLEYBALL!
FOR THREE YEARS...
...LET ME LIVE MY OWN LIFE.
OH PLEASE, MOTHER!
I'LL HELP OUT WITH SEIRYU DURING THAT TIME.

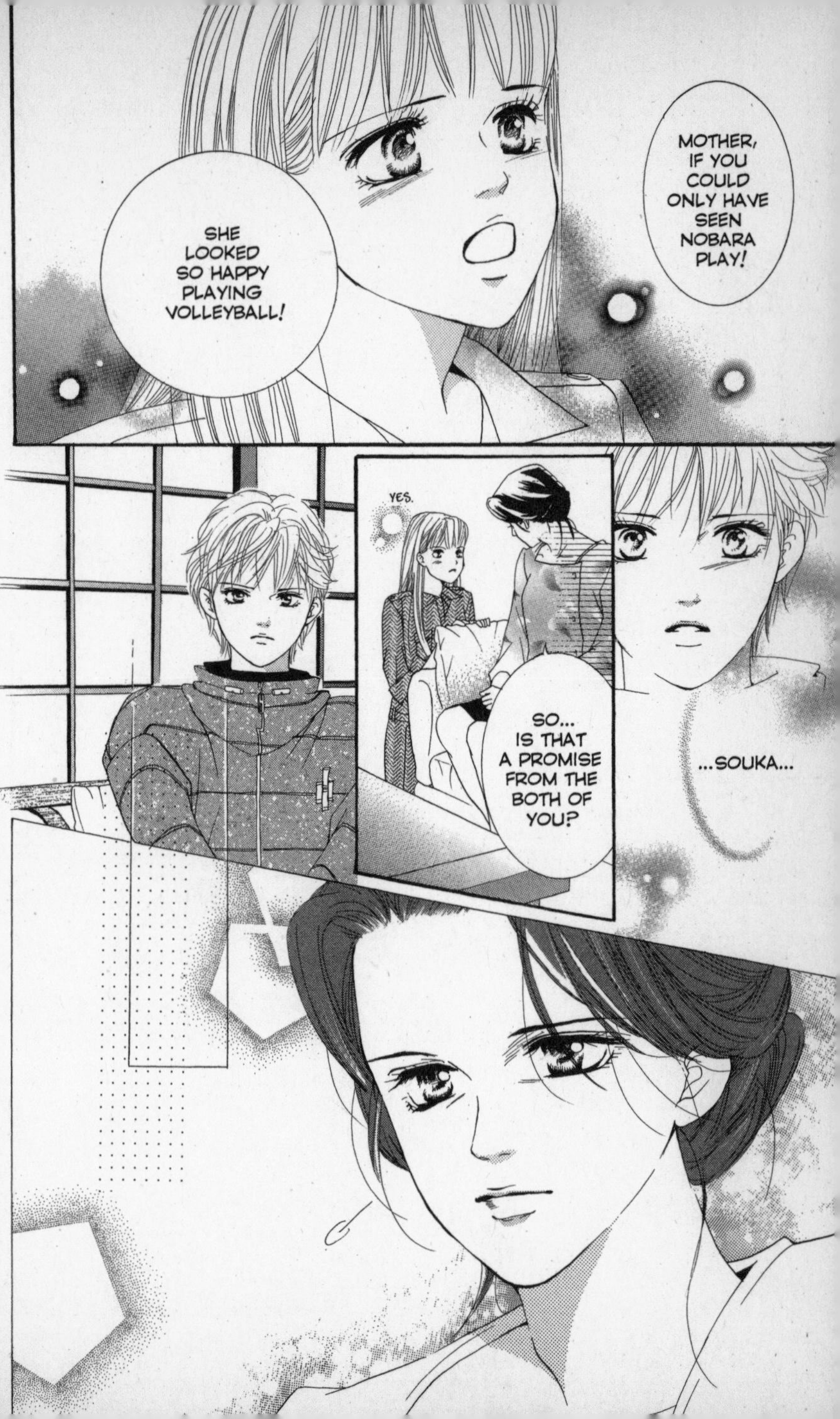
MOTHER, IF YOU COULD ONLY HAVE SEEN NOBARA PLAY!
SHE LOOKED SO HAPPY PLAYING VOLLEYBALL!
...SOUKA...
SO... IS THAT A PROMISE FROM THE BOTH OF YOU?
YES.

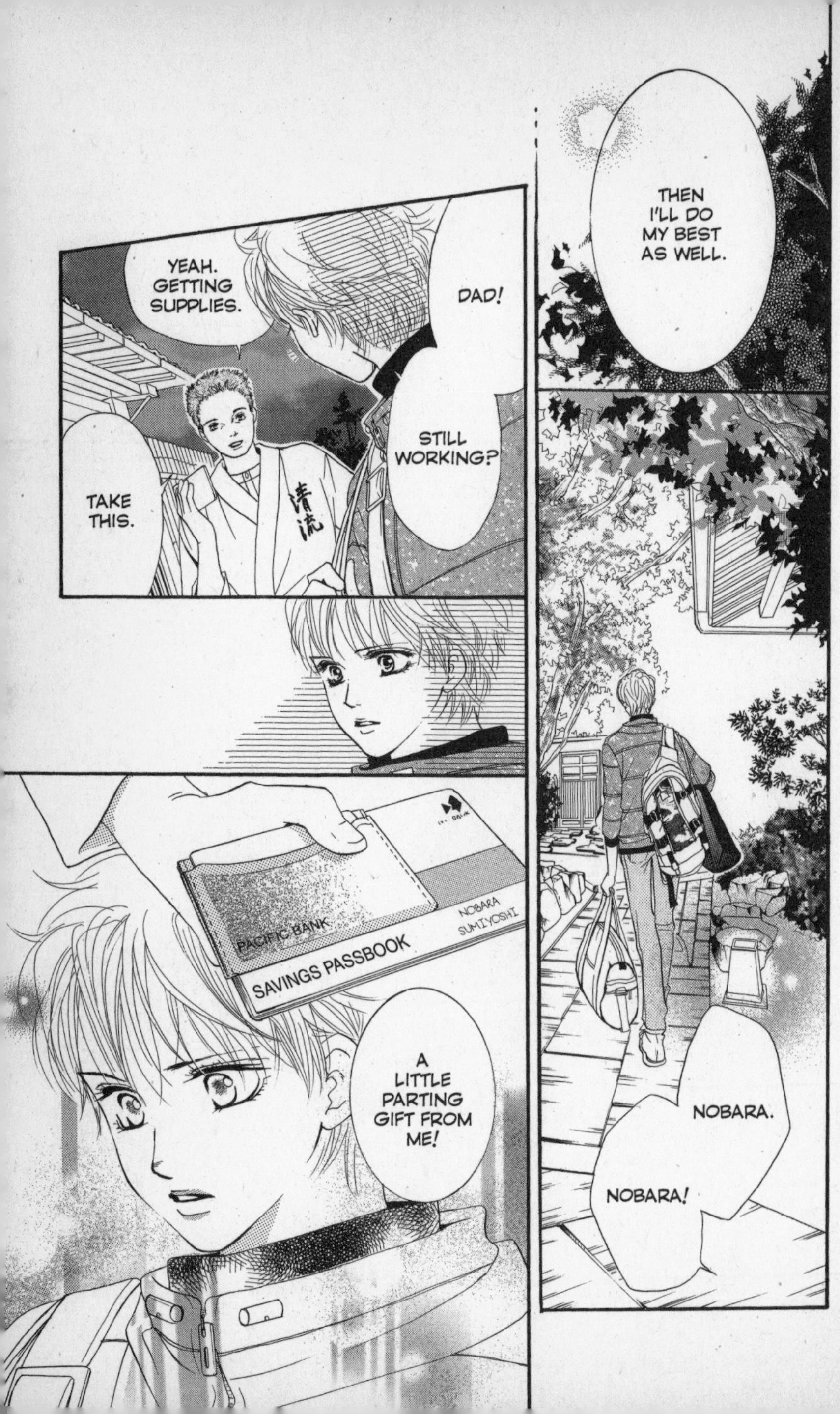
THEN I'LL DO MY BEST AS WELL.
NOBARA.
NOBARA!
DAD!
STILL WORKING?
YEAH. GETTING SUPPLIES.
TAKE THIS.
PACIFIC BANK
SAVINGS PASSBOOK
NOBARA SUMIYOSHI
A LITTLE PARTING GIFT FROM ME!

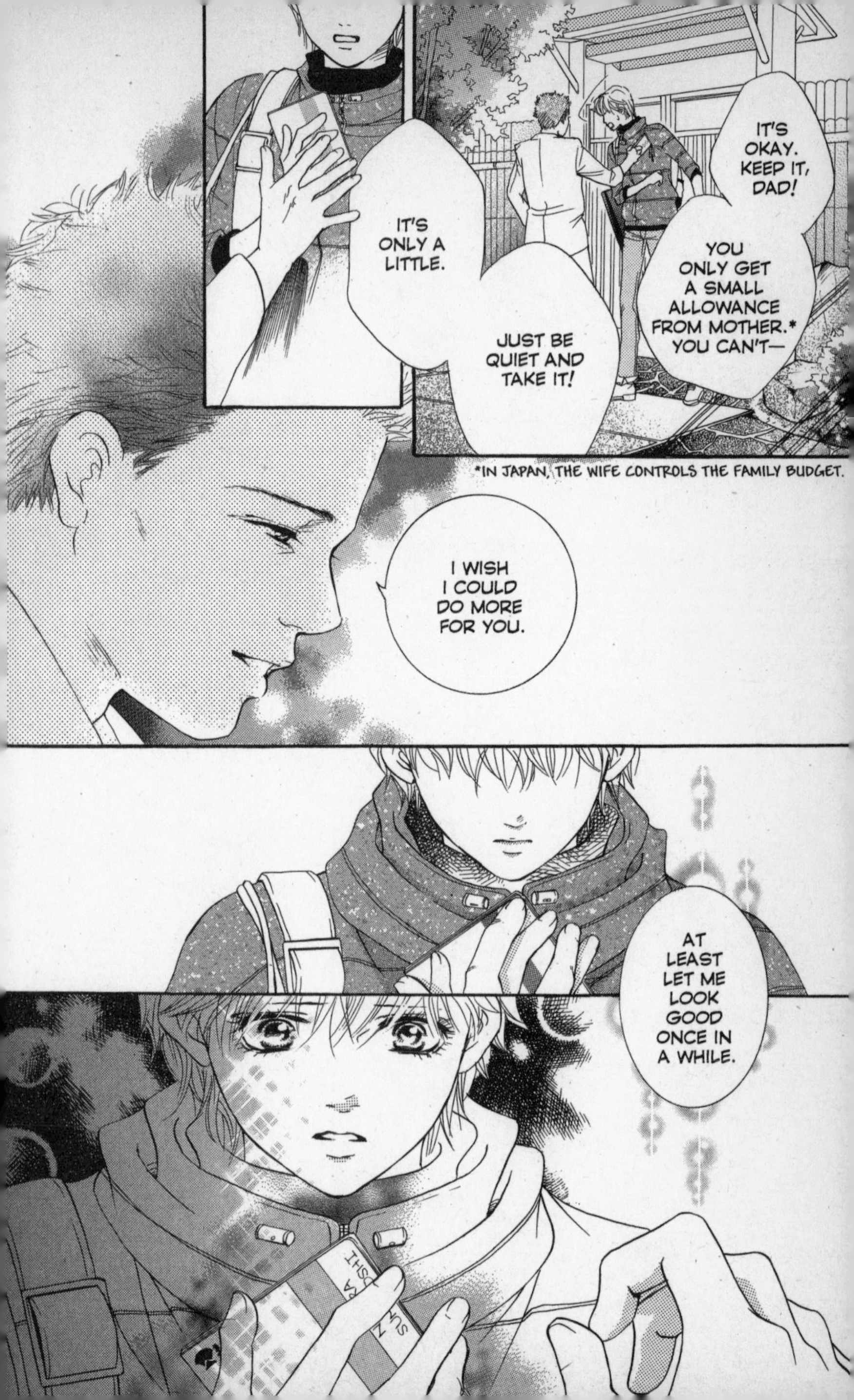
IT'S OKAY. KEEP IT, DAD!
YOU ONLY GET A SMALL ALLOWANCE FROM MOTHER.* YOU CAN'T—
IT'S ONLY A LITTLE.
JUST BE QUIET AND TAKE IT!
*IN JAPAN, THE WIFE CONTROLS THE FAMILY BUDGET.
I WISH I COULD DO MORE FOR YOU.
AT LEAST LET ME LOOK GOOD ONCE IN A WHILE.

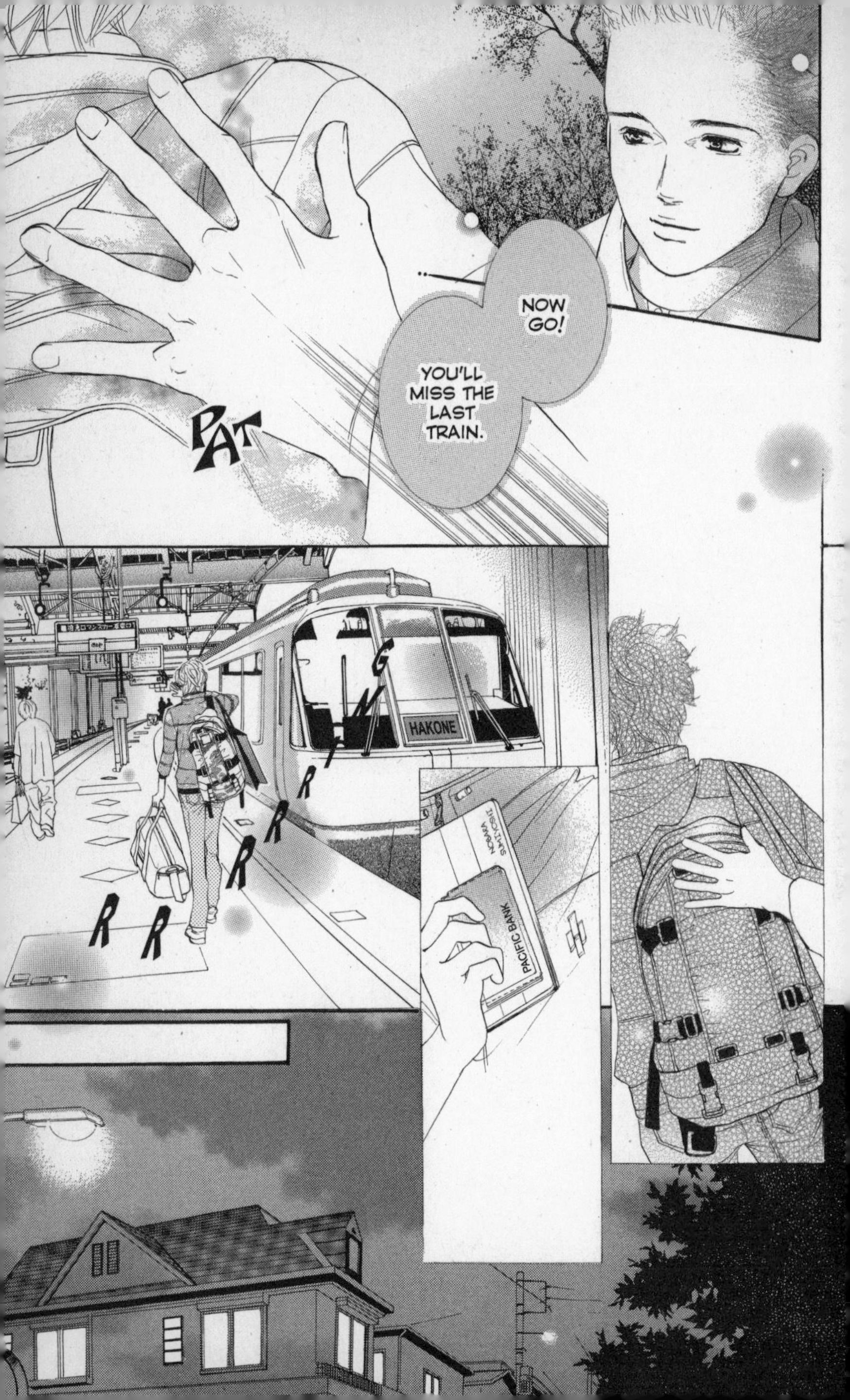
NOW GO!
YOU'LL MISS THE LAST TRAIN.
PAT
HAKONE
GRRRRRRR
NOBARA SUMIYOSHI
PACIFIC BANK

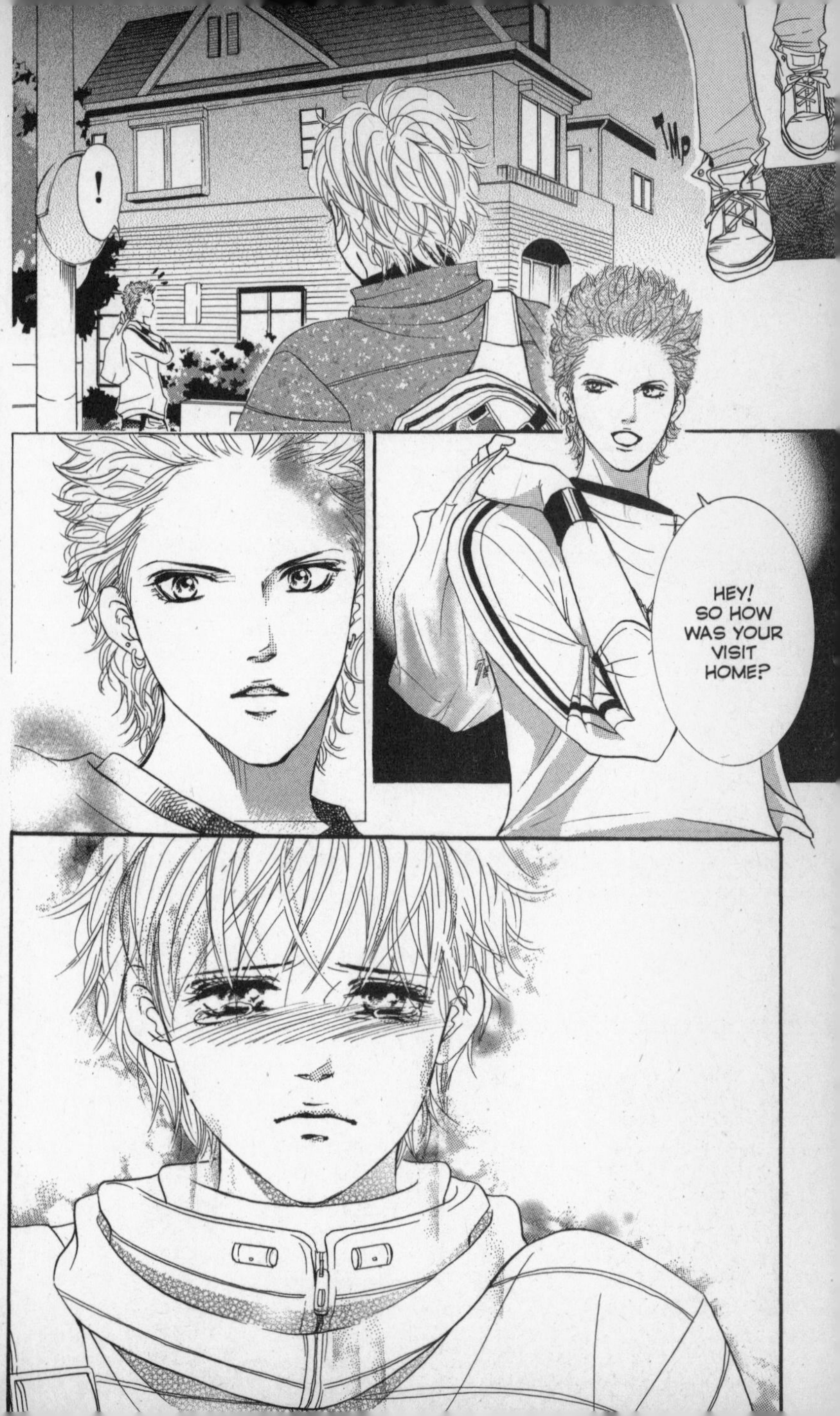
TMP
!
HEY! SO HOW WAS YOUR VISIT HOME?

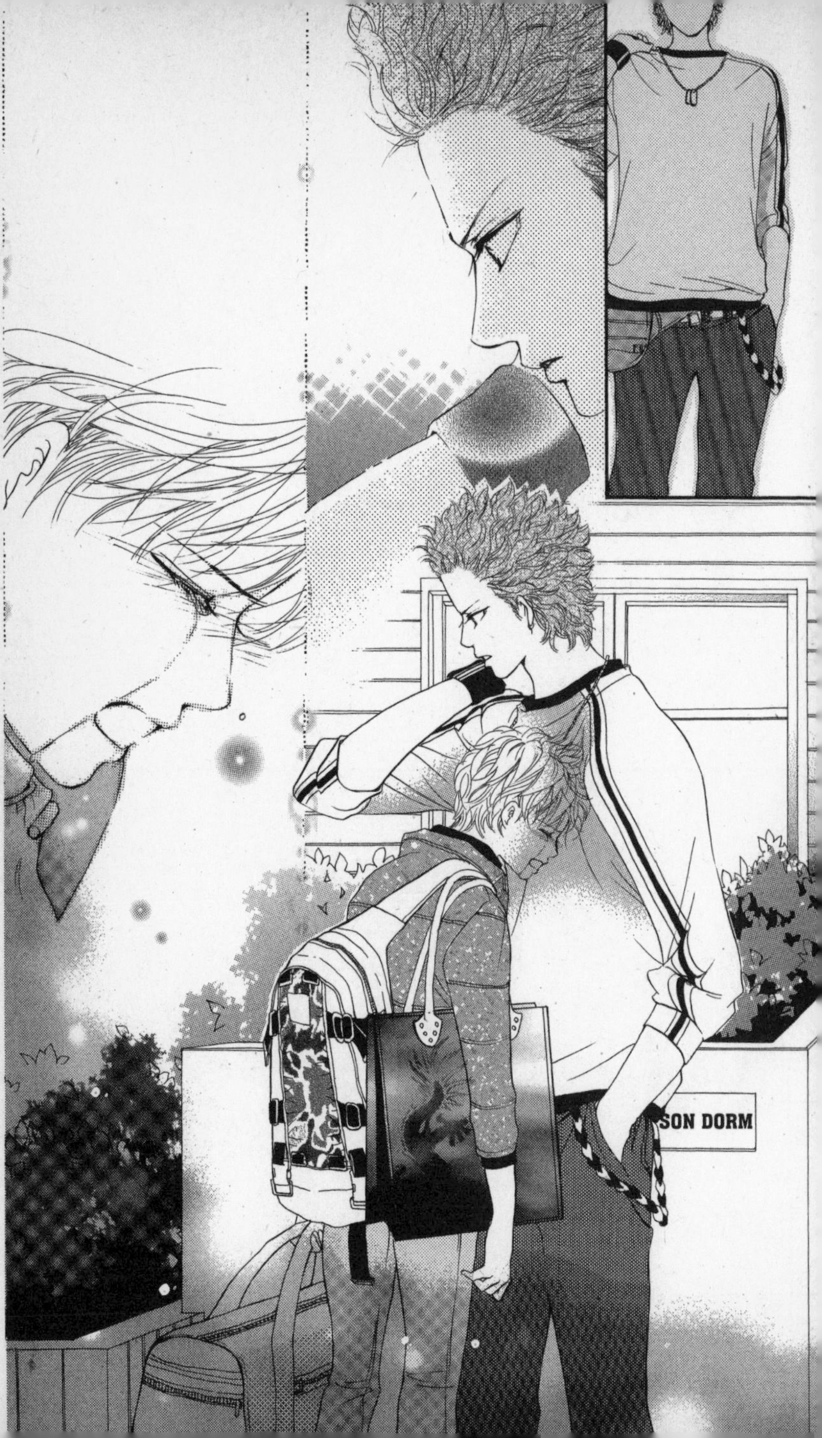
SON DORM

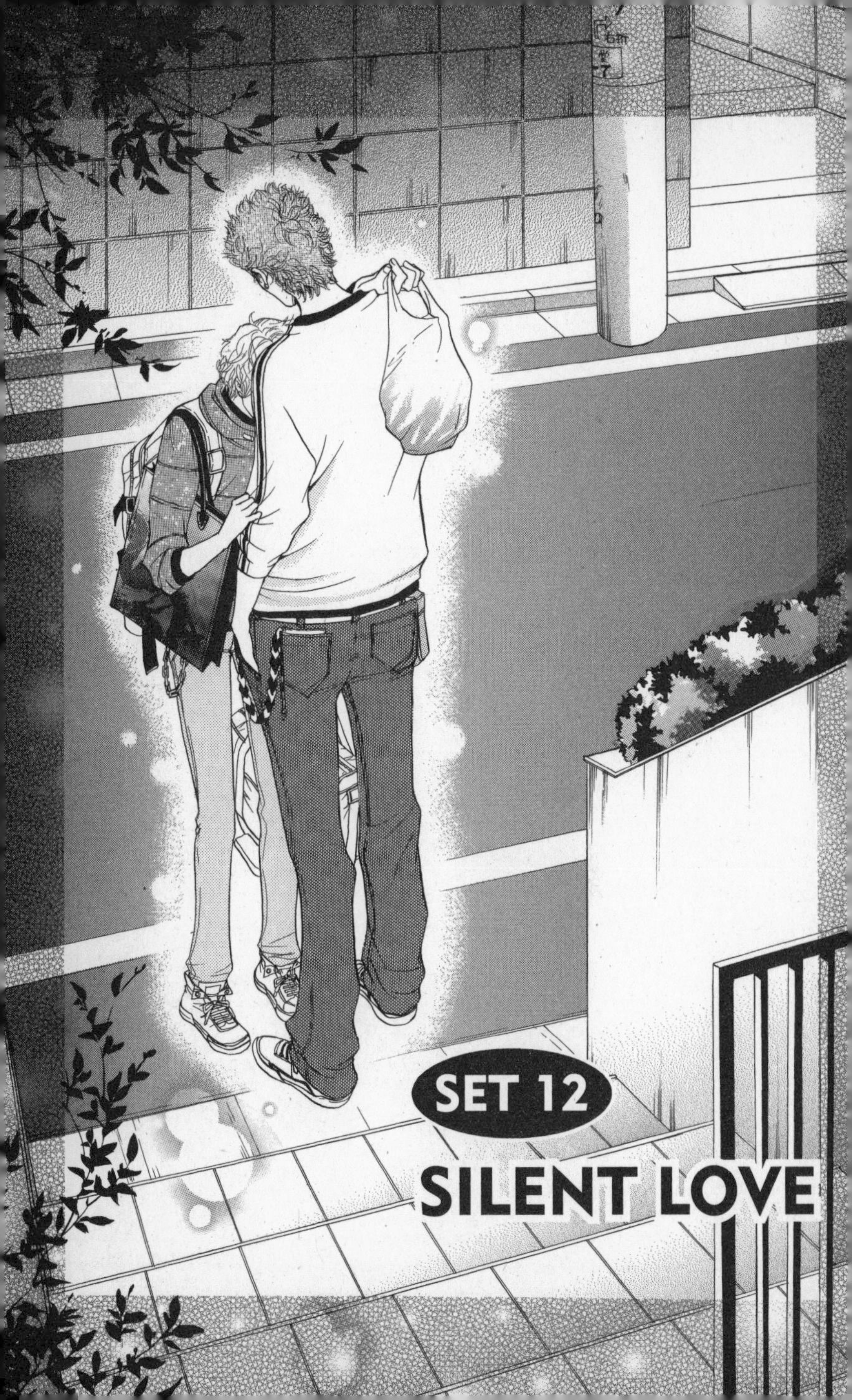
SET 12
SILENT LOVE

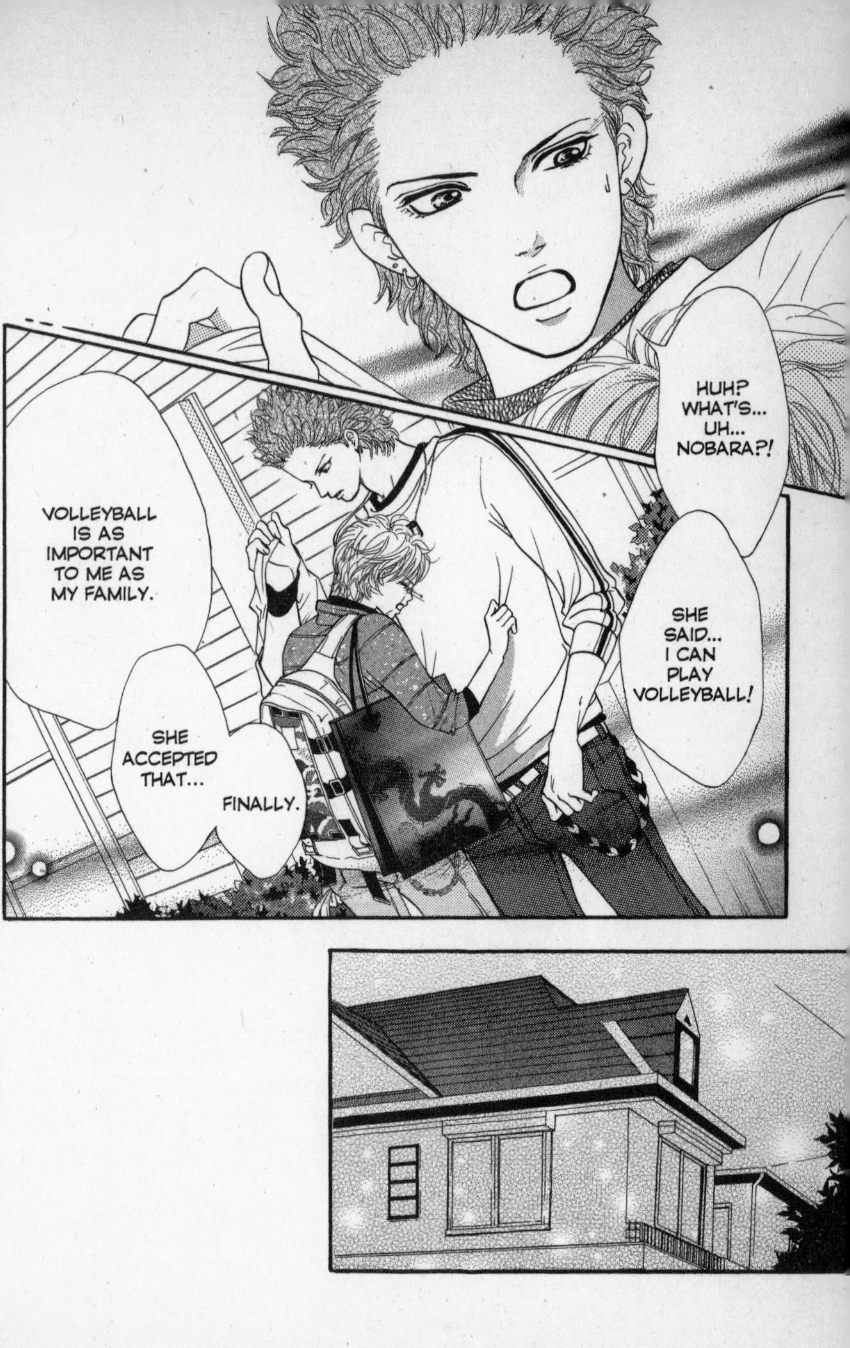
HUH? WHAT'S... UH... NOBARA?!
SHE SAID... I CAN PLAY VOLLEYBALL!
VOLLEYBALL IS AS IMPORTANT TO ME AS MY FAMILY.
SHE ACCEPTED THAT...
FINALLY.

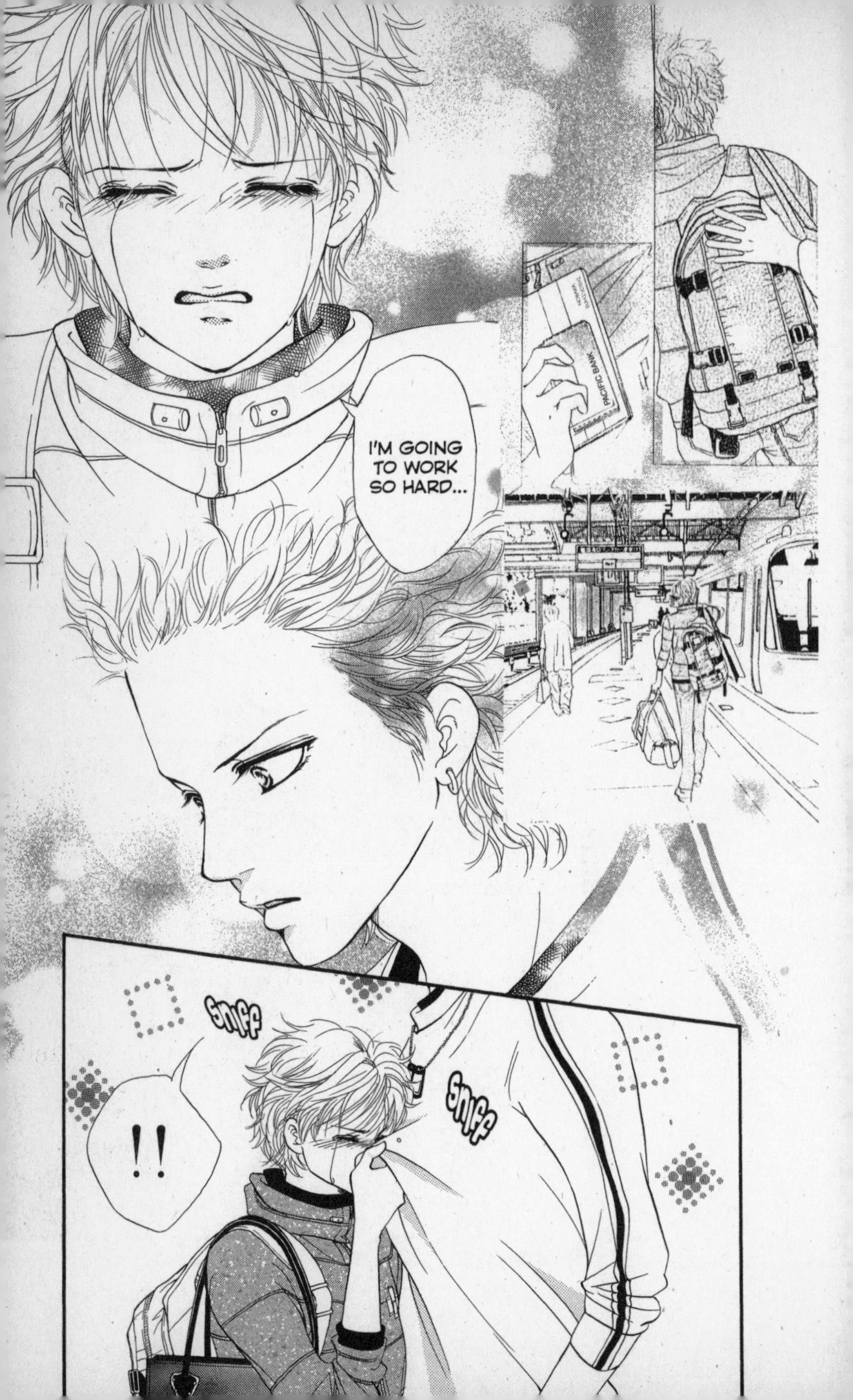
I'M GOING TO WORK SO HARD...
SNIFF
SNIFF
!!

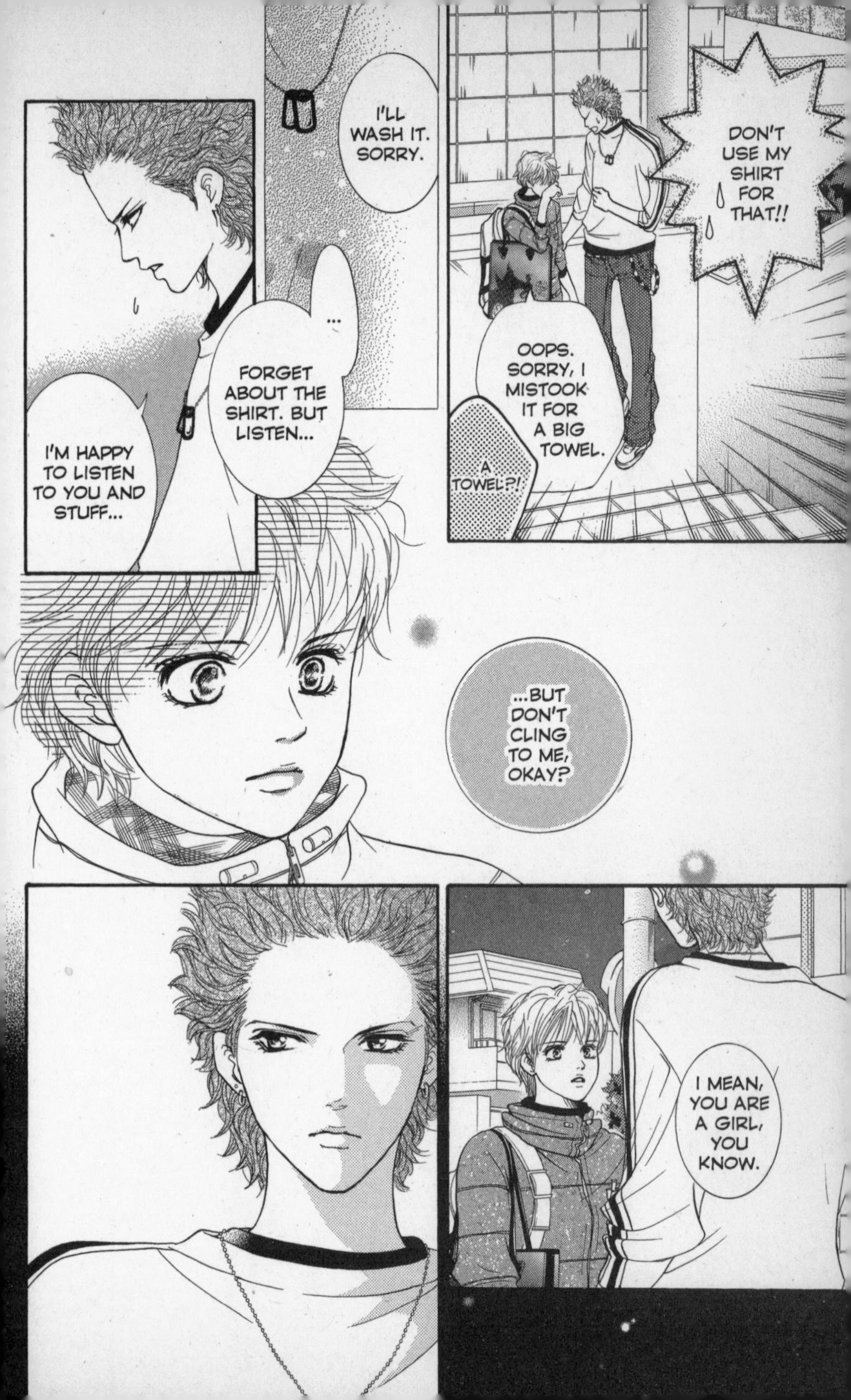
DON'T USE MY SHIRT FOR THAT!!
OOPS. SORRY, I MISTOOK IT FOR A BIG TOWEL.
A TOWEL?!
I'LL WASH IT. SORRY.
...
FORGET ABOUT THE SHIRT. BUT LISTEN...
I'M HAPPY TO LISTEN TO YOU AND STUFF...
...BUT DON'T CLING TO ME, OKAY?
I MEAN, YOU ARE A GIRL, YOU KNOW.

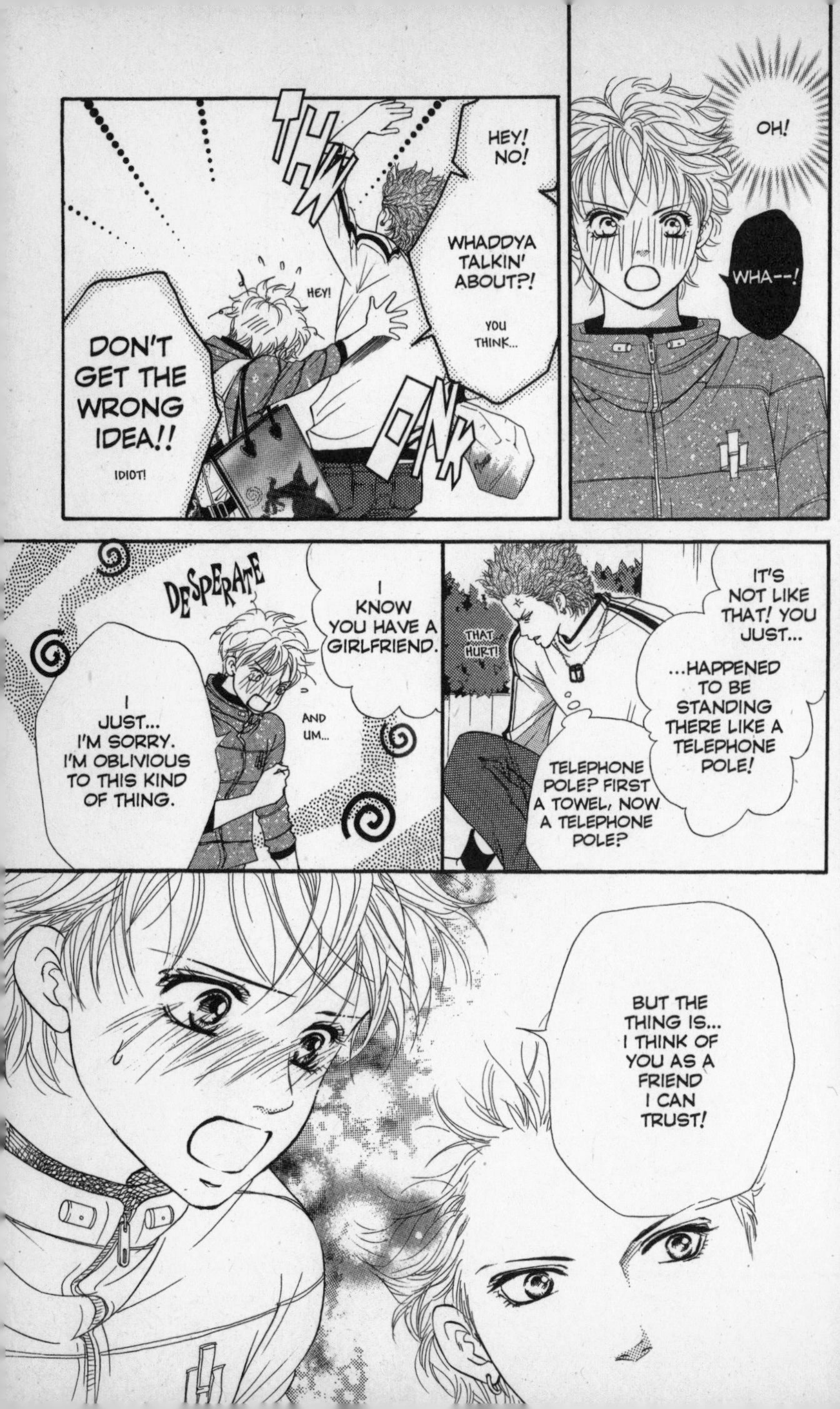
OH!
WHA--!
HEY! NO!
WHADDYA TALKIN' ABOUT?!
YOU THINK...
HEY!
DON'T GET THE WRONG IDEA!!
IDIOT!
IT'S NOT LIKE THAT! YOU JUST...
...HAPPENED TO BE STANDING THERE LIKE A TELEPHONE POLE!
THAT HURT!
TELEPHONE POLE? FIRST A TOWEL, NOW A TELEPHONE POLE?
I KNOW YOU HAVE A GIRLFRIEND.
DESPERATE
AND UM...
I JUST... I'M SORRY. I'M OBLIVIOUS TO THIS KIND OF THING.
BUT THE THING IS... I THINK OF YOU AS A FRIEND I CAN TRUST!

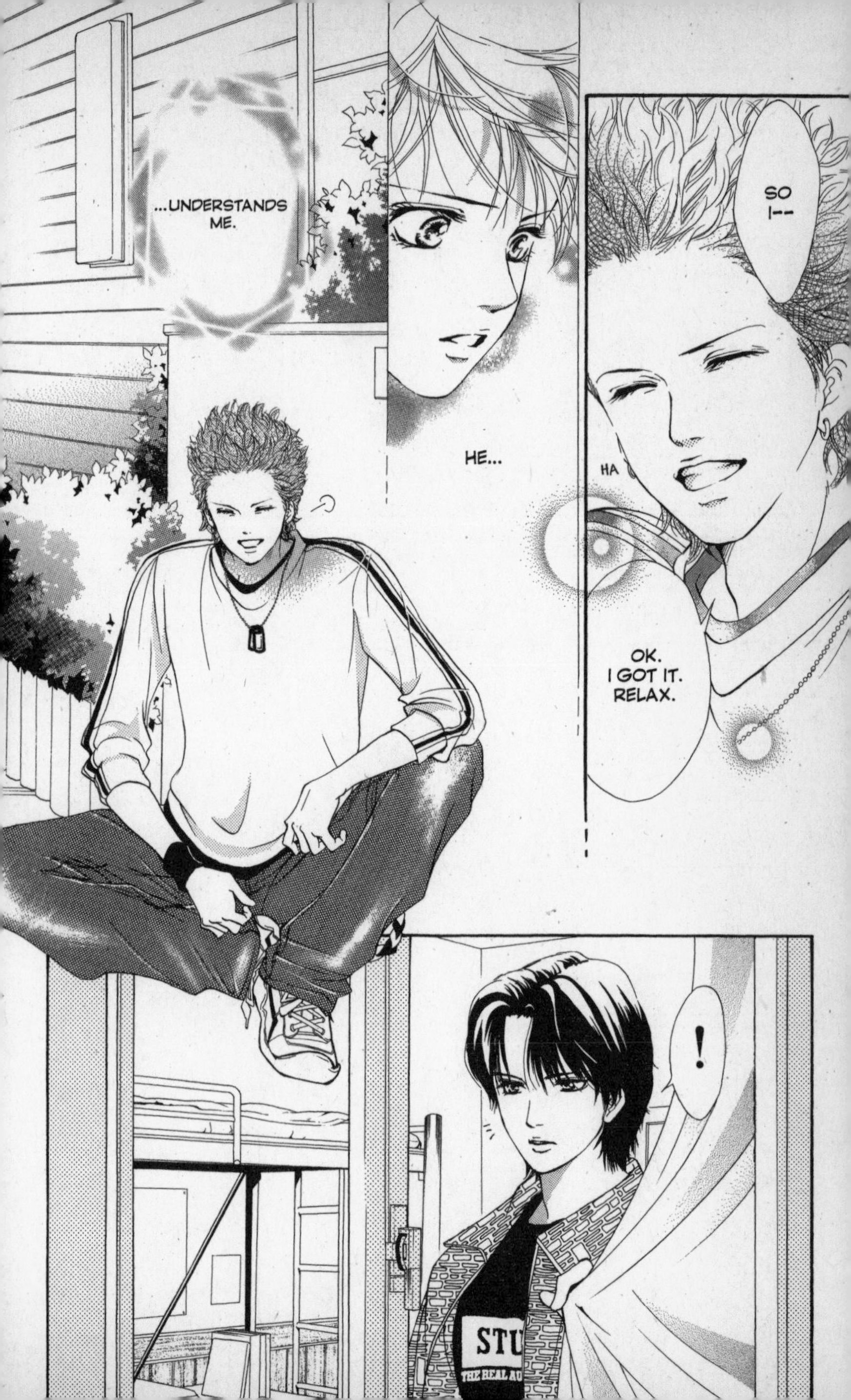
SO I--
HA
OK. I GOT IT. RELAX.
HE...
...UNDERSTANDS ME.
!

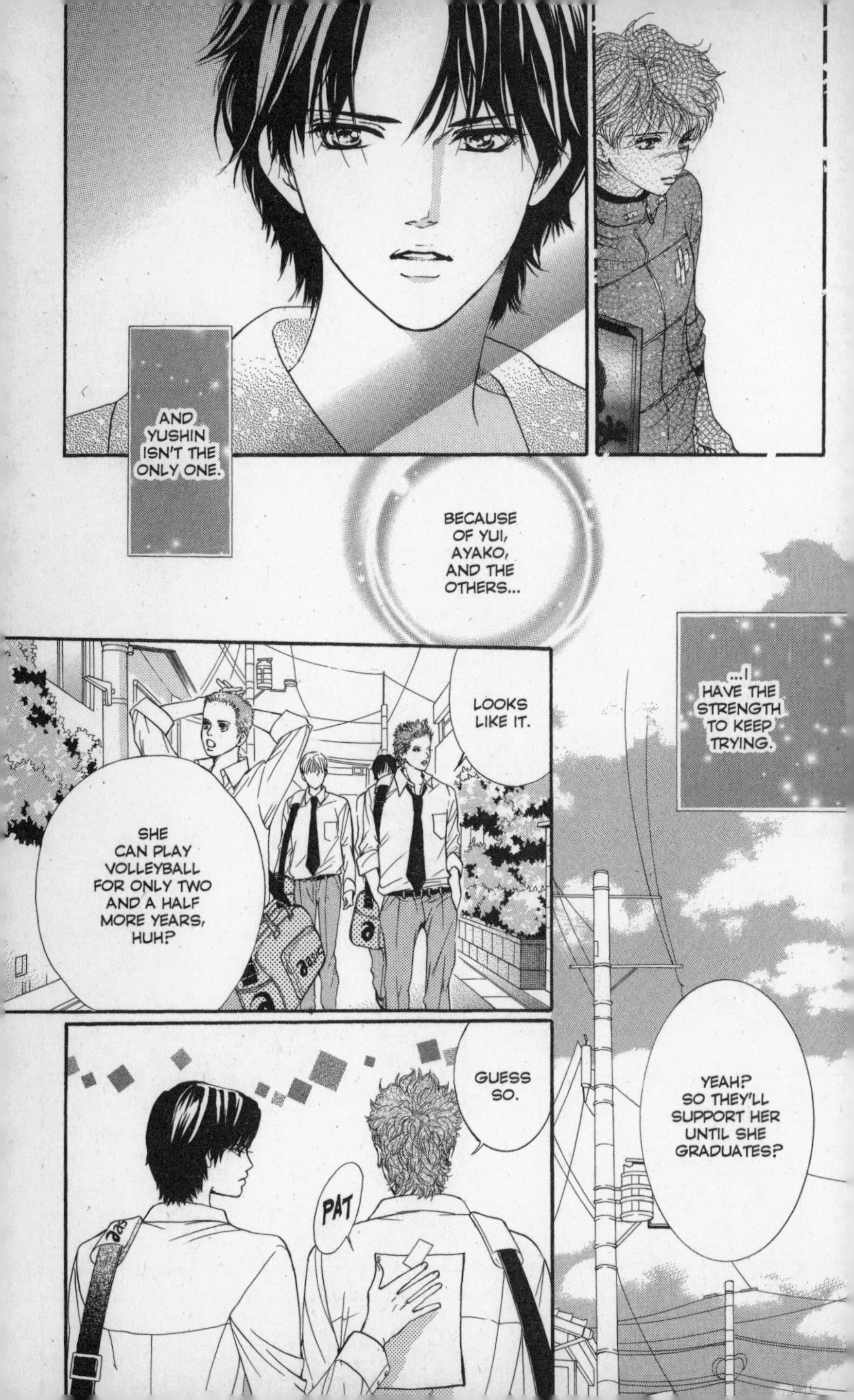
AND YUSHIN ISN'T THE ONLY ONE.
BECAUSE OF YUI, AYAKO, AND THE OTHERS...
...I HAVE THE STRENGTH TO KEEP TRYING.
SHE CAN PLAY VOLLEYBALL FOR ONLY TWO AND A HALF MORE YEARS, HUH?
LOOKS LIKE IT.
YEAH? SO THEY'LL SUPPORT HER UNTIL SHE GRADUATES?
GUESS SO.
PAT

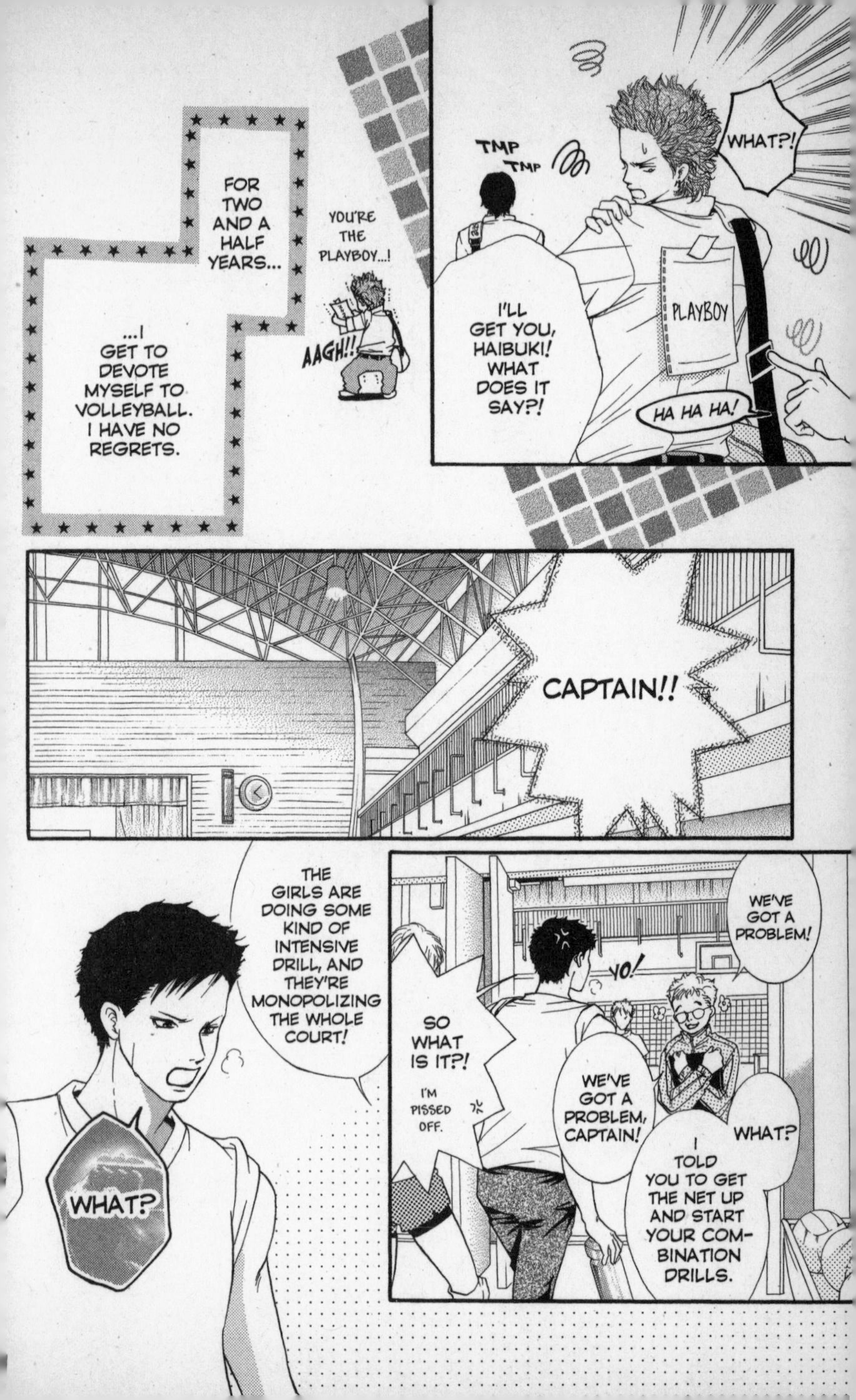
WHAT?!
TMP
TMP
I'LL GET YOU, HAIBUKI! WHAT DOES IT SAY?!
PLAYBOY
HA HA HA!
YOU'RE THE PLAYBOY...!
AAGH!!
FOR TWO AND A HALF YEARS...
...I GET TO DEVOTE MYSELF TO VOLLEYBALL. I HAVE NO REGRETS.
CAPTAIN!!
WE'VE GOT A PROBLEM!
YO!
WHAT?
I TOLD YOU TO GET THE NET UP AND START YOUR COM-BINATION DRILLS.
WE'VE GOT A PROBLEM, CAPTAIN!
SO WHAT IS IT?!
I'M PISSED OFF.
THE GIRLS ARE DOING SOME KIND OF INTENSIVE DRILL, AND THEY'RE MONOPOLIZING THE WHOLE COURT!
WHAT?

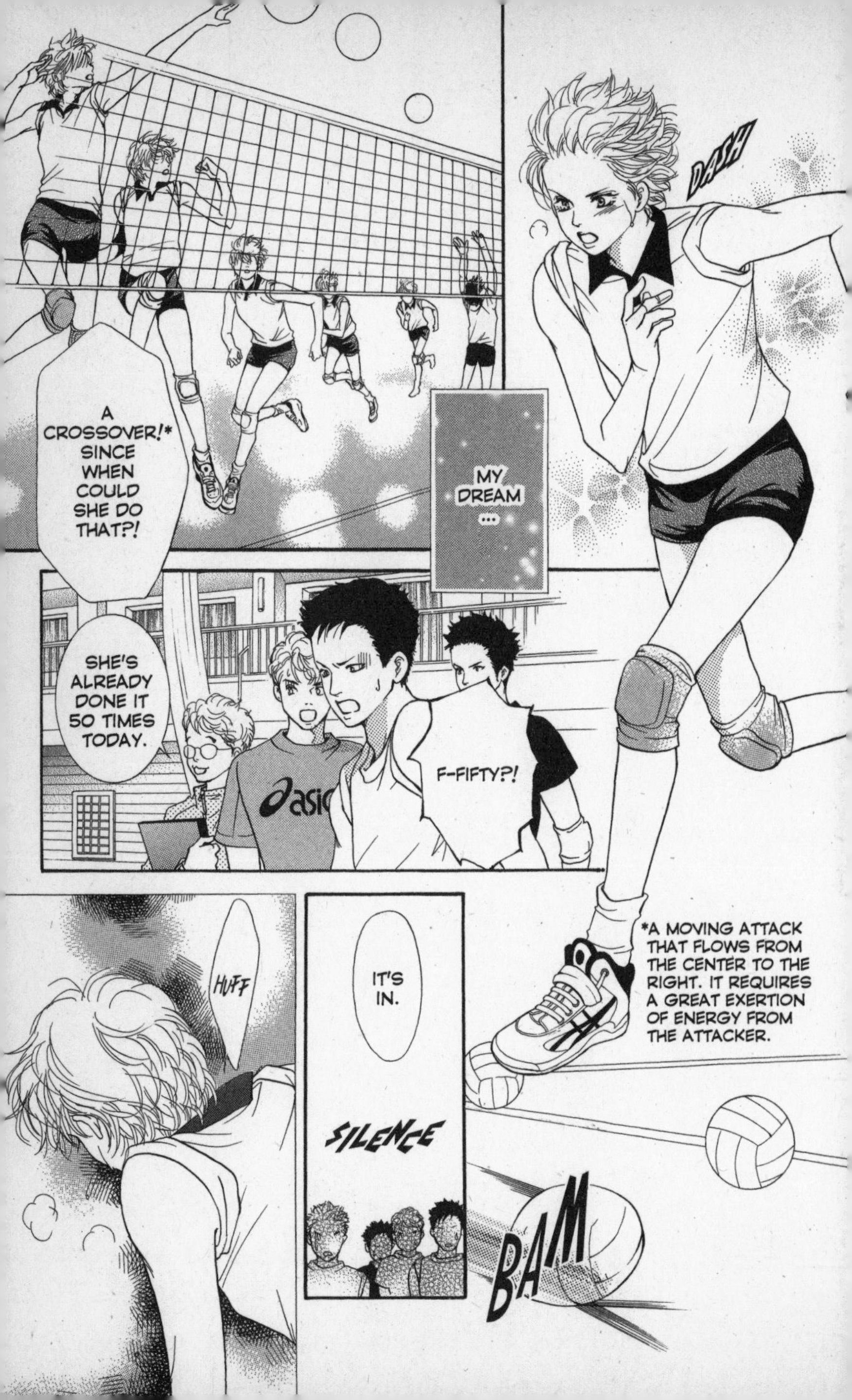
DASH
MY DREAM ...
A CROSSOVER!* SINCE WHEN COULD SHE DO THAT?!
SHE'S ALREADY DONE IT 50 TIMES TODAY.
F-FIFTY?!
BAM
IT'S IN.
SILENCE
HUFF
*A MOVING ATTACK THAT FLOWS FROM THE CENTER TO THE RIGHT. IT REQUIRES A GREAT EXERTION OF ENERGY FROM THE ATTACKER.

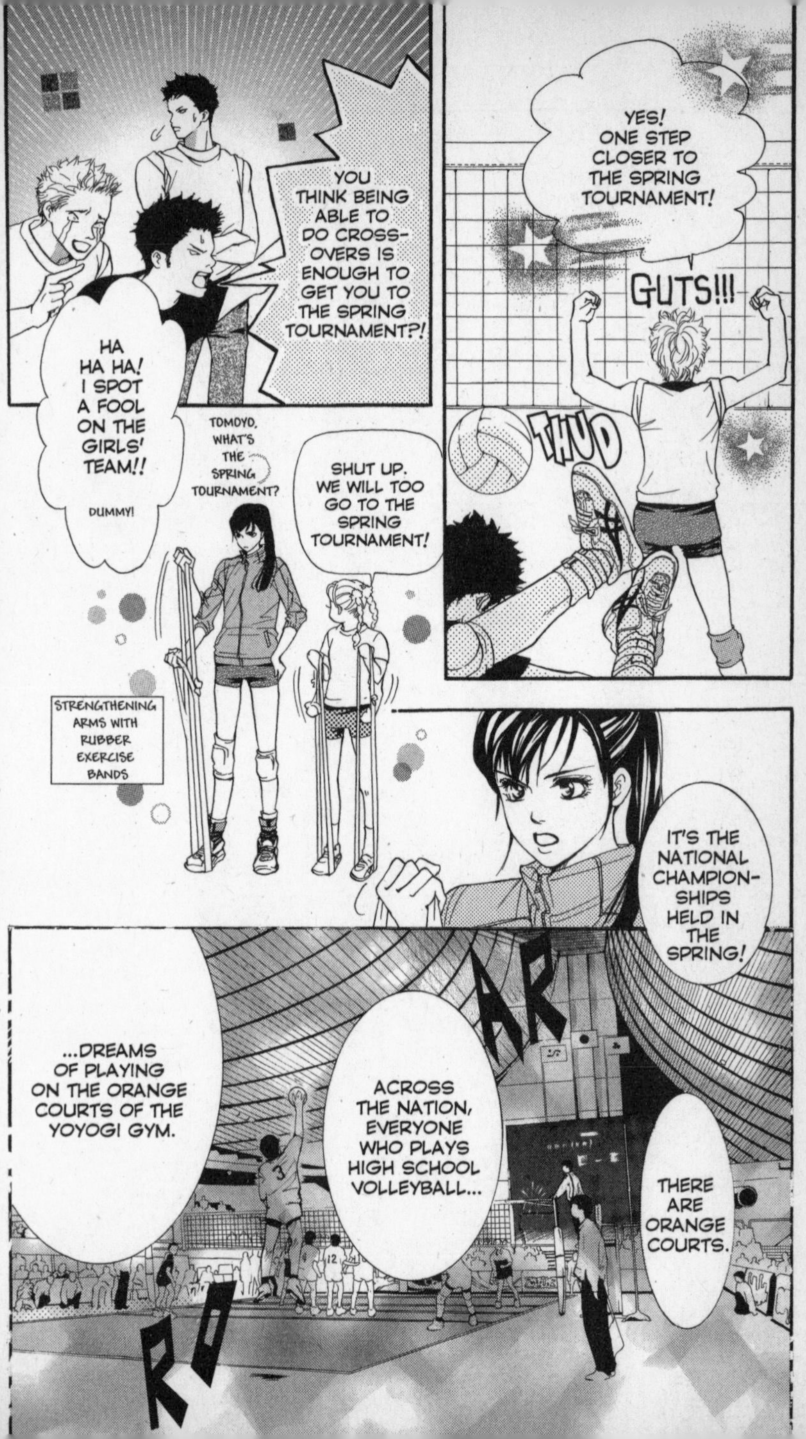
YES! ONE STEP CLOSER TO THE SPRING TOURNAMENT!
GUTS!!!
THUD
YOU THINK BEING ABLE TO DO CROSS-OVERS IS ENOUGH TO GET YOU TO THE SPRING TOURNAMENT?!
HA HA HA! I SPOT A FOOL ON THE GIRLS' TEAM!!
DUMMY!
SHUT UP. WE WILL TOO GO TO THE SPRING TOURNAMENT!
TOMOYO, WHAT'S THE SPRING TOURNAMENT?
STRENGTHENING ARMS WITH RUBBER EXERCISE BANDS
IT'S THE NATIONAL CHAMPION-SHIPS HELD IN THE SPRING!
THERE ARE ORANGE COURTS.
ACROSS THE NATION, EVERYONE WHO PLAYS HIGH SCHOOL VOLLEYBALL...
...DREAMS OF PLAYING ON THE ORANGE COURTS OF THE YOYOGI GYM.
ROAR

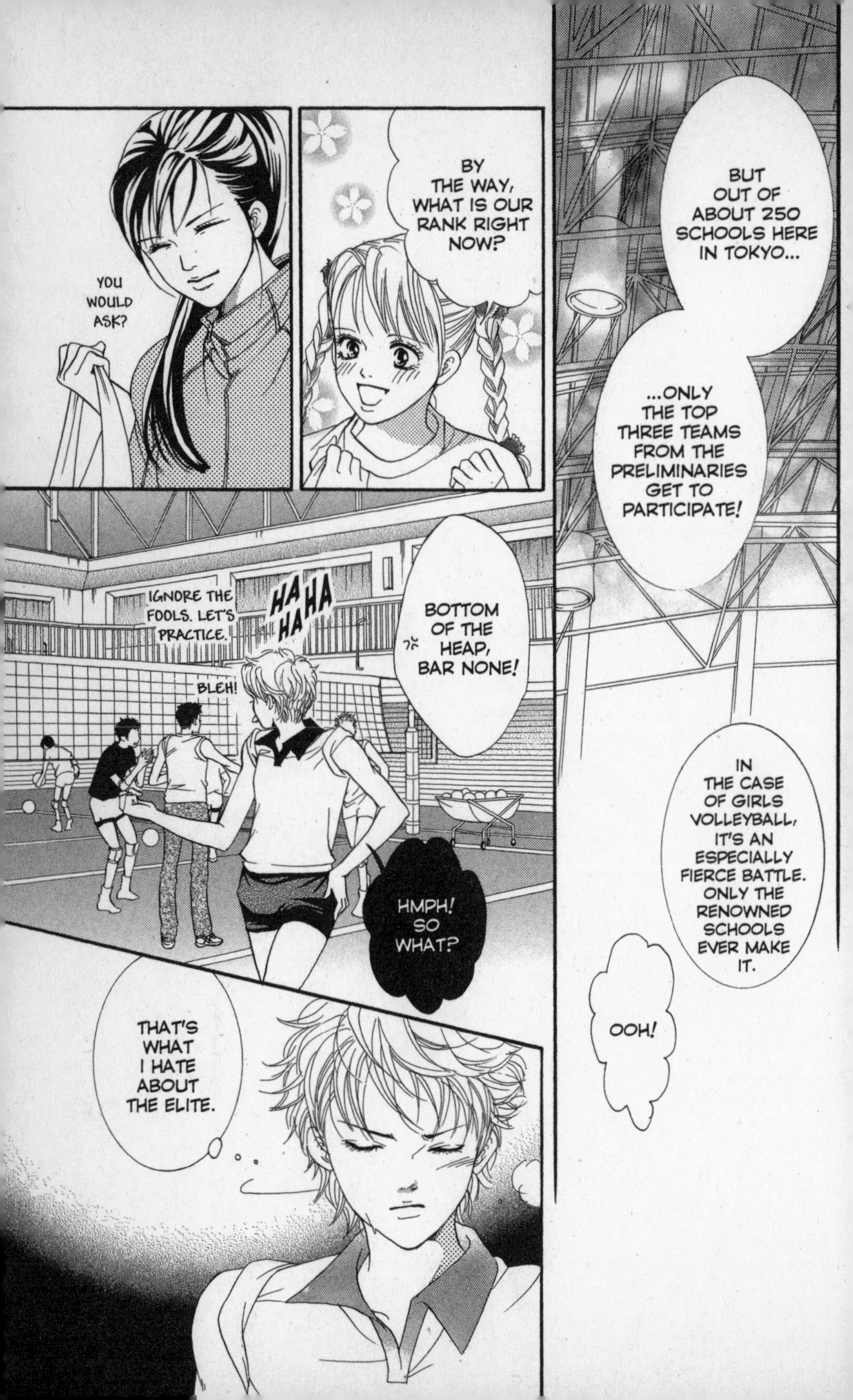
BUT OUT OF ABOUT 250 SCHOOLS HERE IN TOKYO...
...ONLY THE TOP THREE TEAMS FROM THE PRELIMINARIES GET TO PARTICIPATE!
IN THE CASE OF GIRLS VOLLEYBALL, IT'S AN ESPECIALLY FIERCE BATTLE. ONLY THE RENOWNED SCHOOLS EVER MAKE IT.
OOH!
BY THE WAY, WHAT IS OUR RANK RIGHT NOW?
YOU WOULD ASK?
BOTTOM OF THE HEAP, BAR NONE!
HA HA HA
IGNORE THE FOOLS. LET'S PRACTICE.
BLEH!
HMPH! SO WHAT?
THAT'S WHAT I HATE ABOUT THE ELITE.

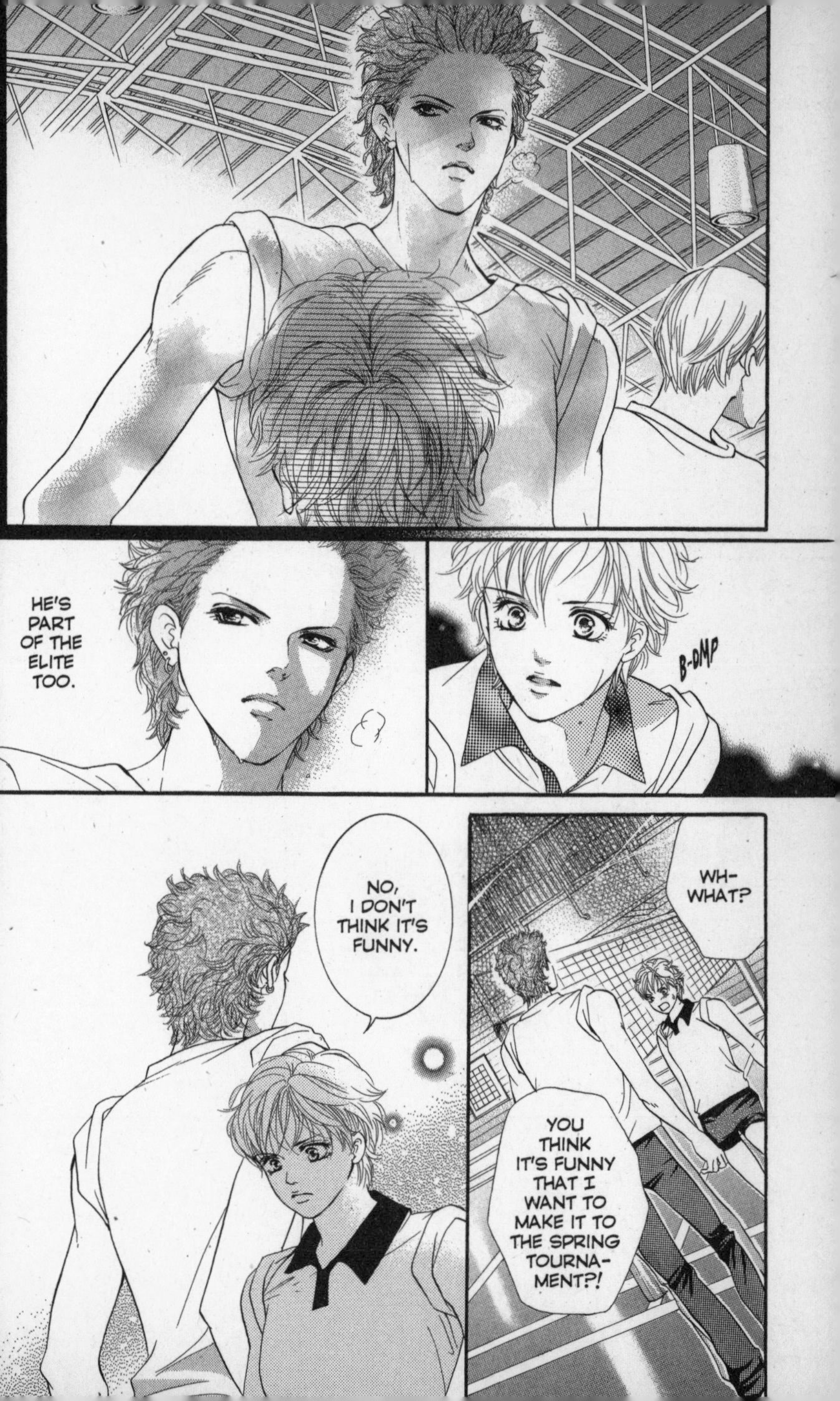
B-DMP
HE'S PART OF THE ELITE TOO.
WH- WHAT?
YOU THINK IT'S FUNNY THAT I WANT TO MAKE IT TO THE SPRING TOURNA-MENT?!
NO, I DON'T THINK IT'S FUNNY.

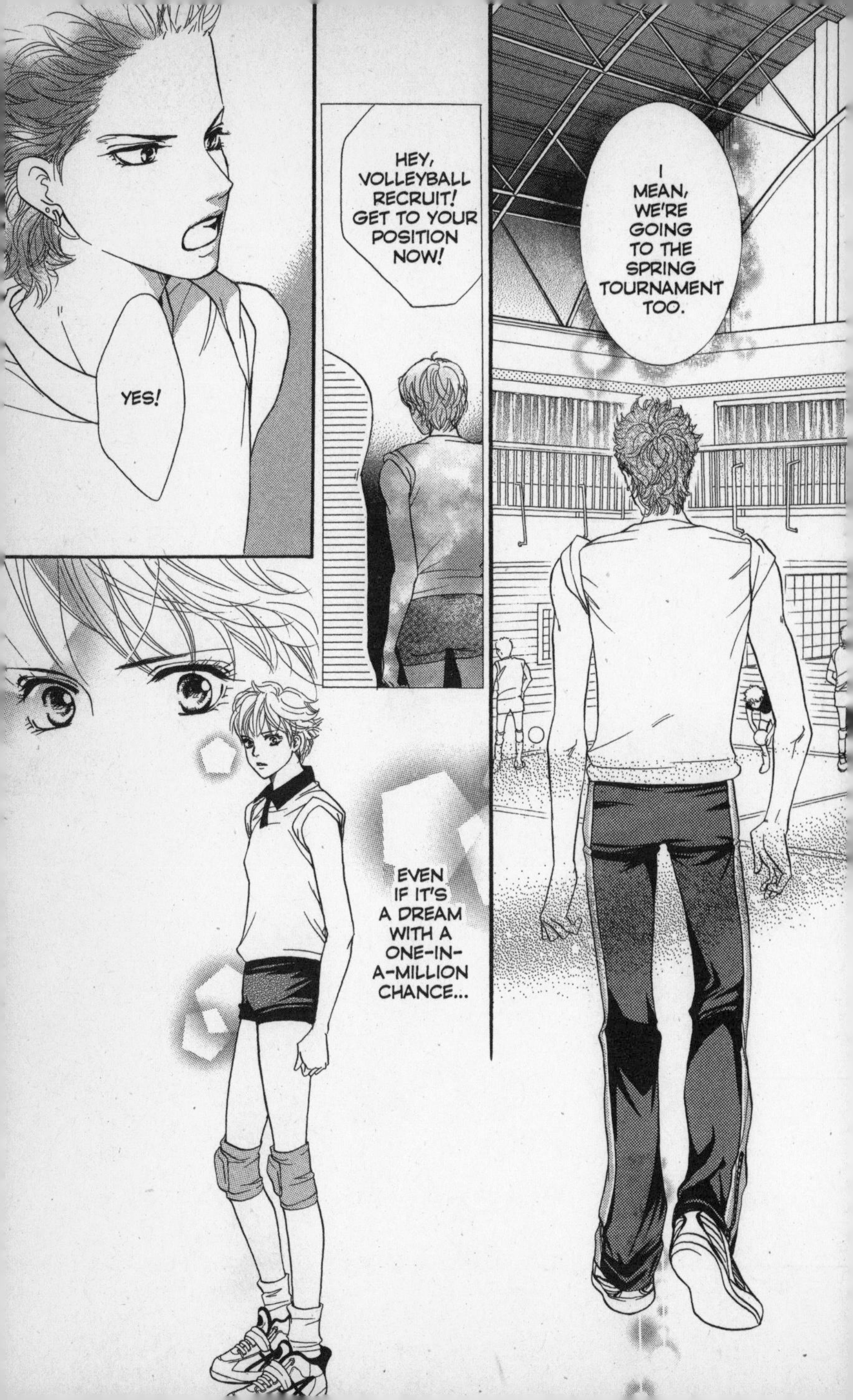

I MEAN, WE'RE GOING TO THE SPRING TOURNAMENT TOO.
HEY, VOLLEYBALL RECRUIT! GET TO YOUR POSITION NOW!
YES!
EVEN IF IT'S A DREAM WITH A ONE-IN-A-MILLION CHANCE...

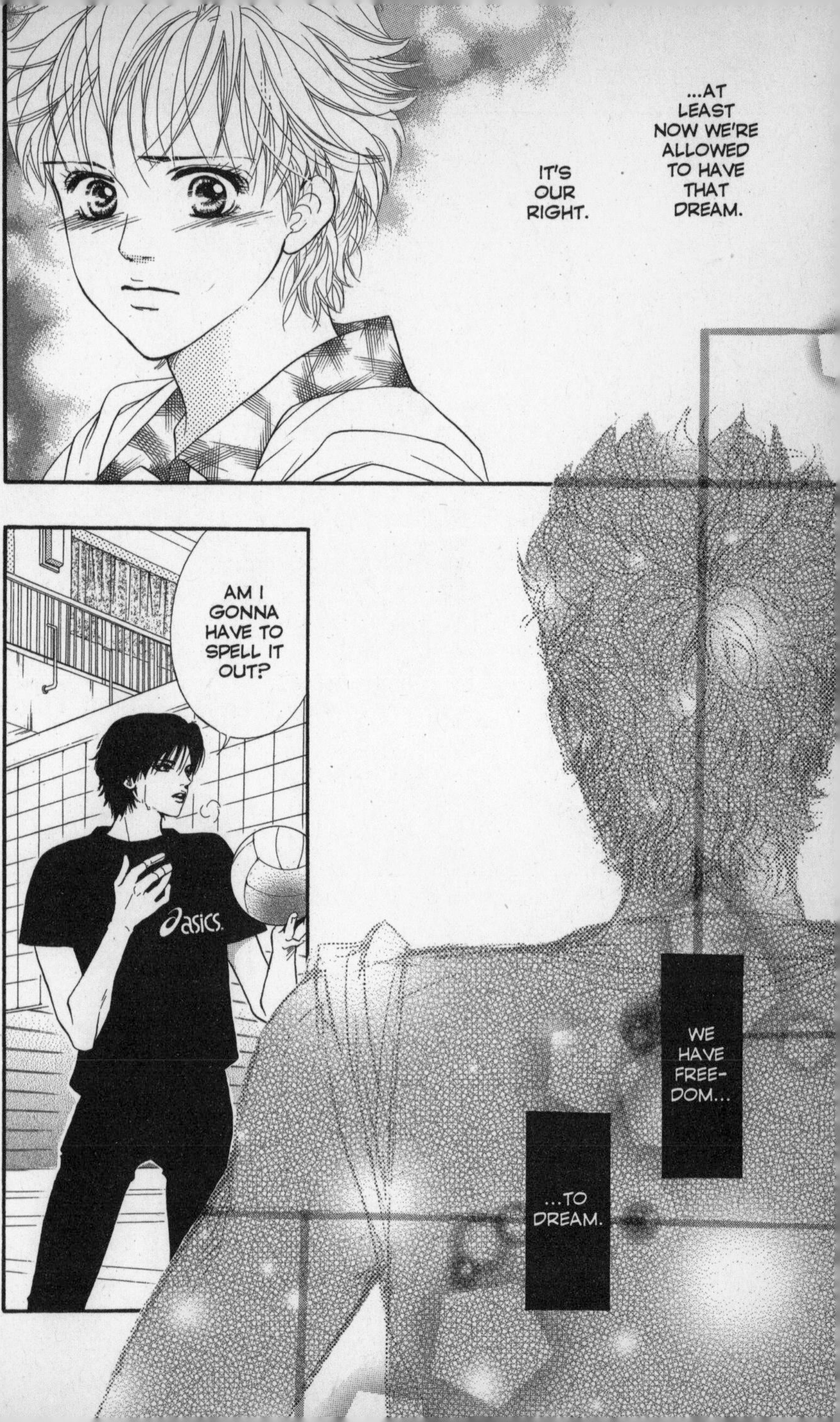
...AT LEAST NOW WE'RE ALLOWED TO HAVE THAT DREAM.
IT'S OUR RIGHT.
WE HAVE FREE-DOM...
...TO DREAM.
AM I GONNA HAVE TO SPELL IT OUT?
asics

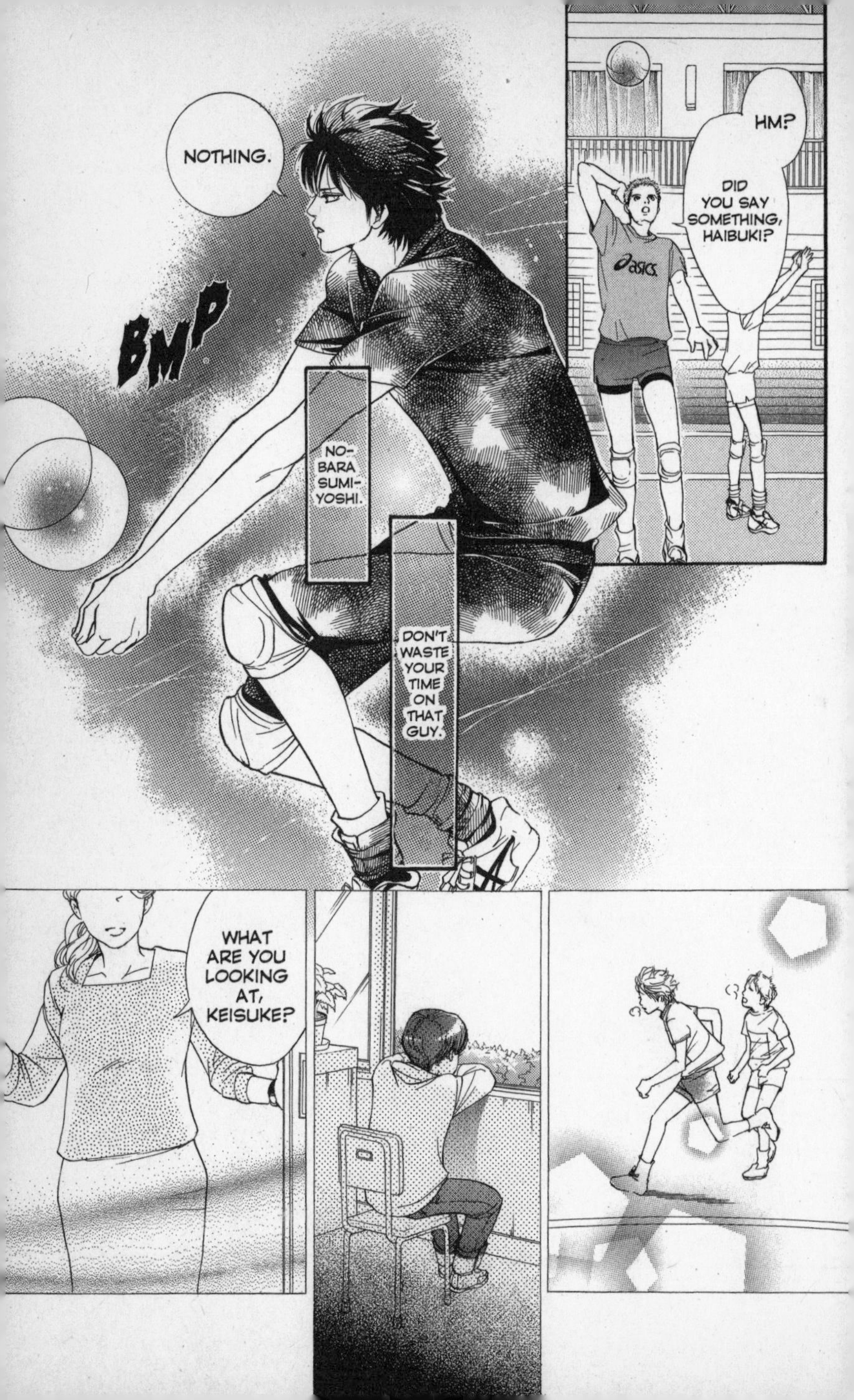
HM?
DID YOU SAY SOMETHING, HAIBUKI?
NOTHING.
BMP
NO-BARA SUMI-YOSHI.
DON'T WASTE YOUR TIME ON THAT GUY.
WHAT ARE YOU LOOKING AT, KEISUKE?

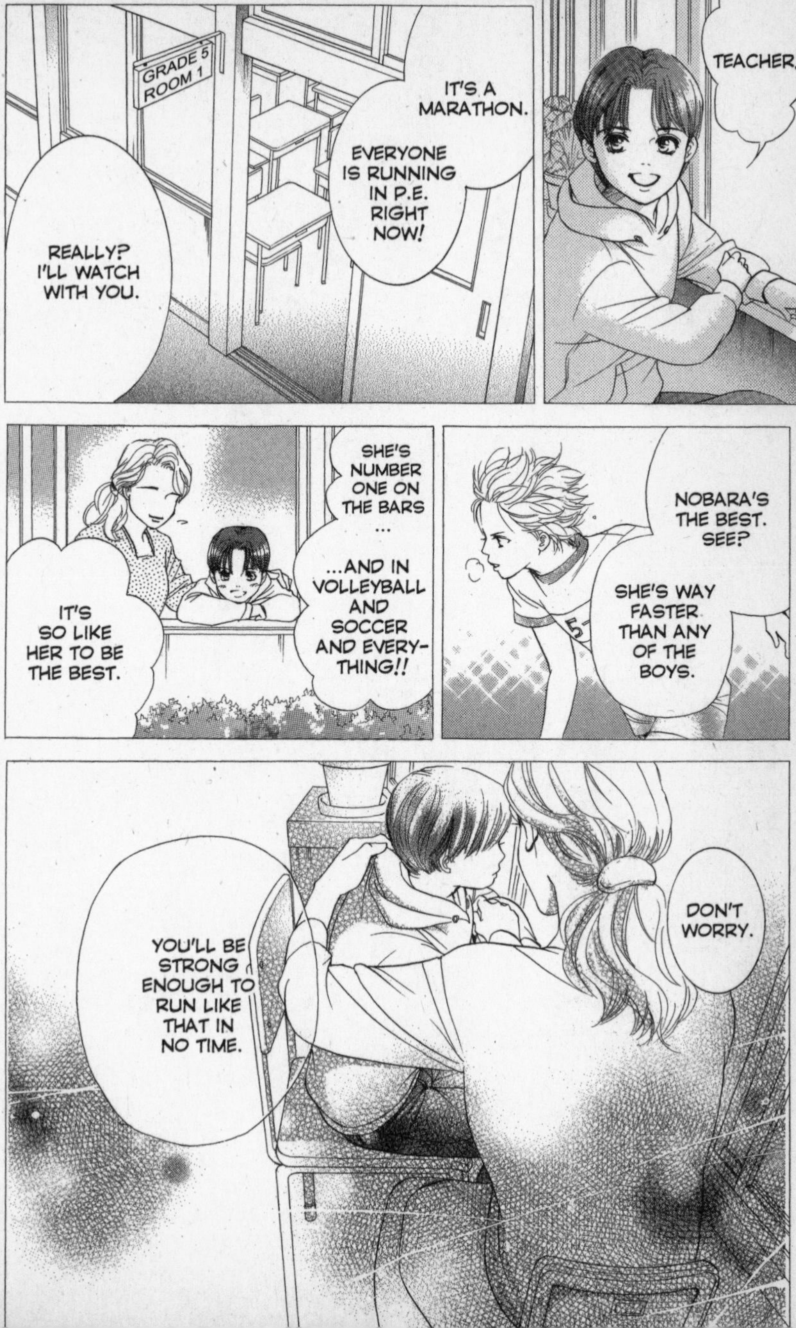
TEACHER!
GRADE 5 ROOM 1
IT'S A MARATHON.
EVERYONE IS RUNNING IN P.E. RIGHT NOW!
REALLY? I'LL WATCH WITH YOU.
NOBARA'S THE BEST. SEE?
SHE'S WAY FASTER THAN ANY OF THE BOYS.
SHE'S NUMBER ONE ON THE BARS ...
...AND IN VOLLEYBALL AND SOCCER AND EVERY-THING!!
IT'S SO LIKE HER TO BE THE BEST.
DON'T WORRY.
YOU'LL BE STRONG ENOUGH TO RUN LIKE THAT IN NO TIME.

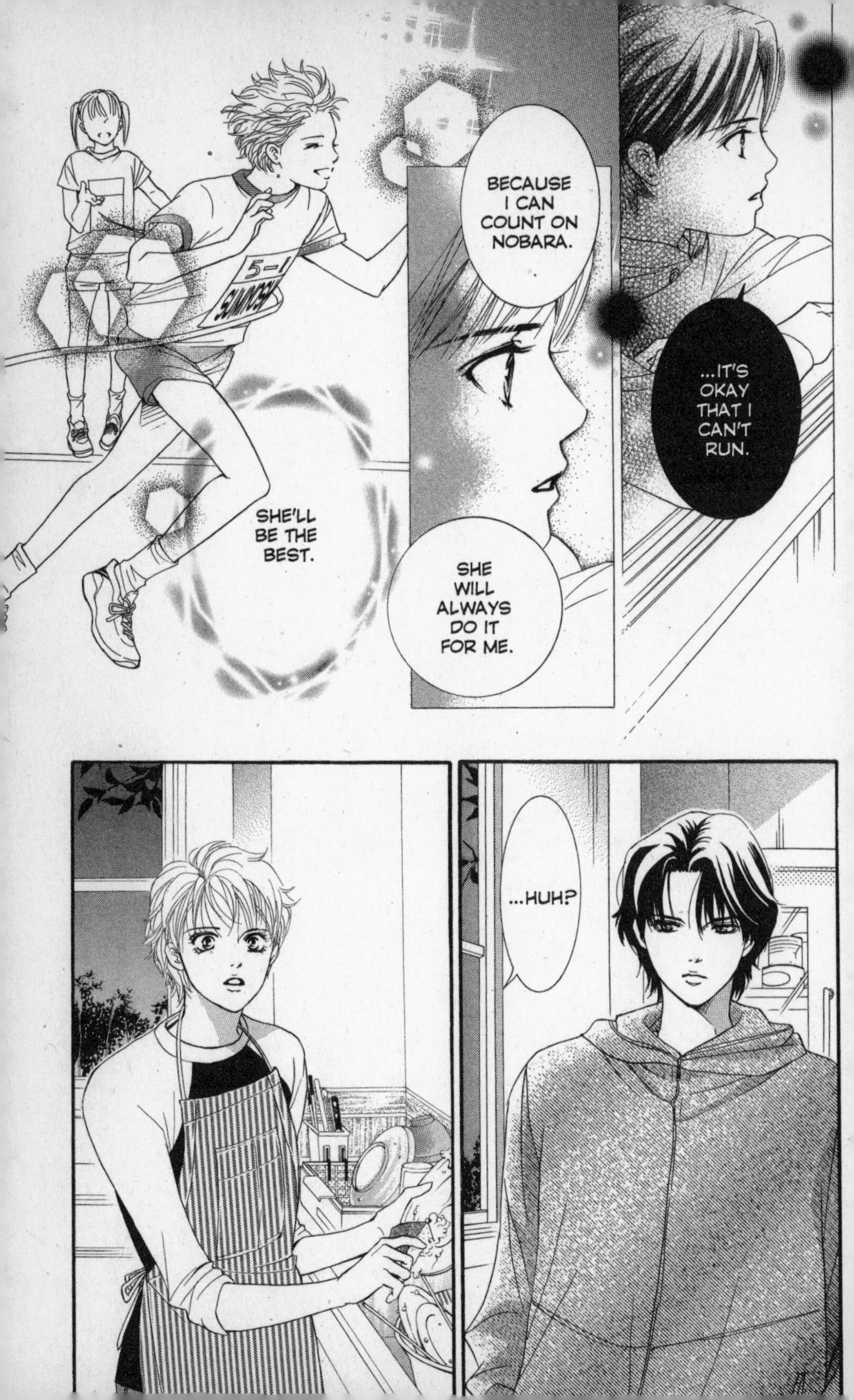
...IT'S OKAY THAT I CAN'T RUN.
BECAUSE I CAN COUNT ON NOBARA.
SHE WILL ALWAYS DO IT FOR ME.
SHE'LL BE THE BEST.
...HUH?

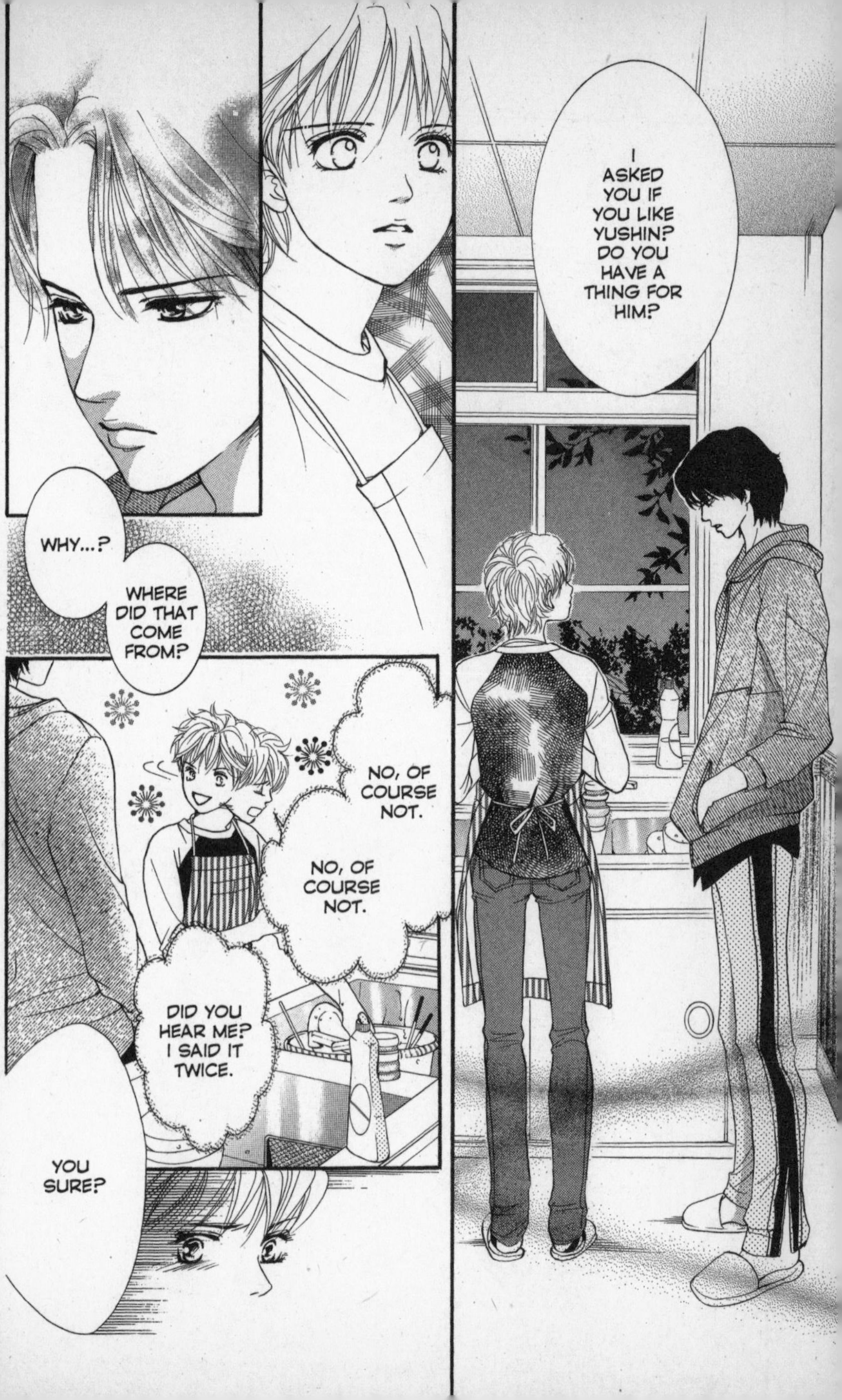
I ASKED YOU IF YOU LIKE YUSHIN? DO YOU HAVE A THING FOR HIM?
WHY...?
WHERE DID THAT COME FROM?
NO, OF COURSE NOT.
NO, OF COURSE NOT.
DID YOU HEAR ME? I SAID IT TWICE.
YOU SURE?

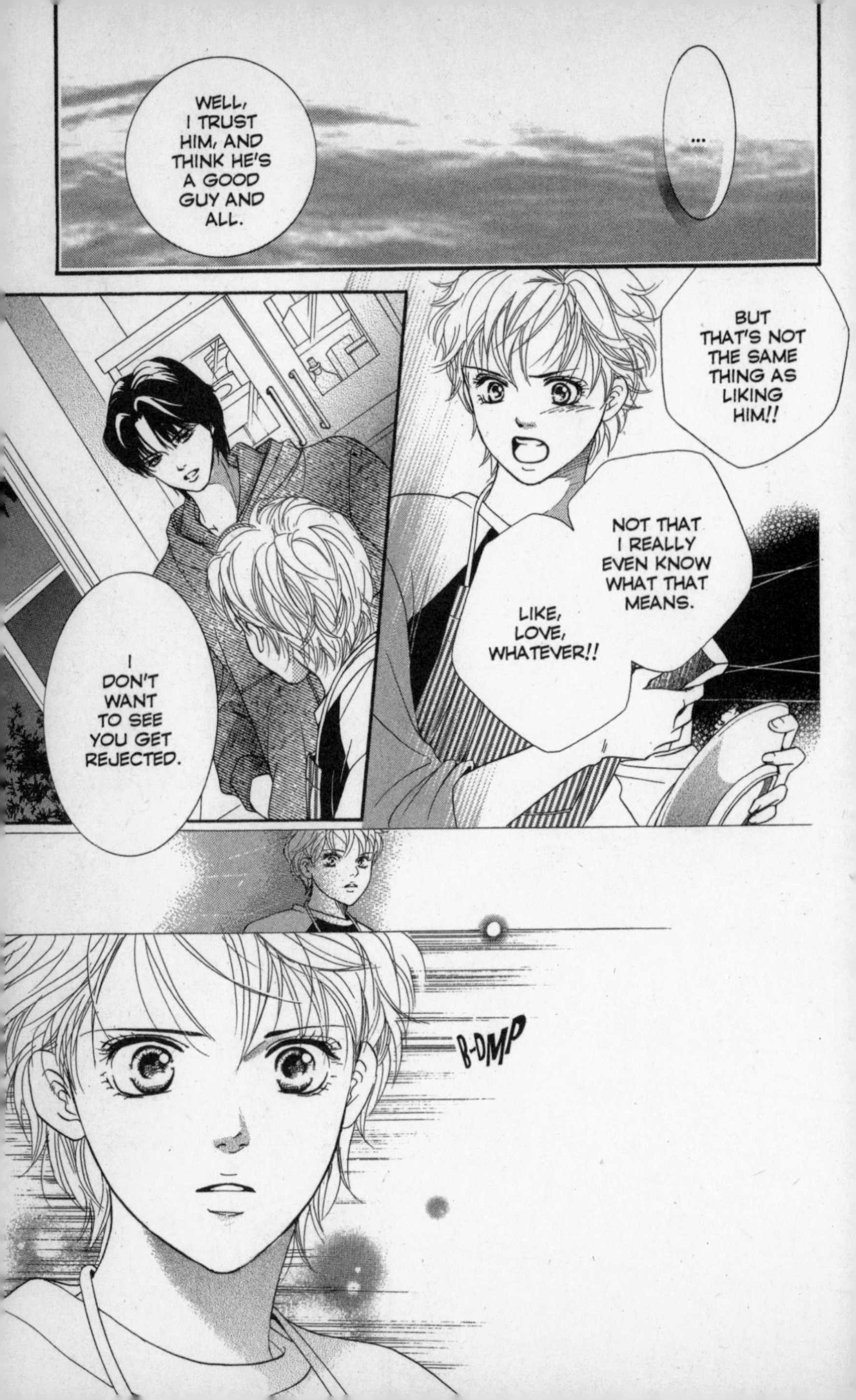
...
WELL, I TRUST HIM, AND THINK HE'S A GOOD GUY AND ALL.
BUT THAT'S NOT THE SAME THING AS LIKING HIM!!
NOT THAT I REALLY EVEN KNOW WHAT THAT MEANS.
LIKE, LOVE, WHATEVER!!
I DON'T WANT TO SEE YOU GET REJECTED.
B-DMP

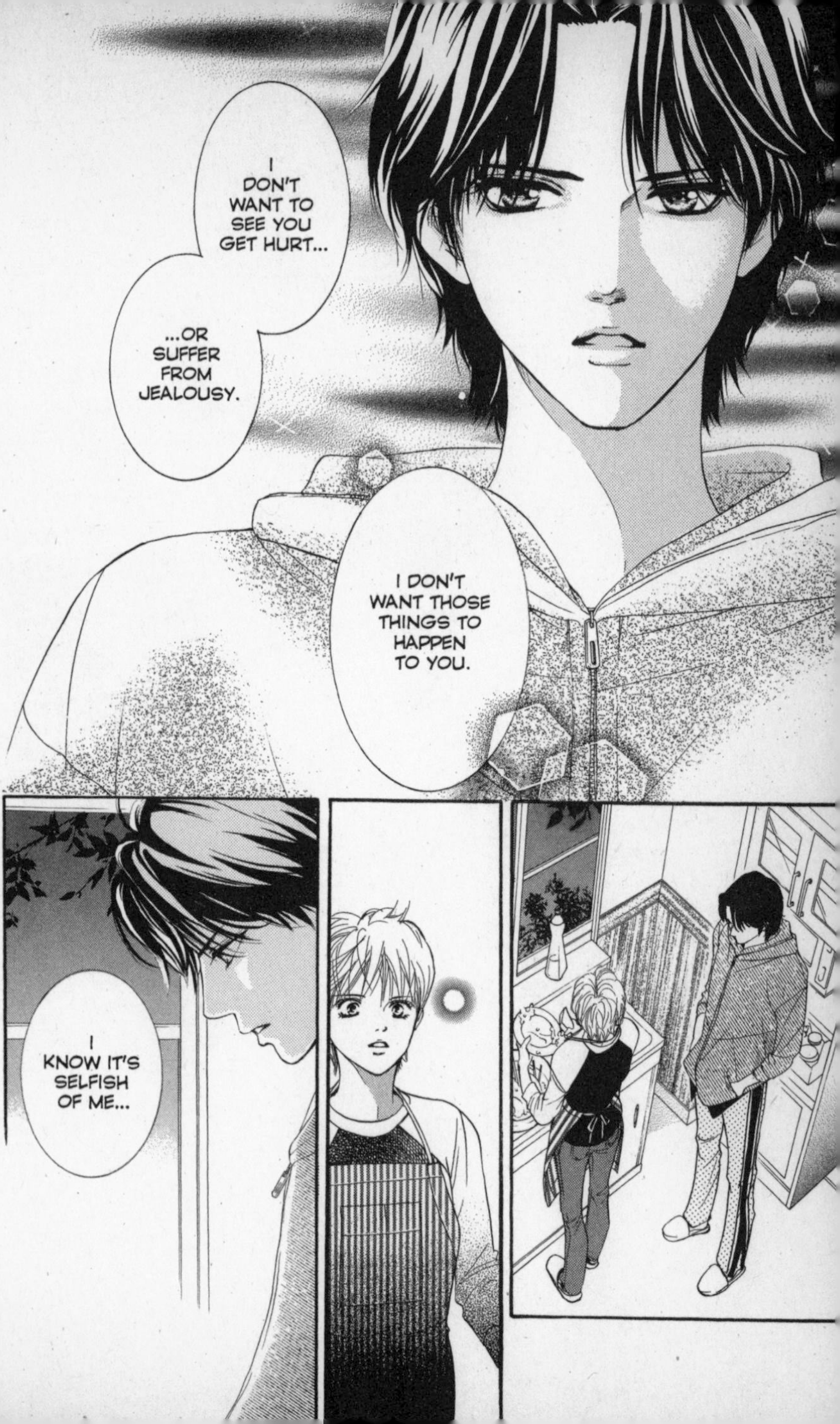
I DON'T WANT TO SEE YOU GET HURT...
...OR SUFFER FROM JEALOUSY.
I DON'T WANT THOSE THINGS TO HAPPEN TO YOU.
I KNOW IT'S SELFISH OF ME...

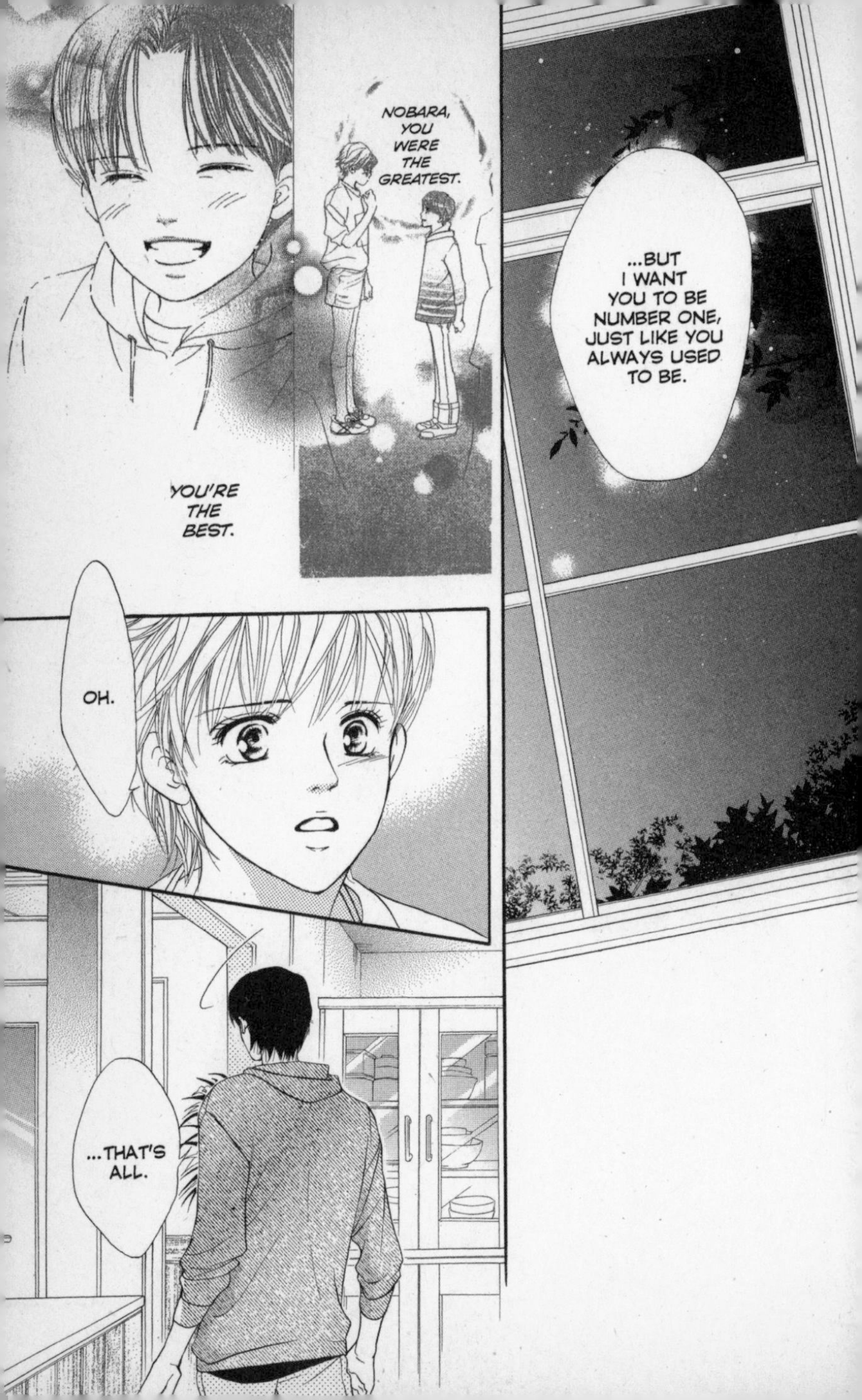
...BUT I WANT YOU TO BE NUMBER ONE, JUST LIKE YOU ALWAYS USED TO BE.
NOBARA, YOU WERE THE GREATEST.
YOU'RE THE BEST.
OH.
...THAT'S ALL.

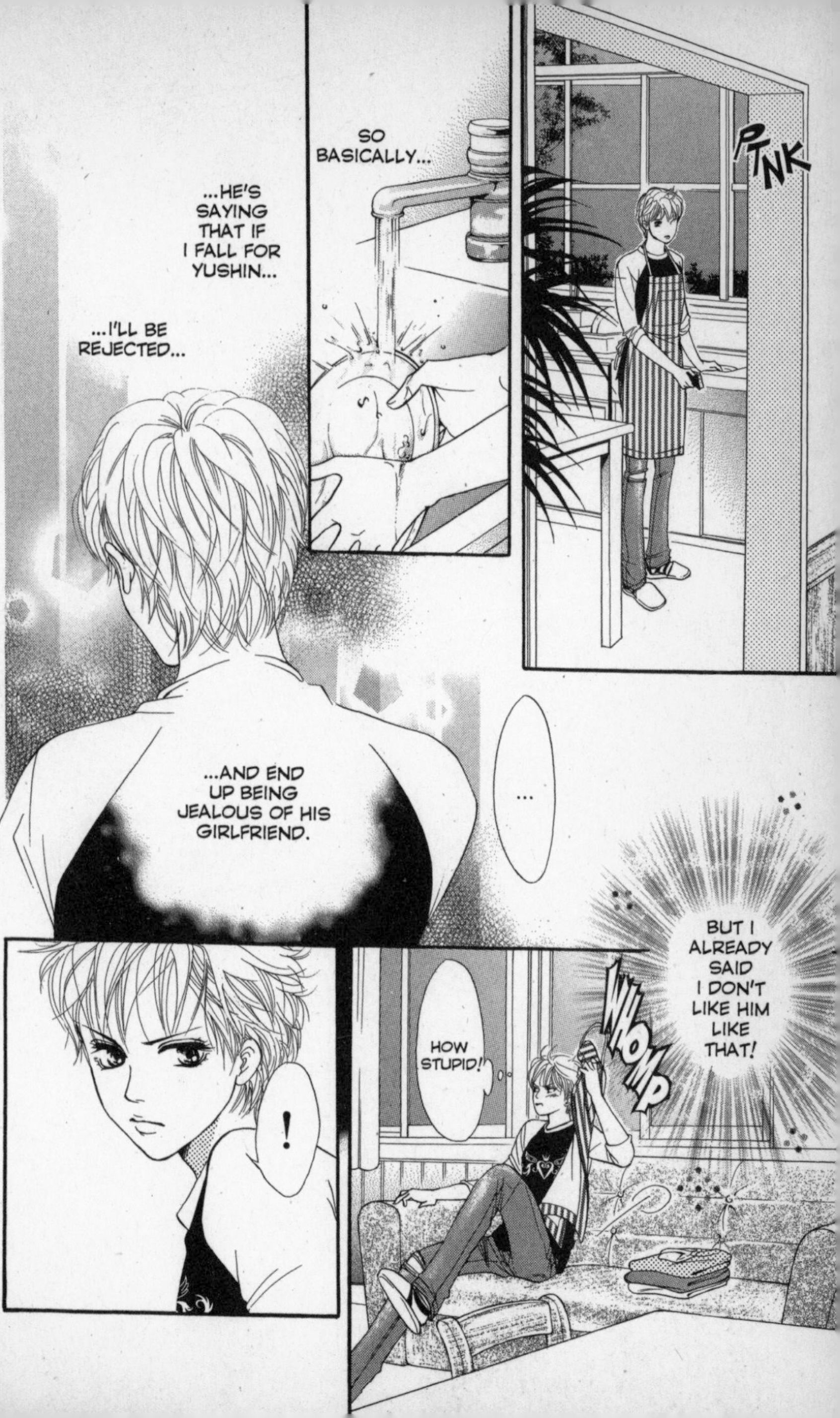
PTINK
SO BASICALLY...
...HE'S SAYING THAT IF I FALL FOR YUSHIN...
...I'LL BE REJECTED...
...AND END UP BEING JEALOUS OF HIS GIRLFRIEND.
...
BUT I ALREADY SAID I DON'T LIKE HIM LIKE THAT!
WHOMP
HOW STUPID!
!

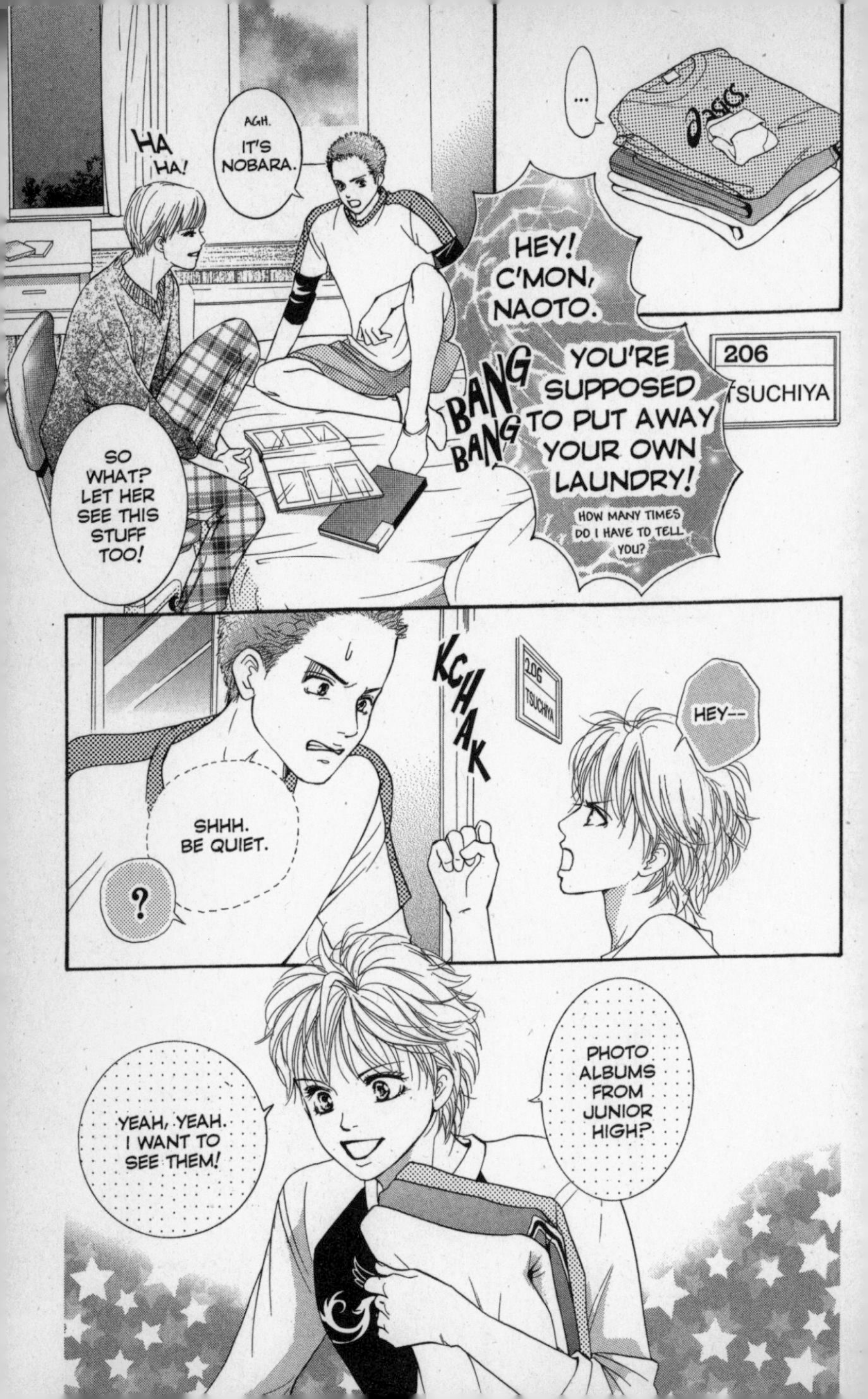
...
206
TSUCHIYA
HEY! C'MON, NAOTO.
YOU'RE SUPPOSED TO PUT AWAY YOUR OWN LAUNDRY!
HOW MANY TIMES DO I HAVE TO TELL YOU?
BANG BANG
AGH. IT'S NOBARA.
HA HA!
SO WHAT? LET HER SEE THIS STUFF TOO!
HEY--
206
TSUCHIYA
KCHAK
SHHH. BE QUIET.
?
PHOTO ALBUMS FROM JUNIOR HIGH?
YEAH, YEAH. I WANT TO SEE THEM!

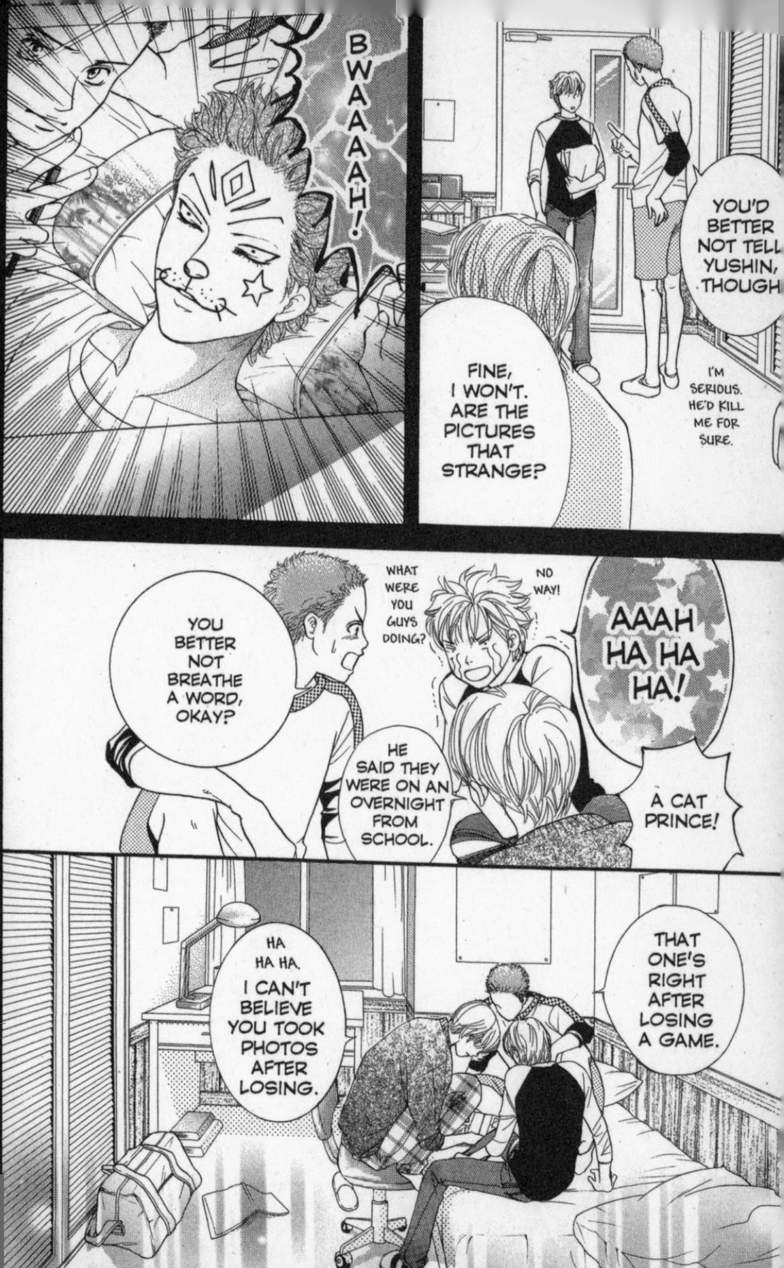
YOU'D BETTER NOT TELL YUSHIN, THOUGH
I'M SERIOUS. HE'D KILL ME FOR SURE.
FINE, I WON'T. ARE THE PICTURES THAT STRANGE?
BWAAAAAH!
AAAH HA HA HA!
NO WAY!
A CAT PRINCE!
WHAT WERE YOU GUYS DOING?
HE SAID THEY WERE ON AN OVERNIGHT FROM SCHOOL.
YOU BETTER NOT BREATHE A WORD, OKAY?
THAT ONE'S RIGHT AFTER LOSING A GAME.
HA HA HA. I CAN'T BELIEVE YOU TOOK PHOTOS AFTER LOSING.

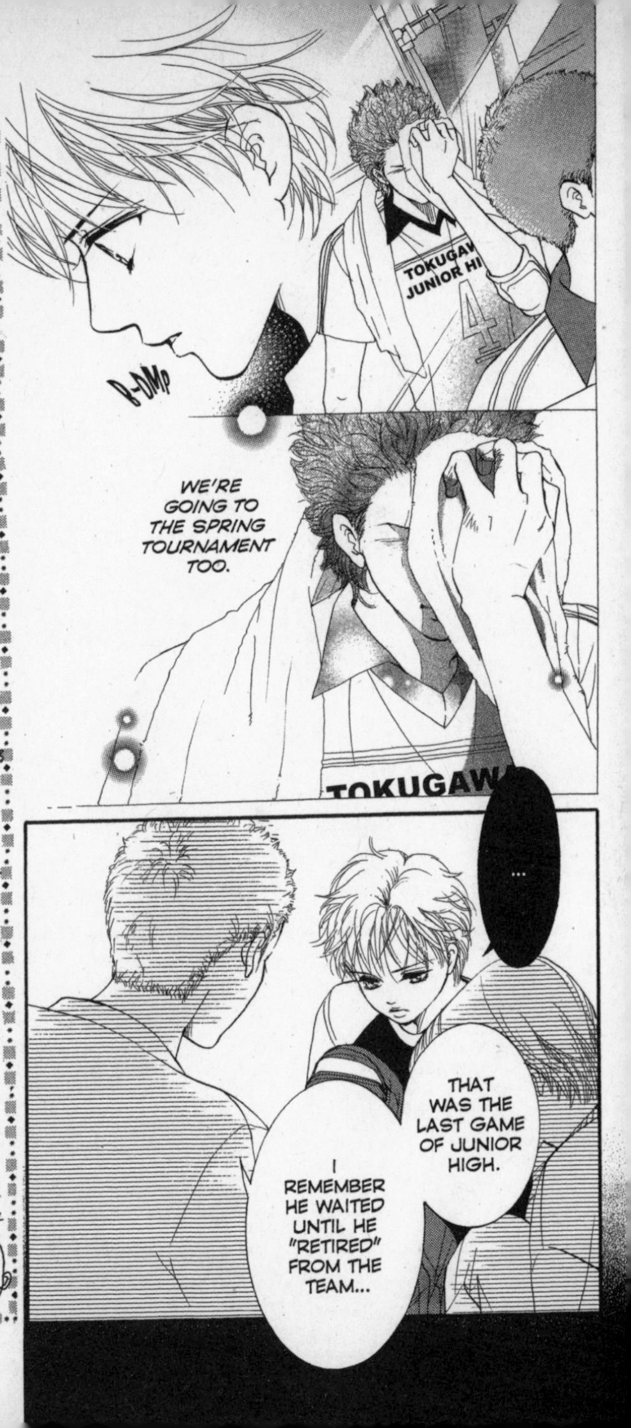
TOKUGAWA JUNIOR HI
4
B-DMP
WE'RE GOING TO THE SPRING TOURNAMENT TOO.
TOKUGAWA
...
THAT WAS THE LAST GAME OF JUNIOR HIGH.
I REMEMBER HE WAITED UNTIL HE "RETIRED" FROM THE TEAM...

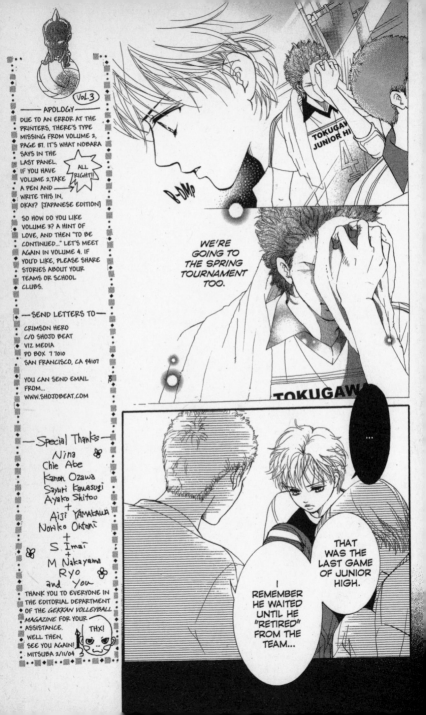

Vol. 3

—APOLOGY—

DUE TO AN ERROR AT THE PRINTERS, THERE'S TYPE MISSING FROM VOLUME 2, PAGE 87. IT'S WHAT NOBARA SAYS IN THE LAST PANEL. IF YOU HAVE VOLUME 2, TAKE A PEN AND → WRITE THIS IN, OKAY? [JAPANESE EDITION]

ALL RIGHT!!

SO HOW DO YOU LIKE VOLUME 3? A HINT OF LOVE, AND THEN "TO BE CONTINUED..." LET'S MEET AGAIN IN VOLUME 4. IF YOU'D LIKE, PLEASE SHARE STORIES ABOUT YOUR TEAMS OR SCHOOL CLUBS.

—SEND LETTERS TO—

CRIMSON HERO
C/O SHOJO BEAT
VIZ MEDIA
PO BOX 77010
SAN FRANCISCO, CA 94107

YOU CAN SEND EMAIL FROM...
WWW.SHOJOBEAT.COM

—Special Thanks—

Nina
Chie Abe
Kanon Ozawa
Sayuri Kawasugi
Ayako Shitou
+
Aiji Yamakawa
Noriko Ohtani
+
S. Imai
+
M Nakayama
Ryo
and You

THANK YOU TO EVERYONE IN THE EDITORIAL DEPARTMENT OF THE *GEKKAN VOLLEYBALL MAGAZINE* FOR YOUR ASSISTANCE.
WELL THEN, SEE YOU AGAIN!
MITSUBA 2/11/04

THX!

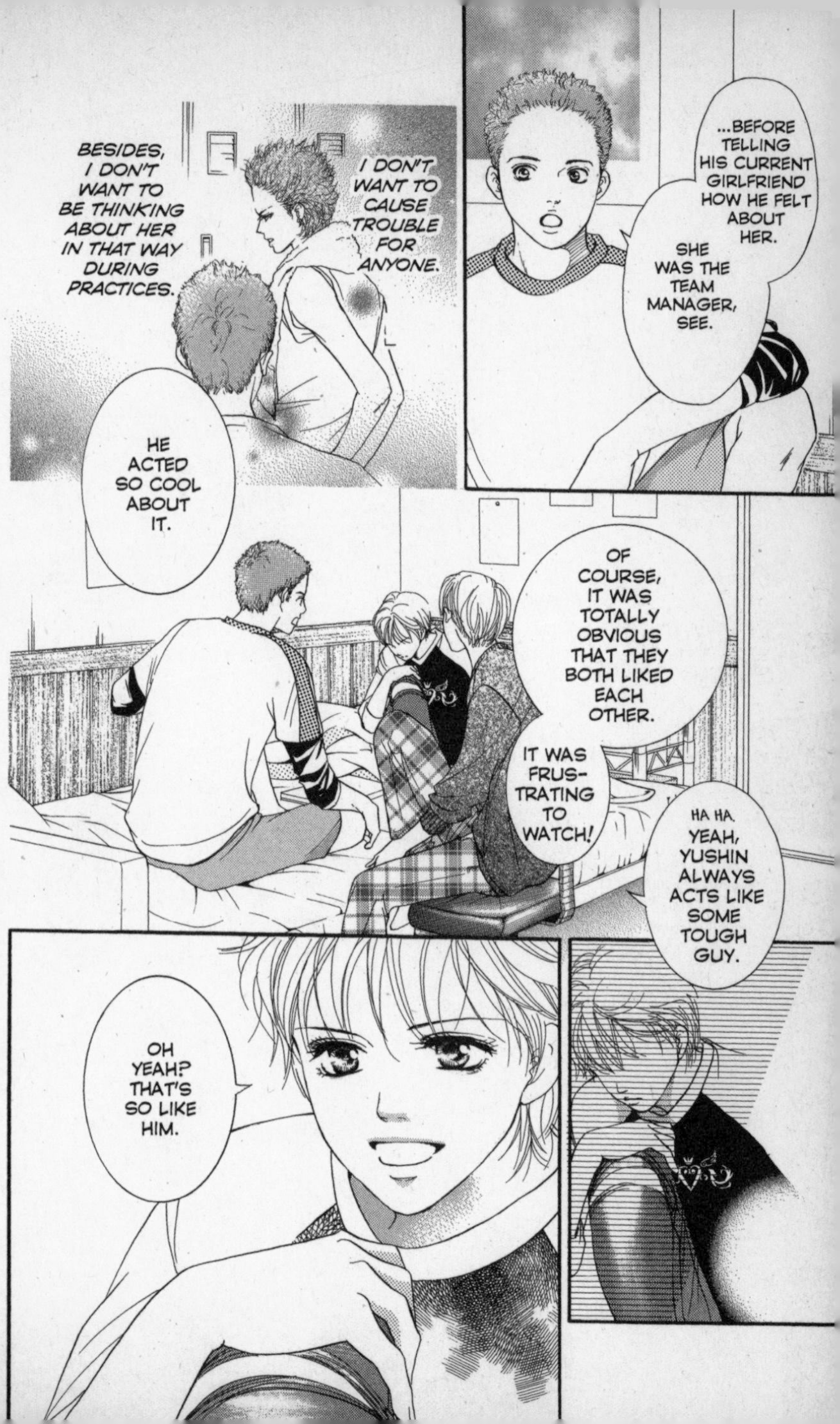
...BEFORE TELLING HIS CURRENT GIRLFRIEND HOW HE FELT ABOUT HER.
SHE WAS THE TEAM MANAGER, SEE.
I DON'T WANT TO CAUSE TROUBLE FOR ANYONE.
BESIDES, I DON'T WANT TO BE THINKING ABOUT HER IN THAT WAY DURING PRACTICES.
HE ACTED SO COOL ABOUT IT.
OF COURSE, IT WAS TOTALLY OBVIOUS THAT THEY BOTH LIKED EACH OTHER.
IT WAS FRUS-TRATING TO WATCH!
HA HA. YEAH, YUSHIN ALWAYS ACTS LIKE SOME TOUGH GUY.
OH YEAH? THAT'S SO LIKE HIM.

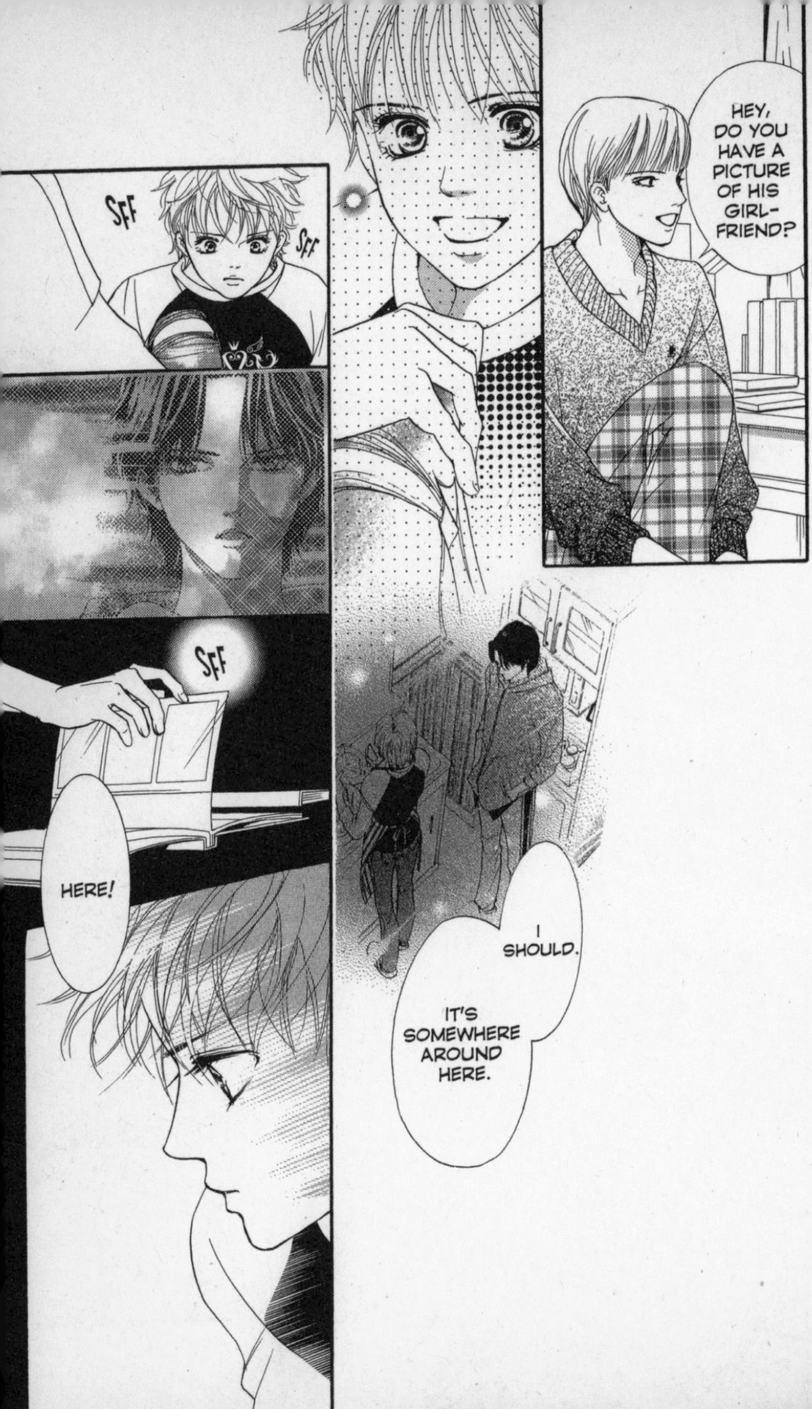
HEY, DO YOU HAVE A PICTURE OF HIS GIRL-FRIEND?
I SHOULD.
IT'S SOMEWHERE AROUND HERE.
SFF
SFF
SFF
HERE!

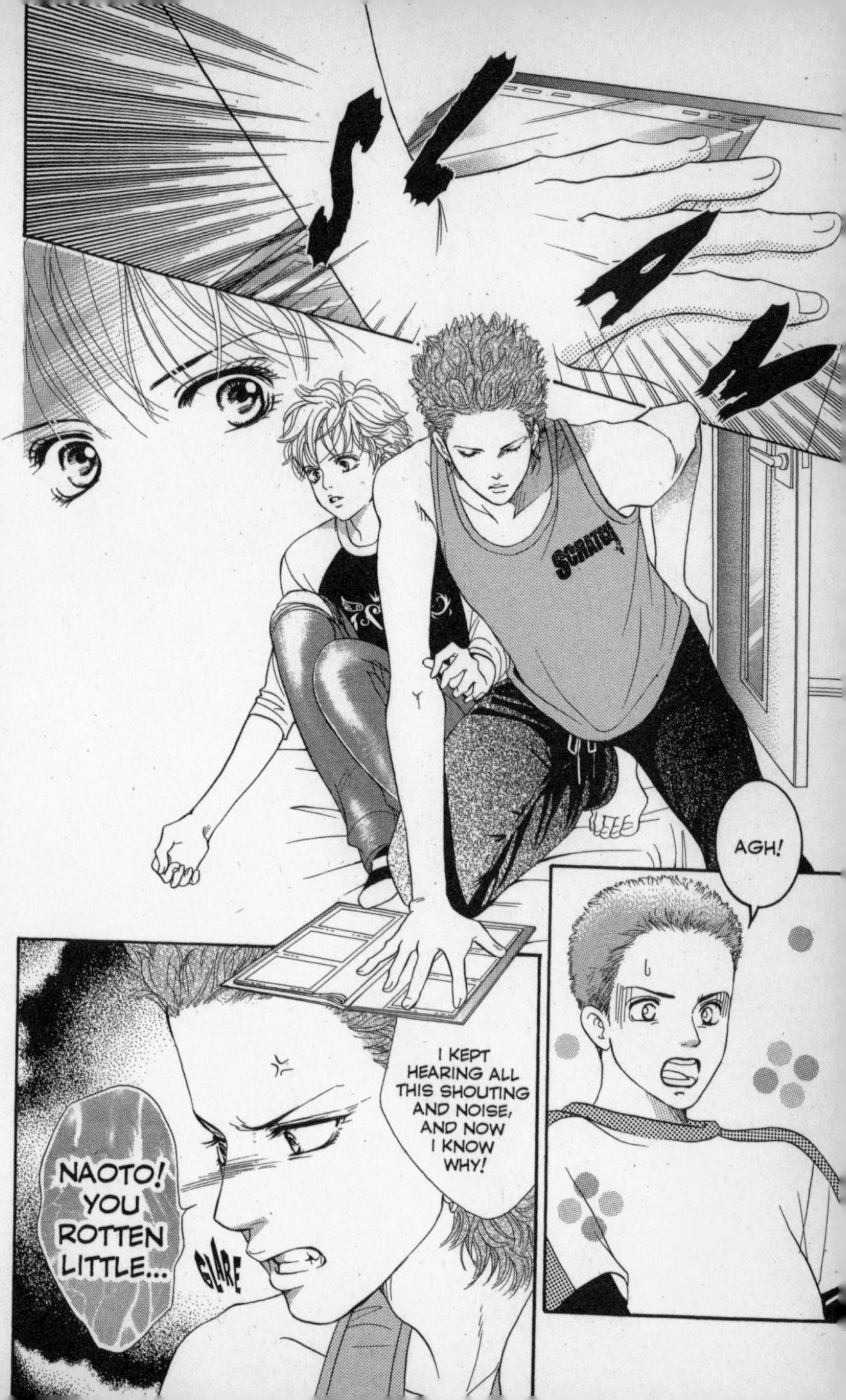
SLAM
SCRATCH
AGH!
I KEPT HEARING ALL THIS SHOUTING AND NOISE, AND NOW I KNOW WHY!
NAOTO! YOU ROTTEN LITTLE...
GLARE

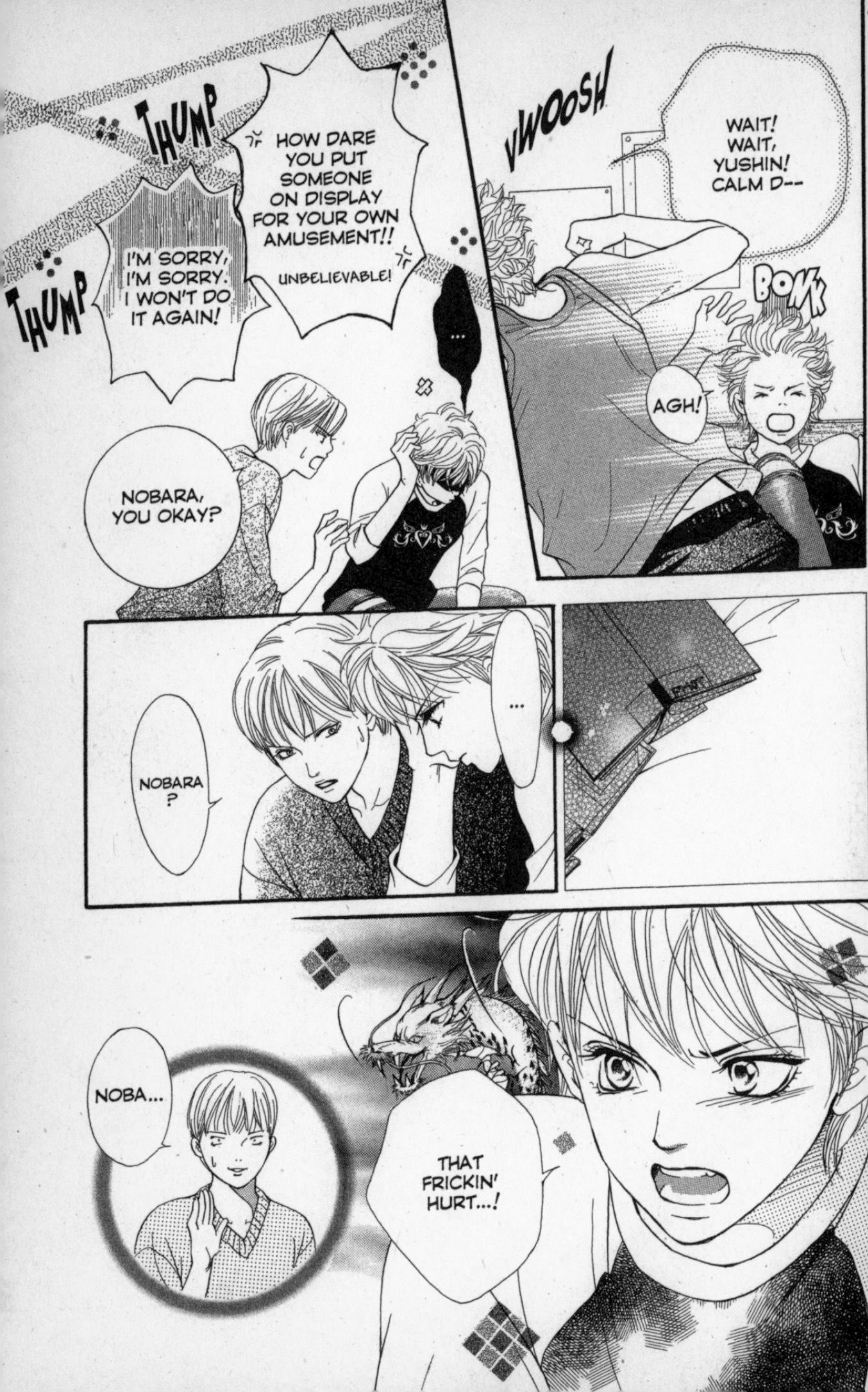
VWOOSH
WAIT! WAIT, YUSHIN! CALM D--
BONK
AGH!
THUMP
HOW DARE YOU PUT SOMEONE ON DISPLAY FOR YOUR OWN AMUSEMENT!!
UNBELIEVABLE!
I'M SORRY, I'M SORRY. I WON'T DO IT AGAIN!
THUMP
...
NOBARA, YOU OKAY?
...
NOBARA?
THAT FRICKIN' HURT...!
NOBA...

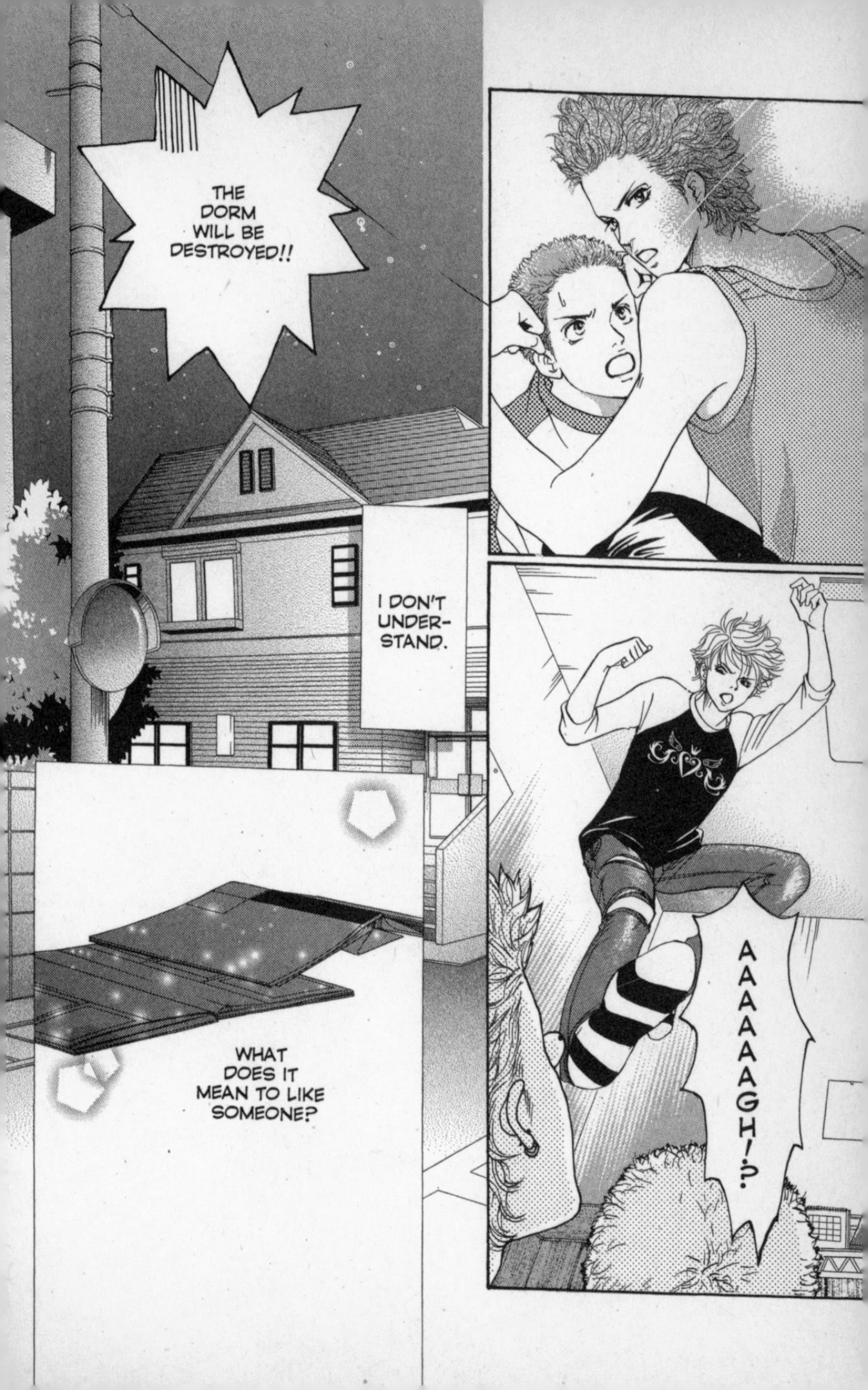
THE DORM WILL BE DESTROYED!!
AAAAAAAGH!?
I DON'T UNDER-STAND.
WHAT DOES IT MEAN TO LIKE SOMEONE?

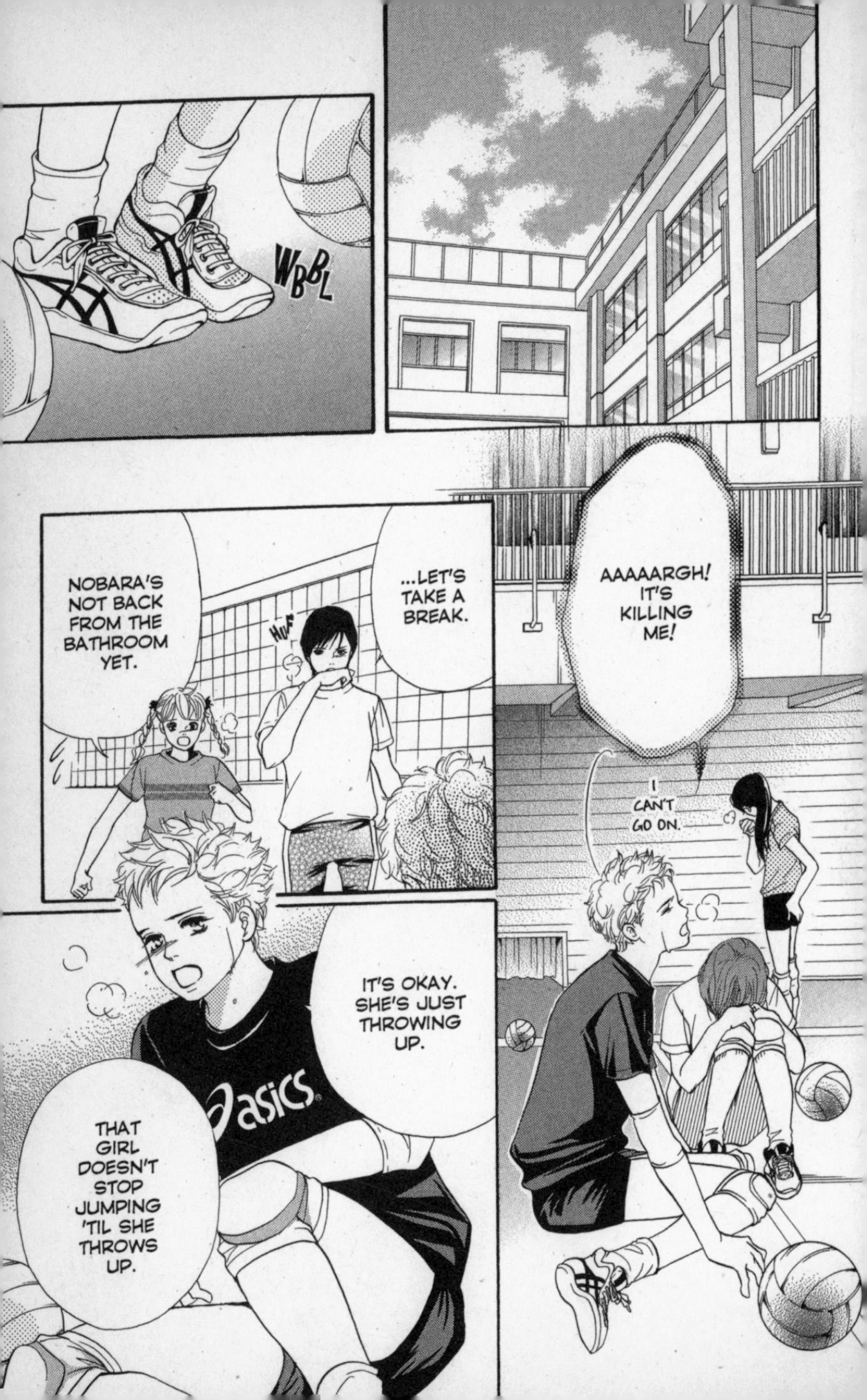
WBBL
AAAAARGH! IT'S KILLING ME!
I CAN'T GO ON.
...LET'S TAKE A BREAK.
HUF
NOBARA'S NOT BACK FROM THE BATHROOM YET.
IT'S OKAY. SHE'S JUST THROWING UP.
THAT GIRL DOESN'T STOP JUMPING 'TIL SHE THROWS UP.

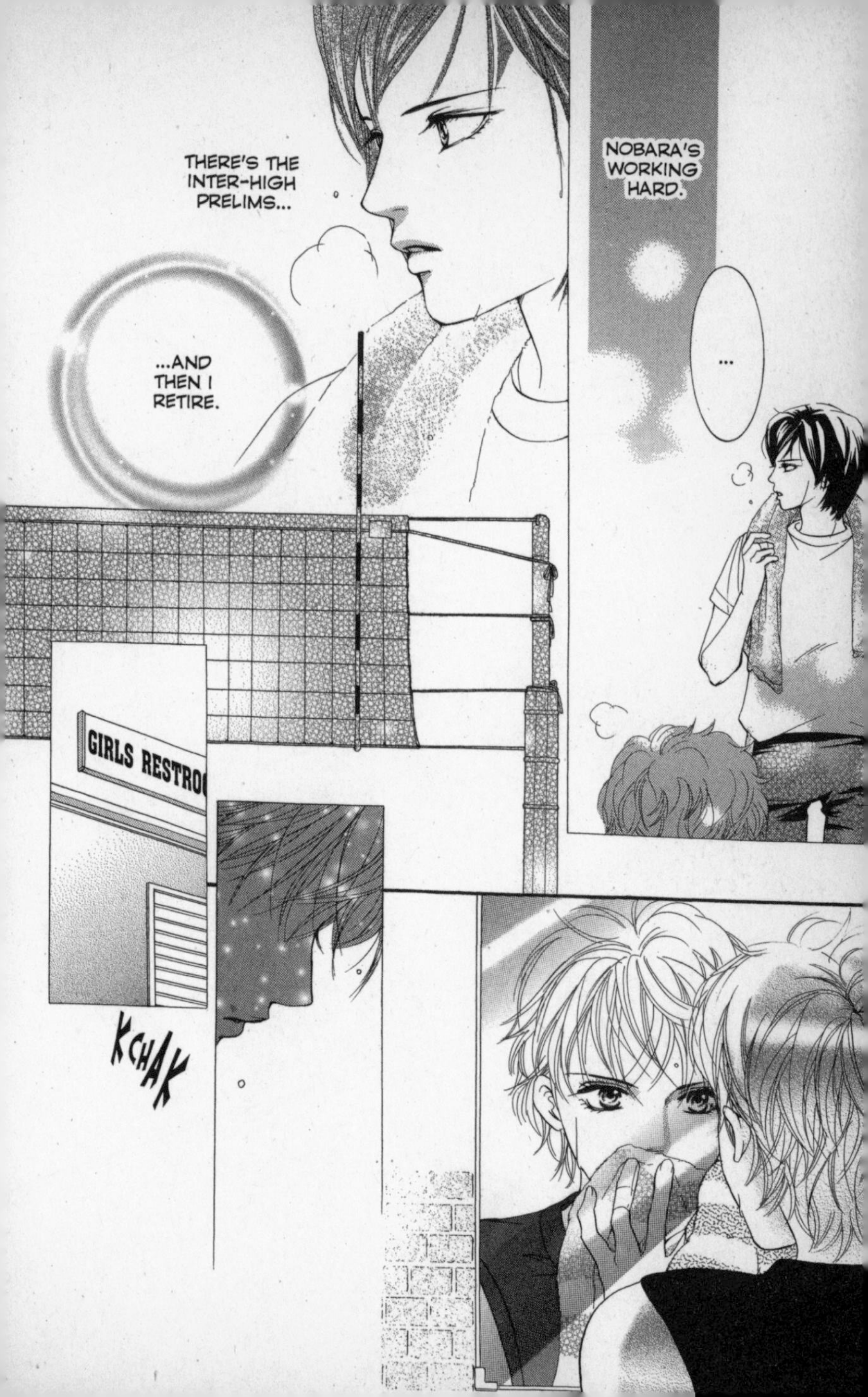
NOBARA'S WORKING HARD.
...
THERE'S THE INTER-HIGH PRELIMS...
...AND THEN I RETIRE.
GIRLS RESTRO
KCHAK

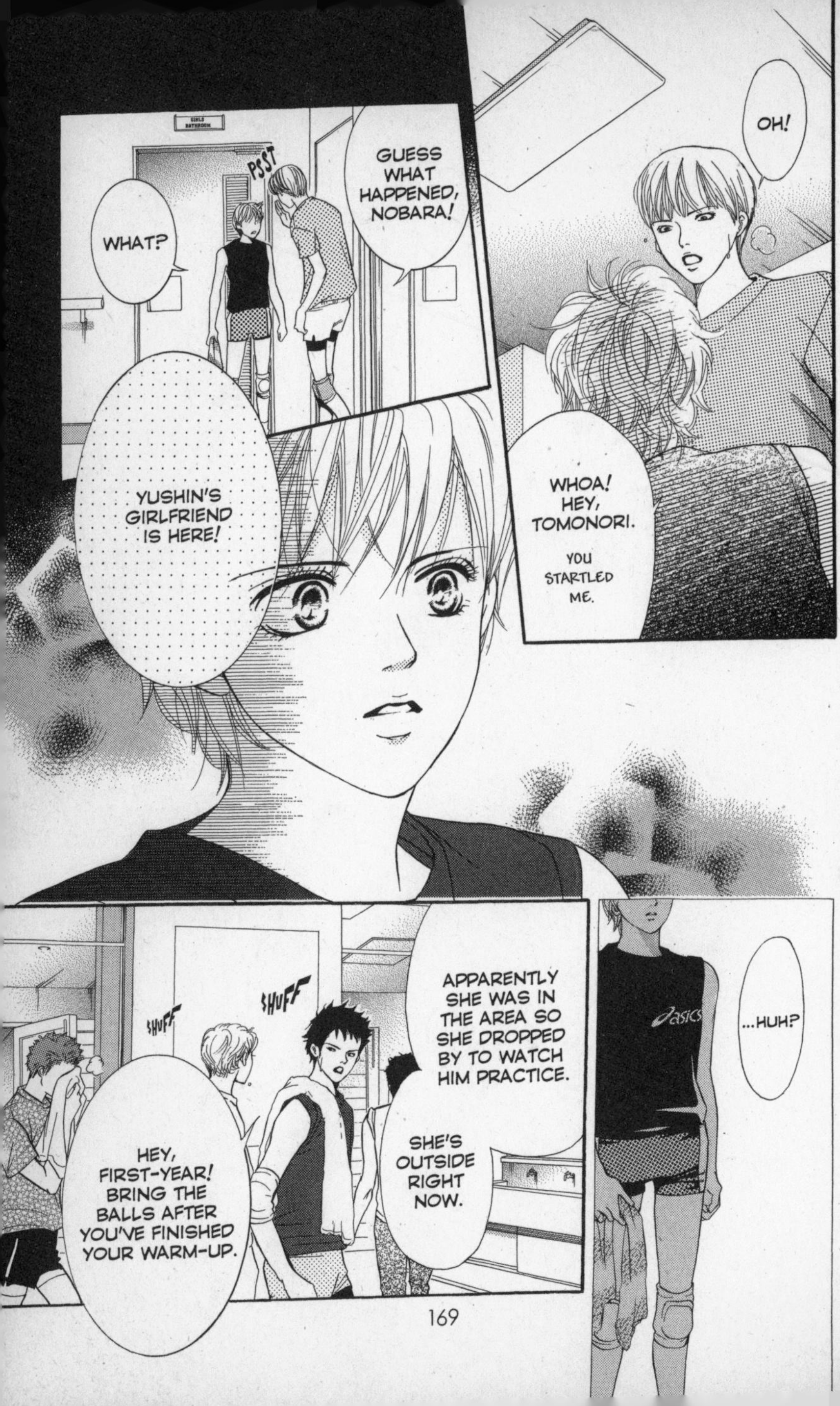
OH!
WHOA! HEY, TOMONORI.
YOU STARTLED ME.
GIRLS BATHROOM
GUESS WHAT HAPPENED, NOBARA!
PSST
WHAT?
YUSHIN'S GIRLFRIEND IS HERE!
...HUH?
APPARENTLY SHE WAS IN THE AREA SO SHE DROPPED BY TO WATCH HIM PRACTICE.
SHE'S OUTSIDE RIGHT NOW.
SHUFF
SHUFF
HEY, FIRST-YEAR! BRING THE BALLS AFTER YOU'VE FINISHED YOUR WARM-UP.

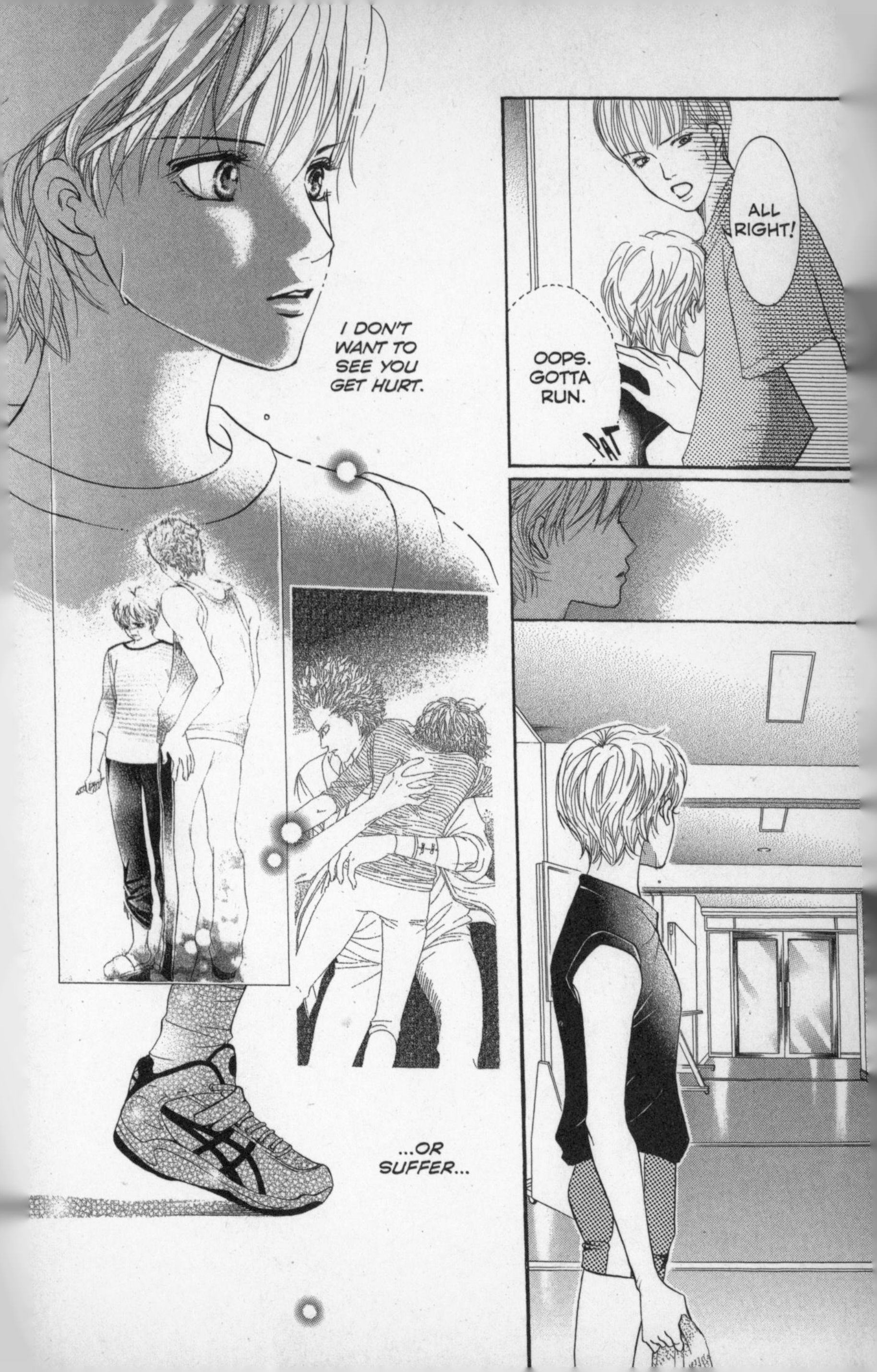
ALL RIGHT!
OOPS. GOTTA RUN.
PAT
I DON'T WANT TO SEE YOU GET HURT.
...OR SUFFER...

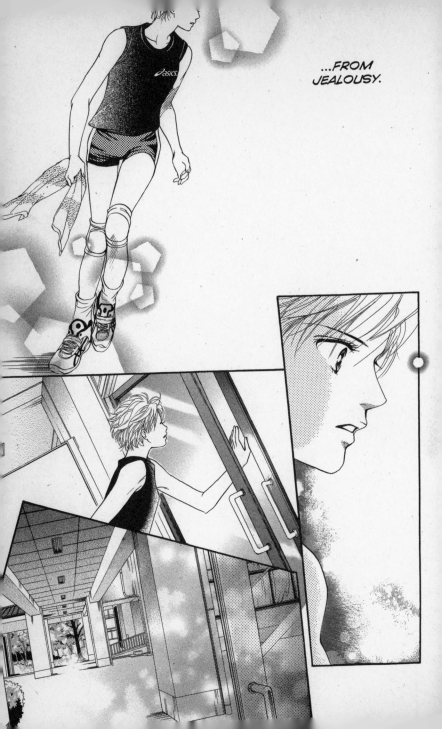

...FROM JEALOUSY.

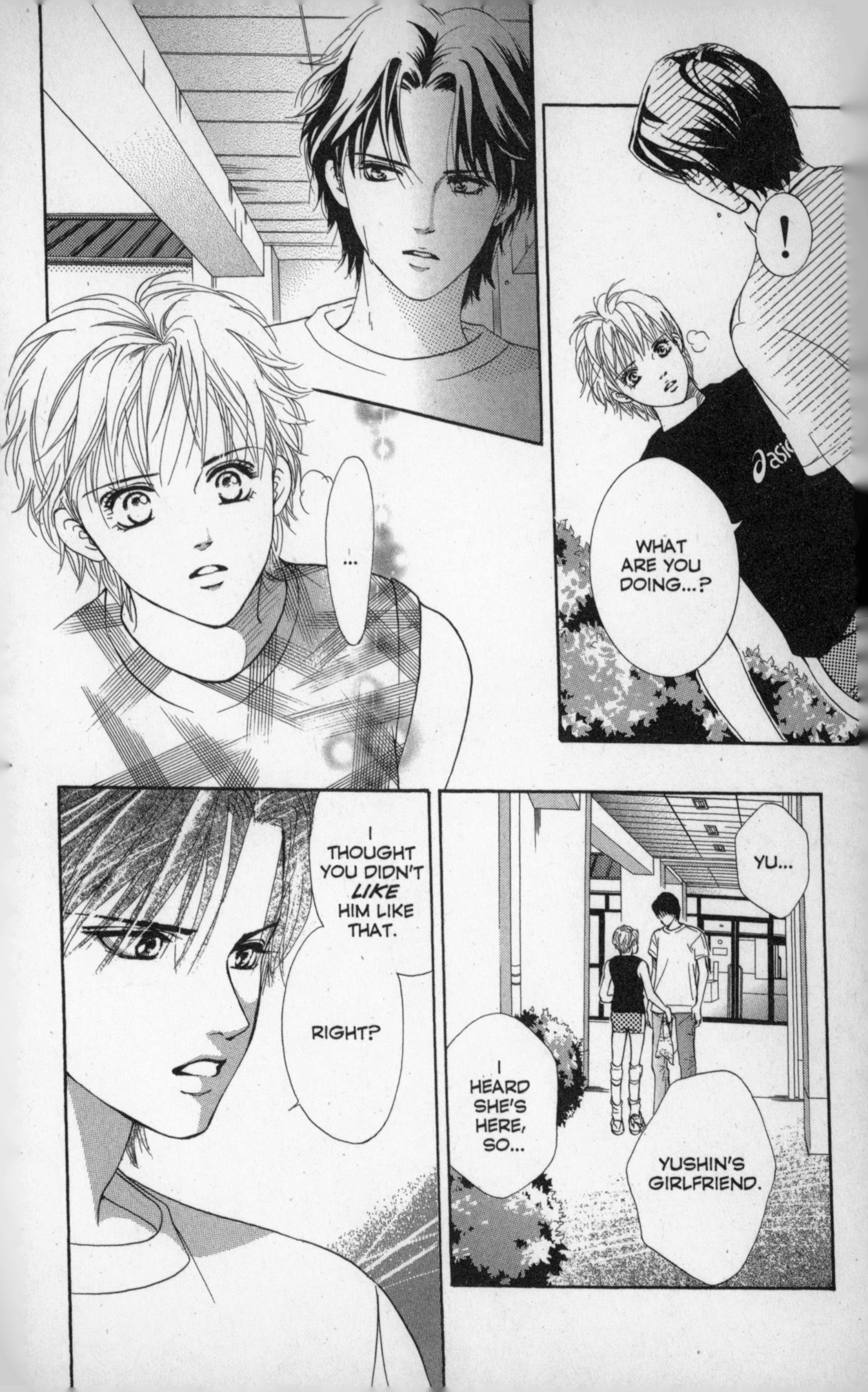
!
WHAT ARE YOU DOING...?
...
YU...
I HEARD SHE'S HERE, SO...
YUSHIN'S GIRLFRIEND.
I THOUGHT YOU DIDN'T ***LIKE*** HIM LIKE THAT.
RIGHT?

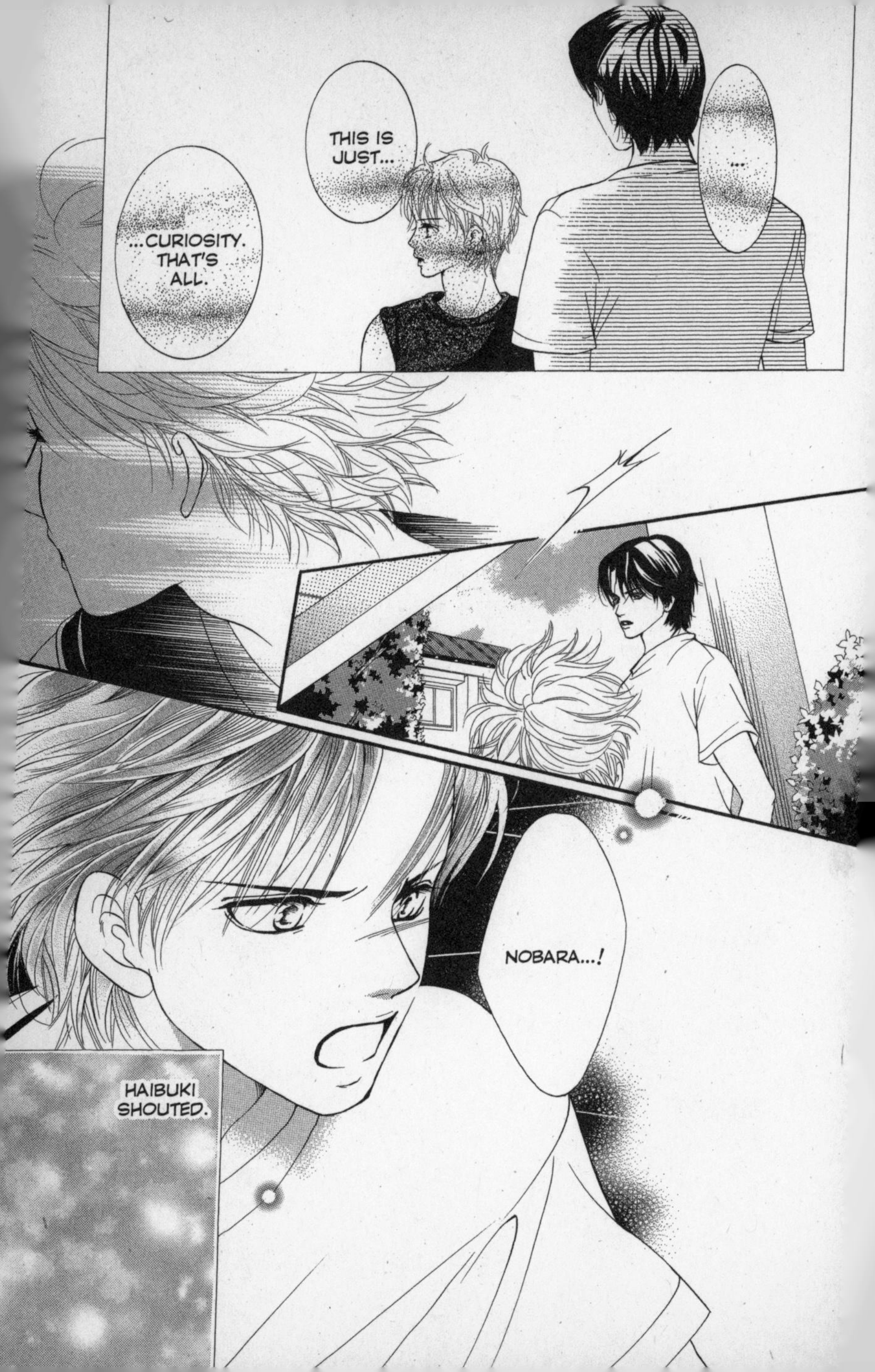
...
THIS IS JUST...
...CURIOSITY. THAT'S ALL.
NOBARA...!
HAIBUKI SHOUTED.

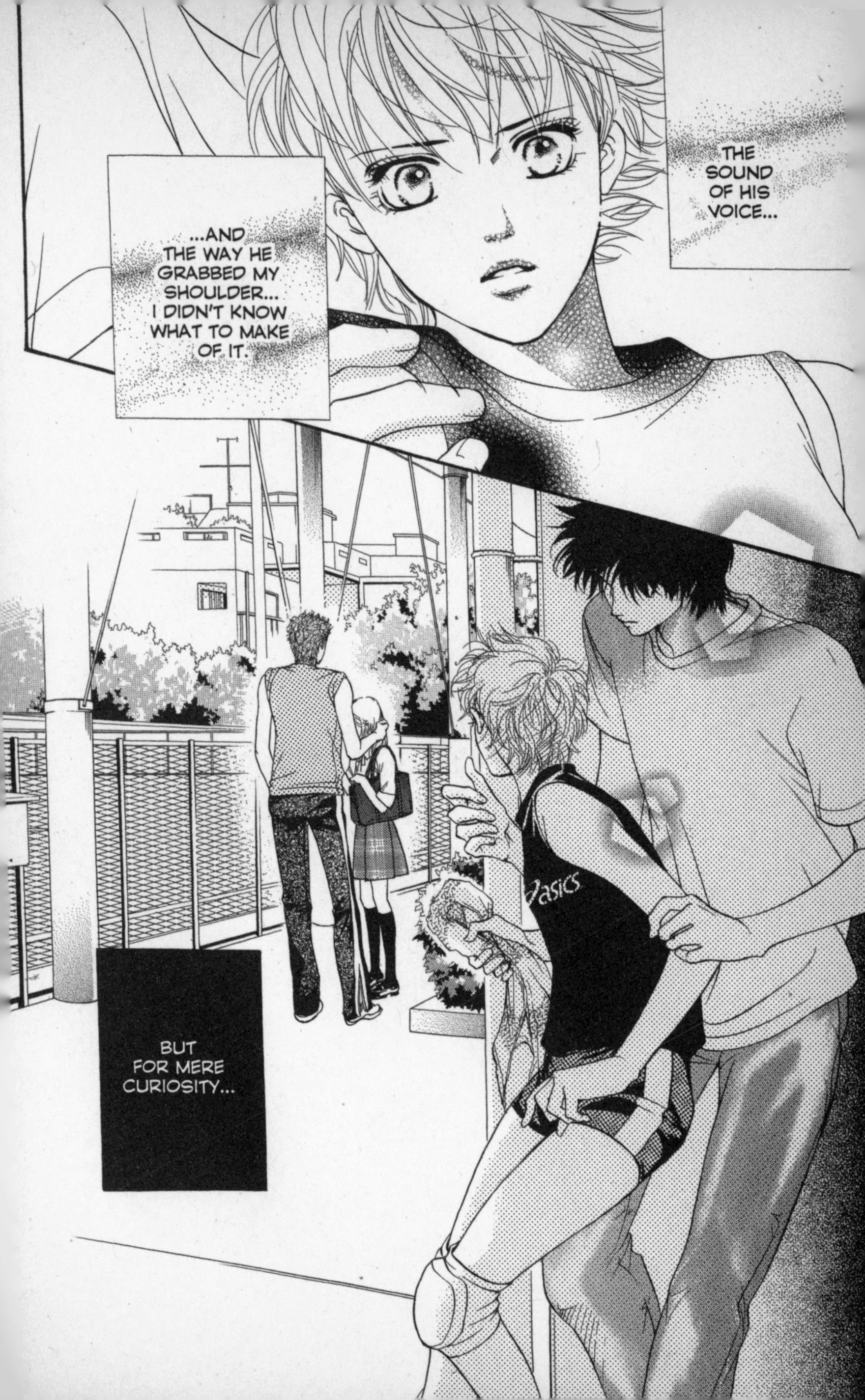
THE SOUND OF HIS VOICE...
...AND THE WAY HE GRABBED MY SHOULDER... I DIDN'T KNOW WHAT TO MAKE OF IT.
asics
BUT FOR MERE CURIOSITY...

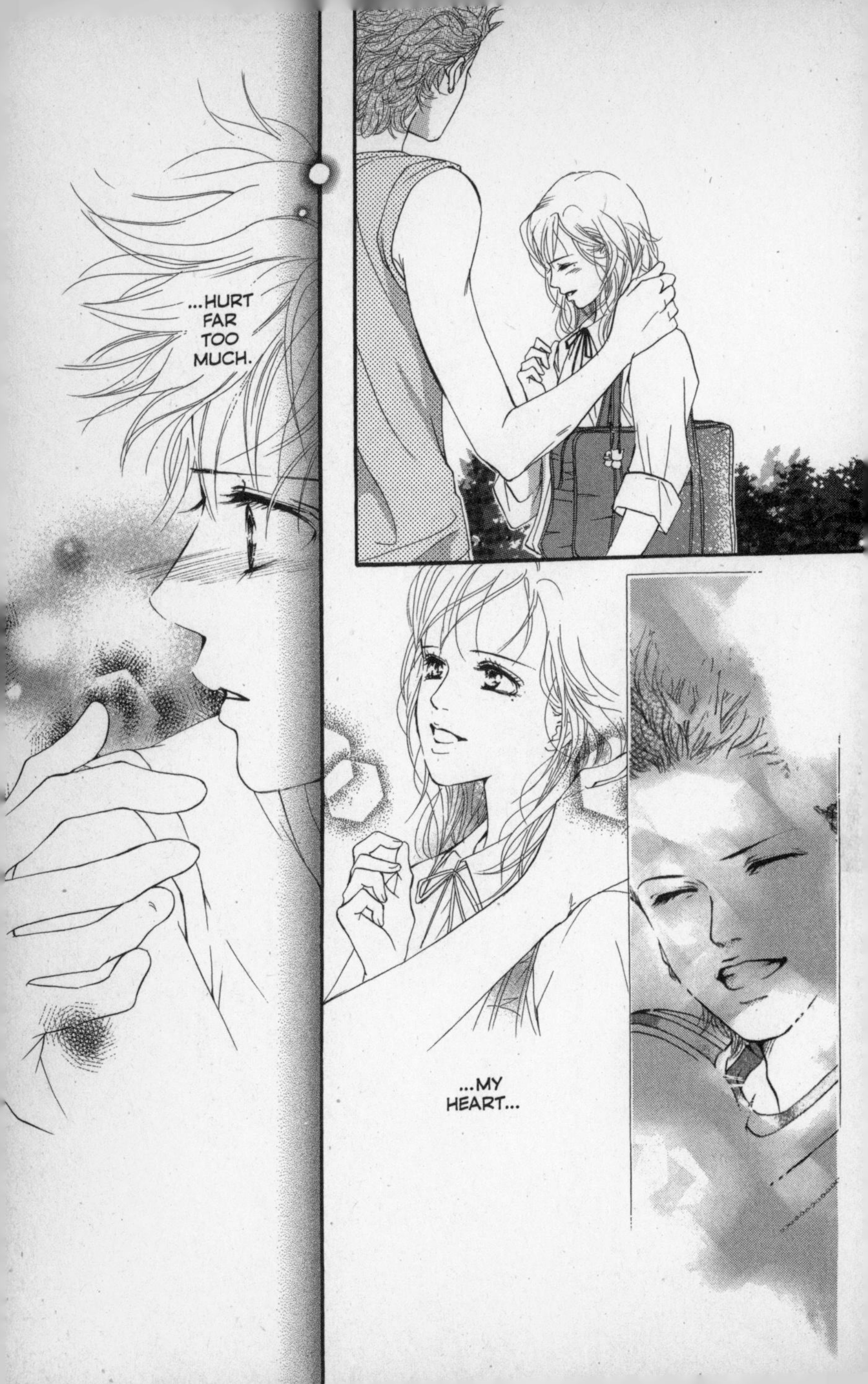
...MY HEART...
...HURT FAR TOO MUCH.

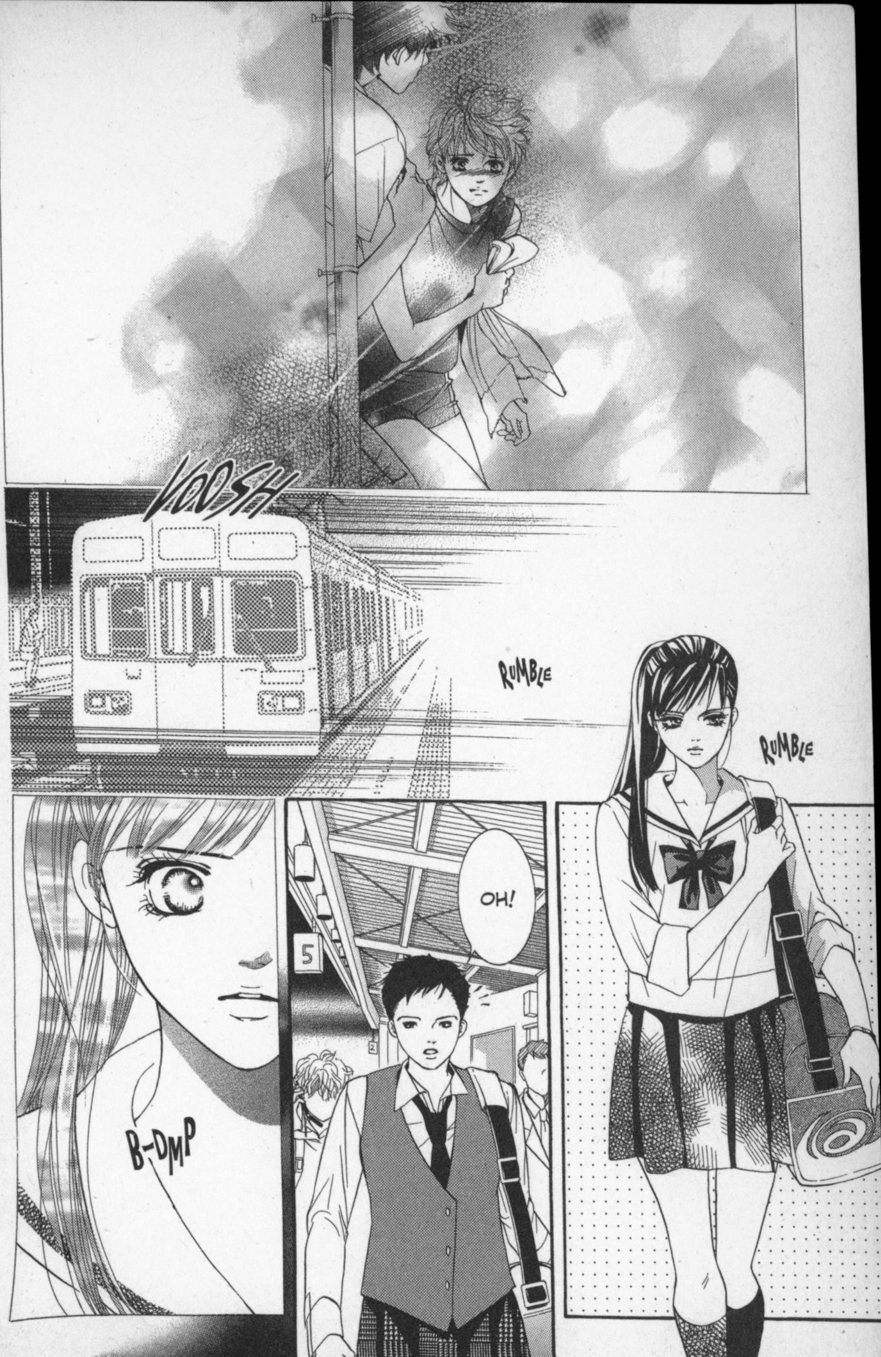
VOOSH
RUMBLE
RUMBLE
OH!
B-DMP

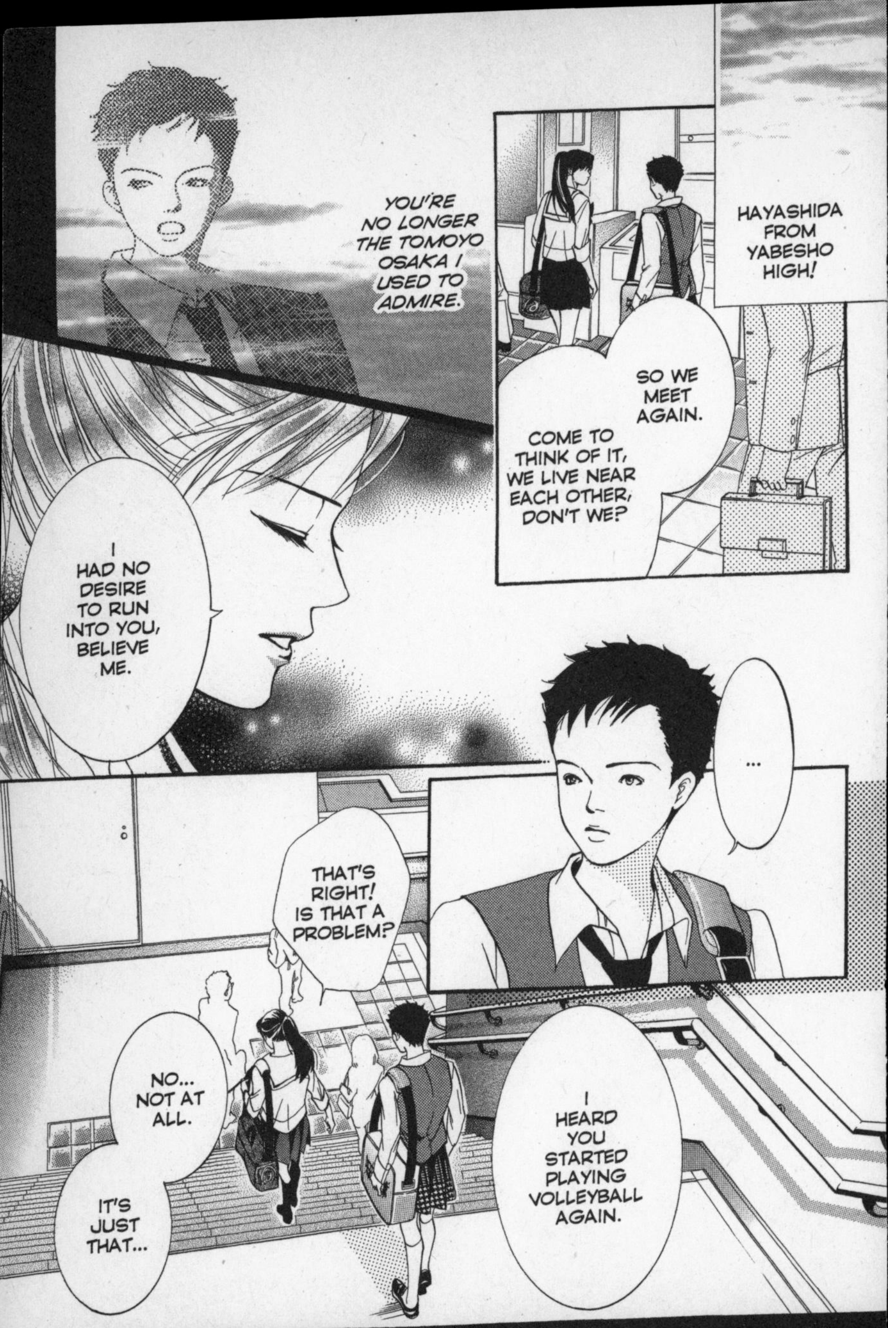
HAYASHIDA FROM YABESHO HIGH!
SO WE MEET AGAIN.
COME TO THINK OF IT, WE LIVE NEAR EACH OTHER, DON'T WE?
YOU'RE NO LONGER THE TOMOYO OSAKA I USED TO ADMIRE.
I HAD NO DESIRE TO RUN INTO YOU, BELIEVE ME.
...
I HEARD YOU STARTED PLAYING VOLLEYBALL AGAIN.
THAT'S RIGHT! IS THAT A PROBLEM?
NO... NOT AT ALL.
IT'S JUST THAT...

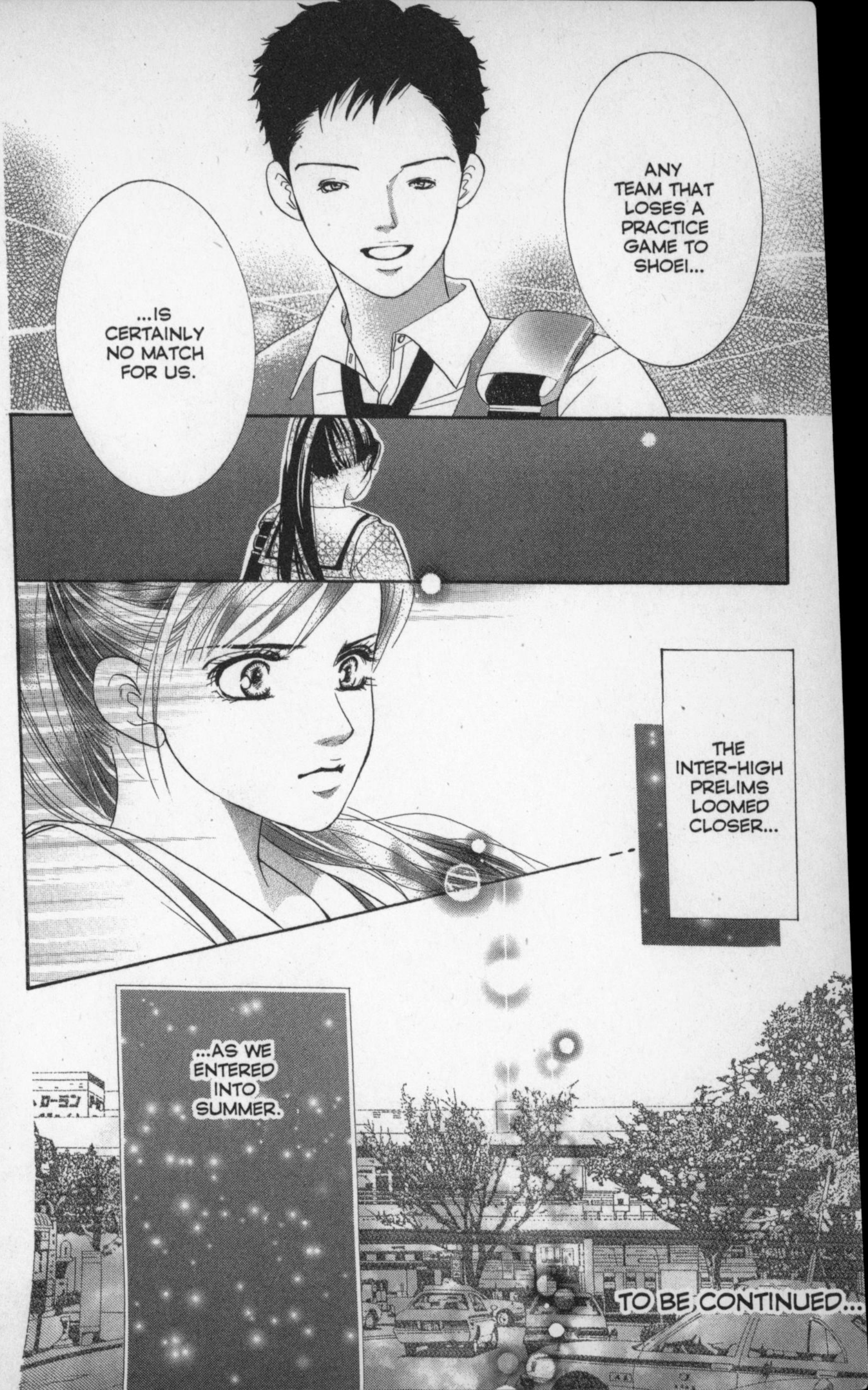
ANY TEAM THAT LOSES A PRACTICE GAME TO SHOEI...
...IS CERTAINLY NO MATCH FOR US.
THE INTER-HIGH PRELIMS LOOMED CLOSER...
...AS WE ENTERED INTO SUMMER.
TO BE CONTINUED...

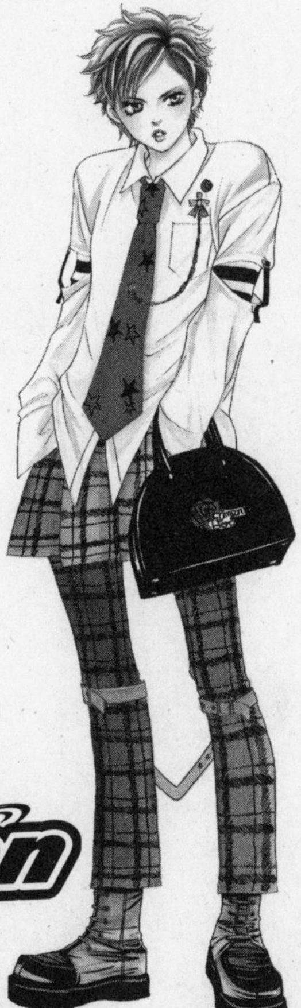

Crimson Hero

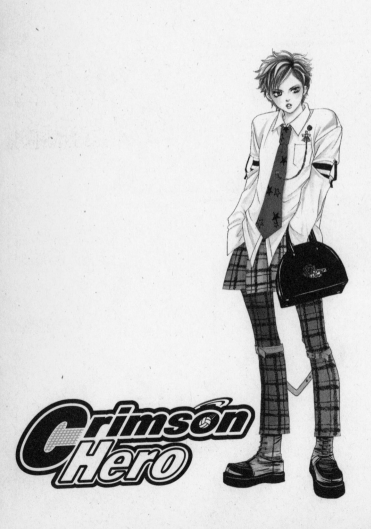

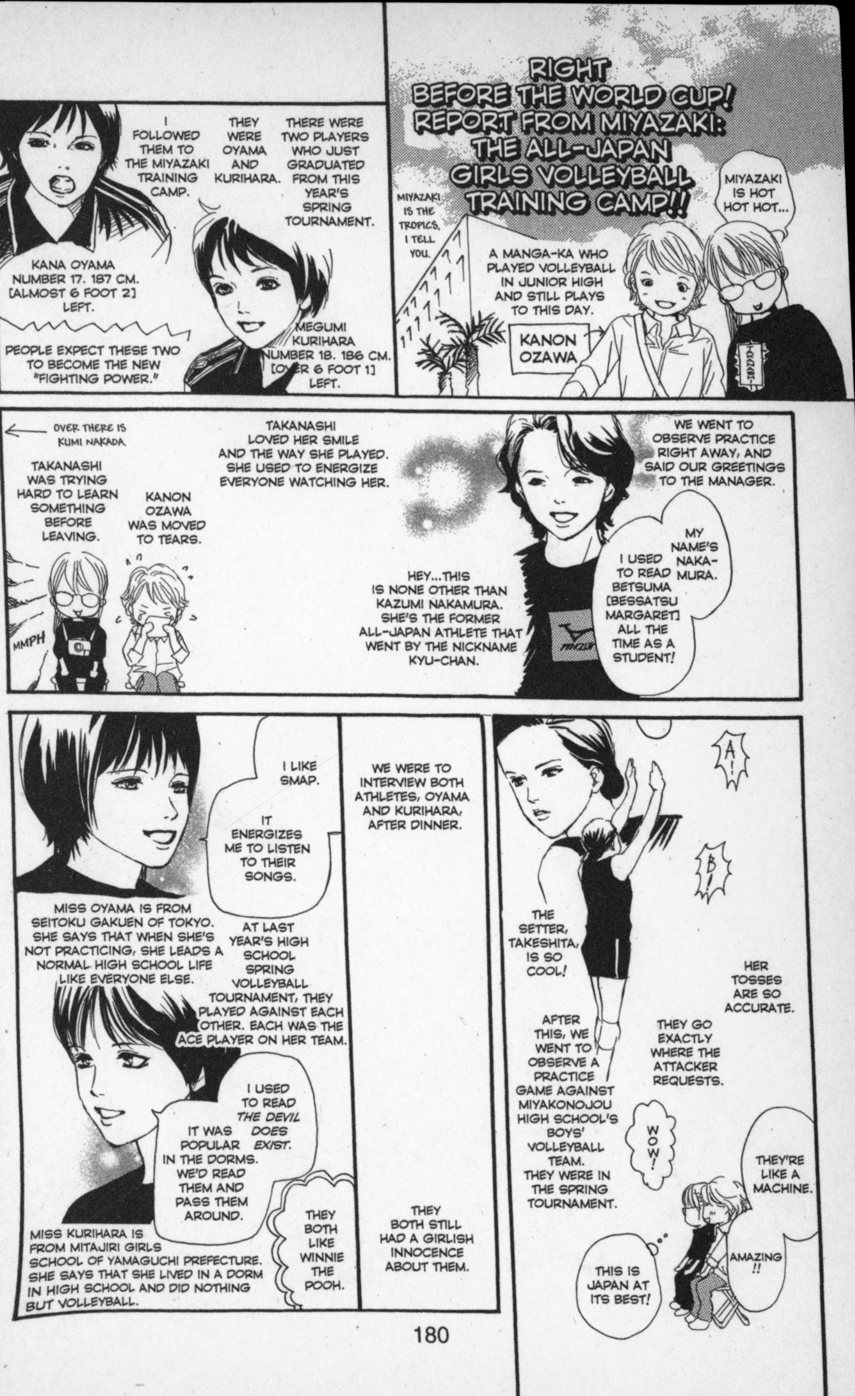
RIGHT BEFORE THE WORLD CUP! REPORT FROM MIYAZAKI: THE ALL-JAPAN GIRLS VOLLEYBALL TRAINING CAMP!!
MIYAZAKI IS HOT HOT HOT...
MIYAZAKI IS THE TROPICS, I TELL YOU.
A MANGA-KA WHO PLAYED VOLLEYBALL IN JUNIOR HIGH AND STILL PLAYS TO THIS DAY.
KANON OZAWA
TAKANASHI
THERE WERE TWO PLAYERS WHO JUST GRADUATED FROM THIS YEAR'S SPRING TOURNAMENT.
THEY WERE OYAMA AND KURIHARA.
I FOLLOWED THEM TO THE MIYAZAKI TRAINING CAMP.
KANA OYAMA NUMBER 17. 187 CM. [ALMOST 6 FOOT 2] LEFT.
MEGUMI KURIHARA NUMBER 18. 186 CM. [OVER 6 FOOT 1] LEFT.
PEOPLE EXPECT THESE TWO TO BECOME THE NEW "FIGHTING POWER."
WE WENT TO OBSERVE PRACTICE RIGHT AWAY, AND SAID OUR GREETINGS TO THE MANAGER.
MY NAME'S NAKA-MURA.
I USED TO READ BETSUMA [BESSATSU MARGARET] ALL THE TIME AS A STUDENT!
HEY...THIS IS NONE OTHER THAN KAZUMI NAKAMURA. SHE'S THE FORMER ALL-JAPAN ATHLETE THAT WENT BY THE NICKNAME KYU-CHAN.
TAKANASHI LOVED HER SMILE AND THE WAY SHE PLAYED. SHE USED TO ENERGIZE EVERYONE WATCHING HER.
OVER THERE IS KUMI NAKADA
TAKANASHI WAS TRYING HARD TO LEARN SOMETHING BEFORE LEAVING.
KANON OZAWA WAS MOVED TO TEARS.
MMPH
A!
B!
THE SETTER, TAKESHITA, IS SO COOL!
HER TOSSES ARE SO ACCURATE.
THEY GO EXACTLY WHERE THE ATTACKER REQUESTS.
AFTER THIS, WE WENT TO OBSERVE A PRACTICE GAME AGAINST MIYAKONOJOU HIGH SCHOOL'S BOYS' VOLLEYBALL TEAM. THEY WERE IN THE SPRING TOURNAMENT.
WOW!
THEY'RE LIKE A MACHINE.
AMAZING!!
THIS IS JAPAN AT ITS BEST!
WE WERE TO INTERVIEW BOTH ATHLETES, OYAMA AND KURIHARA, AFTER DINNER.
THEY BOTH STILL HAD A GIRLISH INNOCENCE ABOUT THEM.
I LIKE SMAP.
IT ENERGIZES ME TO LISTEN TO THEIR SONGS.
MISS OYAMA IS FROM SEITOKU GAKUEN OF TOKYO. SHE SAYS THAT WHEN SHE'S NOT PRACTICING, SHE LEADS A NORMAL HIGH SCHOOL LIFE LIKE EVERYONE ELSE.
AT LAST YEAR'S HIGH SCHOOL SPRING VOLLEYBALL TOURNAMENT, THEY PLAYED AGAINST EACH OTHER. EACH WAS THE ACE PLAYER ON HER TEAM.
I USED TO READ *THE DEVIL DOES EXIST*.
IT WAS POPULAR IN THE DORMS. WE'D READ THEM AND PASS THEM AROUND.
THEY BOTH LIKE WINNIE THE POOH.
MISS KURIHARA IS FROM MITAJIRI GIRLS SCHOOL OF YAMAGUCHI PREFECTURE. SHE SAYS THAT SHE LIVED IN A DORM IN HIGH SCHOOL AND DID NOTHING BUT VOLLEYBALL.

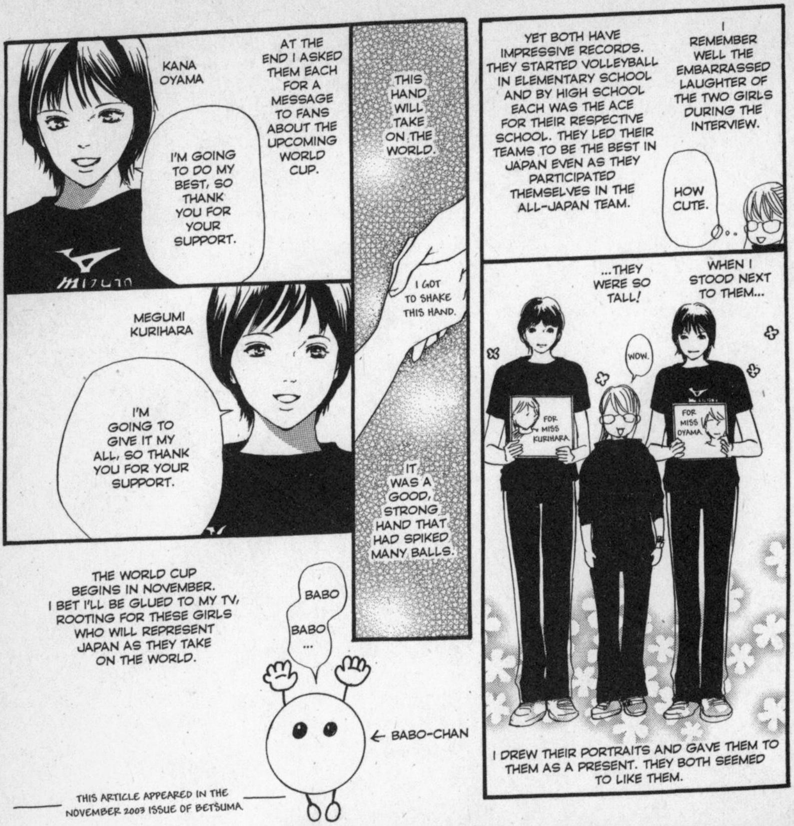
I REMEMBER WELL THE EMBARRASSED LAUGHTER OF THE TWO GIRLS DURING THE INTERVIEW.
YET BOTH HAVE IMPRESSIVE RECORDS. THEY STARTED VOLLEYBALL IN ELEMENTARY SCHOOL AND BY HIGH SCHOOL EACH WAS THE ACE FOR THEIR RESPECTIVE SCHOOL. THEY LED THEIR TEAMS TO BE THE BEST IN JAPAN EVEN AS THEY PARTICIPATED THEMSELVES IN THE ALL-JAPAN TEAM.
HOW CUTE.
WHEN I STOOD NEXT TO THEM...
...THEY WERE SO TALL!
WOW.
FOR MISS OYAMA
FOR MISS KURIHARA
I DREW THEIR PORTRAITS AND GAVE THEM TO THEM AS A PRESENT. THEY BOTH SEEMED TO LIKE THEM.
THIS HAND WILL TAKE ON THE WORLD.
I GOT TO SHAKE THIS HAND.
IT WAS A GOOD, STRONG HAND THAT HAD SPIKED MANY BALLS.
AT THE END I ASKED THEM EACH FOR A MESSAGE TO FANS ABOUT THE UPCOMING WORLD CUP.
KANA OYAMA
I'M GOING TO DO MY BEST, SO THANK YOU FOR YOUR SUPPORT.
MEGUMI KURIHARA
I'M GOING TO GIVE IT MY ALL, SO THANK YOU FOR YOUR SUPPORT.
BABO BABO...
← BABO-CHAN
THE WORLD CUP BEGINS IN NOVEMBER. I BET I'LL BE GLUED TO MY TV, ROOTING FOR THESE GIRLS WHO WILL REPRESENT JAPAN AS THEY TAKE ON THE WORLD.
THIS ARTICLE APPEARED IN THE NOVEMBER 2003 ISSUE OF BETSUMA.

A PHOTO FROM THAT TIME →

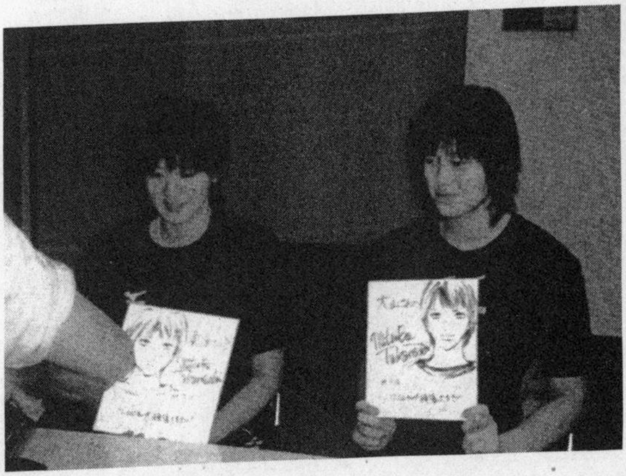

HEH HEH

WASN'T THE WORLD CUP AMAZING?! ESPECIALLY THE GIRLS. I WENT TO YOYOGI TO SEE THE KOREAN MATCH AND I WAS REALLY IN TEARS!! YES I WAS.

I WISH THE ALL-JAPAN GIRLS AND BOYS THE BEST IN THEIR UPCOMING ENDEAVORS.

FEBRUARY 20, 2004
MITSUBA TAKANASHI

♥ I'm so busy!! There's the drama CD, the magazine, the manga volumes, the storyboards, color pages, and research. I can't slack off on any of these things so it's a constant battle against time. No matter how much I do, it's not enough. And I want to work on other manga and do illustrations too. It'd be nice if there were one other me. If only I could self-replicate and morph into two. Then I could do more of the things I want to do.

—Mitsuba Takanashi, 2004

Mitsuba Takanashi debuted her first short story, *Mou Koi Nante Shinai* (Never Fall in Love Again), in 1992 in *Bessatsu Margaret* magazine and now has several major titles under her belt.

Born in the Shimane Prefecture of Japan, Takanashi now lives in Tokyo, where she enjoys taking walks, watching videos, shopping, and going to the hair salon. Takanashi has a soft spot for the Japanese pop acts Yellow Monkey and Hide, and is good at playing ping-pong.

CRIMSON HERO

VOL. 3
The Shojo Beat Manga Edition

This manga volume contains material that was originally published in English in
Shojo Beat magazine, March–June 2006 issues.

STORY AND ART BY
MITSUBA TAKANASHI

Translation & English Adaptation/Naoko Amemiya
Touch-up Art & Lettering/Mark Griffin
Design/Courtney Utt
Editor/Nancy Thistlethwaite

Managing Editor/Megan Bates
Director of Production/Noboru Watanabe
Vice President of Publishing/Alvin Lu
Vice President & Editor in Chief/Yumi Hoashi
Sr. Director of Acquisitions/Rika Inouye
Vice President of Sales & Marketing/Liza Coppola
Publisher/Hyoe Narita

Printed in Canada

Published by VIZ Media, LLC
P.O. Box 77010
San Francisco, CA 94107

Shojo Beat Manga Edition
10 9 8 7 6 5 4 3 2 1
First printing, August 2006

www.viz.com   store.viz.com

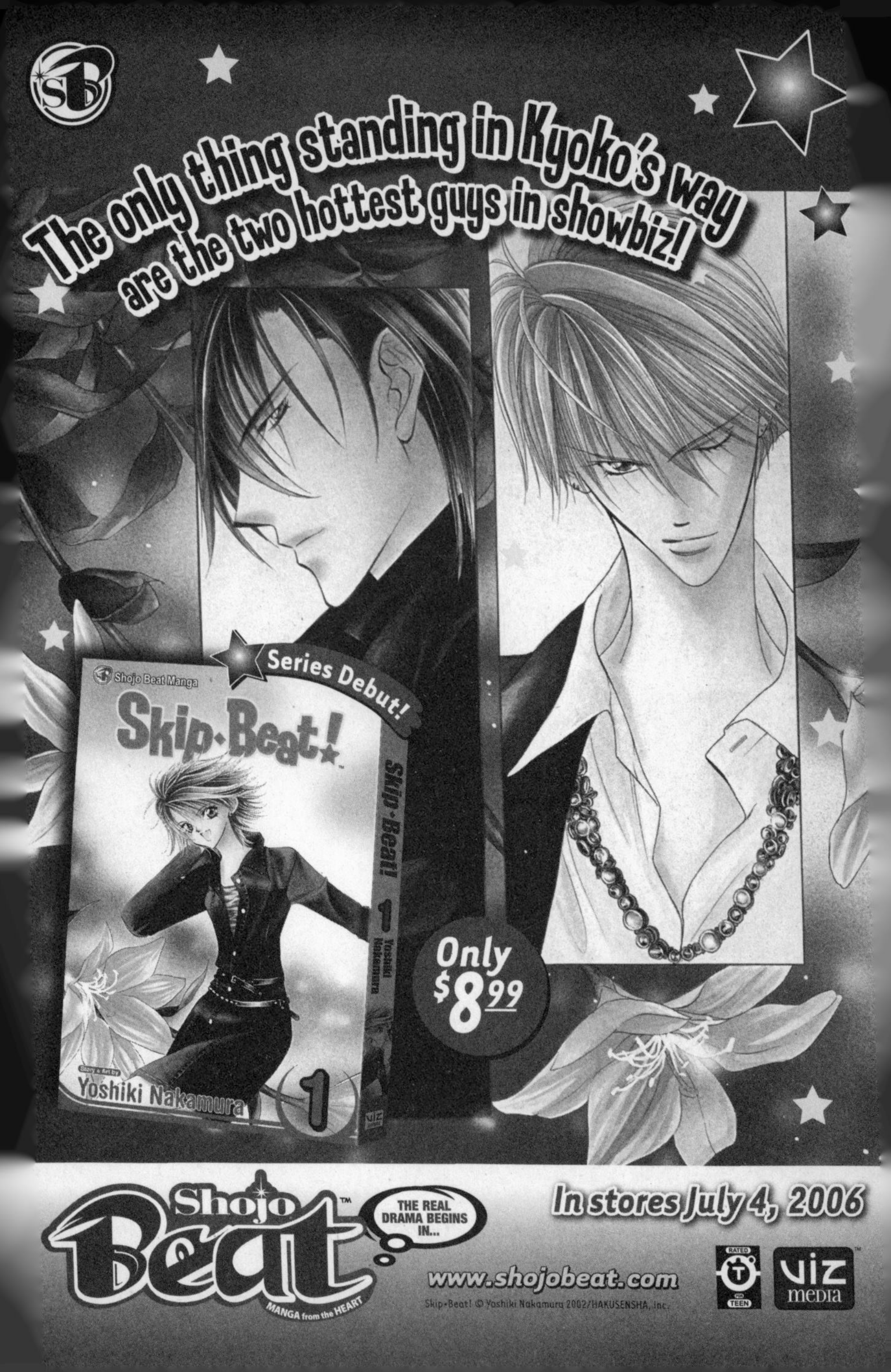
The only thing standing in Kyoko's way are the two hottest guys in showbiz!
Series Debut!
Shojo Beat Manga
Skip·Beat!
Story & Art by Yoshiki Nakamura
1
Only $8.99
Shojo Beat
MANGA from the HEART
THE REAL DRAMA BEGINS IN...
In stores July 4, 2006
www.shojobeat.com
Skip·Beat! © Yoshiki Nakamura 2002/HAKUSENSHA, Inc.
RATED T FOR TEEN
VIZ media

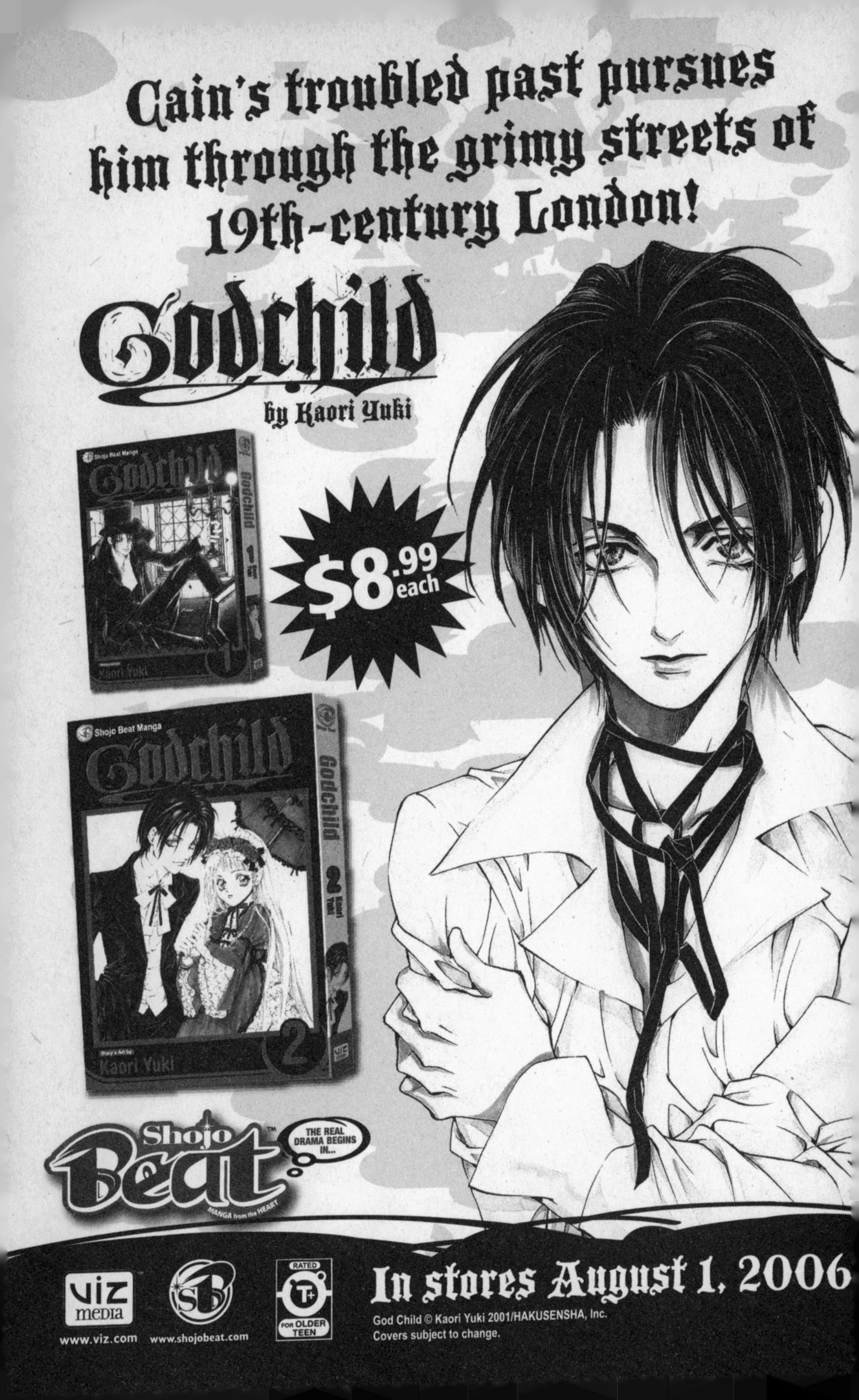
Cain's troubled past pursues him through the grimy streets of 19th-century London!
Godchild™
by Kaori Yuki
Shojo Beat Manga
Godchild
Kaori Yuki
$8.99 each
Shojo Beat Manga
Godchild
2
Kaori Yuki
Shojo Beat™
THE REAL DRAMA BEGINS IN...
MANGA from the HEART
viz media
www.viz.com
www.shojobeat.com
RATED T+ FOR OLDER TEEN
In stores August 1, 2006
God Child © Kaori Yuki 2001/HAKUSENSHA, Inc.
Covers subject to change.

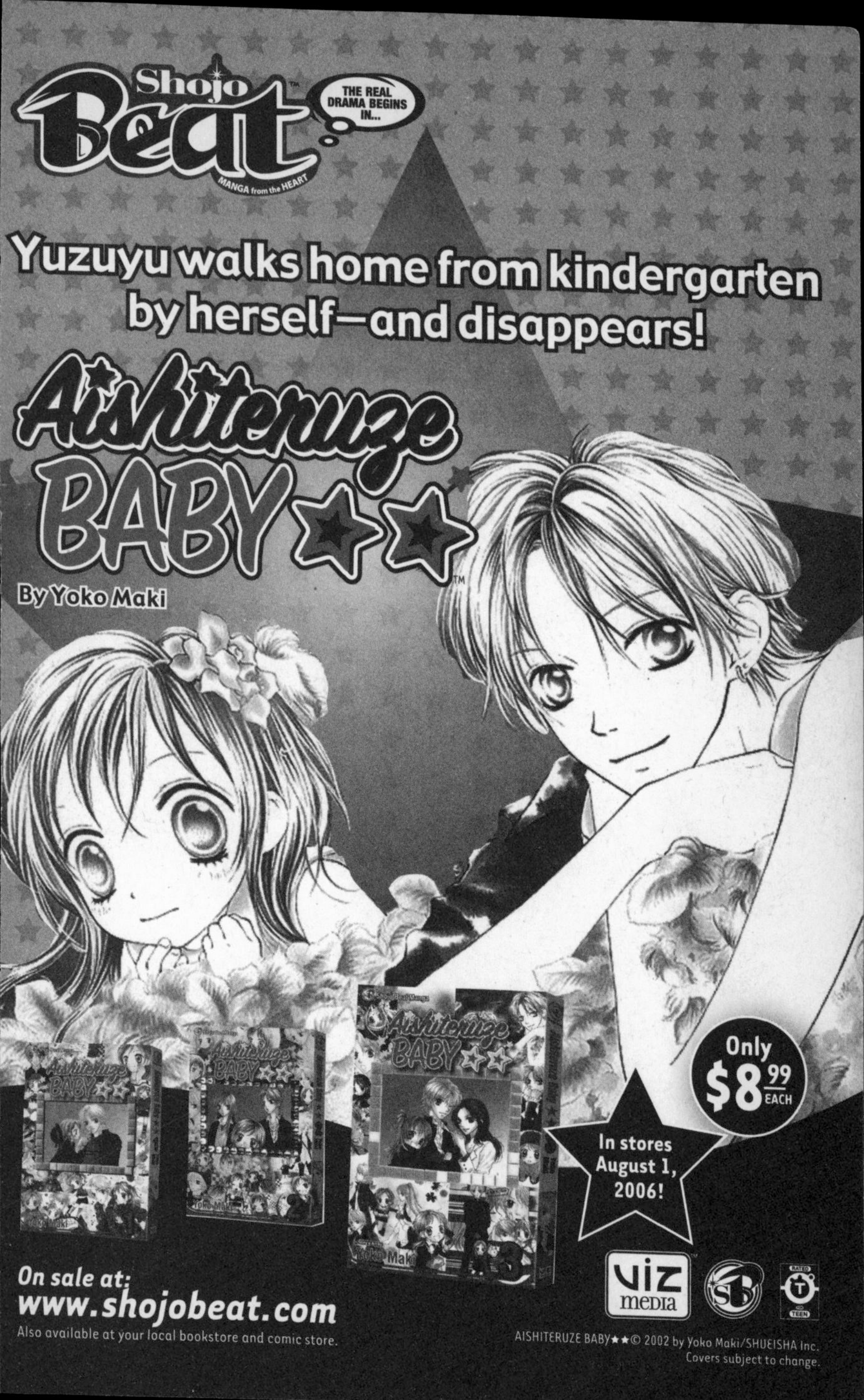
Shojo Beat™
MANGA from the HEART
THE REAL DRAMA BEGINS IN...
Yuzuyu walks home from kindergarten by herself—and disappears!
Aishiteruze BABY★★™
By Yoko Maki
Only $8.99 EACH
In stores August 1, 2006!
On sale at:
www.shojobeat.com
Also available at your local bookstore and comic store.
viz media
RATED T TEEN
AISHITERUZE BABY★★ © 2002 by Yoko Maki/SHUEISHA Inc.
Covers subject to change.

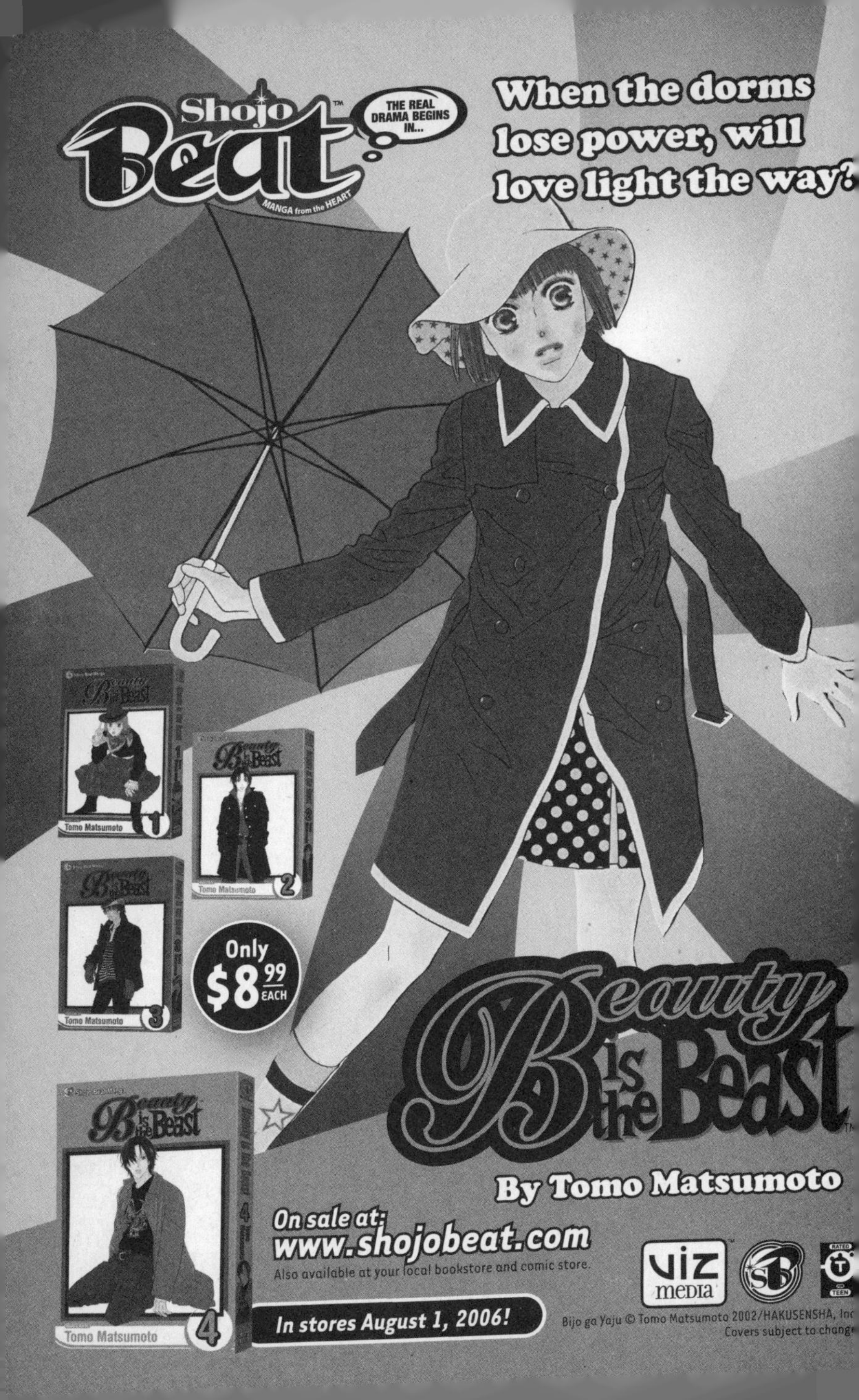
Shojo Beat
THE REAL DRAMA BEGINS IN...
MANGA from the HEART
When the dorms lose power, will love light the way?
Beauty is the Beast
Tomo Matsumoto
Only $8.99 EACH
Beauty is the Beast
By Tomo Matsumoto
On sale at:
www.shojobeat.com
Also available at your local bookstore and comic store.
In stores August 1, 2006!
VIZ media
RATED T TEEN
Bijo ga Yaju © Tomo Matsumoto 2002/HAKUSENSHA, Inc
Covers subject to change

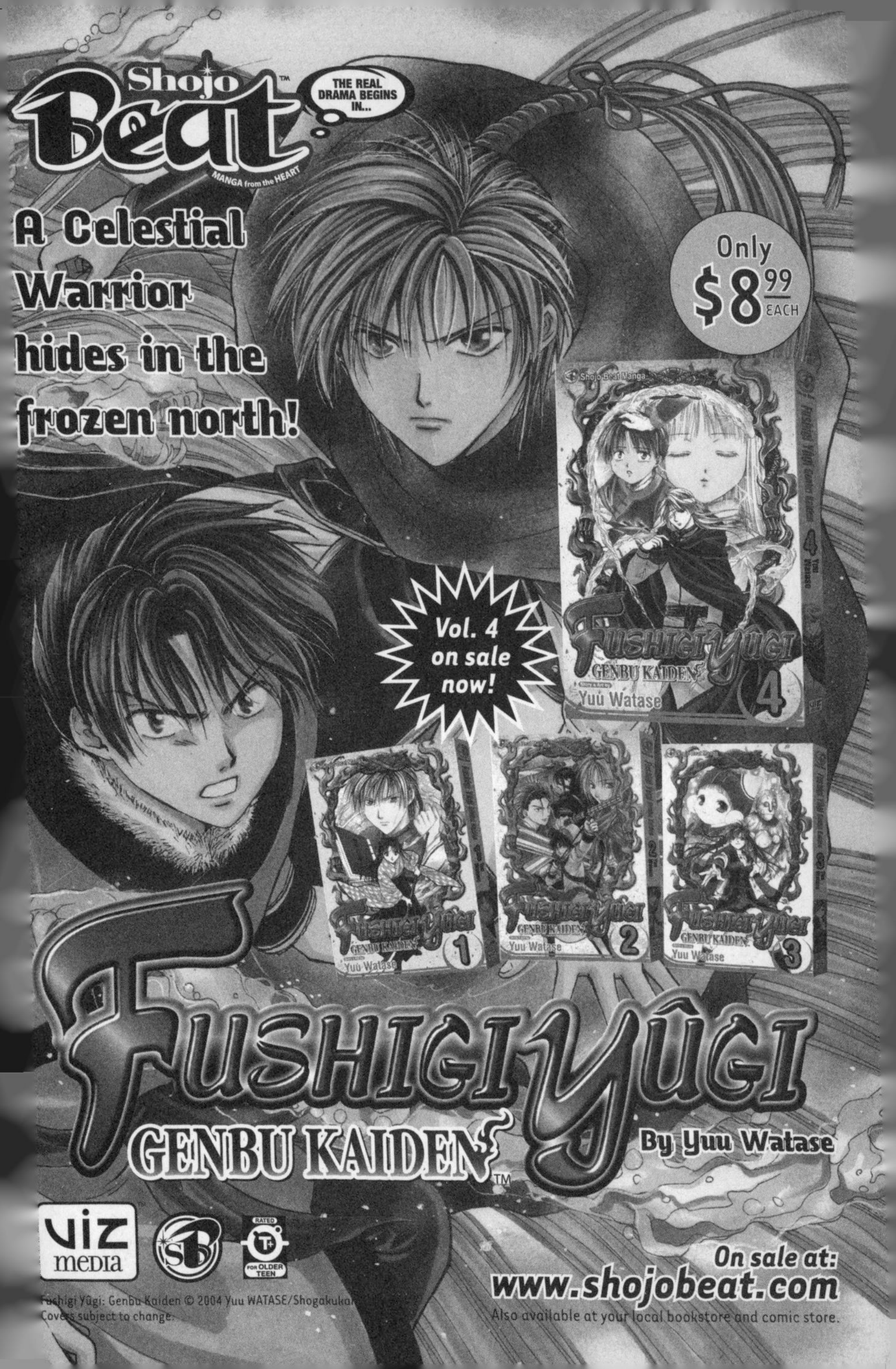

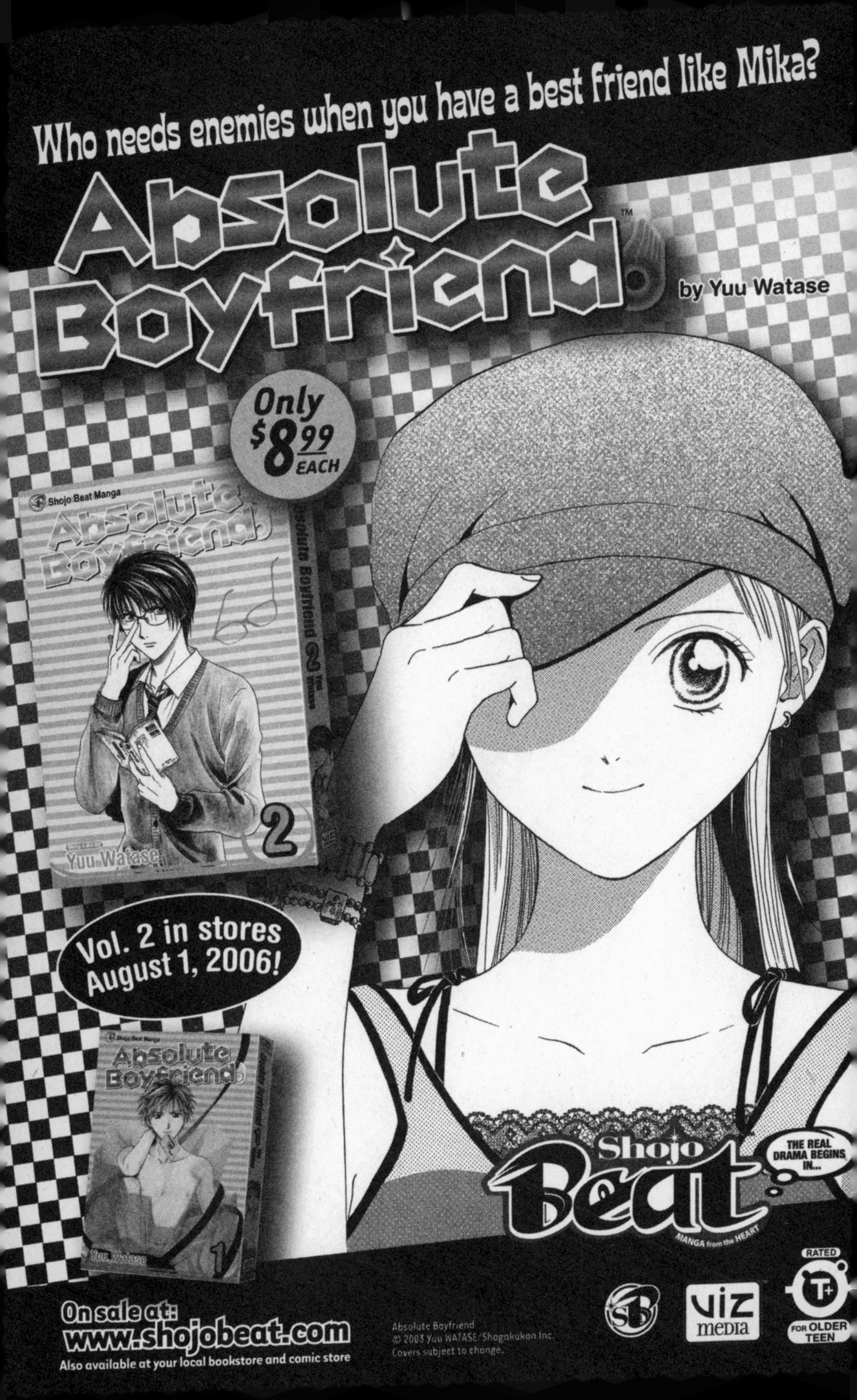
Who needs enemies when you have a best friend like Mika?
Absolute Boyfriend™
by Yuu Watase
Only $8.99 EACH
Shojo Beat Manga
Absolute Boyfriend
Absolute Boyfriend 2
Yuu Watase
Vol. 2 in stores August 1, 2006!
Absolute Boyfriend
Yuu Watase
Shojo Beat
THE REAL DRAMA BEGINS IN...
MANGA from the HEART
On sale at:
www.shojobeat.com
Also available at your local bookstore and comic store
Absolute Boyfriend
© 2003 Yuu WATASE/Shogakukan Inc.
Covers subject to change.
viz media
RATED T+ FOR OLDER TEEN

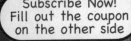